GIANTS OF FAITH

Giants of Faith

GREAT AMERICAN RABBIS

by Rabbi Alex J. Goldman

The Citadel Press
NEW YORK

FIRST EDITION

Copyright © 1964 by Alex J. Goldman

All rights reserved

Published by The Citadel Press
222 Park Avenue South, New York 3, N. Y.

Manufactured in the United States of America
by The Haddon Craftsmen, Inc., Scranton, Pa.

Library of Congress Catalog Card No.: 64-8163

ACKNOWLEDGMENTS

For their generous loan of photographs for this book, the
author wishes to thank the following: American Jewish
Archives, Cincinnati; American Jewish Congress, New
York; Rabbi A. Stanley Dreyfus, Galveston: National Jew-
ish Welfare Board, New York; the Park Avenue Synagogue,
New York; and Yeshiva University, New York.

To my own
Giants of Faith

MY FATHER
Rabbi Julius David Goldman

MY MOTHER
Sarah Esther

CONTENTS

CONTENTS

INTRODUCTION

This is a book of portraits of great rabbis in America who, during the last century and a half, came onto the stage of history, performed their missions nobly and well, and achieved deserved recognition. They charted the course of Jewish history, guided, counseled, and led with the kind of fervor becoming only giants of faith. Their impress on America is indelible, for they were as much a part of this country as they were a part of Judaism.

Hailing from many different environments—Eastern and Western Europe, Italy, America—they all joined here. They were Orthodox, Conservative, Reform; as right as Aaron Kotler, as left as David Einhorn. Although they represented vastly different orientations and made contrasting demands, they all loved their people and all of mankind. Each was recognized and admired by thousands of people of all religions and persuasions. This volume is designed to convey their essence; to make them live even to those unacquainted with their contributions to Jewish and American history.

History, it has been said, is the biography of great men. As we stand, as it were, upon a tall mountain and view the panorama of the past, the great men supply the foci which enable us to understand the ebb and flow of events. This is equally true of Jewish history. Through an examination of the lives of Jewry's greats we are educated in Jewish history itself. A mere mention of names evokes much of that history. It is Abraham and Isaac and Jacob. It is Moses and Joshua and Saul and

Solomon and David. It is Isaiah, Jeremiah, Amos and Malachi. It is Ezra and Nehemiah and Judah Maccabee. It is Hillel and Akiba and Yohanan ben Zakkai and Saadya and Bahya. It is Yehudah Halevi and Ibn Gabirol, Maimonides, Karo and the Vilner Gaon. And so on. The impact of each was tremendous.

So, too, in recent Jewish history. The greats are not only rabbis, but more often than not the rabbinical greats provide the apex of each era's hill. Group several together into something like a century of time and the impact can only be described as formidable. Take a number of rabbis, especially from the middle of the last century, contemplate each one—his service, devotion and faith—and the picture of Jewish history is sharply drawn. Without any one, Jewish history would have been substantially different. Unfortunately there are omissions. Certainly Israel Friedlander, Judah Magnes, Marcus Jastrow, Emil G. Hirsch, Levi Ginsburg, Henry Periera Mendes, Benjamin Szold, Morris Raphall, Alexander Kohut, Henry Berkowitz, Joseph Krauskopf and others deserve to be called "giants of faith." We can only protest that space limitations made hard choices mandatory. Those omitted must be covered in another study.

The reader may react differently to each man described here depending on his own upbringing and religious views. Indeed, such may cause him some discomfort when reading about men whose views sharply diverge from his own. However, he will not be able to deny, if he is intellectually honest, that each made a major contribution to American Jewish life and history. American Judaism is not homogeneous; it is the composite of many views, none of which can be ignored. One cannot deny the profound effect of a Kaufmann Kohler or an Isaac M. Wise on the one hand, nor of an Aaron Kotler or Bernard Levinthal on the other, nor of a Sabato Morais and a Solomon Schechter.

Are they all "giants of faith"? Who is to judge? By what yardstick shall we measure? Shall we compare an Einhorn to Bernard Revel, Schechter to Henry Cohen, Morais to Alexander Goode? Each gave unstintingly of himself for his people and country. Our community is what it is today precisely because they all lived and contributed. Nor did these 18 giants of faith live in isolation. They interacted in and with time and place; they fought and died for their faith.

Each biography tells a broader story than the life it encompasses, for each was marked by destiny. It is the spirit of each that the writer has sought to capture and impress on the American Jewish canvas. The biographical narratives presented are not definitive, critical presentations; nor are they intended to be exhaustive. Rather, they are designed to offer the "feeling" of the character and personality of each of the men. The writer's hope is that the personalized insights offered will stimulate the reader to study the bibliography provided and seek out more detailed information about some or all of the men portrayed.

I should like to acknowledge with deep gratitude the help of the many persons who have read chapters of this book and offered valuable suggestions and made appropriate corrections: Rabbi Isaac Klein, Buffalo, New York; Rabbi Israel H. Levinthal, Brooklyn, New York; Judge Louis E. Levinthal, Philadelphia, Pennsylvania; Abraham A. Levinthal, Philadelphia; Justine Wise Polier, New York; Miss Lili Kohler, New York; Mrs. Edith Steinberg, New York; Mrs. Bernard Revel, New York; Mr. Norman Revel, New York; Rabbi David Max Eichhorn, New York; Rabbi A. Stanley Dreyfus, Galveston, Texas; Mrs. Arthur Hays Sulzberger, New York; Rabbi Aaron Rothkoff, Newark, New Jersey.

Many were generous in helping to secure information about the men studied and to them I should like to offer my heartfelt appreciation: Dr. Stanley F. Chyet, Assistant Director, American Jewish Archives and Assistant Professor of American Jewish History, Hebrew Union College—Jewish Institute of Religion; Mrs. Sylvia Landress, Director and Librarian, Zionist Archives and Library; Mrs. Albert I. Zemel, Chicago, Illinois; Rabbi Ira Eisenstein, editor, *The Reconstructionist*, New York; Mr. Edward Grusd, editor, *National Jewish Monthly*, Washington, D.C.; Rabbi Bernard Raskas, St. Paul, Minnesota; Mr. and Mrs. Max Kopstein, Chicago, Illinois; Mrs. Theresa Kaplan, Columbus, Ohio; Rabbi Seymour Cohen, Chicago, Illinois; Rabbi Eli Pilchik, Newark, New Jersey; Albert Mordell, Philadelphia, Pennsylvania, and Rev. Walter H. White, Chaplain-in-charge, The Chapel of Four Chaplains, Philadelphia.

I sought assistance from a number of libraries and was graciously provided with much needed volumes and documents. I should like to express my thanks to: Mr. Jacob I. Dienstag, Librarian, The Mendel Gottesman Library, Yeshiva University, New York; Dr. Baruch Weitzel,

Librarian, Judaica Department, Free Library of Philadelphia; Mrs. Leah Mishkin, Librarian, Rabbi Saul Silber Memorial Library, Hebrew Theological College of Chicago, Skokie, Illinois; Mrs. Mildred Kurland and Mrs. Sophie Cooper of Gratz College Library, Philadelphia; and especially to Mr. Maxwell Whiteman, Librarian, Dropsie College for Hebrew and Cognate Learning, Philadelphia, for his readiness to help, his incisive and welcome criticisms, and his friendship, and to his capable staff, Miss Miriam Stern and Miss Sarah Mozenter for their painstaking help.

I acknowledge also permissions to reprint selections from: Rabbi Leon H. Elmaleh, the acrostic about Dr. Sabato Morais; Funk and Wagnalls Company, New York, to quote from *A New World Is Born* (1943) and *Steering or Drifting, Which* (1928), both by Israel H. Levinthal; G. P. Putnam's Sons, New York, to quote from *Challenging Years, the Autobiography of Stephen S. Wise* (1949); Justice Justine Wise Polier to quote her father's sermons and addresses; Mrs. Edith Steinberg to quote from Milton Steinberg's books published by Harcourt, Brace and Company, The Bobbs-Merrill Company, and Behrman House, Inc.; to Harper and Row, New York, to quote from *A Rabbi Takes Stock* (1931) and *Crisis and Decision* (1938); the Jewish Publication Society of America, Philadelphia, to quote from *Studies in Judaism* (series one, two and three) by Solomon Schechter; and to Holt, Rinehart and Winston, Inc., to quote from *Anatomy of Faith* (1960) by Arthur A. Cohen.

My sincere thanks also go to Mrs. Mildred Barron for her careful typing of the mauscript.

Finally, my deepest feelings of appreciation are for my wife, Edith, for her love, her constant, unreserved encouragement to write and for the inspiration she has been to me in my career. Without her devotion and counsel, neither this book, nor any other, would have been brought to light.

ALEX J. GOLDMAN

August, 1964

GIANTS OF FAITH

ISAAC LEESER

Passionate Oracle of Orthodox Judaism

[1806-1868]

The Talmud tells that when the famous scholar and saint, Rabbi Zeira, was ordained, he was acclaimed by his colleagues with the words: "Neither powder nor paint nor ornament, but yet how beautiful!" They referred to the fact that the new rabbi may not have been physically attractive but was nevertheless beautiful because of the saintliness of his character and the greatness of his spirit.

Isaac Leeser, educator, preacher, writer, traveler, and unofficial chief rabbi of American Jewry for a number of years, was not physically handsome. Rebecca Gratz, first lady of Philadelphia and one of Leeser's close friends, in one of her letters remarked, drawing on the Talmud (Taanit 7): "Wisdom is safest with ugliness." Smallpox had struck in his youth and in his prime sickness plagued him continually. His inner strength, however, prevailed. Out of a sense of duty and calling he labored wholeheartedly in the vineyard of the Lord and was recognized as the nation's leading exponent of Orthodox Judaism. His passionate earnestness and untiring efforts for his ancestral faith in the middle of the 19th century earned for him respect and admiration. He was its towering spokesman and advocate, as uncompromising in his devotion to the principles of his faith as he was valiant in the face of any and all onslaughts, from Jew or non-Jew, American or European. He was, in his zeal and love, prodigious writing and masterful oratory, a true defender of the faith.

Isaac Leeser was the most dominant spirit of Orthodox Judaism in an era which saw the rise of the Reform movement. The time and the sparse Jewish community begged for organizational life. Leeser zealously sought the union of Israel. He was a teacher par excellence, an eloquent orator, a dedicated educator, and an untiring traveler, traversing the length and breadth of America preaching and defending the faith and the people of the faith he loved so completely.

Leeser is one of the forgotten heroes of American Jewish history. Few know of his Herculean contributions to American Judaism. Few are aware of his indelible stamp on present-day Jewish life. Few realize how many organizations and activities now taken for granted and flourishing were the products of his brain and heart, his keen insight and vision. The American Jewish Committee and the American Jewish Congress can trace their existence to his efforts for unity in American Israel. The B'nai B'rith can look to him as one of its prime movers. The Federation of Jewish Charities of Greater Philadelphia, and indeed the Federations all over America which raise gigantic sums to help Jewish people locally, nationally and internationally, received their impetus from Leeser. The theological seminaries in America of all denominations training rabbis for religious leadership can claim Leeser as their guiding spirit and founder. The Philadelphia Board of Rabbis, and indeed every local and national council of rabbis, might well recall the dynamic fervor of Leeser as he worked for unity and understanding among the spiritual leaders of America. The Jewish Publication Society of America can view with pride Leeser's call for the organization of a society to publish and distribute volumes designed to increase the knowledge of our people. Other organizations, hospitals and charities in America can find their roots in his ever-active mind and heart. Indeed, Isaac Leeser's mark is everywhere on present-day American Jewish life.

Little is known about Leeser's earliest years. No documents record or detail the background of the shy, brooding, reserved youth who, born in Westphalia on December 12, 1806, came to the shores of America at the age of 18. It is known that his mother died when he was of tender years and that his grandmother and father followed her to their eternal reward soon thereafter. It is also known by a note to one of his discourses that he had a deep affection for a brother who died in the prime of life of an illness similar to that which afflicted him. He was deeply disturbed that he could not help his brother because of his own "sufferings of unspeakable intensity and horror."

Leeser attended the gymnasium (high school) at Muenster and was profoundly influenced by the Right Rev. Abraham Sutro, chief rabbi of the diocese of Muenster and Mark. In one of his first volumes, he pays loving tribute to the rabbi in his dedication:

> I well remember the time, when scarcely nine summers had passed over my head, that you arrived among us; and how the first sermon I ever heard delivered, the one you addressed to our congregation, made a powerful impression upon us all, not excepting the little unconscious boy I then was. You, also, as I advanced in life, encouraged my humble striving to excel, and I can never forget the kindness with which you always seconded the efforts of my blessed teacher.

Rabbi Sutro's impact upon the young, sensitive, impressionable Leeser was lasting. Sutro, too, was a zealous defender of traditional Judaism and a resolute fighter against new movements. He was the author of *Milhamot Adonoy* (Battles of the Lord) written in 1836, and certainly the philosophy contained therein was part of his instruction and teaching. Imbibing from him the love for traditional Judaism, Leeser became his counterpart, in America.

He was also impressed deeply in his earliest years of study by Rabbi B. J. Cohen ("guide of my infancy") and Rabbi B. S. Cohen, principal of the Jewish Institute at Muenster in Westphalia, to whom he dedicated his first book, *The Jews and the Mosaic Law,* in which he recalls "the pleasure of daily enjoying a friendly intercourse with you."

Unheralded, unknown to any but his uncle, Zalma Rehine in Richmond, Virginia, Leeser came to America in 1824. His uncle, to whom he later dedicated the book *Instruction in the Mosaic Religion,* had a commercial establishment, a counting house, and Isaac joined the business. He worked hard all day and studied during the night. Soon he became a teacher for Jewish children in Richmond. Love of learning was paramount and his photographic mind and retentive faculty drew in and kept within its recesses the Hebraic studies in which he was involved. He also must have devoted himself completely to a mastery of the English language, because in less than five years after his arrival, his remarkable essays written in flawless English destined him for greater horizons than clerking. Despite poor eyesight, the result of intense and zealous study, he continued to read voraciously and, when able, assisted Rev. Isaac B. Seixas, the minister of the congregation in Richmond. In 1828, a series of articles, originally printed in the *London Quarterly Review* and subsequently reprinted in a New York paper, changed Leeser's entire life and catapulted him from obscurity to fame and to leadership in his era. The article he read defamed Jews and Judaism throughout the world:

> There are great numbers of Jews in Poland; there they literally swarm; they are innkeepers, tradesmen, distillers of brandy, brewers, horse-dealers, money-changers, usurers, as everywhere else; some few of them are farmers of the soil. Their numbers have increased of late years so rapidly as greatly to alarm and embarrass the governments of countries which afford but slender resources for a population so averse to be engaged in tillage. The evil of this immense accumulation of such a people, having one common interest and feeling, both of which are foreign to the interests and feelings of the citizens of the state, is felt, specially by the Russian government.

The writer called Jews "foreign unbelieving moneychangers." The teachings of the Talmud are referred to as "the blasphemous and horrible absurdities of the talmud." The Jews do not accept Jesus as their Saviour. The Jew is arrogant, stubborn, superstitious, contemptible, etc.

Young Leeser, as he read these vicious and slanderous charges, was fired by the compulsion to answer them, but he felt that his youth militated against him and that it was presumptuous for him to come forward as champion of his people when there were others, more scholarly and erudite than he, who should step forward. He imagined that others might be unhappy if he were so aggressive:

> Another opinion may be maintained about my unimportance, and the little good I can do by appearing voluntarily and uncalled for as the champion of the Jews. Indeed this objection is much more reasonable than the usefulness of a defence; but all I can say in reply is, that my intentions are good, and that, if my abilities and standing are not sufficient, let some one more able, and upon a higher station in life, and more known to the public, assume the responsibility, and he may be assured that I shall with pleasure yield him the palm of superiority.

In this way, young Leeser introduced a series of articles which appeared in the *Richmond Whig* and which later became part of his first volume, *The Jews and the Mosaic Law*. He set forth in masterful detail his position as a Jew, rebutting "the calumnies which have been spread abroad through an English Review against the character of the Jewish people and faith." He wrote carefully, methodically, confidently, and with deep feeling born of zeal for his faith. The six essays which rolled off his pen brought him quick recognition. Almost immediately he attracted the attention of Jews all over America. The officials of Mikveh Israel Congregation in Philadelphia promptly offered him the position of hazan (reader). Leeser, only 22 years of age, never ordained officially, accepted the offer. This call to a distinguished synagogue, following on the heels of his magnificent defense of Judaism, brought him quickly onto the public scene. It marked also the opening of a new era in the history of the congregation, which he was to serve faithfully for 21 years.

During these years, the influence of Leeser's learning, labor, and leadership expanded far and wide. Many came for advice and counsel. He undertook long journeys and enthralled hundreds of audiences with his vast learning and articulate presentations. His ravaging sicknesses did not stand in the way of his service to God. He dedicated synagogues, propagated Judaism among its adherents, and defended it and them when attacked.

The years of Leeser's service are marked as among the most prolific and fruitful in the history of the rabbinate. Those productive years saw him as author, educator, textbook writer, publisher, translator, editor, communal leader; and in each area, he excelled. To satisfy the "lamentable deficiency of devotional works" he prepared English translations of Hebrew services—Daily, Sabbath, Fasts, Festivals, and Holy Days, a new version of the Pentateuch, and the first American edition of the Hebrew Bible. Until the rise of Isaac M. Wise, Leeser was the unquestioned leading rabbi in America.

Leeser's arrival in Philadelphia brought with it almost immediately a major change in the congregation. Though he was a strict traditionalist, he introduced innovations, among them the English sermon, the following year. It is he who is credited with the American synagogue practice of a weekly sermon or discourse. He collected all his sermons and essays and published them in a series of volumes called *Discourses, Argumentative and Devotional on the Jewish Religion*. Each discourse opens with a prayer. The prayer ended, the discourse is introduced by the endearing

word, "Brethren." The learned oration—and each is a near masterpiece
characterized by a prophetic fervor almost comparable to that of Jeremiah—concluded, Leeser ends with a prayer. Thus, to Leeser, the discourse may well have been considered part of prayer—study and
knowledge being evaluated as equal to prayer and worship.

Leeser was astute, far-sighted and practical. He noted the emptiness
of educational materials. He realized early that the only way to maintain
the faith and survive was to enlist interest. To keep the youth within
the traditional fold, they had to be taught and taught abundantly, fully,
and on their level. But there were few books and materials available
for children. He knew that he could not bemoan and decry the lack
of education without doing something about filling the void himself.
He thus set out to create a whole literature of textbooks for both children
and adults. He wrote a *Hebrew Reader*—a spelling book. He prepared
a *Catechism for Jewish Children,* subtitling it "A Religious Manual for
House and School." He dedicated it to the gracious Rebecca Gratz, who
with his encouragement and prodding organized the Sunday School
for Mikveh Israel, forerunner and model for the Sunday School system
in America and of the Hebrew Sunday School Society of Philadelphia.
The eminent minister selected 12 general headings: from "Religion
in General" to "The Jewish Creed," from "God and His Attributes"
to "Life after Death," from "The Law Revealed through Moses" to "The
Ceremonial Law." Each chapter follows the same pattern, a question
and an answer. The questions are simple and direct, the answers are
brief and concise; 378 questions, comprehensively covering every phase
of Jewish thought and practice, appear here—the underlying basis of
which is belief in the revealed word of God, the Bible, the binding
character of the Law, and the Thirteen-Principled Creed of Maimonides.

Pedagogue that he was, Leeser was aware that children unassisted
could not fully comprehend and appreciate the approach of the *Catechism*. He therefore exhorted teachers to exercise care and caution and
to offer clear, preparatory explanations before the volume was placed
in their hands for study.

Here are a few examples of the approach he advocated:

What is religion?
  Religion is the knowledge we have of God, and the duties we owe in
obedience to His will.

What do you mean by saying, "I believe in God"?

I believe, that everything I see around me, the trees, the flowers, the earth, the water, also the sun and the moon, and the thousands of bright stars that shine so beautifully in the sky, were made by the great Creator, whom we call "The Almighty God."

What object do you think God had in creating so many varied living creatures, and especially Man?

Their happiness: that is to say, God made them, not for His own sake, since *He* cannot be assisted by them, but in order that *they* might have the means and capacities to rejoice in their existence, and to become better and wiser by education and the knowledge of His will.

What religion do you profess?

I profess the Mosaic Religion, which was revealed by the Lord; and I esteem the same as the true, pure, and unmixed word of God.

Can we see God?

No; God is a spirit and cannot be seen by human eyes.

How can such a Being be known?

Through the spirit dwelling in Man; that is to say, we can recognize or discover a spirit through the working of our soul or mind, which is likewise a spirit.

In what relation do we stand to God?

God is our Father, and we are His children.

What is prayer?

The raising of our thoughts to God, and the expressing of the feelings of our hearts in words addressed to our Maker. . . .

To whom have we duties to perform?

Towards God, through whose favor we live. Towards our fellow-men, who, as well as ourselves, have received life and being from God. Towards ourselves, both as regards our body and our soul.

In 1843, he founded *The Occident and American Jewish Advocate,* the first successful Jewish monthly in America and, in effect, the forerunner of Jewish journalism in the country. The *Occident* existed for a quarter of a century. Its 26 volumes record American Jewish history in its making. There are addresses and sermons in it. There are editorials describing and analyzing every event in Jewish life all over the world. Views of all kinds, in agreement with the editor or opposed, are included. The establishment and organization of synagogues are faithfully recorded. Communal events are described and discussed. The *Occident* has become the primary source for information on Jewish life of its time and clearly mirrors the struggles, controversies, events, and anxieties of the Jewish scene in this crucial period. Reflecting also Leeser's dream of union of all Israel, the *Occident* provided a great unifying influence. It was the undisputed leader in its field until the publication of Isaac M. Wise's *Israelite* ten years later, but it retained its influence and stature.

Through the pages of the *Occident* and other volumes, Leeser, champion of traditional Judaism, spoke out on every major issue, Jewish and American. Together with other liberals, he fought vehemently the introduction of religion into the Constitution. He opposed energetically the use of the Bible in the public schools. He spoke out forcefully against the Sunday Sabbath laws that worked hardships upon those who observed the Jewish Sabbath.

The sense of need for unity was so intense within him that he supported every and any call which urged union. He believed that it was necessary to establish an ecclesiastical authority in America which would have jurisdiction over ministers. This body would have no official association with any individual congregation, but would deal with the group as a whole. He joined Isaac M. Wise in every effort which pointed to the possibility of unity. A famous and nearly successful conference was convened in Cleveland in 1855. While both opposing leaders of American Judaism were present, each to project his view, a compromise agreement was reached. The crucial question revolved around the basic principle of the authority of the Talmud. Rabbi Henry Englander, in his essay on Leeser in the Central Conference of American Rabbis' *Yearbook,* 1918, describes the event:

> Wise had proposed, as the sense of the conference, the declaration that the Bible is the revealed and inspired word of God and the Talmud the logical and legal development of Scripture. Leeser offered a substitute to the effect that the "Talmud contains the divine tradition given to Moses, and that all Israelites must decide all questions according to its decision." Agreement was obtained on the compromise proposition declaring "the Talmud to contain the traditional, logical and legal exposition of sacred Scriptures." Leeser felt that he could accept the compromise with the

mental reservation that the word "traditional" implied a "divine" exposition. Leeser expressed his joy at the view taken in reference to the Talmud by declaring it to be his belief that the 17th day of October, 1855, would be a national holiday if all Israelites in America would adopt the Bible as the rule of faith, and the Talmud as the rule of practice and interpretation of Holy Writ.

Although the attempt at union did not succeed, Leeser continued his efforts all his days to bring it about.

One of Leeser's lifelong concerns was the role of the rabbi in American life. He was perhaps the first leader in America to speak out for freedom of the pulpit and for more privileges for the religious leader of the synagogue. He particularly insisted that the rabbi be fully prepared for his holy ministry. American rabbis, he felt, should be prepared in American institutions. He aspired to develop a rabbinate which would be native-trained and prepared.

We say it with heartfelt sorrow, there is no school either in England or America where a Jewish student of theology could be educated, or whence he might issue forth as an able representative of his religion and a real expounder of the Word.

This he wrote in 1844 in the *Occident*. Soon thereafter he prepared a suggested curriculum for a seminary. Much of his waning effort was exercised toward the realization of this goal. Only one year before his death Maimonides College was founded with Leeser as its president, the first theological seminary for rabbis and teachers in the entire western hemisphere. It did not last, however. With the loss of its moving spirit, it, too, expired. Only four students were graduated before its doors were closed.

Leeser's career is so varied and his spirit so permanently impressed upon the structure of American Jewish life that it is difficult to single out his greatest contribution. He identified himself with every movement for the advancement of Jews and Judaism. Certainly in the field of literature his magnum opus was his translation of the Bible into English, the result of 18 years of effort. While not the first, in fact the fourth, Leeser's rendering of the Bible into readable language was widely accepted and recognized as authoritative. Moreover, it was easy to read and understand, a blessing to those who could not understand the original Hebrew and had to rely on the Christian King James version. Leeser's translation of the Bible remained the almost official work until replaced by the Jewish Publication Society translation in 1917, a combined achievement of Orthodox, Conservative and Reform leaders which in turn is now being replaced by a still newer translation.

When he retired from Mikveh Israel in 1850, Leeser devoted seven years to study and writing. Then when Temple Beth El Emeth was organized by some of his friends, he became its rabbi and served until his death on February 1, 1868.

Leeser was almost as well-known and as much admired among Gentiles as among his own people. He was regarded as representative and spokesman of the Jewish community. When Lincoln was assassinated, Leeser immediately delivered a memorial address before his congregation, and soon afterward was called to Washington to be the principal speaker at a Lincoln memorial service. In 1844 his became one of the first Jewish congregations to observe Thanksgiving. In a service at Mikveh Israel he extolled the blessings of democratic America:

> Yes, this land was blessed, is blessed. Fruitful are its fields, extensive are its forests; through untrodden regions extend its majestic thousand rivers; its sea-shore is crowded with the commerce of the world; its sails whiten every ocean; through its numerous towns resound the shouts of merriment; the people are secure against oppression, if they but preserve the spirit of their laws; peace may be said to dwell in the boundaries thereof, and each man may sit under the shade of his fruit-tree with none to make him afraid.

His demand, however, for equal rights for Jews, knows no peer in passion and vigor:

> Ay, you made us drink, drink deep out of the cup of degradation, you drugged our cup of misery with poison that slays the soul, and now we reel, we stagger under the intoxicating, brutalizing draught; and you mock us! You, the authors of our woe, cry out against the unclean, whom you yourself have rendered so! You offer us your pity, your commiseration! Away with it, we want it not. We have withstood your persecutions upheld by our Maker, we are yet a people, although we are not in Palestine. . . . Yes, we ask not your pity; only we *claim* your justice. To the Christians we would say, "We are your elder brothers"; to Mohammedans, "From us you received the law"; to the philosophical rationalist, "We are the found-

ers of the true system of rationalism"; to the lovers of freedom, "Ours was the first code that called all men equal"; and to all "That we are innocent of evil designs against the gentile states and their laws"; we ask only to be let alone; to be suffered undisturbed to walk the even tenor of our ways; and to pursue happiness in the manner best consonant to our wishes and our wants.

Champion of traditional Judaism, Leeser never faltered in its cause. He may have allowed innovations to be introduced into the synagogue service. He insisted on the sermon in English. He removed the custom of selling Torah honors. He altered the procedure of the blessing called *Mi Sheberach* recited for each one called to the Torah by combining one blessing for all. These were, however, to him not violations of traditional Judaism. The principles upon which Judaism rested were immutable, unchangeable, eternal. Leeser was their passionate defender and proponent and he was consistent throughout his life. In one of his earlier essays he maintained:

> . . . the law given by God through Moses is the citadel in which we must take shelter; but let that rude hand be blasted which should impiously dare to break down the wall which our good pastors and faithful guardians have with so much care built around it.

Leeser felt himself to be one of the faithful guardians, as indeed he was. He did not stray from his path of belief. God, the Creator, had revealed himself through Moses. The Law of Moses was permanent and changeless. It must be observed. Time and again he refers to the certitude of his faith and finds strength therein as he shares his convictions with his listeners:

> There is but one right way, and this way is the one pointed out by the revelation of God. For the man of no principle, except his own vague ideas of right and wrong, can have no guide save interest and expedience; and as these guides are different with different persons, and constantly changing their position with the same persons even, it follows, that to measure the right by this standard would be to admit a constant change in its quality and application; and that which is wrong in one would be right in another; and what was condemned today might meet with our approbation tomorrow. . . .
>
> Where next shall we look for the desired standard? From men in general, let us ascend to the favored few who are endowed with powers of

intellect beyond their fellows, but are they capable of deciding so unerringly as to become our guides? Do their bodies not sicken? Do their thoughts never become clouded? Remains their judgment always unimpaired? And has interest nothing to do in making their opinions turn to the right and left? And lastly, are they infallible in their decisions? . . .

Let us next go into the assemblies of the honored and great ones of the land; but there we shall find confusion even worse confused. Interest there rules with a potent hand; popular favor is to be courted; popular applause is to be won; the million is to be propitiated and each individual bows at the altar of fear and self-aggrandizement. . . .

Let us next go among the religious sects, among whom the earth is divided. But there too the weakness of human nature will astound and baffle us. . . .

Ages of suffering have passed over us, and even now our afflictions are not ended! How many thousands were slaughtered, how many innocents were plundered for no evil they had done, but solely because they bore the hated name of Jew; and who heeded their sufferings? Who cared for the blood that flowed? Who minded how many stakes were kindled? It was but the Hebrew that laid in the dungeon; it was but the Israelite that groaned under the blow; it was but the Jew who shrieked as the flames slowly devoured him! And were it not that we had been dispersed, were it not that persecution could not overtake us simultaneously in all countries, the name of the seed of Jacob had long since perished. But thanks to Him who woundeth and also healeth, and who prepareth the balsam, even before the blow is struck! He caused us, when wandering from our land, to be scattered wherever mankind dwelt, and always caused some to compassionate us, when others laid snares for our feet. So that we were preserved in diminished numbers, but still preserved, a nation one and undivided, to glorify the Name, the honored and fearful, the everlasting Lord our God. . . . Can there be a stronger argument of the truth of the law, which has preserved a handful of people entire, when the mightiest empires have been swept away and have left not a wreck even behind? Let this therefore be our consolation, that we are in possession of the rule of right; a rule handed down to us from heaven; a rule under which in God's own good time all nations will be made happy. . . .

Certainly it can be seen that Leeser's devout feeling for God, His Torah, and His people, includes a profound belief in the doctrine of Israel's selection. Of this there is no question in his mind and he says it unhesitatingly:

. . . the giving of the law was the virtual selection of Israel, and an obedience to this law confers upon Israel the just appellation of God's peculiar people, since at no time has any other people acted according to the law given to them, and never could show any reason why another law should be considered as divine legislation.

We are, it is true, dispersed over every land, in almost every island; but still we are united—the bond of one law, and the belief in one God, keeps us as one, though scattered in every corner. It is in this manner that the God of our fathers has fulfilled the covenant which He made with us; and thus He has proved that His mercies are unending, even to the sinful and the lowly ones. He has also promised that when we are repentant, and return to Him in sincerity, that He would restore our captives, and bring us back to our land. . . .

Leeser is sure, utterly sure that the people of Israel will have their homeland once again. He bemoans the fate of his people in days gone by. In words which convey the torment of the scene he writes of the destruction of the Temples in Jerusalem which gave impetus to the Dispersion, which he is sure will end with glorious restoration:

Rapidly did the flames spread; and on all sides towers were crushed, and walls crumbled into dust; whilst the bodies of the defenders covered the spots where they stood; and the corpses of the priests were thrown in heaps around the altar, and the floor of the temple was made slippery with the gore of the victims, and the headless and severed limbs were strewn about, and the wild shout of the heartless soldier was heard above the noise of the devouring element—destruction reigned all around—and even the voice of the commander, whom the sight of so much misery had excited to compassion, remained unheeded. . . .

The tale of suffering and persecution has been repeated time and time again through the ages, but it is all but a bad dream in the light of God's promise to Israel's children. Leeser speaks in the accents of the thundering prophets of old as he foretells the return of Israel to the homeland, binding the homeland up with the acceptance of the Torah:

. . . Which is the country that the collective nation of Israelites can call their own land? Is it this land, where freedom dwells? Is it the land of the Spaniard, where the name of freedom is almost unknown? Is it the wide desert of central Asia where the barbarous Tatar feeds his countless herds? Is it the country where the Russian despot rules with tyrannic sway?

—No! no! it is the favored land of the East, where the Israelites dwelled of yore; it is the land which God covenanted to give to Abraham, to Isaac, and to Jacob, and to their seed after them; it is the land of the Lebanon, which the dying prophet desired so ardently to see; it is the land where the once beautiful Jerusalem yet stands although in ruins; it is the land where stood in olden days the sacred temple, resplendent once in all the beauty of holiness, but which our transgressions, alas! caused to be twice destroyed, when our people fell into the hands of the enemies! This is the land which is the Israelite's home, and he should always regard himself as having an interest in its soil, although he has been born in exile, in the country of the stranger, far from the banks of the lowly Jordan; for there it was where our national glory reached its highest elevation, and because we have remained scattered and disunited, ever since we were driven thence. Do not misunderstand me as saying that you should not regard the country in which you live as your own, and that you should not endeavor to serve it according to the best of your abilities; for we are commanded by the prophet, speaking in the name of God, "to seek the peace of the city to which we have been banished." As Jews, therefore, and believers in the revealed law and the prophets, we are bound to obey the laws of the land and to uphold the authorities in every instance where their edicts are not at variance with the Commandments of God.

One ought not to suppose that Leeser either expected or pleaded for blind faith. To him, simple belief was not enough. It had to be motivated and expressed. As he stated it:

The religion, by the bestowal of which God has favored us, demands of us two things: namely, believing or faith, and deeds, or in other words, active religion. Without a motive for action we do not act, and consequently without a motive for religious conduct we would certainly not be religious; and consequently if we wish to be religious, or to speak more properly, if we are really anxious to secure that great share of happiness which flows from an obedience to the divine law, we must fortify ourselves previously by an acquisition of such feelings as best conduce to such a desirable consummation; or what is the same, we must endeavor to grow in faith, and strengthen thereby the growth of good deeds; for faith alone cannot be the producer of outward actions, if these actions are to have the least claim to sincerity.

He places the burden of teaching religion squarely in the laps of parents. It is they who will inspire children to mature in the faith, or, either by direct action or default, bear the blame for the wilting of the faith. He speaks boldly and frankly:

> To you, therefore, fathers in Israel, do I address myself; devote some more time to the personal superintendence over the education of your children, and do not leave their future happiness entirely to pensioned strangers, who but too often think themselves absolved from all responsibility. . . . And you, who are mothers in the house of Jacob, listen I pray you, to the advice of a brother, though he be young and not as experienced or as virtuous as many of you. In your power it is to produce a great reformation in the state of our youths. . . . Try your gentle power of persuasion, which you can so powerfully exert; lead your children and your wards in the way they should go. . . .

He urges the study and retention of Hebrew:

> A national tongue binds together the people speaking it in one bond, and cements a union hardly otherwise attainable. . . . Hebrew has always maintained its position in the love and the heart of all true Israelites, and has constituted the bond which has kept united the captivity of Jacob in all parts of the world. . . . The holy tongue is their bond, and by it do they meet as a band of brothers, and all thus unite to call with one voice upon their God, who is truly the Preserver of Israel. . . .

Thus reads Leeser—in words which ring with the resonance of Israel's inspired prophets. This was not a man to keep silent when speech was indicated. It matters not where or when the circumstances, in the pulpit, on the platform, at the convention, in the home, on the street. What must be said, must be said. And he drives his message home whatever the issue, let the chips fall where they may. Like Jeremiah, fired by the love of God and zeal for the faith, Leeser rose on every occasion to fulfill his role as defender of his faith.

DAVID EINHORN

Uncompromising Exponent of Reform Judaism

[1809-1879]

Under a mantle of darkness, September 23, 1777, the magnificently symbolic Liberty Bell was escorted out of Philadelphia and taken to Zion Reformed Church, Allentown, Pennsylvania, where it was hidden under the floor of the stone building for the duration of the siege of Philadelphia in America's Revolutionary War. General Howe's British armies were rapidly approaching the city that had been called the Cradle of Liberty. Thus threatened, the Liberty Bell was removed from the belfry of the State House where the Declaration of Independence had been signed only 15 months earlier and taken to safety.

Less than one hundred years later, April 22, 1861, under a mantle of darkness, a rabbi, his wife and two children were stealthily escorted out of Baltimore, Maryland, and brought to safety in Philadelphia. These were Civil War days. The purpose of this war was the same—freedom—except that this time reference was to freedom within America itself and for human beings of color. The rabbi was among the most outspoken of the spiritual leaders in America who deplored slavery. He was an uncompromising abolitionist, forcefully, unhesitatingly preaching liberty and freedom for all men. But Maryland was a border state, and sympathy was with the Southern cause. Feeling ran high. Mobs poured through the city day after day, burning and destroying.

Before this night, Rabbi David Einhorn had been shown a list of people marked for death on which his name appeared prominently, but he had not been deterred. Friends had urged him to relent, pleading with him to escape. He had refused. Finally a group of young men had volunteered to stand guard around his home. It was only when he realized that the safety of his wife and children was endangered and the lives of the devoted young men who stood guard that he allowed his good friends to arrange the escape.

He felt humiliated and debased as he traveled through the night. He had come to America only six years before, to a land where free speech was guaranteed. Now, as in Europe, it was being denied. One can well imagine his frustration and confusion. He felt, however, that in Philadelphia he could speak fearlessly. He also expected that when mob rule was wiped out and law and order restored in Baltimore he would return to his pulpit triumphantly. Meanwhile, the city where liberty in America was born would provide a platform for him. Fate did not so decree. He never returned to his pulpit. The board of directors, before the lapse of too much time, influenced by Southern sympathizers, advised him that the pulpit was no longer his. His position as rabbi of Keneseth Israel Congregation in Philadelphia was not to be temporary.

This was not the first time this restless reformer had moved on. Ever at the center of controversy, David Einhorn from his earliest days in the rabbinate kept moving—preaching, teaching as he went. Peace was never his portion. He seemed to have been born to combat. Slim and sharp-featured, he looked the fighter he was. But although he made more enemies than friends, he never deviated from principle.

Perhaps this inner strength of David Einhorn, who was destined to become a standard-bearer for Reform Judaism, came from his mother. He was born on November 10, 1809, in the small Bavarian village of Dispeck, near Fuerth. The year of his birth was one that saw the birth of several future leaders of men. Friedrich Schiller, Charles Darwin and Martin Luther were born on the same day. Lincoln, Tennyson, Gladstone, Poe and Mendelssohn all saw the light of day in 1809. Fate had decreed greatness for each in spheres encompassing almost every important area of human aspiration. For Einhorn, fate had decreed dynamic leadership in a turbulent world of rapid change.

David's mother, early determining that her son should be strong and resolute, devoted her energies to bringing him up properly. He early showed a brilliant mind and capacity for learning which amazed and thrilled his teachers. At the age of ten he was already a student at the famed Talmudic Academy of Rabbi Wolf Hamburger, leading scholar of the period. Although his companions were much older than he, his thirsty, incisive mind soon overcame the age differential. For seven years, under the personal tutelage and supervision of the Rosh Hayeshivah, head of the Academy, David's keen mind absorbed knowledge of the Bible, Talmud, and Codes. At the age of 17, the precocious boy was awarded traditional Semicha, ordination. The parchment given at the time usually indicates the scholastic accomplishments of the recipient. Einhorn's tells of his keen mind and great erudition in the most glowing terms. He was thus at the tender age of 17 marked for greatness in a rabbinical career.

He did indeed achieve greatness, but not in the same rabbinical world. Like many others, Einhorn had quietly and privately studied areas of knowledge which were not part of the Yeshivah curriculum, such as mathematics and the classics. Modern culture had captivated many minds, Einhorn's among them. With youth on his side, he decided to further and broaden his education. He moved from university to university, from Erlangen to Wuerzburg and thence to Munich. By the time his university education was formally completed, Einhorn, torn within and without, mixed feelings and views plaguing him, was a changed man. Traditionalism had lost its appeal. Indeed, he became a militant foe of Orthodox Judaism. The admiration and esteem of his former teachers receded as they saw their erstwhile favorite take up with the reformers of his day. With few pulpits open to a radical thinker and outspoken reformer, he was shut out from the active rabbinate.

Ten years of bitter disappointment were to elapse, but his spirit remained undaunted. He studied and prepared. His time for service would come. In 1842, at the age of 33, he became rabbi of Hoppstaedten in the Grand Duchy of Oldenburg. The members of the small congregation were sympathetic to his views and innovations were consequently not difficult to institute. He had finally secured a home base from which to function as rabbi.

David Einhorn was not, however, marked out for serene and peaceful service. Great problems were capturing and confronting thinking men and women. Theological, religious and historical issues were stirring up a whole Jewish generation. Sides were being drawn, controversies shaping up, and Einhorn, though young in years, was in the very midst, participating completely and aggressively in all discussions. No matter his opponent and on whatever religious issue, Einhorn plunged in, supporting his every assertion with rabbinic bases and Talmudic sources.

Hardly had he become the rabbi of Hoppstaedten when controversies on the rabbinical scene erupted. In the great Geiger-Tiktin controversy, in which Abraham Geiger was accused of being a Karaite and a denier of truth, Einhorn, seeing himself as the butt of the accusation also, rose to defend the great thinker. At the same time, when the Frankfort Reform Verein proposed principles which to Einhorn were destructive and abhorrent to Judaism, he unhesitatingly lashed out against it

> . . . at a time when a consolidation of all our forces is greatly needed in view of the many disintegrating and hostile powers that we have to encounter, under the mast of reform aims at a schismatic disruption, nay, at the uprooting and the overthrow of Judaism. It wants to put anarchy in the place of law. Instead of pointing out what is mutable and transitory and what is immutable and permanent, either in the doctrine or the law of Mosaism, it declares the same to be in a process of perpetual and unlimited motion, which is tantamount to saying that it has no divine character at all, that it is human in origin and may culminate in Spinozaism. The apostles of a new religion built on mere negation have renounced not merely the externals, but the kernel, the doctrines of Mosaism; they avowedly reduce the divine wisdom which all the generations of the past have drawn from the teachings of the Law, to the level of treasures attained by the great intellects of all nations. . . .

Einhorn here not only attacks the particular Verein, but he brings out the ideas and principles upon which he is destined to stand as leader of the Reform movement in America later on. He continues in the same vein:

> In all its stages, Judaism shows its capacity for continuous development both as to its form and its spirit, insofar as the latter became ever clearer and purer in the human consciousness; and no Israelite who knows his religion will deny it the power of perfectibility. Its essence, which is truth uniting all men, was from the beginning intended to overcome the exclusiveness attached to the form, which is national; but insofar as the latter served as an armor of protection and as the priestly garb of Israel among the nations, it can not with impunity be cast off until the former in its entire inner force and its all-encompassing extent will have penetrated the

whole human family, and Israel (Mosaism) have fulfilled its priestly mission at the arrival of the Messianic era.

In every major issue, theological and practical, in almost every conference and convention called to ventilate the thinking and suggestions of the new movement, Einhorn played an increasingly large role. He had opinions and knowledge on every issue. His views were listened to and heard. The new movement, revolutionary by its very nature and reflecting the revolutionary temper of the time, sought spokesmen and leaders who would be able to project its spirit, but with basic knowledge and depth of conviction. Einhorn was such a one.

When the matter of the use of Hebrew in the service was discussed, Einhorn was prepared:

While the Talmud leaves no doubt as to the permissibility of the vernacular in the liturgy, he [referring to Zacharias Frankel, who insisted on maintenance of Hebrew in the liturgy] would urge its use in the divine service as a necessity today. Hebrew is the language of the study of the Law. As long as prayer was mainly the cry of the oppressed Jew, the scarcely intelligible Hebrew sufficed. Now people need prayer as the simple expression of their innermost thoughts, convictions, and sentiments. This can only be attained through the mother-tongue. . . . By striking the rock of a dead language we cannot bring forth living waters to quench the thirst of the people.

On the matter of the statements of the Messianic idea in the prayer service, Einhorn is unequivocal:

We stand on the ground of prophetic Judaism which aims at a universal worship of God by righteousness. Israel's political overthrow, formerly bewailed as a misfortune, in reality is its forward move toward its larger destiny. Prayer took the place of sacrifice. From Israel's midst the word of God was to be carried to all parts of the earth, and new religious systems were to aid in this great work. The Talmud moves in a circle, whereas we today believe in progress. . . . The Messianic idea expresses, in my opinion, the hope of both earthly and heavenly salvation. There is nothing objectionable therein. The belief in Israel's election also contains nothing that is repugnant. On the contrary, it should be retained in the service as expressing the claim of an undeniable privilege, as it engenders in the Jew a feeling of reassuring self-consciousness over against the ruling church.

Every question projected—and by its very nature, the early Reform movement questioned everything: thought as well as practice—had the stamp of Einhorn's mind and voice upon it. The changes then wrought and innovations instituted have to some measure been retained. In other words, Einhorn was a framer and former of the Reform movement in Europe as well as in America. All questions which concerned the Reform movement were concerns of Einhorn. To him, the Sabbath "bears the character of a symbol. It is to remind Israel of God, the Creator and the Deliverer from bondage." He urged removal of the Second Day of Festivals because "the whole Jewish calendar derives its sanction from a fictitious authorization by the defunct Synhedrion at Jerusalem. We no longer consider Jerusalem as the center of Judaism. By the abolition of the Second Holiday, which in the Talmud also is in many ways regarded as inferior to the first day, we declare our religious independence of Palestine." The dietary laws should be abrogated because of their "interfering . . . with our high mission as a priest-people to bring our sacred truth home to the people surrounding us." In all, he insisted that Reform's intent was not to undermine the authority of the Bible, rather the laws were not intended for our day and age. To Einhorn, the concepts of the holiness of the Jewish people and the binding nature of the ceremonial laws are superceded by the Messianic era which foresees including the entire human family into the covenant with God.

In 1847, when the position of Chief Rabbi of Mecklenburg-Schwerin became available, having been vacated by David Holdheim, one of the most radical of reformers, Einhorn was elected to the post. As usual, controversy erupted almost immediately. The issue was circumcision, with Einhorn as chief rabbi at the center of the conflict.

Einhorn's prayerbook began to take shape during this period. It was later issued under the title *Olath Tamid* (Perpetual Offering), and eventually became the basis of the official Union Prayerbook. He felt unhappy with the traditional prayerbook because it was not in consonance with the reformers' views toward Zion and Palestine. They sought to stress, Einhorn among them, Israel's election for the Messianic mission for mankind. The Messianic mission of Israel was Einhorn's lifetime refrain:

The task before us is not an easy one, and requires long deliberation, especially insofar as the ardent longing for Zion and the lofty spirit of resignation in view of all the suffering and shame of the centuries past, lent to the Jewish liturgy such rare power of elevation and buoyant hope and such wondrous charm. We must therefore find the adequate form for it in our Messianic hope and not allow it to be absorbed by our aspiration for political emancipation and civic equality.

Einhorn made repeated attempts at unity and peace between Orthodox and Reform in the city, seeming to suggest that each community provide for both religious services. His plans were doomed. He pleaded with the government, defending his liturgical changes and other innovations and views. When after four years he saw that success would not be his, he accepted a call from the Reform Congregation in Pesth, Hungary. Here, his period of duty was astonishingly brief. Again, his service was marked by opposition from Orthodoxy and from the government, the latter hesitating to defend that which was theologically revolutionary. The entire European continent was bathed in revolution and strife. His official duties lasted but two months, and then the government closed the doors of the temple.

Einhorn was not crushed. He stayed on at the homes of friends, developing his theological structure and crystalizing his thinking, as if in preparation for the call which was soon to come from America.

Har Sinai Congregation in Baltimore, Maryland, summoned David Einhorn in 1855. He arrived in America preceded by his reputation. Stories of his scholarship, oratorical genius and dynamic spirit had earlier reached the shores of the new country. Einhorn, for his part, hoped that the new climate of freedom and humanitarianism would provide more ready soil for his liberal ideas. Here in America he could speak without fear. Here there would be a rallying of all like-minded men who were concerned with the future of Judaism and who felt that major changes were necessary. In his inaugural address on September 27, 1855, he was immediately outspoken in the cause of Reform:

We have come to a turning point. Our entire religious and moral life is imperiled. Mere outward forms which render the service more attractive are of no avail. They merely hide the inner decay. Judaism must be reformed from within. The evil which threatens to absorb all the wholesome vigor and marrow must be remedied at the root. Whatever is in a state of decay and has lost its hold on the people must be taken out of the system in order that the religious life be made whole and healthy again. Lest our children emancipate themselves from Judaism altogether, we must emancipate Judaism from such shackles as tend to corrupt the inner life. But in removing the scaffolding we must be careful not to tear down the structure. We want to build up. We do not lack piety. Profound reverence for our religious sanctuary dictates our steps and should direct us to concentrate our energies all the more fully and single heartedly upon the essence of the divine law which is far above the changes of time and place, and which will remain in force, even though the earth wax old like a garment, and the heavens vanish like smoke. We want no self-created cult, no Judaism modelled to suit our taste, no stripping off of Jewish characteristics, no straying away into the empty void. No, on the contrary, we want an Israelitism with all its distinctions sharply brought out as rooted in Sinai, and destined to bring forth new blossoms and fruitage upon the lofty height of a four thousand years' history.

Standing upon the immovable ground of divine revelation, we must turn our entire attention to our system of belief. The more the ceremonial laws lose of importance and dominion, the more necessary is a comprehension of the Jewish faith in its uniqueness as the fountain of our strength, the cause of our endurance throughout the centuries. For ours is the belief in the innate goodness and purity of all things and particularly those beings created in the divine image whose power of self-sanctification is never interfered with by any other force and who need no other mediation for redemption than their own free will. Ours is the belief in one human family, whose members, all being made alike and endowed with the same claim and title to happiness, will all participate in the bliss of that glorious time when the blood-stained purple of earthly kings will forever be consigned to the grave, together with all the garnished lies, selfishness and persecution, and God alone will rule as King over all the nations who will become the one people of God. These doctrines, first presented in the garb of specific Jewish nationality, in order that man should not be dazzled by the splendor of their sublime truth, are still the proud possession of Israel and its hope for the future. These doctrines enshrine treasures of world-redeeming thoughts, and it is our sacred task to unfold and apply them to the realities of life and enrich thereby the heart and the soul. As to the ceremonies, they are to be held sacred and inviolable as long as they awaken religious thought and sentiment. . . .

Two months after Einhorn's dramatic inaugural address with its lofty ideals, the Cleveland Conference, attended by the most prominent rabbis in America, from both the Orthodox and Reform camps, adopted unanimously a pronouncement which agreed upon the divinity of the Bible and acknowledged the Talmud as the legal and obligatory commentary on the Bible:

1. The Bible as delivered to us by our fathers . . . is of immediate divine origin and the standard of our religion.
2. The Talmud contains the traditional, legal, and logical exposition of the Biblical laws, which must be expounded and practiced according to the comments of the Talmud.

Einhorn was stunned. He felt that the very leaders of Reform had themselves undermined and sabotaged the true Reform position. He had many years before revealed his attitude toward the Talmud:

Such an infallibility, such an apotheosis we cannot and we may not grant to the Talmud; however strong our belief in its veracity may be, we must refuse and reject such deification; we address the Talmud in these words, "Israel believes thee, but not in thee; thou art a medium through which the divine may be reached, but thou art not divine."

He had certainly expected all reformers to project similar views. They had not been prepared, however, to go as far as Einhorn. Instead, his Reform colleagues had joined traditional rabbis in a statement which declared the Talmud to be the authoritative interpreter of the Bible and consequently binding upon the Jew. In effect, Einhorn, conservative reformer in Europe, had turned out to be a radical reformer in America. The alignment of Orthodox and Reform was a crushing blow to him. Indeed, it was to be felt for many years as a source of friction among Reform rabbis themselves.

Einhorn's congregation sent a stirring protest against the adoption of the platform. But the position had already been adopted. Einhorn turned his sights elsewhere.

He had long sought a vehicle through which to express his views and those of the Reform movement. Accordingly, in February, 1856, he began to issue a monthly magazine entitled *Sinai* which was destined to exist for some seven years. As his motto he selected Joseph's statement in the Bible which he made when he went out to search for his brothers, "Et Achai ani m'vakesh—My brethren do I seek." The monthly contains many magnificent articles and editorials representing the thinking of David Einhorn and other Reform leaders. The fact that it was written in German, however, rendered it less effective than it would have been had it been printed in English. Herein, in fact, lies a well-recognized major deficiency of Einhorn's position. His basic training and environment having been German and of German influence, he felt that German language and ideas must be basic to the Reform movement. Even the training of rabbis, he maintained, ought to include a period of study in Germany.

While serving his congregation, and at the same time striking out for larger horizons on which to experiment with the views burning deeply within him, Einhorn sought to create a worship ritual which would express the principles of Reform. He had begun thinking of an appropriate prayerbook while still in Europe. The worship service, he believed, required a prayerbook which would reflect the ideas of the new movement. He was not satisfied to move slowly. Isaac M. Wise's prayerbook, *Minhag America,* to him was nothing more than the traditional prayerbook which merely excluded prayers and passages not in harmony with Reform ideology. Thus it was that after many years of thought and arduous effort, he issued his own prayerbook in May, 1856, entitled *Olath Tamid,* meaning Perpetual Offering. The new prayerbook provided his congregation with a worship service which projected his principles of Reform. While it was hailed by many Reform leaders, especially by those rabbis who felt an ideological kinship with Einhorn, the prayerbook was not quickly accepted. Most importantly, it was written in German. To Einhorn, Reform Judaism must be rooted in both German spirit and language. Said he, "Where the German sermon is banned, there the reform of Judaism is nothing more than a brilliant glass, a decorated doll, without heart, without soul, which the proudest temples and the most splendid theories cannot succeed in infusing with life."

Over the years many calls were issued to translate Einhorn's prayerbook into English. Attempts failed until Emil G. Hirsch brought out a translation in 1896. In the meantime, the Central Conference of American Rabbis authorized a prayerbook for the entire movement, entitled the Union Prayerbook. Isaac M. Wise, who had earlier published his *Minhag America,* withdrew his creation, and the new prayerbook modeled after Einhorn's *Olath Tamid* became standard for Reform congregations throughout the land.

Einhorn's concerns were not limited to problems of Judaism and its expression. He felt deeply for the principles America stood for, and those feelings demanded expression when the slavery question moved to the fore. To Einhorn slavery was not only immoral in terms of the Bible, but in violation of every humanistic principle he held dear. It was a crime that must be eradicated. He did not care where he lived. True, Maryland was a border state where mixed feelings were exhibited not only by the general populace but by Jewish people as well. But to Einhorn, it was unthinkable, especially for Jews, to look with any favor upon slavery. Especially, he lashed out against those who quoted the Bible as favoring slavery. He could not restrain his articulate tongue against Jews, who above all others ought to have known the experience of slavery and subjection and yet closed their eyes or openly defended the principle.

Judaism has never adopted and never will an attitude of indifference on the question as to whether human slavery is to gain further ground, or whether the glorious institutions of our country, which had their origin in its inmost essence and nature and have already brought immeasurable blessing to mankind, are, or are not, to be laid in ruins by ambitious and perjured Rebels.

Is not the slavery question, above all things, a religious one? Can a religion which contains regulations with regard to one's treatment of an overloaded animal pass by, coldbloodedly and unfeelingly, a human being who has been mercilessly enslaved . . . ?

Throughout the entire year, humanity, clemency, benevolence, and mercy are lauded as the essence of Judaism. These are very cheap declamations! But whether or not a human being has the right to buy and sell another human being, like an animal, and to tear parents and children away from each other for all time—about this, God forbid!—not a single word is to be uttered, because it might shock the nervous system of the audience. Right there, ardent, pious zeal suddenly fades away—apparently because of fear of unholy politics, but actually because of politics. . . .

Scorning the entire civilized world, the rebellious South wants to overturn the principle of the innate quality of all beings created in the image of God, in favor of the opposing principle of innate servitude, and to see slavery and the law of might recognized as a force in the formation of states, as the basis of civilization. It wishes to tear the glorious Stars and Stripes to pieces, to trample it into the mire, and to set up in its place the bloody corpse of international freedom as an ornament.

If this diabolical undertaking should succeed, who would have more to fear than Israel, the very ancient slave of slaves? And should the religion of Israel, whose world-redeeming and happiness-bringing powers used to be boasted of so much in peaceful times, not have a word of indignation to say against such an outrage? Should it have no word of encouragement to utter on behalf of the highest possession of mankind, and to struggle against the kingdom of lies and of malice . . . ?

His strong views did not gain him friends nor win him popularity. But Einhorn was not one to concern himself with popularity. This was an insipid goal for a man of principle. It was this obstinacy that led to his humiliating departure from Baltimore in the middle of the night, April 22, 1861. To Einhorn, it was a most depressing experience. Imagine, running away, escaping from principle.

But better days were in store for him when he accepted the call of Keneseth Israel Congregation. He resumed publication of his monthly, *Sinai,* and received deserved recognition for his forthright stand for freedom. The Philadelphia Union League Club elected him an honorary member, for instance. He felt that his position had been vindicated. His feelings of love for the great founders of America, his admiration for Abraham Lincoln, he now could express freely without restraint. His shock when learning of the tragedy of the assassination of the great emancipator was reflected in his sermons and magazine writings. Indeed, David Einhorn was writing his own eulogy as American patriot when he eulogized martyred Lincoln.

His five years as rabbi of Keneseth Israel were marked by the continuation of his activities in the realm of thought. He devoted his time continuously to his *Sinai,* his congregation, and to the clearer formulation of his philosophy. He determined to provide a concise and clear understanding of the principles for which he stood. Tirelessly, he devoted himself to this task in the preparation and publication of *Ner Tamid* (Everlasting Light), a book on his system of thought. His views on revelation, prophecy, and the role of the forefathers of the Jewish people are herein given—the experience on Sinai, Giving of the Ten Commandments, described as the basis of the moral order; and Israel, the priest-people, as God's messengers to the world. Israel must retain its individual identity until the mission of bringing all mankind to the One God is fulfilled. Others, more radical than Einhorn, had held that the need for separateness or individual identity was not significant since it interfered with the mission of striving for all humanity.

In 1866, he accepted the pulpit of New York's Adeth Jeshurum Congregation, primarily because the congregation had many German-speaking members. In 1874, this synagogue merged with Anshe Chesed Congregation, to form Temple Beth El, and there Einhorn remained until his death.

As had other leading rabbis in America of all persuasions, Einhorn recognized that a movement cannot long endure without the proper training of rabbis to take places of leadership. In 1869, he succeeded in creating a loosely knit group for the promotion of higher Jewish learning in America, but its success was short-lived. He joined Isaac M. Wise a few years later in the call for discussions to establish an institution of learning in America. He later joined other Reform leaders, with whom he had earlier sharply disagreed, for the same purpose, becoming chairman of the course of studies committee for the Hebrew Union College in 1876.

In the meantime, Einhorn continued his writings. In 1869, *Sinai* having long since ceased publication, he successfully launched the *Jewish Times,* the staff of which included a number of Reform leaders. Encouraged by this success and the recognition that was at long last his, he convened in November, 1869, what was destined to be known as the Philadelphia Conference. Here, reframing of the principles of reform was discussed and new principles were adopted which formed the basis of the 1885 Pittsburgh Platform, official pronouncements of Reform Judaism for half a century until the Columbus Platform in 1937. Dr. Kaufmann Kohler, son-in-law and biographer of David Einhorn and one of the leaders of Reform, summarized them as follows:

They formed the basic union of American Reform Judaism and consolidated the ideas of religious progress both as to the form of divine service and the rabbinical functions outside of the Synagogue. They defined the main issues of Reform Judaism in (a) declaring the Messianic hope to be universalistic and not national, and Israel's dispersion over the globe to have the fulfillment of its world-mission for its object, and not punishment for sin, as was the rabbinical view; (b) consigning the sacrificial cult together with the Aaronitic priesthood and the belief in resurrection of the body to the past, and accenting the selection of Israel as the priest-people of humanity, and the belief in immortality; and finally, (c) urging the necessity of having a large portion of the prayers in the vernacular, in view of the unfamiliarity of the average Jew or Jewess with the Hebrew.

Psalm 90 allots to man three score and ten years and in unusual instances, four score years. David Einhorn's strength was not sufficient to enable him to reach the latter goal. Indeed, he did not quite make the former. One week before its achievement, he quietly expired. He had long felt tired. He had long labored tirelessly, self-sacrificingly, whole-heartedly. As his 70th year approached, he felt the time had come for rest. He had preached for many decades, looking upon it as a sacred and consecrated duty. His last sermon significantly was entitled "Eevri Anochi—I Am a Hebrew," the words Jonah uttered when he was on the ship en route to Nineveh at God's behest. Einhorn was always en route, always moving from pulpit to pulpit in Europe and in America, driven by a compulsion few have matched. He never relaxed. Despite his frequent espousal of unpopular views, Einhorn made his mark on Judaism. Many disagreed with him violently and fiercely, calling him rebel and revolutionary; but they respected his determination, his devotion, his unswerving firmness and earnestness. And all would admit that David Einhorn was a giant of faith.

MAX LILIENTHAL

American of the Americans

[1815-1882]

No giant of faith has ever been accorded as
many descriptive titles as Max Lilienthal—titles which tell the remarkable
story of the man whose passion for liberty and freedom secured him a
place in America's Hall of Fame. Max Lilienthal has been called:

> Great Conciliator
> American Jewish Prince of Peace
> Peacemaker
> Watchman on the Tower of Liberty
> Prophet of Humanity
> Vigilant Champion of American Principles
> Messenger of Peace
> Advocate of Peace
> Messenger of the Lord
> Apostle of Liberty
> American of the Americans

These titles portray not only the greatness of the person, but the
feeling and heart of one of the most fascinating personalities the 19th
century produced. Born in Munich, Bavaria, October 16, 1815, one of
four children of affluent parents, Lilienthal was early destined for
greatness. Greatness meant service to God via a rabbinical career.
Legend tells that just before he lost his mother at a tender age, he promised her faithfully that he would become a rabbi in Israel. Conscientiously

44

and studiously he devoted himself to the realization of this goal. He attended the University of Munich and was graduated in 1837. Concurrently he studied under the guidance of the renowned Rabbi Moses Wittelsbacher and matriculated at the famed Yeshivah of Wolf Hamburger in Fuerth. Rabbi Hirsch Aub, Rabbi of Munich, ordained Lilienthal, conferring upon him the degree of rabbi.

Lilienthal's excellence in his studies at the University of Munich attracted a great deal of attention. His scores on examinations were so unusually high that he was offered a position in the country's diplomatic service. Lilienthal was hard pressed to respond positively. He had earlier determined to be a rabbi and thus serve his God and his people. The offer, however, was attractive and as it came at a time when family financial reverses were such that his assistance was sorely needed, he succumbed to the temptation and accepted. Then he learned that a condition for his assumption of the post was conversion to Catholicism, and he immediately withdrew his acceptance. One can well picture his indignation at the apparent deception and the unbelievable suggestion that he renounce his ancestral faith.

This was not the only time he was the object of conversion attempts. His Christian classmates at the university "wept for his soul" and did not hesitate to suggest that he was a lost sheep because of his religious profession. When he later accepted a post in Russia, the wife of a Russian official, a fanatical member of the Russian Church, recommended conversion, but Lilienthal responded as he must have earlier when the government position dangled before him:

> No, madame, I am born a Jew and feel happy to be a Jew. The purpose of my feeble endeavors is to raise the Jews from their civil degradation to fit them for the higher services and duties of useful citizens, to remove even all the abuses that crept into our religious observances in the middle ages; but our religion, being of divine origin, cannot be changed, and our brethren today, as in times of yore, are ready to sacrifice blood and treasure rather than to yield to any missionary or proselytizing schemes.

Later in America, he was a fearless, outspoken opponent of missionary movements. He had been thoroughly conditioned to them. In his writings he devotes many chapters to converts and speaks bitterly about their loss of "all commiseration for their brethren."

Lilienthal now turned his attention to his rabbinical career. Here, too, he was blocked. The Jewish community, Orthodox in view and practice, had succeeded in convincing the government to issue an order denying congregations the right to select Reform rabbis or, as the document stated, rabbis who were "candidates favoring destructive neology," which meant, in effect, rabbis not of traditional Jewish mold. This decree was part of a larger edict which brought back the most stringent measures against Jews since medieval times. Stymied, Lilienthal looked toward other horizons. He studied and wrote, publishing a number of articles on Hebrew manuscripts. These works brought him into intimate contact with Dr. Ludwig Philippson, editor of the journal *Allgemeine Zeitung des Judentums* and probably the most influential Jew in Germany at that time. The association was fortuitious. It was this close relationship that led to Lilienthal's becoming a diplomat in the employ of the Russian government and a man who, though young in years, became associate and companion of diplomats and statesmen alike. Russia, through her Minister of Education Count Sergius Uwaroff, was seeking a superintendent to direct the destinies of a new Jewish school just established in Riga. Dr. Philippson, to whom the Count had turned for advice, recommended Lilienthal and he accepted.

At the age of 23, tall, stately Max Lilienthal left his home in 1839 for Russia and spent the next five years of his life in the courts of the czars and homes of Jewish leaders as the Crown's representative. The glamor of the high post soon faded as he realized the magnitude of the job he had accepted. It turned out to be an almost impossible undertaking. Here was the first prominent German Jew to see at first hand the wretched living conditions of his fellow Jews in Russia, the restrictions and limitations imposed upon them, and in spite of it all, the sense of unity which seemed to prevail. Their faith warmed Lilienthal's heart time and again as he traversed the country and spent Sabbaths and holidays in their homes.

The unity, however, was not complete. The division of groups reflecting different views was evident. There were the Mitnagdim and the Hasidim, the new group of pious Jews. Jewish life and law remained essentially unchanged in their ancient form. Still, the age of German enlightment spilled over into the solid Jewish community. Sparks of a new era were seen. A group known as Maskilim arose, seeking to bring the new spirit into Russia. They tried to interrelate secular subjects and traditional studies, thereby modernizing the educational system for Jewish children. They spurred representatives of the Jewish community in Riga in 1838 to petition Count Uwaroff to open a new kind of school for Jewish children, actually two separate schools: one for boys and one for girls. Instruction in Bible would follow Mendelssohn's German translation. They suggested that the superintendent be a Jew of a foreign land and his assistant a Christian. The plan appealed to the Count and he, in turn, presented the suggestion to the Emperor, who went along with it.

To this new experimental school Lilienthal came as supervisor filled with the sense of himself as one divinely ordained to perform this task— a feeling that constantly inspired him onward no matter the obstacles. Elected preacher of the congregation, his sermons and lectures attracted large numbers, Jew and Christian alike. It wasn't long before Lilienthal was accepted by the entire community, the suspicion which had been aroused at his arrival replaced by complete confidence in his sincerity.

His success, however, did not allow him to remain in Riga. After but one year, he was summoned by the Count to St. Petersburg to begin a more expanded program of establishing similar Jewish schools throughout the land. Difficult as had been the task in Riga, it was now almost insurmountable. In addition, Jewish people were not convinced that the Emperor had their interests at heart. They knew that his motto was: "One country, one language, one church." They felt that this new plan was but a painless way of luring their children into the Greek Orthodox Church. Lilienthal, youth in his favor, could not believe this to be the intent and purpose of the government, but he spoke frankly to Uwaroff, insisting on assurances of good faith. These he received. This is not to say that the Count was completely honest with him and that he did not withhold his real intent and purpose, but he was persuasive. In one of the edicts a promise was made that there would be no interference with religion. The plan for the establishment of such Jewish schools included the formation of a commission of four rabbis selected by the Jews themselves which would carry out the plan.

Once the edict was announced, Lilienthal set out on a journey to persuade the Jewish leaders in Russia to cooperate. Before leaving, he published his now famous *Maggid Jeshuah* (The Announcer of Salvation) in which he described the plan of the Russian government to organize the commission on Jewish education. He urged the people to help, pointing out that the government might come to believe that the Jews themselves did not want to better their lot if they failed to cooperate. In July of 1842, he set out. He traveled from city to city, meeting the leading rabbis and scholars of the time. His experiences are recorded in the book, *My Travels in Russia,* a glowing document expressive of the depth of his feeling for his people and the gentle spirit and zeal for which he was always noted.

Out of his deep conviction, he persuaded the two leading Jews in Russia—Rabbi Isaac ben Hayyim, affectionately known as Reb Itzele, head of the Yeshivah of Voloshin, the seat of Jewish learning in Russia; and Rabbi Mendel Schneersohn, leader of the Hasidim—to join the commission. Bezalel Stern, principal of the school in Odessa, and Michael Heilprin, a banker of Berditchev, also joined the group. Though their discussions were heated, as expected, reflecting divergent tendencies and currents, their differences did not prevent them from affixing their signatures to a document establishing the schools and approving the books to be used. Count Uwaroff, after signing the document, issued the proclamation on November 13, 1844, which formally established the schools.

When they were at long last opened, it was found that the government had made a basic change in the original plan. Instead of bringing German Jewish teachers to Russia to teach in the schools, as had been agreed, the government decided that the structural base of the schools would be the established Russian schools. Lilienthal was disturbed. He sensed that he had been used as a tool by the Russians. Perhaps the earlier suspicions of the Jews had been justified and Russia had always planned to use the schools as part of a proselytizing scheme. Christians were appointed inspectors of the schools, most of them incompetent.

Whether the Count had been dishonest with Lilienthal or not, no one will ever know. Suffice it to say that almost immediately after the issuance of the edict, he was discharged. The handwriting on the wall could not be ignored. Lilienthal had to accept that the government was less than sincere; indeed had used him shamelessly. There were even attempts made to convert him.

Frustrated and discouraged, Lilienthal, at the age of 29, left Russia for Munich. His successes may not have been glorious, but his reputation preceded him wherever he went. Even in the United States, young Lilienthal was already known.

Having married his childhood sweetheart, Pepi Nettre, to whom he had been engaged for ten years, Lilienthal came to the United States in November, 1845, barely 30 years of age. He was warmly welcomed. His strong features and imposing height, the grace and dignity of his manner and bearing, suggested a man of force and culture. His physical appearance joined his reputation to inspire confidence and admiration.

Probably because of his bitter memories of Russia and his experiences in bearing witness to the wretched lot of his brethren, Lilienthal drank in the free air of America with a special eagerness. He became the ever willing servant, messenger and advocate of his adopted land. From the day of his arrival throughout his life, whenever and wherever America needed a spokesman, Lilienthal was there. His first letter from the United States shows how quickly he became acclimated to the freedom America promised:

My fraternal and friendly greetings from New York, from the blessed land of freedom, the beautiful soil of civic equality! Old Europe with its restrictions lies behind me like a dream; the memory of the repellent Judaeophobia of Russia is like a distant mirage; the frightful images of oppression and persecution are distant from the harried soul. . . . I breathe freely once more, my spirit unfolds its pinions and I would waft exultingly the heartiest kiss of brotherhood to all men who find here the bond of union! . . . Oh, it is necessary that you breathe this free air of Columbia in order that you may be able to understand the pride and joy of her children; you must have shaken off the centuried dust of the old Jewish oppression in order to appreciate to the full the feeling, "I am a man like every other!" . . . the name of this country is union of the states and its motto is union of all forces for a great end, the respect of the rights of each in the great brotherhood. Here nothing is known of the idea of a Christian state which after creating pariahs, brands them as pariahs; here men are known only as men, who respect one another in liberty and equality and work together for the common weal.

Before the lapse of too much time, Lilienthal was elected chief rabbi of three congregations in New York, who after listening to his eloquent and persuasive oratory, combined to create the rabbinical post for him. His first sermon as rabbi of the new unified congregation set

him up as a traditionalist. He probably was. In his writings about Russia
he speaks with deep feeling and love about the ceremonies and rites, the
spirit of the Sabbath and holidays which he shared in the many homes
he visited. He also writes that when he arrived in St. Petersburg, a
city where Jews were not permitted to live, "I did not know where to
get a kosher dinner. . . . At last Mr. T. from Riga arrived and brought
me to a Jewish soldier where I could get a kosher dinner. . . ." Still, his
views were unquestionably away from the traditional. When in Russia,
engaged in a tête-à-tête with the Preacher of Vilna, he said (and later
recorded) :

> My dear rabbi, I have too high an idea of the eternal truth of our creed
> to be in the least afraid of such gloomy consequences. Our creed and our
> people have outlived and outlasted quite other periods than that of a
> desirable reconciliation with the advancement and enlightenment of our
> age. I, on my part, consider it a sin to believe and to assert that our creed
> is not compatible with science and knowledge itself; its principles are
> light and nothing but undimmed light; its doctrines are true and eternal
> as God is; how can you suppose for a moment that by the reconciliation
> with the irrefutable demands of our age the existence of our sacred creed
> will be endangered?

He took the position that he would not institute reforms but that he
would strive for more modern services. Here, Lilienthal created an
impression which later plagued him. Some insisted that he was deviating
from his original stand. David Philipson, his pupil, successor, and
biographer, puts it this way as he analyzes Lilienthal's changing viewpoint:

> Although he thus began as a sympathizer with what is known as ortho-
> doxy, still as he became better acquainted with American conditions he
> recognized the need for reform. In other words, he grew in liberal religious
> thought as the years advanced. His sympathies, however, were never with
> radicalism. He was a conservative reformer, if such a seemingly paradoxical
> phrase is permissible, to the end of his life. It was at first his belief that
> reforms could find their warrant in the Talmud, and he wrote copiously
> to this effect although he later abandoned this attempt. As time went on
> he became more and more outspoken in his reform position.

Under the general title, *The Spirit of the Age,* Lilienthal, the year
after arrival, answered the sharp attacks the Reverend I. Leeser launched
against Reform by penning a series of letters. He begins forcefully:

... you have thrown down the gauntlet to me for a contest on the Principles of Reform. I willingly take it up. . . .

Week after week, for five consecutive weeks, in November and December of 1856, Lilienthal carefully, studiously, developed his answer to Leeser.

... You will agree with me that Reform, nowadays, has gained so much ground that it cannot be haughtily overlooked nor indignantly overlooked. . . . Nor can we despise and decry it as the offspring of license or atheism, for it numbers in its ranks men of the highest standing in the community. . . .

Nor can we nickname the process of Reform "a child of religious indifference."

... Nor can you call it only a fleeting and temporary process that, swept away by the rolling waves of time, will leave no other trace but an unsavory memory. . . .

But we take quite a different view of the pending questions. We call the process of Reform "The Spirit of the Age," the proper and just demand of our time. . . .

It was early seen in America that Lilienthal's approach was a moderate one, fiery but moderate, firm but moderate, forceful but moderate, dynamic but moderate. His moderation, one of his most characteristic qualities, established for him the role of peacemaker and conciliator, a role which he was called upon to play time and time again during his ministry in America. The age was one of opposites, not only among Reform leaders but among Orthodox as well. A moderate approach was necessary. Lilienthal played that part. He believed in what he called "quiet development and orderly progress." This is how Lilienthal himself explained it in an article in *Allgemeine Zeitung des Judentums:*

Our century glorifies results and discoveries, like the railroad, the steamship, and the magnetic telegraph; for their usefulness lies on the surface; our age probes no deeper. We theologians, swept along by this practical tendency, would like to discover spiritual steam machinery and telegrams, so as to bring mankind to God and perfection in a trice. But this is quite impossible despite all the jolting and shaking, despite all the tearing down and building up. Mankind requires time for its development, and whoever would judge it aright must be patient or else he will never comprehend it. If this patience in spiritual matters be necessary anywhere, it is particularly so here, where the seed has been sown so recently and is just beginning to sprout. If one has the gift of quiet, though by no means inactive, looking on he will surely not be dissatisfied with local conditions.

It may be that this approach was impressed upon him by his delightful yet crucial meeting with Rabbi Isaac ben Hayyim of Voloshin when he went to him as representative of the Russian government, urging him to join the commission to establish Jewish schools. In his published descriptions of his travels, he writes of the incident with Reb Itzele, as he was affectionately known. They were discussing the situation and the possible successes to be achieved. The venerable sage, responding to Lilienthal's question: "How do you overcome all the difficulties?", answered:

By patience, doctor, and forbearance. And this is the golden rule I am giving you on behalf of your mission: "You must prepare yourself for the greatest indulgence and leniency if you aim at success." Both with the Russian government and our brethren you cannot succeed by pressing matters to extremes. Time is the best assistant we can possibly have; time and patience will remedy every evil.

Lilienthal's love for America at first sight is one of the most beautiful and touching aspects of his brilliant and dynamic life. While chief rabbi of the combined congregational effort, he instituted a few innovations in the service. He was the first rabbi in America to introduce on Shavuos 1846 the confirmation program—now an accepted part of most synagogues. In October of the same year, he organized the first rabbinical association in America. It was called the Beth Din (Court of Law) and was dedicated to serving Jewish congregations in America. Lilienthal was elected president and Isaac M. Wise secretary. The organization did not last very long. It is significant historically, however, not only because it presaged the organization of rabbis in America, but also because it was at the first meeting of the Beth Din that Isaac M. Wise presented a plan for a Union Prayerbook, his own *Minhag America*. The laudable purpose was to create one prayerbook for all American Jewish synagogues. The purpose was not fulfilled for many years.

In addition to a busy literary career in which he wrote extensively and passionately about his experiences in Russia, Lilienthal established the first day school in America, calling it the Hebrew Union School. It is probably the forerunner of the present day Jewish day schools in America which offer combined curricula of Hebrew and secular studies.

Lilienthal was destined, however, to make his great mark upon Judaism in America and upon America itself not in New York City but in what was then known as the West—Cincinnati, Ohio. The synagogue there, Bene Israel, called Lilienthal to the pulpit after he was recommended by the fathers of some of the boys who attended his day school. He accepted the call, and on July 14, 1855, preached his first sermon. He remained in Cincinnati for 27 years, the quarter of a century bringing to the fore one of the most fascinating characters in the American rabbinate. Here Lilienthal plunged into the task of serving his people, his community, and his land. To each he gave his heart and soul unreservedly and completely.

He introduced changes in the service, not without opposition. He was, however, persistent, though not radical in approach. He insisted that changes were necessary.

> Religion and life must be reconciled . . . [it] is the supreme demand of our times, and the just issue of all proposed reforms. . . . Let us assist time in its travail for the birth of the future. Let us prepare and foster progress. Let us remove abuses by enlightenment and instruction and an impartial posterity will gratefully acknowledge our sincere and faithful endeavors.

He maintained and fostered the generally accepted teaching of Reform that Judaism had a universal mission. The destruction of the Temple in Jerusalem was providential, and the loss of a separate Jewish nationality was the necessary preliminary to the mission of the Jew. America was the new Promised Land. He said years later, maintaining this position consistently:

> We owe no longer any allegiance to Jerusalem, save the respect all enlightened nations pay to this cradle of all civilizing religions. We cherish no longer any desire for a return to Palestine, but proudly and gratefully exclaim with the Psalmist, "Here is my resting place; here shall I reside; for I love this place."
>
> . . . America is our Palestine; here is our Zion and Jerusalem; Washing-

ton and the signers of the glorious Declaration of Independence—of universal human rigths, liberty, and happiness—are our deliverers, and the time when their doctrines will be recognized and carried into effect is the time so hopefully foretold by our great prophets. When men will live together united in brotherly love, peace, justice and mutual benevolence, then the Messiah has come indeed, and the spirit of the Lord will have been revealed to all His creatures.

When his new synagogue was dedicated on August 27, 1869, he combined the fervor of his profession and his devotion to the freedom of America with his undeviating belief in the Reform version of universal Judaism as he spoke these words:

> . . . Since the glorious day of the Fourth of July, 1776, the spell has been broken, and a better morning is dawning for the human race. Since the blessed and immortal fathers of our country, these prophets of modern times, declared it to be "a self-evident truth that every man is entitled to life, liberty and the pursuit of happiness," the old fetters and barriers have been broken down, and all over the old continent, political and religious liberty begins now to become the law of the various countries. God bless America for this glorious redemption. . . . Sunning ourselves in the golden rays of human and universal liberty we have ceased our wailings and cries of sorrow, and our prayers and psalmodies are full of thanksgiving and wishes for the welfare of the whole human race. . . .

Shortly after his arrival in Cincinnati, Lilienthal tried to convene a conference of rabbis in Cleveland. The meeting was held but failed in the face of diverging views. David Einhorn, radical reformer, was opposed to the statements adopted, as was Rev. Isaac Leeser, the leading Orthodox rabbi in America. Peacemaker Lilienthal attempted to bring the parties together, but the divisions were too deep.

It took fourteen years for all the Reform rabbis to meet, which they did in November, 1869. A statement of principles was adopted but not much else was accomplished. Views were still very different, even among the Reform rabbis. It was at a later conference of Reform rabbis that Isaac M. Wise's plan for a Union of American Hebrew Congregations and also for the establishment of a rabbinical seminary was endorsed. Lilienthal, the retiring president of the conference in Cincinnati of June, 1871, in his presidential report called for the appointment of a committee which would consider the formation of a rabbinical seminary. At the same time, he called upon his colleagues to support the newly organized Jewish Publication Society and suggested the idea of circuit rabbis for smaller communities. Two years later, the Union of American Hebrew Congregations was organized and Lilienthal was Wise's strong assistant in its creation. When the Hebrew Union College was finally organized, it was Lilienthal who was the spokesman for the Board of Governors at a special thanksgiving service at the Plum Street Temple in Cincinnati on May 22, 1874:

We Israelites . . . now consider it a supreme duty to afford to our men and especially to our future preachers and teachers the opportunity of acquiring that knowledge which shall fit them to become true and faithful exponents of our religion. Of course, we could have adopted the plan proposed by several good men of sending those who wish to devote themselves to the Jewish ministry to Germany, where the master minds of Jewish theology and literature are diffusing their stores of learning to crowds of Jewish students, and where Jewish colleges are already fully established, thoroughly organized, and richly endowed. But we do not want any ministers reared and educated under the influence of European institutions; we intend to have ministers reared by our glorious institutions, men who love their country above all, men who will be staunch advocates of such civil and religious liberty as the men who signed the Declaration of Independence and understood it, men who are ready to defend this priceless gem against all and any encroachments, and hence we wish to keep our students at home and raise them as genuine Americans on the virgin soil of American liberty. . . .

Our sons, born in America, are proud of the title of Americans, and do not trouble themselves whether their parents hail from Germany or France, or any other part of Europe. They wish to be Americans and nothing but Americans, and as such they will cling and work together. For them, for their future, and not for our foreign, antiquated notions, we are bound to work. Let the dead past bury its dead, and let us foster that harmony, that mutual good will, that forbearance and indulgence which will strengthen our congregations and enable them, without difficulty, to accomplish all the noble objects we must have in view.

While so striving for Reform Judaism in America, Lilienthal continued also to share his vast knowledge and erudition. He wrote many articles, edited the *Hebrew Review,* and founded the first paper for Jewish children, *Sabbath Visitor,* remaining its editor all his life.

In 1878, Lilienthal, not having given up his hope for an association of rabbis in America, succeeded in calling together and establishing a permanent organization under the title, The Rabbinical Literary Association. He became its first president.

Lilienthal served not only his own people directly but also indirectly. He was vastly popular and sought after in the general community. He created a great stir in 1867 when he was invited to occupy the pulpit of the Unitarian Church. This was the first time in the history of America that a rabbi was invited and in fact did preach from a non-Jewish pulpit. This first step forward for Christian-Jewish understanding marked him as a messenger of peace to the non-Jewish world and his untiring efforts along these lines provided the underlying reasons for the good will and spirit of brotherhood which existed between Jews and non-Jews in the city. The respect he enjoyed from all groups elevated him to many positions of high responsibility. He served as a member of the board of education in the city. He was a member of the board of directors of the University of Cincinnati, a director of the Relief Union, and president of the board of trustees of the medical college. He spoke to numerous audiences, and his views were always highly regarded. His fearlessness, his honesty and eloquence kept him always in the forefront as a fighter for the basic rights he believed America offered.

More than any other rabbi of the day, Lilienthal lashed out against any and all who would seek to undermine America's security or threaten freedom. He allowed nothing to stand in his way. It was his incontrovertible, God-inspired duty, as he saw it, to fight to the end, if need be, to preserve America. He called upon the citizenry to be aware of invidious campaigns against their rights. It was his love for America, his enthusiasm for its blessed ideals, that led him to the platform again and again. He soared to heights of exalted feelings as he spoke these words in his dedication sermon at Vicksburg, Miss., on May 20, 1870, about the American principle of the separation of church and state:

The true prophets and apostles of modern civilization were these God-inspired men who, on the Fourth of July, 1776, proclaimed the divine principle of civil and religious liberty. They declared church and state separated forever. They proclaimed the self-evident truth that every man is entitled to life, liberty and happiness; they broke the chains of every fettered race and class; and America, the great child America, became the beacon light for the hopes and aspirations of all humanity. O, God bless America. Heaven's best reward to those immortal spirits, Washington and his compeers, who first asserted man's innate rights and titles, and Israel's lasting gratitude to them and their descendants for ever more.

From the moment he touched the shores of America, he breathed in its pure, free air. He felt it surge through his veins as few others have. This is shown in a Fourth of July address in 1847:

Has any one here ever said to you, as in Germany, you must first become better, i.e., you must first be baptized before we will consider you men and citizens, before we will give you freedom? No, never; this country and its law rest on the principle that man is born free; permit him the full use of his powers, grant him the ways and means to support himself and everyone will be good and brave.

Thus no conditions have been imposed on you here; no reproaches have been cast in your teeth. Here history has begun anew and in this beginning the injustices of Europe are unknown. One God in heaven and on earth and all men His children—yes, all children of His, the all-Merciful, destined for the same rights, the same duties, and the same enjoyments; this is the law of this land, the shout of triumph, the paean of victory of this holiday—free, free, stand we here, my brethren; have we then not sufficient cause to rejoice on this day? Let us strive then to become worthy of this day, of the new freedom, the new law. . . .

He unhesitatingly took Horace Greeley, famous editor of the *New York Tribune,* to task when Greeley wrote what Lilienthal considered a vicious attack. "Sir," he wrote, "the pretension in your paper that we are strangers wherever we reside is false and untrue. We are true citizens of this great and glorious republic, and have, ever since we inhabited this soil, proved by actions that we are true Americans."

Few were so eloquent in Civil War days. In an address entitled "The Flag and the Union" at the Broadway Synagogue on April 15, 1865, when the war ended, Lilienthal's deep love for both flag and union, moved him to unsurpassed heights:

Oh, how dearly we love thee, blessed flag of our country! How proudly we look upon thee, emblem of the home of the brave and the free! How reverently we embrace thee, sacred legacy of our immortal Washington! Is it true that thine own children have forsaken thee, have rebelled against thee, have trampled thee in the dust, nay, afar down in the Sunny South, have buried thee at the foot of a monument of the immortal Jackson, in a dark and silent grave, as if thou, heaven-born child, wert not eternal like the heavens, as if after the Creator's command, "Let there be light," the heavenly stars could be extinguished, and give way to the darkness of chaos and disorder?

Alas! It is so. This day, four years ago, was the gloomiest in the history of our country; it was as if the sun of liberty was setting forever! Monarchs were rejoicing, but the nations were desponding; kings and their myrmidons were shouting, "The people's government is a vision and delusion," but nations were despairing—the last hope of the regeneration of the human race seemed to be lost forever.

Oh, we remember those days of agony and national misery! Morning after morning brought us the heart-rending news, sister state after sister state was seceding; the holy bond of our union was broken. Who dared at that time to look up at this flag, with its then thirty-one stars, without feeling ashamed of the mockery it represented, without being shocked at the insult it offered to the blazing escutcheon? . . .

But over the dishonored flag stood in all its power and fury, watchful, ever ready, the eagle of America. How he screamed in tribulation. How he beat his majestic wings! How he awakened his people to the great words of our Jackson: "The Union must and shall be preserved."

. . . Over the deluge of blood is triumphantly waving the ark of the Union, greeted already by the sweet dove harbinger who is bringing the olive branch of peace, union and universal liberty.

All hail, then, our glorious republic, undivided and indivisible. . . .

Oh! there is but one country, one America; there is but one self-government. Let us swear allegiance to it. Let our motto be forever: "Our country above and before any and all parties."

Seven days later his tone was different. Abraham Lincoln was assassinated during the week. Lilienthal's broken heart, as if a brother had been taken, asks:

Brethren, is this the same flag which by a grateful and victorious people but a few days ago was greeted with the intensest national pride and national joy? Why droop today its brilliant stars, its mighty stripes? Why is it draped in mourning? And this bust, crowned but a few days ago with the laurel wreath of fresh and decisive victories, why does it look so pale? Why, too, is it creped and hidden? Why are we frightened today as we look upon its mild and good features?

Alas, this is a gloomy day!

...Indeed, a great man has fallen in Israel! There never sat in the presidential chair a man who, by his life, as well as by his death, so fully demonstrated the progress of modern ideas and the greatness and glory of our institutions. . . .

We turn away and our heart longs for the object to whom our love and our affection were devoted. We gaze no longer at the hero and patriot—we look at the man and the friend. And what a change—this man who was without pride and ostentation, who had a smile for everyone and everything, a welcoming grasp and winning word—is this the man who was identified with the nation's terrible struggle and its deliverance? Yes, this man was Lincoln. . . .

Yes, illustrious martyr, this is the vow we make. . . .

Smile on! They cannot bury the principle thou hast bequeathed us; thy name shall be as immortal as the truth of thy teaching. Abraham Lincoln, friend of the people, the poor and the slave, farewell! We will cherish and revere thy memory forever; for thou wast great, because thou wast good, and thou wast good because thou wast great. Farewell till God grants us a meeting in eternity.

And so he spoke and wrote down through the years, at every opportunity extolling the virtues of America and the blessings it showered on all its citizens regardless of religion or race. If he saw those virtues threatened, he could not remain silent. So it was that when the Vatican Council of 1869 established the principle of papal infallibility and brought to the fore the sensitive question of primary allegiance, Pope or country, and when Protestant groups campaigned for the governmental recognition of Christianity as the religion of America, Lilienthal let the fire of his heart and feeling speak as he wrote in the *Israelite:*

The brightest gem in the American diadem is religious liberty. All denominations without any distinction have flourished and finely progressed under this divine coat of arms. The American, the native nature's nobleman, is tolerant and free from all prejudice by the very air he breathes. . . .

All we wish and hope and pray for is to live in peace and harmony with all our fellow citizens, no matter how widely they may differ from our religious opinions; to see Judaism as much respected as any other denomination; and that the equality which is granted it by the state and the law of our blessed country may also be fully recognized by the votaries of the various churches.

Again, when the state of North Carolina retained on its books a law which disqualified Jews from office, Lilienthal called on his people to take action. It was wrong, against the Constitution of the United States. To Lilienthal, "vigilance is the price of liberty and it needs concerted and courageous action to thwart all such nefarious schemes."

When the issue of church and state began to plague America, Lilienthal took the lead in the fight to preserve separation. It was a group of Protestant ministers that wanted to petition Congress to insert the name of God in the Constitution and declare the United States a Christian nation. Lilienthal did not restrain his feelings. He wrote in the *Israelite* on December 16, 1870:

> . . . What do the revered gentlemen mean and intend by inserting the name of God in our Constitution? Was the Almighty Ruler of All Nations less God and Father because His holy name was not mentioned in that holy instrument? Was He less worshipped, less revered and adored by the American people because the fathers of 1776 wisely refrained from meddling with religious matters?
>
> Yes, what do they mean and intend by trying to declare by a new amendment to the Constitution this nation to be a Christian nation?
>
> What kind of a Christian nation shall this people be, according to the desire of the revered gentlemen, a Catholic or Protestant one? Which one? These gentlemen do not come out in their true colors; they, of course, mean a Protestant Christian nation. . . .
>
> No, my friends, an old, true adage says, "Let well enough alone." Our country is in no need of a better name than free America, and our people of no better name than that of an American nation. There is glory enough in the name, "I am an American." There is security enough against all threatening dangers in our Constitution. It will protect and shield us against all temporal or spiritual intrigues and machinations. Let us not willfully jeopardize its might and power, its wise and well-meant guarantees; let us cling to it at any price as it reads and stands; let us hold firmly to the entire separation of church and state and our beloved country will not only prosper and succeed as heretofore, but will always lead the van of human liberty and civilization.

In an address at the conference of rabbis when he retired as president June 5, 1871, he underscored the Jewish position regarding the separation of church and state in words that are still timely today:

In these threatening times let us show and prove by our discussions and the declaration of our principles that Judaism is in favor of the complete and unbiased separation of church and state and school; that Judaism by all means of reform tries to adapt itself to the progressive spirit of the age; that it will always be found on the side of those who stand up for the unlimited enjoyment of civil and religious liberty; and that it considers and reveres as one of the boons of civilization that denominational peace, which heretofore characterized the unequaled growth and prosperity of our young and God-blessed country.

Almost as a climax to a lifetime of striving for religious freedom was Lilienthal's complete involvement in the famous case of Bible reading in the public schools. The Cincinnati board of education decided that Bible reading in the public schools was unconstitutional and should be dispensed with. Suit was instituted by an interested citizen in the courts contesting the resolution. The lower court sustained the board's decision and an appeal to the higher court was taken. While the court considered the case, excitement grew in the city and extended throughout the land. Feelings were sharp and tempers short. Meetings were held by both opponents and proponents. To Lilienthal, this question was part of the larger issue of church and state to which he had repeatedly addressed himself so eloquently. He did not refrain from speaking. Addressing a massive audience at Mozart Hall, March 30, 1870, he said:

The Catholics denounce the public schools as godless and the hotbed of every vice and apply every approbrious epithet to them. They demand a division of the school fund. What is to be done? Sectarianism must be removed from the schools, in order that there may be no just ground left for this demand. But look to the Protestant side. The Protestants come now and say defiantly that this is a Protestant country. When I left Europe I came to this country because I believed it to be free, the God-blessed country of all the world.

On one side of this controversy are the Protestants, and on the other are the Catholics. Where in heaven's name are the Americans? . . . I do not propose to answer the question myself, but instead will read from a letter written by Washington in May, 1789, addressed to the United Baptist Churches of Virginia: "If I could have entertained the slightest apprehension that the Constitution, framed in convention where I had the honor to preside, might possibly injure the rights of any ecclesiastical society, certainly I would never have placed my signature to it; and if I could now conceive that the General Government might ever be so administered as to render the liberty of conscience insecure, I beg you will be persuaded that no one would be more zealous than myself to establish effectual barriers against the horrors of spiritual tyranny and every species of religious persecution, for you doubtless remember that I have often expressed my sentiments that every man conducting himself as a citizen and being accountable to God alone for his religious opinions, ought to be protected in worshipping the Deity according to the dictates of his conscience." So wrote Washington. Are we better than he was? Are we wiser than he was? Obstinacy is no wisdom, bigotry is no justice, fanaticism is no righteousness, and any one who unfolds these banners will ruin this glorious country.

Lilienthal, certain of his position, set forth the platform which Jews should establish and pursue in the controversial issue:

1. Bible or no Bible, our children will visit the public schools. Our Sabbath schools and synagogues give us ample room and time to impart to them the required religious instruction.

2. No division of the school fund, no matter under what pretext it may be demanded.

3. Not a single penny out of the public funds for the support of any sectarian institution, be it for charitable or educational purposes.

4. No union of State and Church under any shape and form whatsoever.

These principles will save the Union and restore the denominational peace we have heretofore enjoyed and which we hope will be continued for evermore on the virgin soil of American happiness and liberty.

Three years later, still the untiring spokesman for the separation of church and state, writing in the *Israelite,* he called upon all religious denominations to look to themselves, their own churches, for the religious instruction of children, and not to the public schools:

Let the Sabbath schools of every denomination instruct the children in those doctrines which their denomination teaches and proclaims; this will be a private affair with which we, as citizens, have neither the right nor the intention to interfere. But in our schools, where our youths meet as American youths, we shall try to inspire them with the principles which, when faithfully carried out, will find favor in the eyes of God and man.

Lilienthal's closing years were not happy ones. His own life of service had brought rich rewards and deep satisfactions, but new waves of anti-Semitism were washing over Europe. A sensitive soul such as this could not but be sickened by the reports from Germany and Russia, lands he knew so well—the former his homeland, the latter the country of his diplomatic sojourn. The hurt and pain which this lover of freedom and liberty felt were carried over into his thinking and personal relationships. His overriding love of liberty, however, constantly eased his burden. He spoke of hope and of the future, which he knew would be good, certain as he was that the terrible persecutions and pogroms were but passing phases. In an article entitled "The Jew, a Riddle," appearing in *Hebrew Review,* probably his last published words, he wrote:

> But this storm will pass away. The Jew knows it. During the eighteen centuries of his wandering, he, the riddle, the living mummy, as he is nicknamed, has learned how "to labor and to wait." He will wisely use the interim to adapt himself to altered conditions and circumstances. And he will succeed, for adaptability is one of his recognized characteristics. He will throw off the stained rags of the pariah and don the toga of the free citizen, of the free man, in the noble and proud sense of the word. He will never surrender his abiding faith in a better future of the human race. He will still hope and trust that the time must come in which the doctrine of the common Fatherhood of God and of the common brotherhood of man will not be barren phraseology, uttered either in the pulpit or the forum, but will become a stern reality, an undoubted matter of fact. Then racial antipathy, racial persecution, will be either ridiculed as a nightmare or be pitied as temporary insanity.

He died on April 5, 1882. Perhaps the simplest yet most touching and descriptive tribute paid to him is a paragraph from his student and successor, David Philipson. It summarizes succinctly the life and contribution of a genial, selfless man.

> American rabbi was he in every sense of the word, interpreting the teachings of prophetic Judaism in the terms of American inspiration, and glorifying the Jewish name and Jewish truth in the eyes of all the people. Thus served he his God, his country and his fellowmen, and his name is recorded high on the register of those who throughout the ages fought the brave fight for liberty, right and truth.

ISAAC M. WISE

Architect of Reform Judaism

[1819-1900]

Excitement ran high in the synagogue on Rosh Hashanah. On the surface all was quiet and peaceful. The choir sang En Komocho, introducing the Torah reading service. The erect figure of the youthful, 31-year-old rabbi stepped forward to take the Torah from the Ark. Suddenly the president moved in front of him, blocked his way, and struck him with his fist "so that my cap falls from my head." A riot broke out and constables had to be called to quell the disturbance.

Services for the second day of Rosh Hashanah were held in the rabbi's home and the following week, Yom Kippur, Day of Atonement, services were conducted under the auspices of a new congregation.

The synagogue was Beth El in the city of Albany, New York. The year was 1850; the rabbi, Isaac Mayer Wise; and the new congregation, the fourth Reform Congregation in America, Anshe Emeth.

The storm and struggle embodied in this incident reflect the strivings, disappointments, enthusiasms, frustrations, successes and unparalleled power of the master builder of Reform Judaism in America. That he did not leave the rabbinate for more glowing horizons in the world of law, as his friends encouraged him to do, is a tribute to his unconquerable perseverance as a heroic battler for his beliefs and convictions.

Isaac M. Wise was used to storm and struggle and the exercise of courage and vigor. He had been born into that kind of a world in

64

Bohemia at the beginning of the 19th century. The French Revolution was multiplying its sparks of liberty and freedom and showering them everywhere. The sparks were catching on and igniting. The world was on the march; a new age of enlightenment was changing every aspect of life. In Bavaria, the Jewish community was also struggling. It was striking out for a measure of civil and political equality. It was a difficult struggle. Restrictions on Jews abounded. Yet the Jewish community was virile, active, alive.

The future intrepid leader of Reform Judaism in America was born into this world of tear and toil on March 29, 1819. His father was a minister of one of the congregations in the village of Steingrub—population 534—serving as rabbi, hazan, mohel, teacher and sexton. Isaac Mayer was one of thirteen children and the oldest of seven surviving. His education, as was the custom, began at a very early age. At four, he was a student in his father's school. At six he was introduced into the world of the Talmud and within three years imbibed so much that his father knew no more to teach him. Higher education was not available in the immediate area, so the boy had to leave home. At the age of nine he went to the home of his grandfather, Dr. Isaiah, in Durmaul, where he continued his intensive studies of the Pentateuch and Talmud. Evenings he spent studying with his learned grandfather.

At 12, his grandfather died, and Isaac Mayer, determined to become a rabbi, set out for Prague, capital of Bohemia and center of Jewish learning. He recalls vividly all these early experiences in his *Reminiscences*—how he began his journeying at 12 years old on foot, with a small bundle of clothes and a pitiful 27 kreutzer in his pocket. On the way, he stopped to visit a cousin who gave him five florins. At Pilsen, his uncle added ten more. When he arrived in Prague, he matriculated at the Beth ha-Midrash (School) which adjoined the Alt-Neu Schul (Old-New), the famous Synagogue of Prague. For support, he depended on the prevailing custom called "Teg" or day-board, the practice of affluent Jews to provide poor and deserving students with support so that they might pursue their studies. Perhaps this personal experience was later reflected in his own fatherly concern and provision of home hospitality for the students of the Hebrew Union College.

He remained in Prague for two years. During this time, Professor

Moses Koref, a teacher of mathematics, became interested in him and instructed him privately in arithmetic, algebra, and geometry, thereby laying the foundation for his scientific training. He also studied under Rabbi Loeb Glogau and Rabbi Samuel Freund, the latter being one of the great Talmudic scholars of the period.

After two years he moved on to Jenikau and attended the most famous Yeshiva in Bohemia, conducted by Rabbi Aaron Kornfelt. Here, Isaac Mayer was introduced to the progressive world. The government had decreed about this time, in 1837, that rabbis could not be ordained unless they attended the gymnasium and university. The ruling actually opened up for Wise and others a world hitherto unknown to them. The world of Goethe, Schiller and Herder, Wise absorbed thirstily. He then continued his education at the University of Prague, earning his livelihood as a tutor. At 19 years of age he passed the examinations of three gymnasium courses. He pursued further studies at the University of Vienna, and in 1842 at 23 passed the rabbinical examinations before the Beth Din, the rabbinical court of Rabbis Rappoport, Freund and Teweles. They conferred upon him the title of Rabbi by granting him traditional Semicha, ordination.

Wise held one rabbinical post in Europe. When the community of Radnitz, near Pilsen in Bohemia, asked Chief Rabbi Solomon Rappoport to recommend a competent rabbi, he suggested Isaac Mayer, as a "new light." On October 26, 1843, the "new light" was inducted into office.

His career might have been complacent, quiet, and serene if he had the temperament and nature to live a peaceful life, but an inner restlessness and compulsion drove him. He soon came under the influence of many minds who agitated his own thinking processes. He was profoundly influenced by Gabriel Riesser, a great fighter for freedom, and by Samuel Hirsch, whose philosophy of religious liberalism was projected the year Wise was entering the rabbinate. The young rabbi was developing his view of the mission of Israel as the standard-bearer of pure monotheism—the very center of Judaism. Israel was an eternal witness to God and monotheism. Israel was God's collective chosen servant selected to bring the world to an understanding of Him. In his recollections, Wise admits the burning influence:

Rappoport [Chief Rabbi of Prague, who ordained him] taught us the method of research, Sachs gave us the rules of pulpit oratory, Riesser made us feel free, and Hirsch led us to think free.

The combination of these four men and their influences joined forces with Wise's vast knowledge, innate capacity for organization, indomitable energy, and unique power of pen and tongue, to spell success and recognized leadership.

His fervent belief in democratic doctrines and freedom came to the fore, and he would neither quell his views nor hesitate to assert them. A reprimand came from the governor of the district when the young rabbi mentioned the emperor only casually on the latter's birthday rather than expound on his virtues. But the governor could not intimidate Wise. He also stood up to the government regulation which then allowed only a certain number of Jewish marriages to be solemnized. *Familiantenrecht,* the right to marry, it was called. Convinced that such a law was wrong, he disregarded it and officiated for anyone who came to him.

In May of 1844, he married Theresa Bloch, a former student and daughter of Herman Bloch. Ten children were to be born of this union which was to last, by the will of God, for 30 years. Their first child was born February 22, 1846.

The year before, while visiting Frankfurt, Wise attended the famous Second Rabbinical Conference where, for the first time, he heard debated questions about synagogue service, the use of Hebrew, prayers about Palestine, and many other questions. He did not know then that he himself would introduce these innovations into his own synagogues and make them part of the Reform ritual.

The Conference had a lasting influence on him. He could no longer be satisfied with the small community he was serving. He felt the need of wider horizons in which to work. In Prague, he found a collection of American-English prints and a set of journals about the years 1780-1790, crucial years of American independence. They were the letters of Richard Henry Lee, of Virginia, on the adoption of the Federal Constitution of the United States. "That literature made of me a naturalized American in the interior of Bohemia. It inspired in me the resolution to go to America, and against the will of my friends I did go and my family with me."

In May of 1846, he set sail from Bremerhaven and 63 turbulent days later arrived in New York. His arrival marks the opening of a new era not only for him, but for American Jewish history. The next half century and beyond were to see a transformation of Jewish life in America which in large measure revolved around and resulted from the life, deeds, thoughts, and efforts of Isaac Mayer Wise.

His hopes and spirits high, Wise arrived in New York on July 23, 1846. They were dashed almost immediately on arrival.

> The whole city appeared to me like a large shop where everyone buys or sells, cheats or is cheated. I had never known before a city so bare of all art and of every trace of good taste; likewise I had never witnessed anywhere such rushing, hurrying, chasing, running. In addition to this there was the crying, blowing, clamoring and other noises of the fishmongers, milkmen, newsboys. . . . All this shocked my aesthetic sense beyond expression. In the first few days I heard the sound of music but once in the streets. . . . Everything seemed so pitifully small and paltry; and I had had so exalted an idea of the land of freedom that New York seemed to me like a lost station by the sea; on the first day I longed to be away from the city.

His keen disappointment and initial shock were blunted, however by Dr. Max Lilienthal, to whom he brought a letter of introduction. Lilienthal's warm welcome encouraged and inspired him with hope, which is what he desperately needed during his first few trying days in America. Lilienthal sent him to preach and dedicate synagogues in New Haven, Syracuse and Albany. The traveling refreshed him, and shortly after a second sermon in Albany, he was offered the pulpit of Beth El. The congregation was Orthodox and the pattern of the service traditional. Wise's appointment as rabbi heralded another era for him and for the congregation. He served in Albany for eight years (1846-1854), eight difficult, stormy years separated into two clearly defined periods. The first period was his ministry with Beth El, where he soon tried to introduce new practices and was met by strong opposition, the kind of opposition which grew and grew until it exploded in the scene described at the outset of this story. The second period gave Wise peace and opportunity to develop himself and formulate his plans.

Destiny had a hand in Wise's difficulties, disappointments, and decisions. Shortly after coming to Albany, he attended Dr. Max Lilienthal's call for the organization of a synagogue body under the name Beth Din, Court of Jewish Law. He was assigned a specific responsibility, the preparation of a Minhag America, an American prayer ritual. Such a ritual to him would be more than a set of rules for departure from the traditional pattern. It meant to him a Judaism as a religion symbolic of the new freedom of the age and adapted to the spirit of rationalism and science, political and social reform in the making in America and Europe. Jews who came from Europe and established synagogues in America were following other rituals—the Minhag Ashkenaz, German Ritual; Minhag S'forad, Spanish Ritual; Minhag Polen, Polish Ritual. Wise gladly assumed the task. He realized quickly, however, that success would not come from the Beth Din. Time was not yet ripe for organization.

Back in Albany, he delivered a series of two lectures about his Minhag America and a friend sent transcripts to Rev. Isaac Leeser, editor of the *Occident* and leader of Orthodox Judaism in America. Leeser printed the lectures in his monthly journal. The two began a correspondence which led to Wise's writing for the *Occident*.

In December, 1848, Dr. Wise's eloquent call for the organization of a union of ministers and congregations was issued. In this now famous document one can see the organizing mind of Wise as he envisioned the goals he actually achieved—a union of rabbis, a union of congregations, and a rabbinical college.

. . . It is one of the holy demands of our religion to walk in the ways of God. God is a unity. Wherefore all mankind will one day be united for one great end, to worship in truth the Most High, to adore His Holy Name with humanity and purity. Then will also be fulfilled that God's name will be one. To bring about this sublime unity God has selected the people of Israel. Wherefore we may justly say our cause is the cause of mankind. Now, in order to fulfill our sacred mission, to send our important message to mankind, it behooves us to be united as one man, to be linked together by the ties of equal views concerning religious questions, by uniformity in our sacred customs, in our form of worship and religious education. We ought to have a uniform system of our schools, synagogues, benevolent societies, for all our religious institutions. . . . You see we have no system for our worship, nor for our ministry, and we are therefore divided in as many fragments as there are congregations in North America. It is lamentable but true that if we do not unite ourselves betimes to devise a practical system for the ministry and religious education at large, if we do not take care that better educated men fill the pulpit and the schoolmaster's chair, if we do not stimulate all the congregations to establish good schools and to institute a reform in their synagogues on modern Jewish principles, the house of the Lord will be desolate or nearly so in less than ten years. . . . Something must be done to defend and maintain our sacred faith. Nor is it too late. Everything can be done if we are united before God.

Wise was disappointed by the lack of response to his earnest call. It was at this time that he issued his well-known statement to a reader of the *Occident* who imputed to him mercenary motives, calling him an agitator, a reformer and an office-seeker:

To be sure, I am a reformer as much as our age requires, because I am convinced that none can stop the steam of our time; none can check the swift wheels of the age; but I always have the Halacha for my basis; I never sanction a reform against the Din [law]. . . .

We will go on and erect a memorable monument in the history and bring about that our children and grandchildren may still look upon it with confidence; that the house of Israel may have a solid centre to maintain its sacred faith, to justify and develop our principles before the eyes of the world.

The call was not successful. It was to take another quarter of a century for success to come.

In Albany, acting perhaps impulsively and without properly laying the groundwork and preparing his congregants, Wise took bold, firm steps as he organized a choir, abolished the women's curtained gallery, excluded certain prayers from the service, introduced the organ, the weekly sermon, and confirmation for both boys and girls. The anticipated opposition was forthcoming. Wise later admitted:

. . . struggle and ill-feeling were bound to ensue. True, I might have acted more skillfully and discreetly; but being by nature fiery, earnest and fearless, I gave expression recklessly to all my principles and views, for which the majority of my hearers could by no possible manner have been ripe and ready. In addition to this, I had the peculiarity of pointing out vices, faults, and weaknesses so sharply and vividly that in every sermon someone felt that he had been attacked, and harbored ill-will toward me on that account.

Oppostion does not always take the shape of reasoned objection. Feelings and emotions were aroused and expressed. The changes were sharp and sudden. Anger and ill will intensified against Wise when a personal loss struck his family and he refused to budge from his zeal to reform and reconstruct. His youngest child at two years of age died suddenly. Shaken but adamant, Wise refused to observe some of the traditional customs which append to a loss.

Furthermore, Wise engaged in a public refutation of a Christian clergyman who called upon Jews to become Christians. In a series of articles he attacked the doctrine of miracles, the divinity of Jesus, and the concept of a personal Messiah in general. Here he was projecting himself not alone as a defender of his people. His views were construed as an attack on Christianity, and it was feared this would affect the neighborly relations existing in the community between Jews and Christians. It was one thing to hold such views but quite another to come out with them publically and so strongly.

The road of Wise's ministry was indeed strewn with difficulty. Undoubtedly it affected Wise. His doctor recommended a breathing spell, a trip. So at the age of 30, in 1850, disillusioned, grieved, obsessed by a premonition of death, Wise set out on a brief journey which was to change his perspective and become a turning point in his career. His low spirits gave way to new hopes. He was invigorated and refreshed. He spent some days in Washington listening to the Senate and meeting the statesmen of America. His reputation had preceded him. He met with William Seward, Clay, Sumner, and Daniel Webster. The first rabbi to visit a President of the United States, he was introduced to President Taylor and Vice-President Fillmore. It was this experience which moved him later to write:

> My sojourn in Washington had an Americanizing influence on me. I felt that I was one of the American people although I had not yet been naturalized, and from that time I said "we," "us," and "our" quite unconsciously whenever I spoke of American affairs. I felt greatly uplifted and aroused by this intercourse with the greatest spirits of the country. . . . The intellectual eight-day combat stirred me mightily, enlarged my horizons, refreshed my mind. . . .

He spent time in Charleston, South Carolina, where he engaged in debates with Rabbi Morris Jacob Raphall, one of the leading

Orthodox rabbis in the country, and also delivered sermons in the synagogue on the Sabbath. It was at the end of his visit to Charleston, at a public debate between Dr. Raphall and Rabbi Poznanski, the Reform rabbi, that Dr. Raphall dramatically and unexpectedly turned to Wise and Poznanski and asked: "Do you believe in the personal Messiah? Do you believe in the bodily resurrection?" Wise unhesitatingly and quickly replied, "No." Raphall picked up his books and left the auditorium. The debate was over.

Wise returned to Albany rejuvenated, certain that he was on the right road and convinced more than ever that he would succeed. Trouble, however, awaited him. He had probably forgotten the obstacles and antagonisms he had left behind. His absence had not cemented a divided community. However, when he arrived in Albany, he found that the Charleston synagogue had elected him rabbi. He was happy about it and anxious to leave Albany, but friends and relatives persuaded him not to go because of the horrors of yellow fever in the South. Reluctantly Wise succumbed to the pressure and withdrew his acceptance. In turn, Beth El re-elected him for a period of three years. Dissension, however, continued to rear its ugly head. Dr. Raphall, as a result of his encounter with Wise in Charleston, branded him "no longer fit to act as a rabbi or religious teacher." Three months after he agreed to the new contract, the crisis was reached, a crisis which was to result in the founding of Anshe Emeth in Albany.

Strangely enough, the immediate cause of the public incident described at the beginning of this biographical sketch was the issue of the Sabbath. Synagogue policy required that no board member was to keep his store open on the Sabbath. One of the board members, a friend of the president of the congregation, violated the rule. Wise was determined to preach from the pulpit about this violation against the wishes of the president. The result was a severe breach in which Wise was condemned on a number of counts relative to his views. A thorough investigation was demanded, and Wise was told to submit his defense in writing by a certain day. When he refused the board suspended his salary. Two days before Rosh Hashanah, a special meeting of the board was called. When the meeting was adjourned on a technicality, Dr. Wise's friends left, but the remaining minority heard the charges brought by the president and declared the rabbi's contract void. Wise denied the validity of the decision and refused to leave the pulpit. On Rosh Hashanah during the service, the president took the action he felt justified in accordance with the decision of the rump meeting.

The new congregation, Anshe Emeth, gave Wise his first unhampered opportunity to institute the reforms he had in mind. His congregation supported him completely and the ensuing four years were peaceful, quiet and fruitful. He had time to think and write, and he wrote prodigiously, concentrating on his views of Judaism. Some of the articles were published in the *Occident*. Clarifying some of his views, he sums them up:

> Judaism is based on four leading ideas, and has therefore four principles with which all doctrines, dogmas, maxims, ceremonies, and observances must correspond as consequences with their respective causes, otherwise must be rejected as anti-Jewish and foreign to our system. These four are: (1) One God; (2) Man the image of God; (3) Man accountable to God; and (4) God has chosen Israel to promulgate these divine and sublime truths to mankind at large. These four truths are plainly announced in the Pentateuch, re-echoed by the Psalmist and by each of the Prophets. Nature and history do not contradict them, but they are the living witnesses, they bear the strongest evidence to the verity of all these four dogmas, and every Jew believes them and defends them with his life, liberty, and property; and if he ceases to do so, he has ceased to be a Jew.

In the fall of 1851, Wise severed his association with the *Occident* and began to write for the *Asmonean*. Many articles appeared during the 18 months he wrote for this new weekly, essays defining more clearly his views on reform, papers dealing with Jewish rights, and works defending basic American principles and doctrines. He wrote sharply about the discriminatory practices against Jews in Switzerland, calling upon his people to take united action and to ask Congress to intervene on behalf of the oppressed Jews. He wrote repeatedly about his favorite topics, organization, union, and the need for properly educated and trained rabbis. He utilized the calm and peace of his ministry to study and devoted much time to a work entitled *The History of the Israelitish Nation from Abraham to the Present Time*. He also began working on a subject close to his heart, the nature of Christianity and all religion, his researches culminating in *The Origin of Christianity*. The book was severely criticized. He had excluded miracles, stating that they had no place in history. He also refuted the idea of a personal Messiah, maintaining that the prophets had emphasized a Messianic Era. Here Wise was reacting to the age in which he lived. Having seen the striving for freedom in Europe and America, he had become convinced that history was at the dawn of the Messianic Era. It was in America where fulfillment would be realized. America— with its ideals, hopes and aspirations, goals and doctrines, the complete separation of church and state, emphasis on individual liberty and conscience, opportunity for all—was the harbinger of the Messianic Age.

While he was occupied writing and ministering to a willing congregation, Wise surprised his membership by accepting a call from Bene Jeshurun Congregation, Cincinnati. Albany, especially in the second half of his eight years there, had given him encouragement and inspiration; but he felt that he was limited, confined. When the congregation in Cincinnati offered him a life contract, he accepted the call. He describes the feelings he had of his last days in Albany:

> I was attached to Albany with all the fibres of my heart. It was my first home in the new world. I had so many true and tried friends in the old city on the Hudson. Every child, every tree was dear to me, but my school days were over, I had to go out into the world. I had attended two schools in Albany for nearly eight years; the school of experiences, of bitter struggles and brilliant triumphs, and the school of learning, whose lessons I had learned with tireless industry. I had no fortune, but I was very rich; I had many warm friends, a wife and four children, much self-reliance, and a firm faith in God and the truth. A dreaming optimist, an idealist such as I always was requires no more than this to be happy.

Wise came to Cincinnati on April 26, 1854, at the age of 35 and remained there for the rest of his life, 46 years of service which brought him fame and fulfillment: fame because of the institutions he founded and lived to see flourish, and fulfillment because of the satisfaction of seeing his views and energies recognized. It was in Cincinnati that Wise came forth as leader of the moderate Reform group. It was here that he was most productive, where his great genius of organization was expressed. His congregation, originally Orthodox, was cooperative and allowed itself to be used as his laboratory and institutional experiment. He was, however, more cautious now than he had been earlier in Albany. Innovations were introduced slowly after the groundwork was thoroughly laid, even with a congregation sympathetic to him. He had learned bitterly the lesson of patience.

In Cincinnati, he was devoted not alone to his synagogue, to his people and family, but to his community as well. He was called upon by the community to serve, and serve he did. He was a member of Cincinnati's board of examiners, of the board of directors of the University of Cincinnati and its academic committee.

His people, however, received his most concentrated efforts. His people needed union, and Wise set his sights on the organization of a Union of American Hebrew Congregations, which he achieved in July of 1873. Wise looked again and saw the need for a rabbinical college where young men would be trained to assume the role of rabbis in America and he saw success in the fall of 1875 when the Hebrew Union College was dedicated. He set his sights still further when he determined on a union of rabbis. Waiting until there were graduates from the Hebrew Union College, the Central Conference of American Rabbis was called into being with Wise serving as first president of both the College and the rabbinical group. The president of his congregation was the first president of the synagogue union. These three institutions couple with his *Minhag America,* which he graciously withdrew when the Union Prayerbook was adopted in 1895, being the first to introduce it to his congregation; add thereto a life of intense devotion to country and faith; add further a vital weekly called the *Israelite;* join his love for family, and we have the portrayal of Isaac M. Wise. He has the distinction of being one of few who achieved almost complete fulfillment in life—*almost* because there must always be some discontent to induce and inspire further effort and striving.

Almost on arrival in Cincinnati in 1854, Wise began to make plans for the publication of a Jewish weekly and soon afterward founded the *Israelite,* the only Jewish weekly west of New York. The weekly became the avenue through which Wise spoke his mind, prolifically, frankly and honestly, sharing his views on Judaism, America and religion with all the world. He wrote on the most widely diversified themes—on every phase of the Bible, Talmud, Jewish history, philosophy, ethics, and every aspect of the kaleidoscopic changes in Jewish life and thought. The *Israelite* was a vehicle of defense of the Jews when strong action was called for. It urged adherence to the fundamental faith of the Declaration of Independence, the belief that all men are created equal; the doctrine of separation of church and state, which must remain inviolate; and the principle that discrimination be allowed against no one because of his religion or creed. It was almost an anti-defamation league in itself.

Wise was a vehement spokesman in the important Swiss question. The United States and Switzerland, in November of 1855, had ratified a treaty stating that citizens of Switzerland and of the United States would be treated with reciprocal equality. This sounded proper, but each of the governments was federal, and some of the cantons (states) in Switzerland had restrictive regulations against Jews. Wise issued call after call in the *Israelite,* with banner headlines bordering on the sensational, urging meetings, resolutions, and the sending of letters to authorities. The matter was settled in 1874, when the Swiss government made religious freedom part of its constitution. In the meantime, the *Israelite* had agitated uncompromisingly for Jewish rights and gained wide recognition as a militant weekly.

The ever-watchful guardian also joined the attack against the infamous and discriminatory Grant Order Number 11, issued on December 17, 1862, which stated expressly:

> The Jews, as a class, violating every regulation of trade established by the Treasury Department, also department orders, are hereby expelled within twenty-four hours. . . .

Major-General U. S. Grant had assumed command of the Department of the Tennessee on October 25, 1862, including northern Mississippi and portions of Kentucky and Tennessee. He began at once to prepare for the siege of strategically important Vicksburg. His preparations included limiting of trade with the Confederacy and while he wanted to reduce all commercial traffic, the Treasury Department, itself pressured by merchants, refused and made plans to regulate trade. A large influx of speculators moved in and made enormous profits out of buying cotton. Secretary of the Treasury Salmon P. Chase tried to tighten the regulations but the speculators continued apparently unhampered. They bribed army officers and succeeded in other illegal maneuverings and manipulations. Some of the speculators were Jewish and Grant assumed that the entire traffic involved Jews. On November 9, 1862, he forbade travel south of Jackson, "the Israelites especially, because they were such an intolerable nuisance." On December 17, he wrote to the Assistant Secretary of War, C. P. Walcott, that the regulations were being violated "mostly by Jews and other unprincipled traders" and at the same time issued the order mentioned above.

The *Israelite* took up the cudgels at once. Fortunately, Lincoln acted with alacrity and almost immediately had the order rescinded. But the *Israelite* was on guard, which meant that Isaac M. Wise was on guard.

The editor skimmed editorials and articles from all sources. He wrote prolifically. He has been criticized bitterly for being indifferent to the slavery question and for taking no positive stand on the issue. The *Israelite* had little to say on the entire issue, either before or after the Civil War broke out. Only when hostilities between North and South began did Wise write an editorial, entitled, "Silence is our Policy":

> They say civil war has commenced. . . . What can we say now? Shall we lament and weep like Jeremiah over a state of things too sad and too threatening to be looked on with indifference? We would only be laughed at. Or should we choose sides with one of the parties? We cannot, not only because we abhor war, but because we have dear friends and near relatives, beloved brethren and kinsmen in either section of the country, that our heart bleeds in thinking of their distress, of the misery that might befall them. Therefore, silence must henceforth be our policy, silence on all questions of the day until conciliation shall move the hearts of millions to a better understanding of the blessings of peace, freedom and the union.

The ever-recurring Bible reading in the school question stimulated Wise to sharp attacks and defense of the separation of church and state principle. In November of 1869, the Cincinnati board of education prohibited the reading of religious books, including the Bible, in the city schools. A violent controversy ensued. Wise's views were clearly and forcefully stated:

> We are opposed to Bible reading in the schools. We want secular schools and nothing else. Nor has the state a shadow of right to support any other. As Jews we do not want any one to teach our young ones the religion of our fathers. We do it all ourselves.
>
> From a general standpoint, however, we are opposed to Bible reading in

the school. The American people consists of a conglomeration of national-
ities and sects united by the Constitution and laws of the United States, the
common interests and the love of liberty and independence. The gist of the
whole is, we agree to disagree on every point except public government,
which we agree to support, maintain, and obey. . . .

The public schools are institutions for the education of free, intelligent
and enlightened citizens. That is all. To this end we need good secular
schools and nothing else. The state has no religion. Having no religion, it
cannot impose any religious instruction on the citizen, adult or child. The
Bible is a book of religion—all admit this. By what right is it imposed on
the public schools?

"The government is a secular institution," he editorialized in *The
American Israelite* of April 10, 1890. "It cannot and dare not legislate
on matters of religion and conscience."

"Liberty, justice and peace are impossibilities in countries where
Church and State are united," he wrote on June 18, 1897, in the
Israelite.

Almost at the same time the *Israelite* saw light. Wise also founded
a German weekly, *Die Deborah,* a smaller publication in which he
published his more personal articles, memoirs, novels, and poems.

Unquestionably the *Israelite* was one of the primary means through
which Wise achieved his successes. It was his most potent agency for
spreading far and wide his deep convictions and beliefs. Once he
established the *Israelite,* he began—or, more accurately, renewed—his
efforts for union. He proposed the creation of a college and, indeed,
the following year, 1855, Zion College was opened. It, however, did not
last because of a lack of funds. That same year Wise issued a call for a
conference of rabbis and laymen. Nine rabbis signed the proclamation
and the conference was held in Cleveland. The purpose of the conference was to discuss (a) the union of American Israel on theory and
practice, (b) a plan to organize a regular synod composed of delegates
of congregations, (c) a plan for a Minhag America and (d) a plan
for scholastic education. The conference, Wise hoped ardently, would
unify all groups, Orthodox and Reform. The great issue of the authority
of the Talmud came up for discussion, and Isaac Leeser, the Orthodox
leader, joined the others in a compromise declaration which said:

The Bible as delivered to us by our fathers, and as now in our possession, is of immediate divine origin and the standard of our religion. The Talmud contains the traditional, legal, and logical exposition of the Biblical laws, which must be expounded and practiced according to the comments of the Talmud.

Leeser was able to accept the statement, having in his mind the reservation that the word "traditional" can mean divine. The meeting was, however, a failure. No further conference was held. Attacks against the conference came from two main sources: the radical Reform group of the East on the one hand, and the Orthodox rabbis on the other. They were simply too far apart. The radical reformers, led by David Einhorn, were violently opposed to the recognition of the Talmud under any circumstances. They looked upon such a statement as a step backward in the onward march of reformers. Cleavage prevented success not only from both extremes but from within the Reform group itself. The dissension within the ranks was not to be dissolved until more than a generation later. Greatly distressed by the failure, Wise later wrote of the experience in his *Reminiscences:*

A split among the reformers, whose principles were not yet definitely fixed, appeared to me an event painful and fraught with misfortune. It depressed and discouraged me completely; for without union among the reformers, who were in the minority, no progressive measures could be hoped for from the synod. There was hope for the victory of the reform element only on the condition that its leaders were united. All the efforts for union were shattered, for the moment, at any rate, by these protests. Like Jeremiah I sat on the ruins.

Though disappointed and disturbed, Wise did not hesitate to persist. His inner compulsion was reflected in his determination to try again and again. He wrote editorial after editorial. He spoke in city after city, pressing, pressuring, demanding, urging, pleading. He saw early that there would have to be a change in his technique. First, there would have to be a union of congregations before a college could be founded and there would have to be a college before a union of ministers could become a reality. He worked harder and harder, repeatedly underscoring his aims, constantly emphasizing his goals. After almost two decades, early in 1873, he was imbued with the feeling that success was just around the corner.

It is coming. It is coming after all, the college, seminary, theological faculty, or whatever it may be named, and the union of American Hebrew Congregations. . . . A committee has been appointed to prepare a call for a general convention. . . . Which congregation will stand back? Common sense suggests none. . . . This or that body may stand back for a time, all reforms have met with opposition, but none will be able to resist the united actions of many for any length of time. . . .

His approach decided upon, he preached with renewed vigor in the pages of his *Israelite*. Finally, after much hindering from the radical East, on July 8, 1873, delegates from 34 congregations convened in Cincinnati and established the Union of American Hebrew Congregations. Its main purpose was to establish "a Hebrew Theological College to preserve Judaism intact, to bequeath it in its purity and sublimity to posterity, to Israel united and fraternized, to establish, sustain, and govern a seat of learning, for Israel's religion and learning."

The great organizer's joy was expressed in an editorial the following week:

For a child was born unto us. . . . The child was born in peace, brotherly love, and beautiful harmony. The new chapter in our history begins with peace and sends forth the ancient salutation Shalom Aleichem, peace to all of you. The first object of this union is the Hebrew College.

This object was realized on October 3, 1875, when the formal opening of the Hebrew Union College was celebrated. Wise was the first president, and a great college president he was. His administrative ability was superb. His recollections of his early days in the Yeshivah came back and he became father to his "boys," who looked upon him as a venerable sage, a wise counselor, and a kind father. He helped them financially and guided their every step. Every Passover Eve, they joined him and his family at the Seder. The boys became rabbis and the nucleus of Wise's rabbinical organization.

A touching tribute reflecting adulation and love describes the experience of the first graduation. Rabbi Henry Berkowitz writes:

The venerable form of our revered master seemed to rise to majestic stature as he stood in this consecrated place. . . . It was one of those rare moments of exaltation when our beings are thrilled with a sense of the sublime. Into the souls of us who were favored to receive the hallowed *Semicha* by the pressure of his lips upon our brows, there entered a solemn consecration to the tasks for which he sent us forth and that has made his deathless spirit abide with us in every impulse and motive of our life's work.

On July 10, 1889, the Central Conference of American Rabbis, consisting then of 30 rabbis, was organized. The president of the College was elected first president.

For ten years more, Wise labored in the vineyard of the Lord, securing the foundations of the organizations he brought into being. On March 26, 1900, at 81 years of age, he breathed his last. The simple tombstone on his grave tells the story of his life, from early toil and struggle to fulfillment, achievement and happiness; from a harsh youth in divided Europe to a glorious ending of life in blessed America:

ISAAC M. WISE

BORN IN STEINGRUB, BOHEMIA, MARCH 29, 1819

DIED MARCH 26, 1900

RABBI OF K. K. BENE JESHURUN

FOUNDER OF

THE UNION OF AMERICAN HEBREW CONGREGATIONS

THE HEBREW UNION COLLEGE

THE CENTRAL CONFERENCE OF AMERICAN RABBIS

Perhaps the stone should also have added the words "Editor of the *Israelite* and Author of *Minhag America*" to have completed the chapter outlines of his life.

Wise—an intensely human man, unconquerable optimist, indefatigable worker—lived a full life, not only chronologically. He was prolific with pen and eloquent in speech. He allowed no subject of human concern to be hidden from his active mind and busy pen. Whether he agreed or opposed, he spoke out fearlessly. Friends he had. Enemies he had also. Leaders of men who strive persistently, as if driven by divine compulsion, needs must meet obstacles in terms of people and events. Nothing, however, blocked his way to his goal. His achievements tell the tale.

His views incurred the wrath of many. He was called radical, traitor, heretic. He was accused of denuding Judaism, removing customs and ceremonies in favor of his own concepts and doctrines. He was a violent opponent of Zionism, looking upon it as a political scheme and a mystic

form of heresy. Herzl was "a false prophet and a man without religion."
Zionism was in complete disagreement with the concept of the mission
of Reform Judaism. He even encouraged a resolution following his
presidential address on July 8, 1897, at the meeting of the Central
Conference of American Rabbis held in Montreal, which clearly bears
his stamp:

> Resolved, that we totally disapprove of any attempt for the establishment
> of a Jewish state. Such attempts show a misunderstanding of Israel's mis-
> sion, which from the narrow and political field has been extended to the
> promotion among the whole human race of the broad and universalistic
> religion first proclaimed by Israel's prophets. Such attempts do not benefit,
> but infinitely harm our Jewish brethren where they are still persecuted, by
> confirming the assertion of their enemies that the Jews are foreigners in
> the countries in which they are at home and of which they are everywhere
> the most loyal and patriotic citizens. . . .

He could not see a Jewish state as a haven of refuge for the persecuted Jew experiencing the vicious pogroms in Europe, especially in
Russia and Rumania. It was not necessary, he held. Anti-Semitism was
on the way out and would soon disappear.

He bore vehement opposition from within his own ranks when he
accepted the divinity of the Mosaic origin of the Torah, more especially the gift of the Ten Commandments to Moses. He defined the
theology of Judaism in this way:

> The theology of Judaism is the science of the conceptions of Deity in the
> human mind and their logical sequences in conformity with the postulate
> of reason as laid down in the Torah of Moses, expounded, expanded and
> reduced to practice in different forms, at different times, by Moses, the
> prophets, the hagiographers, the sages, and the lawful bodies in the con-
> gregations of Israel.

His theology revolved around three guiding lines: (1) his unalterable belief in the Mosaic origin of the Pentateuch and of the direct
inspiration of the Decalogue [Ten Commandments], (2) his devoted
adherence to Maimonidean rationalism, and (3) his profound and firm
belief that Judaism was the predestined religion of all humanity.

His *Judaism—Its Doctrine and Duties,* written in 1872, a small but
concise catechism in which he describes, in answer form (the questions

appearing at the bottom of each page), his views of Judaism, contains his most cherished beliefs, simply and clearly given. The preface says that Judaism is a scriptural and rational religion, eminently humane, universal, liberal and progressive, in perfect harmony with modern science and philosophy, and in full sympathy with universal liberty, equality, justice and charity. He urges Hebrew as an essential in the preservation of Judaism in its purity; it must therefore be the principal study in Hebrew religious schools. Here are a few samples:

What is religion?

Religion is the inborn desire of man to know God and His will, in order to worship Him.

Where are God's words preserved?

God's words are preserved intact in the twenty-four books of Sacred Scriptures called the Bible.

Why is Israel's religion claimed to be the true religion?

Israel's religion, also called Judaism, is the true religion, because its doctrines are taken from the revelations of God in His works and words.

How many cardinal doctrines are there in Judaism?

Four. First: God is the first cause of all existence, the fountain of life, love, and reason, the Preserver and Governor of the universe. Second: God's grace is revealed in His government of universal justice. The righteous are rewarded according to their righteousness, and the wicked are punished according to their wickedness, if they do not repent, and in due time amend their conduct. Third: Man is the son and image of God. He is gifted by the Creator with the impulse to attain human perfection and the capacity to reach happiness, here and hereafter; thus to fulfill his destiny on earth and acquire eternal bliss. Fourth: All men have the destiny to enter the covenant of the Lord; to be redeemed of their errors, iniquities, and consequent misery; and to be united before God in truth and justice, freedom and peace, philanthropy and godliness.

How many covenants are recorded in Sacred Scriptures?

Three covenants between God and man are recorded in Sacred Scriptures: (1) the covenant with man, (2) the covenant with the fathers; and (3) the covenant with Israel.

How many duties are in the Decalogue?

There are four kinds of duties contained in the Decalogue: to God, to one's self, to man, and to other creatures.

The small volume, containing 257 questions and answers, covers in 22 chapters the gamut of Jewish doctrines and thought from attributes of God and man's duties to God to man's duties to man and to himself; from the Sabbath and the holidays to the Law and all religious observances. Each answer is verified and attested to by a passage from the Bible.

He wrote for children as he wrote for adults—articles, essays, editorials, novels and poems. An amazingly large number of utterances came from his ever active mind, both from his facile pen and his silver tongue.

Isaac M. Wise's long life was filled with work and adventure. He once wrote in self-reflection: "I have written much, worked much and have been more lauded and abused than any other man of my age." But even his detractors could hardly deny that he stands out conspicuously as a giant of his generation.

BERNARD FELSENTHAL

Teacher in Israel

[1822-1908]

Bernard Felsenthal was the first rabbi of Sinai Congregation, first Reform congregation in Chicago, center of the great American Midwest. He came to this title and position not through ordinary, normal channels of matriculation at theological seminaries and rabbinical ordination, but through study for the sake of study and ordination at the hands of David Einhorn and Samuel Adler, contemporary leaders of Reform Judaism, who, recognizing his vast erudition and qualities of leadership, set the crown of ordination upon his head, addressing him as Morenu Harav—our teacher, the rabbi.

Bernard Felsenthal lived the greater part of the crucial 19th century and was a living part of its turmoil and upheaval. He played a primary role in the formulation of Reform Judaism in America, often anticipating in thought, word and deed what were destined to become the premises, practice and doctrines of Reform. Yet he had the courage and flexibility to alter and modify his convictions when the times seemed to demand different approaches and actions. Convictions were not made to be stagnant. They were important, to be sure, but could be reviewed and re-evaluated. The *status quo* was not for Felsenthal.

How best describe him? Perhaps an examination of his photograph will yield clues to the personality of this extraordinary man. We see him in a reflective pose suggestive of his innate modesty and humility. A shock of gray hair is combed to the right on his imposing brow. A short, thick beard, also gray, lends force to the expression of gentle contemplation.

The high forehead and deeply set, dark brown eyes, set off by heavy black eyebrows, indicate a restless intelligence. Thin-rimmed, old-fashioned eyeglasses do not dim the soft fire of the eyes. He must have looked almost the same all his life. The sculptured features are such as remain relatively constant from the freshness of youth through the weathering of age. And Bernard Felsenthal lived to a ripe old age, his figure readily recognizable as he strolled Chicago's streets. Slightly taller than the average man, he could be identified from quite a distance by his erect posture and the high silk hat and Prince Albert coat he invariably wore.

Cyrus Adler called him "a beautiful soul, noble, lovely personality," words normally reserved for soft, gentle souls. And that he was. This, however, did not diminish in any way his determination and perseverance as a pioneer of Reform and as one of the most outspoken preachers in the pulpit. His frankness in word and philosophy is reflected in his addresses to audiences of all faiths and persuasions. He spoke what he felt, and he felt deeply. He acted as he believed, and he believed profoundly.

In one of his first sermons, Felsenthal said:

> Believe me, I beg you, when I say that my *greatest* happiness in life would be to perceive that around me congregate boys and girls, men and women, saying, "You are our beloved teacher and friend, your words have not fallen on barren ground, we listen to you, and we strive to heed your words and to conform our lives to them." I beg you repeatedly, encourage me in this way.

This statement captures the essence of the man, this teacher who spent his youth with books, books of all kinds, drinking in the purity of their knowledge and making them a part of his very being.

Born in 1822, the oldest of four children, one a sister, Bernard Felsenthal spent his earliest childhood in Münchweiler in the Rhenish Palatinate, the province of Bavaria. His father was a small shopkeeper who also owned a small farm or vineyard. His Jewish education began at an early age and continued under the instruction of Rabbi Moses Cohen in Kaiserslautern. Gradually he amassed a vast store of Jewish learning, although his earliest hopes were entirely unrelated to rabbinical aspirations. He studied for the sake of study. Torah L'Shema. Torah was not a means to an end; it was an end in itself. His passion for Torah increased as his years multiplied and he moved smoothly from Hebrew to Semitic languages, from Jewish history and thought to their background in, and relations with, the religious history and religious philosophy of the world. His later writings reveal erudition at its ultimate as he quotes with ease from all Jewish sources; sources of knowledge which became his capital investment in the earliest days of his life and which formed the basis of his thirst for further and deeper study as well as for his leadership in the world of religion.

At 13, Bernard Felsenthal went to the *Kreisgewerbschule* in Kaiserslautern, where he pursued a general course for three years and then continued on to the Polytechnic High School in Munich. As a young man, his hopes were directed to government civil service and to this end he majored in mathematics, a subject he loved all his life. He read profusely, devoting all his time to the book. No time was wasted. Pleasures were discarded. He immersed himself in the world of books. He was fortunate in that lack of financial worry joined his intense love for knowledge and freed him to live the life of the student.

At 18 he realized that for a Jew to pierce the prejudiced wall of government service was almost impossible. So he shifted his plans, enrolling in the teachers' seminary at Kaiserslautern in 1840. Two years later, 1842, he became a village teacher. Officially he retained the post for a dozen years, but actually he remained a teacher all his life, whether on the platform, in the pulpit, at a convention, in a discussion group, or on the street. As a teacher in the village school, he taught not only Hebrew language and literature, Jewish religion, history and customs, but also mathematics, geography, German, and general history. One must also suppose that his deep love for Lessing and Goethe, his masters and heroes, became part of his personal curriculum though perhaps not of the official curriculum. Love for education, children, school, nurtured in the earliest years of his life, found fruition here. He wrote:

> The impressions which one carries from the schoolroom are deep and lasting. Whoever casts an introspective glance into his spiritual being, whoever seeks to discover the inner springs of his own conduct, whoever recognizes clearly what it is that has made him such as he is and no other, what it is that makes him behave in such and such a way and not otherwise, will also acknowledge that the school as well as life has helped to form him.

In later years he often would muse on his brief 12 years in the schoolroom. The joy of his teaching experience had profoundly influenced him as he sought to influence others.

In 1854, in the sweep of German emigration to America and the seeking of freer air to breathe and greater opportunities, Bernard Felsenthal with his father and sister came to the United States. His arrival points up not only a significant chapter in his life, but an important chapter in the history of the young Reform movement as it struck out for adherents from the East toward the South and the West. Bernard Felsenthal was part of that West.

Louisville, Kentucky was the first brief stop the family made; then Lawrenceburg, Indiana; and a year later, Madison, Indiana, where Felsenthal became teacher to a Jewish family. The small Jewish community of 8000 conducted a vigorous Jewish life. The Orthodox congregation, small though it was, had its rabbi and religious school, where secular subjects were also taught. The tranquillity of the town's Jewish people was jarred when in February, 1856, Felsenthal addressed the people and suggested radical changes in the Sabbath services. The reaction was volatile, as he later wrote. One man, father of a child under his tutelage, exclaimed: "What! A man with such notions expects to read prayers for us on Rosh Hashanah? Such a person wants to teach our children Judaism?" This was Felsenthal's introduction to the Jewish scene in America. Implicit here was the destination this Madison address would lead to. Reform Judaism's principles were being enunciated.

Felsenthal betook himself to writing. He contributed to Isaac Mayer Wise's *Israelite* and David Einhorn's *Sinai*. His address had brought him closer to these leaders and to Samuel Adler. He was now being sought and welcomed as a new light on the horizon.

Felsenthal did not remain long in Madison. The following year, 1858, he went to Chicago, then a teeming city of 80,000 souls. His first employment was as a bank clerk for Greenebaum Brothers, also from Bavaria. Early recognizing Felsenthal's primary interests, they outfitted a small room behind the office as a study, and here the budding champion of Reform in the Midwest studied, thought and wrote.

Felsenthal's arrival brought about him a small circle of people who believed with him in the new Judaism and within two months they organized the Judischer Reformverein (Jewish Reform Society), Felsenthal becoming its secretary and guiding light. The Society became also his platform. He early presented to them Jewish Theses, a series of statements which contained and which were forerunners of Reform principles and which the Society adopted as their guiding principles. The following year, 1859, Felsenthal published one of the most significant and comprehensive pamphlets of the Reform Jewish age, "Kol Kore Bamidbar, A Voice Is Calling in the Wilderness," in which he gave fuller and deeper expression to his views on Judaism. Here he pleaded for a regeneration of religious life; for adaptation of the ceremonies and rites to modern and Western conditions; for the willing recognition of the opportunity which the Dispersion had brought to Israel for the spread of its sublime ideas.

> There is a time to tear down and a time to build up. Thus speaks the holy book imbued with the spirit of God. Our age, in so far as it concerns itself with Jewish religious life, is evidently intended rather to build up than to tear down. But what shall be built up, what shall be constructed anew? The inner, deep-seated belief in God, the moral sense in all the relations of life, the attachment to and love of Judaism, the teaching of Moses freed of all heathenism and foolishness; with this must be combined the excision of all statutes and observances intended for other times, places and conditions. . . .
>
> Doctrines which we have recognized as true, but which have lost in great part their hold on our contemporaries, must be implanted anew and more firmly; institutions which have had a hallowing influence on the religious nature, and which are likely to enhance the religious life, must be retained, suitably changed, or, when necessary, created anew, according to the needs and circumstances.

He conducts a dialogue:

> "The Bible is not the source of Judaism!"
> "It is not? Well, that is heresy, indeed."
> "Softly, my orthodox friend. We say the Bible is not the *source* of Judaism, but we consider it a product of Judaism, and we concede without reservation its most splendid and holiest product. But Judaism is older than the Bible. Judaism originated at the moment when God breathed into the first man the breath of life. *For the kernel of Judaism is natural religion in the soul of man.*"

He extols the use of Hebrew:

> Hebrew in the synagogue is a tie which unites all Israel. There are stronger ties, to be sure; nevertheless, this, too, is not without importance. There is, however, another argument for the retention of Hebrew. It is the "holy tongue," the language spoken by our God-inspired singers and prophets, and its sounds makes a deep impression on the soul of every Jew, elevating, purifying, awakening reverence. It provides an element of mystery in the service which we would not willingly dispense with. Mystery within proper limits—we do not say mysticism—has its place in the spiritual life of man, more especially in the service which we dedicate to an incomprehensible God. Is not the soul itself strange and mysterious, full of unknown and inscrutable depths?

He stresses the right of each individual to search after truth:

> Every Israelite has the right and duty himself to search for the sources of religious truth with the aid of his God-given intellect. For truth is not inculcated in us by ethics; the human spirit is not penetrated from without, rather from within outward shines the light of divine truth.

The pamphlet, carrying the impact of a large volume, exerted a marked influence in Chicago. The almost immediate result was the organization of Sinai Congregation in June, 1861. Bernard Felsenthal became the rabbi, though with reservation and hesitation, but encouraged by Einhorn and Adler who testified as to his scholarship and religious leadership. Felsenthal remained rabbi of Sinai until 1864. The prevailing custom of electing a rabbi for one year did not find favor in the teacher's eyes and he felt it better to look elsewhere. Shortly, with new neighborhoods developing on the so-called West Side of Chicago west of the Chicago River, a new congregation was formed called Zion Congregation. Felsenthal became its rabbi and served it for 23 years.

His life became stabilized as he devoted himself to synagogue, community and country. He was active in B'nai B'rith and used its platform as a means of speaking his mind on matters Jewish and American. Believing firmly in the fraternal order and its ability to help advance the Jews of America, he worked on many of its committees, attended conventions, and spoke in its behalf. A group of young men and women gathered about him to form the Zion Literary Association, affectionately known as Zion Lit., where open discussions on significant subjects stimulated the intellect of its truth-seeking members.

Not only did the Jewish community look to him for leadership, but the non-Jewish community as well. From his writings one will be completely convinced of his faith in interfaith relationship and effort, and his feeling of relatedness to the Christian community was expressed frankly and openly. One of the interesting yet disturbing incidents of his life in that time is related by Dr. John Haynes Holmes in his biography of Robert Collyer. Dr. Collyer had invited Felsenthal to take part in the dedication exercises of the new Unitarian church only to find later that there was a minority of considerable size among the Unitarian membership to whom the sight of a Jew on their platform on that occasion would be unwelcome. It seemed best to withdraw the invitation and this was done frankly and received by Felsenthal in a friendly and understanding spirit. Yet one can read between the lines and imagine his hurt on hearing the invitation withdrawn. Certainly as a man of feeling Felsenthal must have felt this experience deeply. Perhaps it brought to mind his desire of early youth to go into government service in Bavaria and being slapped down with the counsel: "So far shalt thou go, and no farther."

Felsenthal spoke out vehemently against the Western Hebrew Christian Brotherhood attempts to convert Jews. Speaking on the B'nai B'rith platform, he struck hard at them but harder at his own people: "But who are the missionaries of the Jews? Shall we do nothing for the spread of Jewish ideas?"

Though he did not insinuate himself aggressively into the general community, he did not hesitate to make his voice heard when the occasion demanded it. Thus, employing a refreshingly modern approach, he raised his voice in objection to the attempt made by a group of Chicagoans to persuade the board of education to reintroduce Bible reading into the schools. To him it was "an inexcusable, an undemocratic, an un-American tyrannizing of the minority."

> Even if we should admit (which we however do not) that it is but a minority who favor the exclusion of the Bible from the schools, would it not be an unexcusable, an un-American tyrannizing by an accidental majority to force their religious views and practices upon an unwilling minority?

With greater vehemence he lashed out against slavery, calling it "the most shameful institution on earth." And when the well-known issue of Jewish field chaplains came to the fore, Felsenthal immediately wrote to Senator Wilson of Massachusetts. Inadvertently the law regarding field chaplains read that they be "regularly ordained ministers of some Christian denomination." The word "Christian" was quickly, with President Lincoln's hurried intercession, change to "religious," thereby legally allowing the appointment of Jewish chaplains.

Felsenthal served admirably, leading and guiding the new congregation, until 1887, when he became Rabbi Emeritus and was succeeded by Rabbi Joseph Stolz. The congregation had begun to demand more and more English preaching and Felsenthal, master of the written word, had never completely mastered its spoken form. The language which he was most comfortable in speaking remained German. Now, freed from duties, he began to devote longer hours to his writing table. His pen became his more forceful vehicle for participation in Jewish affairs. He had entered not a period of solitary retirement, but one of scholarly refinement. For the next decade, Felsenthal's life revolved around his writings and involvement with people and guiding them. He immersed himself in the 12th Street neighborhood, which had recently seen the influx of thousands of immigrants fleeing Russian pogroms and persecutions. They needed help in this new country and Felsenthal felt a close tie with the Jews of other parts of the world. They were refugees and they were Jews—two facts which underscored their need for help. He became their confidant. He consulted with any whose advice might prove useful. He helped organize schools, encouraging the new arrivals to learn English rapidly. A society grew out of these schools which in appreciation they called the Felsenthal Educational Society. Yiddish was not his language. He deplored it, but Hebrew he loved and encouraged. He looked sympathetically upon the Orthodox rabbis who led the new immigrants, understood them, respected their religious devotion, thought of them as brother Jews. They, for their part, loved him because he met them on terms of absolute equality. They spent many hours in his home. He spoke out for them on a number of occasions, one of the most significant being the time he demanded that kosher food be made available to Orthodox patients in hospitals and that the religious practices of the Orthodox be faithfully considered.

The rabbi's daughter recalls vividly the respect these patriarchs had for her father:

There were many and touching proofs of the affection in which my father was held by the Orthodox Jews of Chicago. On two great days which stand out in the memory of those closest to him, his seventieth and his eightieth birthdays, delegations came from Orthodox congregations and societies to express their joy and to offer congratulations. They sent him flowers; they presented him with resolutions; they made him beautiful speeches. As if it happened yesterday, I remember the visit, on the afternoon of January 2, 1902, the day my father was eighty, of a group of gray-haired old men who came to tell him how they and their friends delighted to do him honor. They stood with my father in our living room, while one, their spokesman, came forward and made his speech of congratulation in Hebrew. My father answered in Hebrew. I remember the sound of the ancient language, even more impressive in our home with its new-world, twentieth century look, than in the synagogue; the patriarchal appearance of the visitors; my father's happy expression, as he stood, vigorous, keen-eyed, listening and speaking. I remember the quiet and the dignity of it all. To my father, I believe it was one of the very happy moments of his life.

The modest rabbi continued to write during his retirement. While, in the main, he concentrated on serious themes, he also wrote with lightness and humor, as, for example, the articles, "Rabbi Patrick," and "How Old Is Lekho Dodi." It was during this period of so-called retirement that Felsenthal, interested in history and historical development, suggested to Dr. Cyrus Adler, in 1888, the organization of the American Jewish Historical Society, now the largest of its kind in the world and one of the most significant Jewish institutions we have. He wrote for the Society and served on its executive council for many years. He was equally interested in the Jewish Publication Society of America, founded in 1888, and served on its publication committee, reading manuscripts and giving counsel and guidance.

Retirement, indeed! While the first decade was marked by renewed energy on his part, the following decade was even more vigorous, for it was in his last decade of life that Bernard Felsenthal, concerned for his people suffering the torments of persecution, embraced Zionism and its cause. He was proud of the fact that he was among the Zionist advance guard. He wrote to Dr. Judah L. Magnes in 1905, asserting that he was as early as 1897 a firm exponent of Zionism, not only in thought but in word and deed.

I do not know whether you are aware of the fact that I really was the very first one among the non-Polish American Jews who came publicly forward as an advocate of Zionism. Several months prior to the *first* Basle Congress, the *American Hebrew* in its issue of May 7, 1897, published a letter from me, in which I strongly called upon American congregations and societies to send delegates to the Congress, and in the months following I defended the stand I took in a number of articles in the *American Hebrew,* the *Jewish Exponent,* etc. Should you ever publish in the *Maccabean* or elsewhere a few historical documents bearing on the subject, my first article, I think, should have a place among them. I am really proud to think that I was the Zionist *avant-garde* among non-Russian Jews in this country.

In the article in the *Jewish Exponent* to which he referred, he wrote that he favored colonization in Palestine as the best method of ameliorating the conditions of Jews in Eastern Europe. He answered the current objections to the Zionist movement and said:

I do not bother my mind with the question whether or not in the near or in the more distant future a Jewish state will be a possibility. For the present I, for my part, have no other object in view than that the Jews now living oppressed and persecuted be helped in reaching a better and higher level of living. . . . But suppose that in fifty or a hundred years there would be such a Jewish state—would this be such an unfortunate turn of events?

The year 1897 was a crucial one for Felsenthal because thereafter he could write of almost no subject other than Zionism, a development which earned for him the wrath of other Reform rabbis, most of whom were anti-Zionist. They accused him of deserting his earlier convictions about the universal character of Judaism and the concept of the Jewish mission to all the world. According to them, he was disloyal as well as inconsistent. Felsenthal denied all this. To one who asked him sternly, "When did you change your views?" Felsenthal replied with equal severity, "I have never changed!" He believed that the mission idea was still valid but that it was not necessary for Jews to remain dispersed in order to fulfill this mission. "A small and well-organized nation can work more efficaciously for good than many millions scattered and disorganized," he declared. As he looked at the world and saw how frightful were the conditions under which Jews lived, his heart was moved to deep emotion:

And they who in their boundless misery implore us for help are our brothers! They are flesh of our flesh! But since, curiously enough, there are still many who deny the obvious fact, the scientific and historical fact, of our blood relationship, let us, on their account, use other words: There are millions of our co-religionists who are living under unspeakable conditions of oppression. There are millions of Jews in Russia, in Rumania, and in other countries, who are threatened with extermination, with annihilation, with ruin—who will be destroyed not only physically, but also spiritually, morally, religiously—if help does not come soon. O help them! save them! do not delay!

One of the most touching expressions of Zionist literature came from the old man of Lake Michigan, who in 1898, the year of the World Zionist Conference in Basle, Switzerland, wrote to Professor Richard Gottheil:

Those high-minded and generous-hearted enthusiasts whom you will see in Basle—extend my greetings to them, and tell them that on the shore of distant Lake Michigan there is an old man who longs for the blessed ful-fillment of their hopes. "Dreamers of the Ghetto" Zangwill has called them; them also. Would to God we had many thousands of such dreamers! The world needs them, in this domain and in many others. What would have become of humanity, what will become of humanity, without dreamers such as these?

Bernard Felsenthal was not satisfied merely to write about Zionism. Aged though he was, he eagerly assumed taxing responsibilities. He was a member of the actions committee of the World Zionist Congress. He was vice-president of the Federation of American Zionists and adviser to its executive committee. He belonged to the Chicago Zionist Society and, though an octogenarian, attended meetings and spoke with the intensity and vigor of youth. His principles of Judaism, written in 1901, clearly point to the basic themes of Zionism and the Jewish state. The principles were remarkably close in thinking and approach to Theodor Herzl's projected *Judenstaat* (Jewish State). When the founder of politi-cal Zionism died, all the world mourned, and among them a co-worker in Zionism, Bernard Felsenthal.

The words he wrote in the *American Hebrew* on January 13, 1899, under the caption "As to a Jewish State" were prophetic indeed.

The Jewish State, as understood by me, will be a state based upon Jeffer-sonian principles of democracy. The ancient Mosaic theocracy cannot be re-established; nor can the Talmudical principles of government find realization in the new Jewish state. Christians and Mohammedans and others will have and will enjoy equal rights with the Jews there, and, the Talmudical laws notwithstanding, the Gentiles will be just as much entitled to occupy official positions and to be eligible as legislators in town councils, in provincial lawgiving assemblies, etc., as the Jews will be. If, in the course of time, the Jews will form seven-eighths or perhaps a still larger part of the population, it is natural and likely that the majority, or perhaps all, of the offices and the seats in legislative bodies will be occupied by Jews. Neither the Mosaic constitution nor the Talmudic constitution can be in force in new Zion. In theory and in practice it will be a modern state. And it will be an ideal state, such as there never was anywhere and at any time. "Onwards and upwards to the heights of the prophetic ideals!" will be the motto of new Zion.

As to the mutual relations of the new Jewish state and Jewish communities scattered throughout the world, I think such will consist only in reciprocal moral influence. Neither party can claim or ought to claim legal power, ecclesiastical or of any kind, over the other party. But I hope and expect that a newly established Jewish state in Palestine will exercise an influence over the Jews in the Diaspora by awakening in them the spirit of a stronger attachment to Judaism, a deeper, purer, and healthier religious sense, a lifting up of the minds of many from low and vulgar materialism to a higher and nobler Jewish idealism. On the other side, I hope and expect that the Jews in the new state will receive from their brethren who remain in Europe and in America much aid and much furtherance in Western culture, in the ways of cultivating methodically the fields of science, in the applying of new discoveries in mechanics, chemistry, electricity, and other fields, etc.

And so I conclude with part of a stanza in a well-known Hebrew hymn: "Shake off the dust of the centuries, O my people! Put on the garments of thy glory, O my people!"

Felsenthal's 80th birthday in 1902 was marked by an outpouring of congratulations from Jews and non-Jews from all walks of life. One Jewish organization sent a laurel wreath in gold inscribed in Hebrew, *Tzadik katamar yifrach,* "The righteous shall flourish like the palm tree"; George Kohut penned a sonnet in his honor which appeared later in the *Menorah Monthly;* Naphtali Herz Imber, famed poet and author of "Hatikvah" ("The Hope"), dedicated to him the English translation of his immortal poem, now the national anthem of the State of Israel;

David Einhorn

Isaac Leeser

Isaac M. Wise

Max Lilienthal

and the Hebrew Union College conferred upon him the honorary degree of Doctor of Divinity as a mark of recognition of his attainment, his zeal and his devotion to the cause of Judaism in America.

Felsenthal, in his later years, had serious misgivings about his earlier absolutes. Perhaps he had been too rigid, too sure. Although his basic convictions were retained, he felt that they could and should be constantly thought through and re-evaluated. Disappointment in Reform plagued him. In a letter to Rabbi S. N. Deinord on March 1, 1907, he declared:

> We must not utterly cast aside all great traditions of our past, nor consent to mow down ruthlessly everything that is characteristically Jewish. . . .
>
> A generation has risen up to whom Jewish rites and customs and usages are as unknown as those of the Hindus. . . .
>
> It will one day be recognized that what we call "Reform Judaism" is not the highest and finest and best thing to be found in modern Israel, is not that which is most worthy of our devotion. The thought often comes to my mind that this extreme Reform we have in America, which knows no limit, will lead gradually to the extinction of Israel and its religion. . . . Do you not agree with me that our Reform friends are preparing a "beautiful death for Judaism?". . . .

Felsenthal continued to believe in Judaism as an ever-evolving and developing religion, but Zionism would set the pace. It could reunite Jews in a land of their own. It would give Judaism the chance continually to adapt itself in its outward forms to time and circumstance.

Though his vigor was taxed, he did not desist from firm action when the opportunity demanded. In 1904, one of the most significant conferences of Reform Judaism was convened in Louisville. The issue was that of establishing a synod to rule over Jewish people. Opposed in principle and practice to any restraint on individual freedom, Felsenthal went to the conference and addressed it with vehemence.

> It is to be hoped that no Conference of Rabbis and no similar body will become guilty of destroying the oneness of Israel and of creating a schism by efforts to establish a synod and to formulate a creed. Beware! A synod may enter—*may* enter? No, it *will* enter as a forceful dividing wedge into American Israel, and inevitably it will lead to a schism. Beware!

His appeal was accepted with respect and reverence and carried the day against the establishment of any kind of synod. Here, too, younger men who had heard of the dynamic Felsenthal gathered about him, referring to him as the "aged yet youthful master."

Four years later, in January of 1908, the "aged yet youthful master" breathed his last. History would tell of his contribution to Judaism and America. Felsenthal's pronouncements and example have as much force and validity today as they had then. He lives on in those who have studied his life and consciously emulated him and through others who, unbeknown to themselves, have been influenced by his thought and deed.

SABATO MORAIS

Pillar of Strength and Determination

[1823-1897]

Sabato Morais, vigorous, fearless exponent of traditional Judaism in America for a half-century, founder of the Jewish Theological Seminary of America, and thus among the founders of Conservative Judaism in America, did not believe in American Judaism. He believed in Judaism in America. There is a difference. There was no more possibility of American Judaism than there was of German Judaism, Polish Judaism, French Judaism, or English Judaism. Such terms were designed to sever Israel from her past. Judaism was Judaism everywhere. Sabato Morais' intense loyalty to God, Torah, Talmud and the hallowed traditions of the Jewish people would not allow Judaism in the new country to be built upon less than a solid foundation. The word "allow" is to be taken literally. Morais was determined, courageous, sure. His stand was equally determined, courageous, sure. Judaism was Judaism everywhere, all over the world.

Father to the fatherless, friend to the poor, helper to the lowly, advocate of justice, champion of Judaism, scholar, student, messenger of God—this was Sabato Morais. His striking physical appearance was softened by a poetic countenance and silken curls, while his patriarchal beard and fiery, deeply set eyes commanded the attention he invariably held by the force of his personality. His every utterance demonstrated his earnestness. For truth he stood up, no matter the climate or opposition. For truth he brought his whole being and power to bear. And the sincerity and humility which characterized this pursuit of truth won

99

him universal love and admiration. He was the first Jew awarded an
honorary doctor of laws degree by the University of Pennsylvania.

Sabato Morais wrote prodigiously about every subject of life, but his
special love was reserved for great Italian Jewish scholars. In a sense, he
was a hero-worshiper. His favorite was Samuel David Luzzatto, master
of the renaissance of Hebrew literature. As one reads of Morais' reverence for his hero, he sees a picture of Morais himself emerging. Morais
writes of Luzzatto:

> Endowed with extraordinary abilities, inspired with love for his re-
> ligion and his people, ever intent upon perpetuating and spreading
> the knowledge of sacred literature, Luzzatto was the man among his
> contemporaries best qualified to fill that important station. The zeal that
> he brought to bear on the discharge of his official duties is attested by
> the work of his hands. . . .
>
> The vigor of his gigantic mind lent additional strength to his
> bodily frame. He would not suffer aught to prevent the accomplish-
> ing of his self-imposed obligations. To improve his brethren, to dis-
> close the transcendent charm of their literature, he eagerly seized every
> moment he could spare from his high calling. . . .
>
> Alas! that very few in this material age emulate his perseverance
> and unwearied zeal in the pursuit of learning. . . .
>
> He omitted no occasion by which he could enhance the value of our
> precious heirloom. He dived into the ocean of time and drew forth
> sparkling jewels. . . .
>
> Not that he gloried in his achievements, but he rejoiced in the
> consciousness of having labored for a noble end. Yes, to enlighten Israel
> and sanctify the Lord had been his early vow, and he fulfilled it to the
> last. He laid upon the altar of his religion man's most precious offering,
> his lifetime and his faculties. . . .

So does Morais write of Luzzatto, words that could as well be a portrayal of himself. Intellectual acumen, a sense of vision, keen observa-
tion of Jewish life, loyalty to God and his people, all were characteristics of Morais as much as they were of Luzzatto. He lovingly quotes
from Luzzatto's own words a reference to teachers and rabbis:

> My soul was deeply impressed with the imperative necessity of
> supplying the minds of the future teachers and shepherds of Israel
> with clear and just ideas of the morality of Judaism, so that they might,

in due time, impart in its own purity that religion, which, when drawn from its primary source, to wit, the Holy Scriptures, is eminently social and promotive of the most healthful state of civilization.

There is here the seed of Morais' contribution to Judaism, the contribution which has earned him special recognition as one of the greatest giants of faith our people have been blessed with in modern times— the founding of the Jewish Theological Seminary of America, fountainhead of Conservative Judaism.

Morais' loyalty to his God and tradition was early instilled. Indeed, loyalty seems to be a virtue in which he specialized—loyalty to homeland, to heritage, to God, Torah, people, America. In every address, every essay, the word appears and reappears.

Sabato Morais was born in Leghorn, Italy, on April 11, 1823, one of nine children and the oldest son. Loyalty was almost innate. His father, a republican patriot and ardent champion of Italian freedom and national unification, suffered persecution for his liberal political views. He was known to have exclaimed, "Even the boards of my bed are Republican." His grandfather, after whom he was named, had earlier proclaimed: "Up for liberty; down with tyrants." Love of freedom was ingrained. Of Spanish-Portuguese origin, the Morais family had come to Italy centuries before and were distinguished and respected.

Loyalty to Judaism, as well as to freedom, was reflected in Sabato's home environment and early Jewish education. His pious mother wished her oldest son to become a rabbi in Israel, and he, for his part, strove to fulfill her wish, though not early drawn to the rabbinate. When he lost his mother at the tender age of 15, his ambition intensified. He studied locally under Rabbis Funaro and Curait and then advanced to Talmudic studies under the personal guidance and tutelage of the Chief Rabbi Abraham Baruch Piperno, who bestowed traditional ordination upon him. Semitics he studied with Professor Salvatore de Bendetti. A quick mind and a brilliant grasp of languages enabled him early to master Hebrew and Italian literature, Arabic, French and Spanish. The same brilliance and self-discipline allowed him to study continuously while supporting his family. He taught and tutored and matured.

When he was 24 years of age, he applied for the post of assistant hazan (reader) in the Spanish-Portuguese Synagogue of London. Although he impressed the congregation and officials deeply, he did not

land the position, the officials feeling that his English was not satis-
factory. They should have realized that one who had mastered so many
other languages would easily learn English. However, the following
year he was invited to become the Hebrew teacher of the orphans' school
in the same congregation. He came to England in 1846 and spent five
years there, quickly mastering English and earning the respect of the
community.

Morais' early devotion to Italian freedom drew him naturally to those
who had similar feelings. He made many lasting friendships based on
this bond, notably with Sir Moses Montefiore and Giuseppe Mazzini.
Throughout their lives, these friendships continued, joined as they were
by passionate love for freedom, though oceans and lands separated them.

Morais' passion for freedom was soon to be felt and known all over
America. In 1851, five years after he came to England, the pulpit of
historic Mikveh Israel Congregation in Philadelphia was vacant. Isaac
Leeser had resigned. Morais hesitated, but friends persuaded him to
apply and to hazard the journey. The young, vibrant preacher was an
immediate success. He preached on March 22nd, and less than three
weeks later, on April 13th, he was elected to the post, chosen over older
and more experienced men.

Morais served the congregation all his life, from 1851 to 1897, almost half a century, and the most crucial half-century in the history of
American Jewry. This was the epoch which formed Jewish life and set
its structure and pattern for generations to come. Morais is inextricably
bound up with it and is one of its creators. But for him, American Jewry
and world Jewry were vastly different. Morais profoundly affected the
course of Jewish history. He stopped the sweeping tide of Reform Judaism in America. He plugged the dikes holding the waters of Torah,
held them in, stirred them up and reinvested life in them. He then
cemented the cracks and made the Judaism of the ages secure. Undisputed leader of the traditional and Orthodox forces in America, he
was the rallying point even of those who had despaired of traditional
beliefs, customs and ceremonials in a new country and changing environment and age.

About him he drew many disciples who became renowned in Jewish
life and in American life. Cyrus Adler, Mayer Sulzberger, Heinrich
Graetz, Moses Dropsie, names which are part of the fabric of American
Jewish life, were inspired by Sabato Morais. The thousands of rabbis

and teachers of Conservative Judaism who carry the message and tradition of historic Judaism throughout the world come from the life's blood and toil of Sabato Morais.

History would have been different, and Jewish life cannot be pictured, without the story of Sabato Morais. His deep sense of loyalty carries on. Not only for Jewish life, but for American life as well, Morais' arrival in America carried implications. His deep love of freedom, born out of love for Italy, was transferred to America. Freedom was freedom everywhere and for all people, as Judaism was Judaism everywhere for all Jews.

Mikveh Israel Congregation learned quickly that their rabbi would stand up for principles. He could not be stifled, nor would he cower under pressure. He would be heard. Among others, Morais fought for freedom of the pulpit. The synagogue podium was a platform from which the rabbi was to speak his heart and his feeling. This freedom must not be repressed. Sabato Morais must be accorded a large measure of credit for the shift of leadership in the synagogue from the congregational laity to the rabbi. The process was long and painful, and its success is a tribute to Morais and others like him who spoke unhesitatingly of themes that they, by right of spiritual leadership, thought appropriate for the congregation and for Judaism.

One of the most dramatic *causes célèbres* in American history saw Morais taking an unusually firm and fearless stand, the famous Mortara Case of 1858. In Italy, a child by the name of Edgar Mortara was abducted by nuns from his Jewish parents to be brought up Catholic on the grounds that he had been secretly baptized by a Catholic nurse. The case stirred world Jewry to indignation. Rabbis and Jewish leaders, joined by some Christians, condemned the act. Meetings and conferences were called all over America to protest. Sabato Morais called upon President James Buchanan to intercede with the Pope. When the President refused, Morais, to the shocked consternation of his congregation, refused to read the traditional prayer for the President in the synagogue on the following Sabbath. The omission of this prayer, long part of the service, reverberated louder in silence than it ever had in observance.

One can almost picture the scene that Sabbath morning. The synagogue is filled with Sabbath worshipers. The service is being conducted by stately Hazan Morais, a magnificent prayer shawl draping his shoulders over the flowing silk gown which the ladies of the synagogue had sewed for him. His sweet voice chants the melodious prayers of the Spanish-Portuguese tradition. The hymns captivate, though they are the same week after week. Inevitably, a different feeling is generated by the songs and hymns each time they are heard. The Torah reading service is over. The time has come to return the Holy Scroll to the Ark. This is the time set for the pause to invoke God's blessing upon the President of the United States. Morais, though his service proceeds with outer calm, is tense within. The President has refused to help in the tragic Mortara case. He cannot ignore this. He must, as a rabbi in Israel, express his indignation and anger. There has been an injustice, and in his own homeland at that. The moment arrives. Pause. The congregation waits for the prayer. Pause. The hazan, without announcement, skips the prayer, continuing with the psalm which follows. The congregation is stunned. Could it be an error? They look at each other, then back at the hazan. One look at him tells the story. Sabato Morais has taken a stand. This was his trademark as a rabbi in Israel.

On every major issue in life, Morais took a firm stand. Injustice invariably stirred him to action. The slavery issue which plagued America and tore it apart found Morais at the forefront on the side of freedom, for emancipation for the Negro and preservation of the Union. He whose father had been imprisoned for his political views, he who was a close friend to the great Mazzini, felt compelled to speak out for freedom. He allied himself with the abolitionists, though many of the members of his congregation were pro-slavery and he was cautioned by a large number of them to temper his expressions. He refused. They insisted that he stick to religious topics alone. Morais could not divorce the question of slavery from the realm of religious and moral subjects. Again he refused. The climax of differences was reached in 1814 when Dr. Morais referred to the State of Maryland, where slavery had just been abolished, as "Merry Land." The group petitioned the directors of the congregation to curtail Morais' freedom to preach. The group had sufficient influence to limit temporarily his passionate anti-slavery sermons. Meanwhile, however, the distinguished and powerful Union League Club of Philadelphia elected him an honorary member for his courageous stand. Unhesitatingly he joined a public march for freedom, in which his participation attracted much attention.

Morais felt a deep admiration for Abraham Lincoln. On the Sabbath of April 15, 1865, when the horrible news of Lincoln's assassination flashed across the country, Morais delivered a passionate prayer in the synagogue. But since it was the Sabbath, no signs of mourning were permitted until sundown. The surrounding neighborhood, aware of his views and feelings, and while insisting on public displays of the American flag, did not disturb his Sabbath.

When Jews were victims of Russian oppression in the 1880's, Morais was again in the forefront. He sought aid for them through his friend, Chevalier Veneziani, who interested Baron de Hirsch in helping to establish agricultural colonies. Morais was friend, counselor and confidant to the new immigrants.

In 1890, his personal involvement helped arbitrate and settle a long strike by Philadelphia clothing workers, Russian Jews, against German Jews who were the manufacturers. He employed a procedure and technique which predated arbitration standards now common. On the Day of Atonement of that year, he quoted the words of that morning's Prophetic portion from Isaiah: "On the day of your fast, you exact all your gain. You fast only to strife and contention and to smite with the fist of wickedness. Will you call this a day of fast and a day acceptable to the Lord?" He continued quoting, "Is not this the fast which I have chosen to let the debt-burdened go free . . . to break your bread with the hungry; to bring the evicted into your house. . . . Prayer and oppression go not together. . . ."

Morais had arrived in America at the middle of the century, 1851. Three years earlier a major immigration wave had brought many Jews who had spread throughout the land. Wherever they journeyed they were confronted with cataclysmic changes taking place. New circumstances brought new problems. The Reform movement was growing and their leaders were militant and aggressive. They were taking firm root in the soil of Free America. Orthodoxy did not have a large number of leaders. Isaac Leeser had been the recognized leader of the right wing, which was trying to stem the Reform tide. Sabato Morais joined with him, affirming the need for basic religion. Traditional observances must be maintained; they were not anachronistic, obsolete. Jewish law was the framework of Jewish life and its vitality must be preserved. Without it all is chaos.

In one of his masterful sermons, delivered before Congregation Mikveh Israel in 1885, he fearlessly opposed the expressed desires for change called for by many in his congregation. He hesitated neither to confront the issues nor to provide frank answers:

"Why do you stand still when all are moving on?" This question is put to me by men and women of Israel, who have a right to an answer. . . .

I might urge an alteration of the organic laws made by the founders of this religious body, and possibly bring it to pass. But the principal impediment would yet remain. My conscience would rise to the defense of sacred ground. The still, small voice within would speak and rebuke the presumption of encroaching upon that which the wise and the upright have established. For, you ought to know, my fellow believers, that the authors of a number of our prayers are the prophets and sages of old. . . . Those devotional effusions being read in the language sanctified by the sounds of the words heard at Sinai, opened among all the adherents of the Mosaic code a current of spiritual magnetism—if I may employ the term—reaching from one end of the world to the opposite end. However circumstances may have affected the Jew socially or politically, he felt on entering a Synagogue, that he was still bound in faith, in hope, and destiny to the whole household of Jacob.

Now that "minor sanctuary" is undergoing such changes, that Hebrew hailing from a foreign land will scarcely recognize it. And I am asked to help in disfiguring what our fathers thought it wise to make. To this I might again briefly reply that when I put on the ministerial robe, I enlisted in the service not only of a small body of brethren, but of the entire Jewish Church. And that I could no more trespass against the orders of my superiors, the Rabbis, than the sentinel desert his military post.

But the demands of our rising generation are pictured to me. The absolute necessity of yielding, to prevent a further estrangement from Judaism, is advanced as an argument against my persisting in the same course. That appeal does affect me deeply . . . but what, if whilst engaged in saving a few, I expose the many to danger? If I cause a whole congregation gradually to lapse into gentilism, by too close an approximation to its rites and practices? . . .

The cause should be ascribed not to my inactivity. . . . It should rather be attributed to the increasing defection of your teachers, O American Israelites; and to your sinful negligence, O Jewish parents! . . . and you, parents, have aggravated the evil. You are, undesignedly perhaps, aiding to sunder apart a strong link which binds together the dispersed of Judah. For you do not regret the sums expended to train your children in all the accomplishments of the age, but you rest satisfied if your son can, at best, learn by rote a portion of the Pentateuch when he attains his religious majority; if your daughter can memorize a verse or two in Deuteronomy, containing the Shema. . . . Can you not foresee the end? Why, it stares us in the face! The next generation will not be recognized as the disciples of Moses and the Prophets: so complete will be the transformation wrought by the changelings. I may be unable to prevent it, but I shall not deliberately hasten the disruption of our brotherhood.

Impressed with the views of Zacharias Frankel, the founder of the Positive-Historical School which held that Judaism could adjust to changing times and traditions without affecting its own integrity, Morais became its foremost exponent and vehicle. The School called for a positive approach of reverence and understanding toward traditional Judaism. Judaism was not to be surrendered to the demands of mere convenience or conformity. The Positive-Historical School is the forerunner of Conservative Judaism, giving it its philosophy and framework for action.

Together with Isaac Leeser in 1867, Morais founded Maimonides College in Philadelphia, the first Jewish college in the Western Hemisphere; for six years of its existence serving as professor of Bible and Biblical literature. Financial support was lacking, and the doors of the college were closed in 1873. But America did not remain long without a Jewish college. Two years later, in 1875, Reform Jewry organized and established the Hebrew Union College in Cincinnati, an institution to prepare and train rabbis for America. Sabato Morais, acknowledged leader of the Orthodox wing of Judaism, hailed the new college. He hoped that even a seminary under Reform auspices might train rabbis of the more traditional persuasion. This attitude demonstrates his liberalism, existing as it did alongside his commitment to historical Judaism. He was not unwilling, for the sake of *Sholom Bayit,* peace within the household, to allow for some changes within traditional outlines. For instance, he was ready to sacrifice the Sephardic (Spanish-Portuguese) ritual that he loved so dearly for an American ritual based on the Ashkenazic (Germanic-Polish) pattern. In any case, when invited to become affiliated with Hebrew Union College as official examiner, he unhesitatingly accepted. However, his high hopes were soon dashed, and the split Morais had wanted to avoid became inevitable. He was stunned to learn that the first graduating class of the College was celebrating at a non-kosher dinner. Shortly thereafter, Reform Jewry officially proclaimed the Pittsburgh Platform as the basis of its principles and doctrines. The Platform, which rejected traditions hallowed by time because they were "not adapted to the views and habits of modern civilization" and "originated in ages and under the influence of ideas entirely foreign to our present mental and spiritual state," affected such basic traditions as Kashruth, Sabbath observance, Hebrew prayers, references to Zion, etc. Hope for a unified Jewry was no longer possible. A series of crises began, each of which had to be confronted head on, else Orthodox Judaism was doomed.

Once again, Morais accepted the challenge. The answer lay in the establishment of an institution of higher learning which would represent traditional Judaism. Help was needed from other rabbis. He was 63 years of age at this crucial juncture of his life, and he felt the need of a younger man to help him. New York City, the center of Jewish life and immigration in America, would be the institution's logical home. Rabbi H. Periera Mendes, minister of the Spanish-Portuguese Congregation in New York, oldest synagogue in America, was just the man to work with him. Accordingly, he traveled to New York to present the plans to the younger leader, who happily was more than willing to cooperate. It has been said that the young rabbi even offered to exchange pulpits so that Morais could personally supervise the new institution. It has also been said that Mendes suggested Dr. Morais become the senior rabbi while he, though he had served the congregation for many years, would become associate rabbi. In any case, they agreed to speak from each other's pulpits on succeeding Sabbaths to bring the message to the people more forcefully.

Dr. H. Periera Mendes later reminisced:

One day, Dr. Morais, a man whom I had learned to hold in high esteem, a man older than my honored father, called on me in New York to propose changing our action of meetings, debates, press-communications, accusations, recriminations, effervescence and indignation with no tangible result, into action that might mean, under God, something that would advance the cause so dear to us both, namely, the preserva-

tion of Historical and Traditional Judaism, with provision for upholding the ethical values of our religion, by establishing a Jewish
Institute of Learning, by educating, training and inspiring teachers,
Rabbis who would stand "for the Torah and the Testimony" as cried
our prophet of old (Isaiah VIII:20).

He came with a definite plan of procedure ready. He proposed that
he and I, as head of the oldest congregation in the country, should take
immediate action to awaken the two Jewish communities of New York
and Philadelphia to the need of the hour, to create a Jewish College or
Seminary on the lines above indicated; that we exchange pulpits for this
purpose; that we take immediate action.

I eagerly and enthusiastically embraced all his propositions. . . .

I well remember that when the Scroll of the Law was placed on the
reading desk, Dr. Morais honored me by calling me to read a section
of the Scriptures—lesson of the Sabbath. I ascended to the reading
desk. In courtly fashion he presented me with the silver pointer, to
guide in reading the lines. I bowed, but I resigned the honor to him.
The verses were of a Menorah or seven-branched candlestick, whose
beautiful and soft light was to pervade the Mikdash, the sanctifying
center, and whose beams were to reveal the Shechinah, the Divine Presence
on Earth. [The portion of the Torah for the particular Sabbath dealt with
the establishing of the Sanctuary in the wilderness and the various articles
of the Sanctuary.]

I felt that I acted rightly in handing over to Dr. Morais the honor of
announcing the crowning meaning of our proposed Sanctuary or Seminary
which we fondly hoped would kindle the light of the World, the light of
God, the light of the Torah, the light for Israel, the light that one day
"shall reach all nations of Earth."

Years of effort were begun. Plans drawn up to enlist support. Without
neglecting his beloved congregation and their families, Morais pushed
doggedly on.

In January of 1886, joined by six other rabbis, Sabato Morais issued
the call, the first concrete step in the organization of the Seminary. The
proclamation was significantly headed with the caption, *"To learn and
to teach, to observe and to practice."* The words *to observe* and *to practice*
were written in capital letters. The announcement declared that:

It is imperative to make a strong effort for the perpetuation of historical Judaism in America. . . . It is proposed to found an institution in
which Bible and Talmud shall be studied to a religious purpose.

For two months he traveled from city to city along the East Coast, at the end of which period he was excited enough with prospects of success to write, "The prospects for the Jewish Theological Seminary are providentially brightening."

Morais' plans were thorough and comprehensive. He had completely formulated purpose and intent.

The tuition will not be one-sided—precluding the free exercise of intellectual faculties—but abstruse questions, apt to mislead, will be set at rest by arguments as cogent as it is given to learned and believing preceptors to advance. The Seminary will strive clearly to demonstrate the possible connection of orthodoxy—or Conservatism, if the word is preferred—with broadness of views. In fact, it will have no claim to general support, unless it shall disclose that an Israelite can obey Sinaic precepts and traditional rules and nevertheless mingle in fellowship with his countrymen, seek the welfare of the land in which he lives, and cultivate the arts and sciences which the present age fosters. The unhistorical assertion that liberality of thought and action implies the abandonment of ancestral practices and the construction of a novel system void of all its Hebrew characteristics, must be refuted by living testimonies. The blatant talk—nowadays very noisy—about the incompatability of Judaism and Americanism—so to term it—will cease when broadly cultured ministers shall preach the sanctity of the ordinances, and shall strengthen their lessons with their example. To reach that end, eagerly to be sought after, the assistance of all my brethren who "believe in the Lord and in Moses His servant" is solicited for large means are imperatively demanded to establish the Jewish Theological Seminary on a permanent footing.

To Morais, the new institution was not designed to form a new movement within Judaism. It was to be and reflect Judaism itself. There was no quarrel with Orthodoxy. The effort was designed to counteract Reform. Morais had even suggested that the new institution be called the Orthodox Seminary, but his colleagues prevailed upon him to accept the more inclusive title, Jewish Theological Seminary of America. In a passionate sermon in Baltimore, at Chizzuk Emunah Congregation, Morais spread the word of the new institution like the prophet of old:

A seminary of sacred learning will be set up. I acknowledge now with resolute boldness, lest I be charged at any period hereafter with having agreed to entangling compromises, I acknowledge that as far as it lies in *my* power, the proposed seminary shall be hallowed to one predominating purpose—to the upholding of the principles by which my ancestors lived and for which many have died. From that nursery of learning shall issue forth men whose utterances will kindle enthusiasm for the literature of Holy Writ, but whose everyday conduct will mirror forth a sincere devotion to the *tenets* of Holy Writ. The language in which the poetry of the soul chose to be clothed; the language which has in all truth annihilated distance and held a people, scattered throughout the habitable globe, in one eternal embrace, the language unexcelled in terseness and vigor, must be revived. . . . I lay great stress upon the need of a conscientious cultivation of the Scriptures with the exegesis thereof, because I contend that those revered volumes must chiefly serve as the armory supplying Conservatism with weapons of defence. . . .

Brethren: In every stage of our history, when Judaism seemed to be gasping for breath, salvation providentially arose and the Torah lived. I am not disposed to denounce its deadly foes—unhappily abounding among men who should bare their breasts and receive the wound rather than pierce their fathers' creed with barbed arrows; but you all know by what perils our ancestral tenets are beset. You know that the covenant which Abraham—looking through a vista of unending ages—asked even ourselves, his late descendants, ineffaceably to seal, is exposed to the risk of being branded as infamous. The Sabbath of the Decalogue—the manifestation of God's creative will and Israel's testimony of that will, is declared beyond the reach of human obedience. The Passover, whose every ceremony evoked historical reminiscences of sublime import, is allowed to see leaven in the dwellings of persons in the public service of our religion. The Day of Atonement, formerly infusing a spiritual awe, is denied its conciliatory powers and willful transgressors are reassured against the Scriptural punishment with which that day threatens them. The feast of Tabernacles—a faithful chronicler of forty years' eventful history, is relegated to obscurity, because its arrival finds the disciples of Moses inextricably engaged in "the fall trade." Superfluous it would be to allude to the laws which prohibit the eating of flesh with the blood thereof, of animals and fishes and amphibious creatures designated in the Pentateuch as an abomination to Israelites. You all know with what indifference the appointed guardians of that sacred book trespass against it, and with what untenable reasonings they preach the abrogation of its behests. None of you can be ignorant of the causes which embolden the reckless and the disaffected, but you can thrust back a fearful evil approaching with rapid strides, you can deliver posterity from recreancy, and keep it in our sacred

fold to the glory of the One God. A bulwark of defence to our belief
is being raised. In New York it shall tower high. You understand me,
brethren. Efforts to promote a study conducive to godly actions have taken
the initiative in that city. . . .

Trained by preceptors loyal to conservatism, real professors, making
declaration of their fealty to Jewish doctrines—the scholars shall follow in
the wake of their teachers, preaching the eternity of the revelation of
Sinai, the venerableness of oral impartings, resuscitating the national
language, commending the books which have preserved it, widened its
scope and beautified it. But above all, those scholars shall luminously prove
in their demeanour their belief in the immortal enunciations of Asaph.
"God established a statute in Jacob, and appointed a Law in Israel which
He commanded our fathers that they might make the same known unto
their children."

One year later, almost to the day, Sabato Morais presided majestically
and with deep satisfaction over the formal opening of the Seminary.
Eight students were registered. One of them, Joseph H. Hertz, was to
rise to international fame as chief rabbi of the British Empire.

Although the institution was now a reality, Morais did not relax.
Three times a week, unfailingly, he traveled to New York—this despite
his age, an age at which one normally eases into retirement. Instead,
Morais was rejuvenated. His Benjamin, as he lovingly called the
Seminary, recalling the patriarch Jacob and his last son, gave him new
life and fervor; and he moved heaven and earth to assure its lasting
success. Every department had his personal impress. Every area of
learning received his personal attention. His hand and heart were felt
in every aspect of the institution, including the library, which in honor
of his 70th birthday, April 18, 1893, was named for him. The course
of study was directed to meet the challenges of the day and the comprehensive goals to which Morais had dedicated his life.

Friendship between founder and students was intense and warm.
They were not youths to be patronized, rather friends and future colleagues. Morais was at once father, counselor, friend, and hero.

After so many years of labor, he looked forward eagerly to the first
graduation ceremony. How disappointed he must have been when he
realized that illness would prevent him from seeing with his own eyes
the graduates receive their ordination. He had worked in the vineyard
of the Lord all these years, and when the moment of triumph arrived,

he had to depend on reports from others. Yet he approached the hour of consecration with thrilled anticipation:

Joy it is to me to cherish the hope that the future leaders in Israel, issuing from this beloved institution of ours, shall have received a complete training in America, that its language will become the vehicle of their sacred instruction, that their faultless diction will enhance the dignity of the pulpit, while a store of Biblical and Talmudical knowledge, unfolded in their lessons, shall feed and strengthen the intellects open to the acceptance of the verities which flow from the written and the oral Law.

When my soul is cast down and agitated within me, because of serious losses sustained in the realm of our literature; when I lament over the paucity of numbers really able to replace those that have gone forever; when, contemplating what happens in our midst, I, like Jeremiah, am almost forced to predict evil, a Bat Kol—a voice from above—cries: "Do not despair; salvation may yet arise from the Lord who rewards sterling sincerity."

Aye, honesty of purpose was the foundation stone of our edifice. Selfishness was not suffered to darken its threshold. One thought swayed the minds of the Hebrews who conceived the creation of our high school of learning; to shield Judaism from extinction by raising around it a wall of defence in the strong characters of the disciples, sworn to keep sentry at our citadel.

Time was running out for the great soul of Sabato Morais, humble man of God. His mighty spirit had made its permanent impact upon Jewish life in America and throughout the world. The seeds he sowed, the plants he nurtured, grow high and sturdily. They have spread everywhere, sending the fragrance of Torah and learning to all corners of the globe. His love of Judaism, the Judaism which came as a precious heritage from Israel's noble past, was intense. No ordinary attachment to Torah was his. His bond with Torah was complete and wholehearted. No pedant, no ivory tower dweller, Sabato Morais was a keen, dynamic observer, watchman of the tower of Torah, fearless champion of his people, giant of faith. He lived by his faith; a faith based on knowledge, which in turn was made alive by that faith. This faith, coupled with the duty of preserving unbroken the continuity of Israel's traditions, made for the essence of the man. The tributes paid him are suggestive of the stellar role he played in preserving the values of Judaism. Words from the Book of Daniel, for instance, were applied to him:

And they that are wise shall shine as the brightness of the firmament, and they that lead the many to righteousness, as the stars forever and ever.

His son Henry pronounced the passage dealing with Elijah's ascension into heaven:

"O my father, my father, the chariot of Israel and his horsemen."

and

The law of Truth was in his mouth, and guile was not found upon his lips; in peace and in uprightness he walked with Me, and many he turned aside from iniquity.

His successor, Rev Dr. Leon H. Elmaleh, wrote an acrostic, bearing Sabato Morais' name in Hebrew. The English, carefully selected passages from the Bible, tells the story of Sabato Morais:

ש I have observed Thy precepts and Thy testimonies; for all my ways are before Thee.

ב Thy words have I laid up in my heart, that I might not sin against Thee.

ת Let Thy hand be ready to help me; for I have chosen Thy precepts.

י Let Thy tender mercies come unto me, that I may live; for Thy law is my delight.

ם I have not turned aside from Thine ordinances; for Thou hast instructed me.

ו I will lift up my hands unto Thy commandments, which I have loved; and I will meditate on Thy statutes.

ד The beginning of Thy word is truth; and all of Thy righteous ordinances endureth forever.

א Happy are they that are upright in the way, who walk in the law of the Lord.

י Let those that fear Thee turn unto me, and they that know Thy testimonies.

ת I hate them that are of a double mind; but Thy law I love.

Generations to come will bear witness to his saintly character, his zeal for Judaism, and his work for Jewish learning in America.

KAUFMANN KOHLER

Matchless Champion of Reform Judaism

[1843-1926]

No one would have believed in 1843 that Kaufmann Kohler, scion of a distinguished rabbinical family in Bavaria, would one day become the foremost exponent of radical Reform Judaism in America. This was the year Kohler was born. Nor would anyone have believed 20 years later, 1863, that Kohler was marked for such a destiny. Nor would anyone have believed in 1926, in America, that Kohler, after a long, fulfilling life of leadership in Reform Judaism, had been originally and for 21 years of his life a devoted son of Orthodox Judaism.

What happened to cause the change? What was the crucial year's trauma that brought about the switch from devout belief in traditional Judaism? It was the year 1864. The place, the University of Munich. Kohler had just entered the University. The first years of his life— May 10, 1843, was the date of his birth—were passed in an atmosphere of genuine Orthodoxy in Fuerth, Bavaria, seat of a great Yeshivah, rabbinical academy and stronghold of Orthodox Judaism. The town was known for its Jewish printing press which provided the student of the Torah with complete editions of the Talmud, the Shulchan Aruch with its commentaries, and a large casuistic and liturgical literature.

Kohler was the descendant of an intense and illustrious Jewish background. His father, Moritz, in common with his friends, studied Talmud in the synagogue every morning after services, and every evening he prepared for the next day's session. Kohler always cherished having his father's set of Talmud. At five, in keeping with Jewish tradition, Kohler was initiated into the Torah by his father. His mother, Babette, who died at 91 and on whose tombstone her adoring son inscribed the words from the Song of Songs: "I am asleep but my heart is awake," was the daughter of David Loewenmayer, teacher and cantor of the Sulzbuerg community. Kohler lovingly recalls: "She loved to quote in her conversation and correspondence from her favorite poets, Lessing and Schiller, so that fondness for the German classics was ingrained in my soul early in life simultaneously with love for Hebrew literature."

At ten, Kohler was sent to Hassfurt to study Talmud with Eisle Michael Schueler. He vividly recalls how he was teased by his peers because he was at such a tender age unable to fast on Yom Kippur, the Day of Atonement, and was called "Yomkippur-fresser"—Yom Kippur eater. The following year, at the ripe age of 11, he determinedly fasted and achieved the rank denied previously. He remembers nostalgically the Bar Mitzvah speech he delivered and how, to the pleasant surprise of his parents and teacher, he selected the discourse for the week's portion of the Torah from the work of his ancestor, entitled Pardes David.

He also studied under the personal tutelage of other leaders of Orthodox Judaism: Rabbi Wolf Hamburger, Rosh Yeshivah of the famous Fuerth Yeshivah; Dr. Marcus Lehmann of Mainz, Rabbi Jacob Ettlinger of Altona, and finally, under Rabbi Samson Raphael Hirsch, revered leader and pillar of Orthodox Judaism in Germany. The influence of these greats was profound and lasting, especially that of S. R. Hirsch, of whom Kohler wrote in his reminiscences: "The man who exerted the greatest influence upon my young life and imbued me with the divine ardor of true idealism . . . was Samson Raphael Hirsch. . . . His strong personality was such as to work like a spell on his hearers. Whether he spoke in the pulpit or expounded Scripture to large audiences, or led us through the discussions of the Talmud, there was a striking originality and a fascinating power of genius in his grasp of the subject. . . . Every Saturday night in my letter to the dear ones at home I gave a faithful synopsis of the sermon I heard in the morning. . . ."

The first two decades of Kohler's life were spent drinking the waters of Torah from such wellsprings of Jewish knowledge. Even in the beginning of his third decade in life, Kohler was still filled with the spirit of his masters' and parents' teachings. Nor did he deviate from his training while at Frankfurt attending the gymnasium (high school) even though Abraham Geiger's two sons were classmates of his. "Nor did I ever enter any of the Reform Temples either in Frankfurt or Mainz, having been taught to regard them as a Tiflah—a perversion of a house of worship."

The great change took place in 1864, at the University of Munich. The cause—a sudden awareness that what he had learned at the feet of Samson Raphael Hirsch was not completely true in terms of his new studies. Kohler recalls later that the change was foretold by one of his experiences. While at Frankfurt he went to a Jewish philanthropist, A. H. Goldschmidt, to ask for a grant for University students. When Goldschmidt learned that he was a student of S. R. Hirsch, he remarked prophetically: "A pupil of Samson Raphael Hirsch, the Orthodox rabbi, you come to me for a stipend? I will grant it, feeling certain that before you have finished your university course you will have ceased to be a follower of Hirsch."

He was a student of philology and taking a course in Arabic at the time. S. R. Hirsch had taught him, as was generally accepted, that Hebrew was the original language of the human race. When his studies did not agree, he began to wonder whether Hirsch might not have erred in other areas. The insinuation of this questioning and the tug of the modern spirit brought much mental anguish to Kohler. He sought to drive the thoughts out of his mind, but they continued to plague him. What disturbed him most was his deep affection, love and admiration for his revered teacher. "I passed days and weeks of indescribable woe and despondency; the heavens seemed to fall down upon me and crush me; and the strange tone of my letters puzzled my dear parents so as to make them suspect me of having fallen into bad company." One can almost picture him sitting in his room, studying intently by candlelight the languages of the past, and see the torment and pain in his face as he experienced these first conflicts with his master's teachings. Which way to turn? What to do? Where to seek comfort and help? He felt himself shaken in his faith and he fought to retain it. But his continued studies overpowered him and he gradually lost faith in what he had previously been taught. Although he approached many for guidance, help did not come. Hopefully, he went to his master S. R. Hirsch for clarification, but the most he received was the assurance that the doubts gnawing within him would pass. He was experiencing a normal questioning period. In the end all would turn out well and be as before. "I rallied strength and traveled to Frankfurt to lay my doubts and scruples before my revered teacher; but instead of having these satisfactorily removed, I received the remarkable answer: 'My dear Kohler, he who wants to journey around the world must also pass the torrid zone; proceed and you will come back safely.' "

Kohler was not satisfied. S. R. Hirsch did not help him and he never went back, but his inquisitive mind persisted in formulating questions. The new knowledge ignited by doubt drove him out of the paradise of his childhood. Doubt followed him to the University of Berlin where the process which had shaken his faith continued uninterrupted as he listened to lectures on psychology and ethnology. His earlier views of Judaism and religion all but disappeared, though he fought this loss. He sought out Zunz and Steinschneider who at the time were lecturing in Berlin but found them inaccessible. He went to others, seeking after truth, but none could help him. He was being driven from all his old moorings. "I had no friend of prominence in the big city to confide in during these days of anxiety and doubt," he wrote later. "Nor did I have a real Jewish home to keep the cherished memories of old fresh in me." But though his struggle was lonely, it did not remove him from Judaism—as had the doubts of so many others.

From the University of Berlin, Kohler went to the University of Erlangen for his doctor's degree. His thesis, offered at the age of 24, was entitled *Der Segen Jacob*. It was a critical study of the Blessing of Jacob (Genesis 49), and created a stir in Jewish circles, not only because of its erudition, but more particularly because of its critical approach. It demonstrated how far young Kohler had traveled from the teachings of his teachers in but a few years. Young Kohler suggested for the first time that the prophetic movement had its beginnings in the Torah, the Pentateuch, not only in the second section of the Bible, the Prophets. He applied the principle of historical evolution to the whole Pentateuch, and thus opposed the accepted and prevailing Jewish view of the Mosaic origin of the Bible. He used his introduction as a vehicle for discussing the meaning of religion and the need to re-evaluate its goals and ideals constantly in terms of present-day living. Here the seeds of Kohler's later views were sown and nurtured.

Kohler's firm, strong, unexpected view, unpopular with the traditionally minded, brought condemnation in its wake. Even his old master Rabbi Lehmann turned against him with bitter vehemence. Kohler said of this period: "I went through the pangs of Jeremiah when I saw my parents, who had built such hopes upon my future, exposed to fanatical animosity and reproach for not discouraging me." The book was banned.

Meanwhile, Kohler's anti-traditionalism had attracted the Reformers. Abraham Geiger, the dominant thinker of Reform, tried to persuade him to enter the academic world. Kohler followed his advice, entered the University of Leipzig, and began to study Oriental philology. But he was not cut out for a quiet ivory tower. His spirit demanded expression. He had to speak. He had to preach. He needed to share the academic learning he had imbibed with the outside world. He could not keep it within, nor could he confine it to the book. Later he wrote that his spirit was not unlike that of Jeremiah, whose inner fire insisted on bursting into flame. It could not be quenched.

Unhappy in Europe, unable to occupy a pulpit there, the young theologian had but one solution—America. Geiger encouraged him to go to America and recommended him to leaders of the new Reform Movement here. Kohler corresponded with them and in late summer, 1869, went to Detroit, Michigan, and became the rabbi of Congregation Beth El, having received his rabbinical diploma from Dr. Aub before he left Berlin.

Kohler's greeter upon his arrival was Dr. David Einhorn, acknowledged leader of the Reform movement in America at that time. Einhorn's striking personality and congenial family circle paved the way for Kohler. The following year Kohler married Dr. Einhorn's daughter Johanna, his lifelong helpmate, to whom in 1916 he dedicated one of his volumes, *Hebrew Union College and Other Addresses,* with the touching inscription: "To my all-beloved wife—my faithful helpmate in all my activities and aspirations—in loving devotion."

Kohler's spirit came to the fore immediately upon his arrival. He launched himself as an exponent of Reform. His first sermon, the inaugural address, was entitled: "The Qualities of a God-called Leader of Israel." He took Moses as his guide, and his two prime qualities, humility and compassion. Underlying the whole sermon was his deep feeling that he was to serve with all his heart and soul. A new age was dawning and a new era made new demands. He felt compelled to help meet these demands. To this end he devoted his life. "Firmly believing that a benign Providence had assigned to me the task of working for a complete harmonization of modern thought with the ancient faith in the land of my destination, I prepared mind and heart for entering my duties as American Rabbi."

Knowledge of his spiritual ardor and strength soon spread throughout the land. He came to be regarded as the leading theologian and intellectual champion of the significance and purpose of Judaism as interpreted by Reform. The young rabbi dedicated himself to the task at hand, writing and lecturing on all questions related to the issues of this new movement.

Kohler remained in Detroit for two years. In 1871, he was called to the pulpit of Sinai Congregation, Chicago, the first Reform congregation in the Midwest, organized by Rabbi Bernard Felsenthal. His arrival was marked by drama. The large city had just been laid waste by one of the most disastrous fires in history. Years and years of effort had literally gone up in smoke. Kohler, sensitive as he was to human feelings, sought to bring comfort to a discouraged people. In his first sermon he rose to heights of glory as he brought his message of hope and confidence. He selected as his text the refreshing words of Isaiah: 61: "To give to them a garland for ashes, the oil of joy for mourning, the mantle of praise for the spirit of heaviness." The text proved to be a boon to the disheartened citizens. The new rabbi had understood the existing feelings and had held out hope and instilled new courage. He foretold a great rebuilding and an era of prosperity based on the spirit of community living and unity. One can well imagine the impact. Here was a new preacher seeing his new home demolished by the destructive forces of nature and taking the cue from its ashes. The pain was lessened; the melancholy spirits brought back to life. Kohler had scored.

Kohler served Sinai Congregation for nine years, from 1871 to 1880. Passionate in his zeal to spread the Reform idea, he wrote and lectured both on popular and intellectual levels. He remained ever a student, but a student who had to share his knowledge and with it his feelings. He offered a new German translation of the Song of Songs which contained also an analysis of its content and style. In 1876 he published *A Jewish Reader for Sabbath Schools,* primarily designed for the young.

It was Kohler who first introduced Sunday services in Sinai Congregation. He maintained that he had no thought of doing away with the traditional Sabbath but sought rather a more propitious opportunity to teach and to make religion an active influence in the lives of his people. He felt that, in view of the lessening number of Sabbath attendees, more people would be subject to the influence of Judaism on Sunday mornings.

His first sermon on Sunday morning, January 18, 1874, he called "The New Knowledge and the Old Faith." He utilized the occasion to interrelate science and religion. The age of Darwin and evolution had struck hard. Many religionists were falling by the wayside, believing that science and religion were diametrically opposed. Kohler took the opposite stand. There was no conflict between the two, he insisted. Nor was science destructive to religion. The reverse was true, he said. The more one studies and views the greatness of the universe, the marvels of nature, the more he acquires profound faith in God's greatness. Judaism had nothing to fear, he maintained—neither from science nor from anything else. H. G. Enelow, writing Kohler's biography, describes his views: "Religion and science were partners in the spiritual life of mankind. Like sun and moon, each had its place in the sky of the human spirit. Increase of knowledge does not mean diminution of the content of faith. The light of faith must shine ever more brightly in the sun-like radiance of science. Religion and science must illumine each other, and become as one. Not mutual belittlement but reconciliation and unity is their goal. Harmony of mind and spirit—of the whole man —that is their aim."

Kohler was not afraid that Darwinism would lead to atheism.

I have a higher conception of the wisdom of the Eternal than if I believed that He must from time to time rush in to help or improve His own work; for, the eternal laws of nature are His eternal wisdom, His immutable will. He were not the Eternal were He forced ever to change His will.

He reaches a climax of thinking and feeling when he strikes hard and firmly:

We do not die to the old faith. We let the science of the new age quicken our spirit anew and declare before the world the works of God and the goal of mankind.

In 1879, when Dr. David Einhorn, his father-in-law, retired, Beth El Congregation in New York invited Dr. Kohler to occupy the pulpit. He served the new congregation with the same zeal and ardor as theretofore. He was determined to expound the principles of Reform, insisting that Judaism is a religion which has gone through a process of development in the past and is capable of further evolution, that it is a mobile and not a fixed faith, that it contains a most valuable spiritual message for modern man, and that moreover, religion, as such, is needful to mankind and nothing else can take its place. Judaism, he felt, was the religion of the future.

In the year 1885, Dr. Alexander Kohut, Orthodox European leader, arrived in America and threatened the efforts of Reform Judaism by declaring that he who does not accept the principles of the Mosaic-Rabbinical view of Judaism, that is, the traditional view of Judaism, forfeits the name Jew. Dr. Kohut was renowned as a scholar and his words jeopardized Reform. The challenge was real. Though the summer season was approaching, and though Kohler welcomed the challenges of an eminent scholar, he took up the cudgels to defend his efforts and the works of other Reform leaders. "The gauntlet thrown into our face must be taken up at once." In a series of carefully worked out sermons, later printed in English under the general heading, *Backward or Forward,* he defended his thesis of the evolutionary nature of Jewish religion and demanded that the process of adjustment be maintained. He called for a reconciliation of Judaism with the needs and knowledge of the new age.

More significant than their delivery was the result. The sermons led to the convening by Kohler in the fall of that year of the Pittsburgh Rabbinical Conference. The Conference adopted a set of guiding principles for Reform Judaism which remained intact as the most authoritative corporate declaration of Reform Judaism until the Columbus Conference in 1937. The Pittsburgh Platform, as it is called, set down all the principles of Reform Judaism.

Kohler served Beth El until 1903, continuing as a prolific propounder of Reform Judaism and a diligent student of Judaism. He spoke everywhere and on all topics. He wrote unceasingly, both popular pieces and critical analyses. He wrote about the Sabbath and mixed marriages, on proselytes, marriage and divorce, and the ceremonies of Judaism. He wrote biographies of great leaders: Moses Mendelssohn, Maimonides, Rashi, Zunz, Philo, Lazarus and others. One of the greatest achievements of his pen was his contribution around 1900 to the massive and magnificent *Jewish Encyclopedia*. Kohler served as editor in the departments of philosophy and theology and contributed 288 articles.

While devoted to this basic work, Dr. Kohler was invited to become the president of the Hebrew Union College in Cincinnati. He accepted wholeheartedly and as president infused a new spirit into the Reform seminary, building many new structures and enlarging facilities. He assumed his office on October 18, 1903, and in his inaugural address, "What a Jewish Institution of Learning Should Be," established his approach to his post:

It is no small matter, I know, to be successor to Isaac M. Wise, the founder of this college, whose powerful personality achieved wondrous success where many other great leaders failed. Nor indeed do I flatter myself that I possess the qualities that made him the leader of leaders and the master builder in American Israel. In one thing, however, I dare say I am not behind my illustrious predecessor, and that is in ardent love and zeal for Israel's sacred treasure, the Torah. Ever since I sat, a young pious lad, at the feet of my sainted teachers, Rabbi Samson Bondi in Mainz, of Jacob Ettlinger in Altona, and Samson Raphael Hirsch in Frankfurt-am-Main, and others, it was my highest ambition and aim to lift up the standard of the Law and disseminate its truths; and while under the influence of more extensive study and independent research, my views have since undergone a mighty change, the well-spring of my love and enthusiasm has not dried up, and with unspeakable joy and thanksgiving to God do I hail this hour as the realization of my holiest dream. But, with the Psalmist, I exclaim, "Not unto us, O Lord, not unto us, but unto Thy name belongeth the glory!" It is the diadem of the Torah, the crown of Jewish learning, that I long to see again placed upon the brow of modern Israel. "The Torah is thy life and the length of thy days." The Torah, the fount of light and joy, the comfort and mainstay of the Jew in darkest time and amid direst distress, must again occupy the central place in our hearts and homes and be rendered the life-center of the Jewish community.

With the Torah as the rallying point of the race, the Jew is unconquerable and irresistible; without it he is bound to go down and be lost, whether it be in free America or under Turkish or British suzerainty.

The Torah establishes his claim as the God-chosen servant of humanity; his material success only provokes jealousy and hatred, notwithstanding all his philanthropic endeavors. To the promotion and propagation of the Torah, to the sending forth of the Testimony, the message of Israel's God sealed upon the lips of disciples, I shall, under God's guidance, consecrate my life and my labors for the rest of my days.

Kohler looked jealously upon the role of the priest, prophet and preacher he would now mold:

. . . the modern preacher's task is one of the greatest, hardest, and most trying ones. His office is a trust, not from the people to whom but from God for whom he speaks, and unless his powers and authority are felt and recognized as coming, not from man but from God on high, unless he voices that which is holiest, dearest, and truest to all, he is no lawful heir to priest and prophet. For into his hands is committed the future of humanity. His hands are to mould the destinies of homes and communities. He is the appointed guardian of souls.

For 18 years he served, never allowing his presidency to be a mere administrative post. He maintained his concern for the intellectual development of Judaism. Writing many critical studies such as *The Origin and Functions of Ceremonies in Judaism* and *Mission of Israel,* he also was one of the editors of the new translation of the English Bible issued by the Jewish Publication Society, which had earlier issued his own translation of the Book of Psalms.

Kohler's magnum opus was his *Jewish Theology Systematically and Historically Considered,* briefly called "Jewish Theology." Here, Kohler covers every aspect of Jewish theology. No phase of religious thought or practice is overlooked. Every topic is discussed honestly and frankly and marked by a rare blending of learning and feeling. A classic in its field, it first projects definitions of the general concepts of theology and Judaism. It then conveys the essence of Judaism and its underlying beliefs. The final section presents Jewish teachings about God, Man, and the Mission of Israel. With amazing brevity and precision, Kohler tells the story of Judaism. Judaism and Jewry are one and the same; they belong together. "Without Judaism, Jewry is a body without a soul." Throughout history Judaism has come into contact with many and varied currents of thought. There have also been varied and different currents within Judaism itself. The core of it all, however, the essence of it all, says Kohler, "is the doctrine of the One only holy God and of the upbuilding of His Kingdom of truth, righteousness, and peace in the world, and the development and propagation of that doctrine is indissolubly linked with it as the historic mission of the Jewish people." Judaism is to him a progressive, ongoing religion. It has gone through many processes of evolution and has survived. Its goal has always been to sanctify the life of the Jew, infuse it "with spiritual radiance and ethical power, and make Israel the priest-servant of mankind" so that the Kingdom of God may be brought about.

When he retired from the presidency of the Hebrew Union College in 1921, his days of retirement remained productive and fruitful. Kohler continued to write, spending many days and hours on a subject which had interested him all his life: *The Beginnings of the Synagogue and the Church and Their Interrelation.*

He looked back over a fruitful life which had seen his mental vigor applied to a variety of scholarly interests and studies. Always in the service of the spiritual ideals of Israel and their expression, his erudition covers a remarkable range. Over 2000 articles from his pen have been catalogued. He wrote on "Hellenism and Judaism," "The Tetragrammaton and Its Uses," "The Psalms in the Liturgy," "The Sabbath and Festivals in Pre-Exilic and Exilic Times." He delivered addresses on "The Mission of Israel," "The Synagogue and the Church in Their Mutual Relations," "Human Brotherhood," "Harmonization of Laws of Marriage and Divorce," "The Faith of Reform Judaism," "The Kaddish," "Jewish Wit and Humor," "Jewish Superstition," "Zionism," and many other topics.

His intense belief in the mission of Israel "to unfold and spread the light of the monotheistic truth in its undimmed splendor, ever to be living witnesses, and also to die, if need be, as martyrs for the Only One and holy God, to strive and battle and also, if need be, to suffer for the cause of truth, justice and righteousness, and thus to win the nations, the races and creeds, all classes of men by teaching and example, by a life of mental and moral endeavor as well as of incessant self-sacrifice and service for Israel's religious and ethical ideals" allowed no room for Zionism. He admitted that he was a determined opponent of Zionism though he denied that he was anti-Zionist. He recognized

the centrality of Zion in Jewish history and its importance to the oppressed and persecuted Jews.

It was his only hope and source of strength. When he welcomed the
Sabbath bride, or recited his daily prayers, when he built a new home, or
suffered a great loss in his family circle, the remembrance of Zion hallowed his joy and his grief. His whole life was centered on Jerusalem.
No lover ever sang the praise of his beloved with such ardor as the great
mouthpiece of mediaval Judaism, the inspired Bard, Yehudah Halevi, did
that of his love, Jerusalem. Not on the streams of Babylon or Spain only,
but in all lands and ages, the Jew, with ashes strewn on his head, clad in
mourning, wept and prayed for Jerusalem. Who dares say that this was a
mere dream and illusion? The hope for Zion was the soul and life-blood
of the Jew. For it he willingly suffered and sacrificed everything. It embodied his faith, his law, his truth, every idea and principle he lived for.

But, he repudiates Zionism as a political scheme as he continues:

Is it the realization of this glorious hope of Israel that the Herzls
and the Nordaus and the whole band of Zionists stand and work for? Do
they come in the name of Israel's God, in the name of Israel's holiest
truth, with the message from Him who redeemed and shielded us all
these thousands of years, that we should hail them as workers of divine
salvation? There is nothing religious, nothing lofty and spiritual about
the whole scheme. . . . Their very use of the name of Zion is a pro-
fanation and an abuse. . . . The question now is whether we, the People
of the Book, the people that for 3500 years stood for the world of ideals,
can afford to sacrifice our past, to sell our birthright, for a piece of land.
. . . The main reason for our most strenuous opposition to Zionism is
that we deny the very fact that we are still a nation in the political sense.
Judaism is a religious truth entrusted to a nation destined to interlink all
nations and sects, classes and races of men. It is a historical mission, not
a national life. . . .

But even now Zionism must be credited with a great achievement.
It has become the bugle call to rally the lost. It has stirred up the national
sentiment in many a Jew thus long alienated from his race and his faith.
It has imbued the timid with new courage, and filled the despondent
with self-respect. It has reclaimed many indifferent Jews for the common
cause, and made wounded race-pride work for the higher interests of
Judaism. It certainly has roused a sense of manhood in the Jew. Will
cheap Zionism only utter the cry: "Hear, O Israel!" and not strike the

higher keynote: "The Lord our God! The Lord is One" ? . . . . Judeans is the name of our club, by which we have been banded together for the common interest of Jew and Judaism. Zionism divides us. . . .

His last article was a contribution to the Hebrew Union College Annual, 1925, in which he advocated the establishment of a chair in the history of religion or comparative religion. The last words of the article, which may be taken as his last written words, aptly sum up Kohler's personality and character:

It is high time to. . . . cry out with Moses of yore, "Would that the whole people of God become prophets, as He lays His spirit upon them." Yes, prophets we need, men of the spirit, men of vision, not of mere mentality, men who proclaim Judaism as did the great seer of the exile, as the light of the nations and as the covenant interlinking the peoples, the races and the creeds. The College must give us men who embody in their life the faith they preach, and who make their Jewish hearers feel that our truth is the power that is to conquer the world.

Kohler, knight of the spirit, unbeknown to himself when he wrote these words, offers an excellent self-description. Born preacher, prodigous scholar, dynamic leader, indomitable idealist, Kohler was a man of faith. His faith brought him fulfillment and gratification.

Looking back upon my years of preparation and my years of activity as American Rabbi, I feel like saying in the words of Scripture: "I have wrestled wrestlings for God, and have prevailed."

SOLOMON SCHECHTER

Prince of Learning, Exponent of Conservative Judaism

[1850-1915]

The towering personality of Solomon Schechter overpowered an awaiting generation in America at the beginning of this century and changed the course and destiny of Jewish life for generations to come. His influence is permanent and indelible. To all, he was the master, in intellect, scholarship, charm and vigor. Everywhere he commanded respect and a hearing. His appearance was such as to be appropriate to his role of prophet and sage. In his youth his leonine head was covered with a shock of curly auburn hair, repeated in the beard he kept as trim as its texture would allow. Determined lips, penetrating blue eyes and firm stance added to the picture of a man of force and vitality. A scholar's scholar and a rabbi's rabbi; guide, counselor, father and friend—this was Solomon Schechter.

Key words often provide succinct descriptions of great men, telling their story in brief. The key words to portray the fabulous life of Solomon Schechter, interpreter of Israel's soul, are: Genizah, Seminary, Catholic Israel. They summarize the life and deeds of this illustrious leader of American Jewry.

"Genizah" literally means hidden. It refers to the fantastic treasure trove of manuscripts and fragments Schechter discovered, brought out of a Cairo synagogue archive, analyzed, evaluated and edited. One hundred thousand parchment fragments he brought to England in 30 large sacks. In his life he could only begin to study them. It will take generations to complete the study, but his knowledge of their contents

Sabato Morais

Bernard Felsenthal

Solomon Schechter

Kaufmann Kohler

filled a gap of ignorance about Jewish life, philosophy, history, literature, liturgy, and language covering the first thousand years of this era. Schechter's discovery and editing earned for him a permanent place in the hall of fame of the greatest scholars the world has known.

"Seminary" refers to the Jewish Theological Seminary of America, fountainhead of Conservative Judaism, which Schechter served as president and prime mover. For years the Seminary was not popularly known by its official name. Schechter's Seminary was one of the names often used. Furthermore, the mere mention of Schechter with the possessive, Schechter's, was enough to suggest the institution from which Conservative Judaism drew—and draws—its strength and inspiration.

"Catholic Israel," a Schechter creation, refers to his view of Judaism and the people of Israel. It comes from the Hebrew, K'lal Israel, meaning community of Israel, and emphasizes the unity of the congregation. While Judaism has no hierarchy nor any other form of strict organization, it does have an inner unity. It has a solidarity with the congregation throughout the world. Judaism has no geographical boundaries. It is one and indivisible everywhere. The unity is based on the generally recognized consensus of loyal and devoted Jews, which is expressed not through any formal vote or plebiscite, but rather in the way a scholarly or scientific consensus is expressed—through general acceptance. Schechter's view stressed Judaism's continuing process of historic development, that it cannot live without the Torah, that it must keep Hebrew as a universal tie, that it cannot either break away voluntarily from its past nor can it remain fixed and unchanging in the old ways. Judaism cannot shed its national character, on the one hand, nor can it be transformed into a secular nationalism on the other. Israel, Schechter maintained forcefully, is not a nation in the common sense of the word—by virtue of racial or political combinations; it is a nation only by reason of its Torah—an assertion he drew from Saadya Gaon.

These key words are clues to the vigorous life of this man of the spirit who hailed from a small town in Rumania saturated with the mystic spirit of Hasidism, drawn to the scientific spirit by men whose influence molded his aggressive championing of Torah with understanding of its meaning. Having come to maturity under the influence of the greatest minds of the day, Christian and Jewish, Schechter came to

America to lead a counter-reformation in the period of the development of American Judaism.

He was born in the little town of Focsani, Rumania, in December of 1850. His father, a shochet (ritual-slaughterer), and therefore a recognized and respected citizen, was a Hasid, coming from that part of the Hasidic movement which stressed learning and study in addition to ecstatic expressions of piety through song and dance. The other part emphasized only the joyous expression of religion. He belonged to the group known as HaBaD, each letter being the initial of a Hebrew word (H stands for Hochma, wisdom; B stands for Bina, reason or understanding; and D stands for Daat, knowledge). A twin, given the Hebrew name Shneur Zalman after the founder of the sect to which his father belonged, Solomon was one of six children. Like the others, he was a healthy, vigorous youth, but surpassed in agility and dexterity his brothers and sisters. He was an active boy, often to be seen racing in the streets or jumping over fences and porches. But his mischievousness and boundless physical energy did not inhibit the development of his equally active mind. At the age of three he was able to read the Bible, studying with his gentle, pious father, from whom Schechter acquired his own piety and love of learning and Torah. At five, he knew the Pentateuch, the first five books of the Bible. At ten, the gifted boy went to a Yeshivah in Piatra where he became expert in Talmud. At 13, he was sent to study under the guidance of the great Talmudic scholar Rabbi Joseph Saul Nathanson in Lemberg, Poland. He studied diligently until he mastered the Law and especially the Midrash, the maxims, legends and homiletical interpretations, and was highly commended for his zeal, knowledge, and originality.

In 1875, Solomon went to Vienna. It was here that he first came into real contact with European culture of the day. However, his time was spent primarily in the Beth ha-Midrash, the House of Study, which he attended for four years. Talmudical studies were supplemented in this relatively modern seminary with history, exegesis, and homiletics. It was not the kind of Yeshivah he had attended earlier, with its almost complete concentration on Talmud. Here his mental horizons widened. These four years, 1875–1879, were important ones for Schechter. Others at this age and in the face of cultures foreign to them fell by the wayside, and defected from the ranks of Judaism. Although Solomon Schechter did not sever himself totally from his traditions, he revealed his own youthful rebellion in a satire on Hasidism which he published anonymously. He was to regret the writing, if one can judge from a later essay on the subject, which spoke warmly of the beauty and idealism of Hasidism.

Schechter's parental and home influence; his own open, brilliant, eager mind; and three great men who steadied him, paved the way for his massive contribution to the history of Judaism. The three were: Isaac Hirsh Weiss, Meir Friedmann, and Adolf Jellinek. They introduced Schechter to the mysteries of historical science as applied to Jewish lore. Under their direction Schechter developed his method of studying and investigating the Talmud scientifically and critically.

From Weiss, great investigator of Halachah, legal portion of the Talmud, Schechter learned the highly significant place of tradition in the continuous development of Judaism. He learned from Weiss the need to study constantly the tradition and know it at firsthand rather than to depend on the knowledge and evaluations of others. From Weiss also, Schechter became able to perceive the Talmud as an organic entity and not a splintered series of unrelated subjects.

From Jellinek, rabbi of the Great Synagogue in Vienna and founder of Beth ha-Midrash, Schechter learned a great deal also. In his long walks with him and as his library assistant, he learned the mystical notion of the concept Keneset Israel, community of Israel, from which later was born the idea for, and term, Catholic Israel.

From Meir Friedmann, master of the Agadic or homiletical part of the Talmud, he learned the intricacies, rabbinical exegesis, and the spirit and soul of the Midrash. Through Friedmann, Schechter also imbibed the faith behind the law, equally important to an understanding of the legal aspects of the Halachah, Law of the Talmud.

Thus, both Weiss and Friedmann had their part in forming the later Schechter, who blended traditional Talmudic scholarship with modern methods, adding his own touch of Hasidic mysticism.

In 1879, at 29, his teachers ordained him Rabbi in Israel, including in the Semicha document words of praise proclaiming him worthy of the position of rabbi and scholar. His appearance changed, having shed the long garb and side curls customary among the Hasidim, he sought further knowledge. He turned to the German Academy for Jewish

Science in Berlin, where he came into contact with the great scholars of that center of learning. There were: Israel Lewy, authority on Jerusalem Talmud and prominent Talmudic critic; Moritz Steinschneider, the greatest bibliographer of the time; Jacob Freudenthal, the great professor of philosophy; Heinrich Graetz, great historian, and others.

In 1882, Claude Montefiore, scion of a famous Anglo-Jewish family who had been studying Jewish lore in Berlin where good Jewish teachers were rarely lacking, decided to continue his Jewish studies in England. A dear friend of Schechter's, Dr. Pincus Friedrich Frankl, one of those who drew Schechter to Berlin in the first place, recommended to Montefiore that he persuade Schechter to join him in England as his teacher. Schechter consented. Half his life was over. This half had been the detailed, painstaking period of preparation for what was to come. He had studied assiduously. He had mastered the Talmud, Midrash and all of Jewish lore. He had developed modern scientific methods of study, analysis and criticism. He was now a blend of many cultures, ready to enter the arena of active life in England.

Indeed, though it took some persuasion to get Schechter to go to Great Britain as teacher to Montefiore and his family, he was ready for the change. His intellectual curiosity drew him to the precious manuscripts available in the magnificent libraries in England, especially the British Museum and the Bodleian Library of Oxford. He had been told that the first housed over a thousand rare manuscripts and more than 10,000 books, and the second had the tremendous number of 3000 manuscripts. The scholar in him drew him to these gold mines of learning. In addition, he had long felt frustrated in Germany, and even before that in the other countries in which he had lived. He felt locked in. He needed room, freedom. His memories of the limitations on the freedom of his people in Europe were sharp and vivid. He longed to erase them. England seemed to be the answer.

England was Schechter's first real home. He spent 20 years there. They were years of learning and scholarship as well as recognition, for here he gained international fame. He quickly became the center of a small group of Jews whose names are engraved in history: Moses Gaster, Israel Zangwill, Israel Abrahams, Lucien Wolf, Asher Myers, Joseph Jacobs, Professor Meldola, S. G. Asher, Arthur Davis, Herbert Bentwich, John Simon, and Solomon J. Solomon. They called themselves Wanderers, not because they were wandering Jews, but because each felt the freedom to wander into another's room and engage in a discussion, debate or conversation. Informality was emphasized—no constitution, no organization, no minutes—and yet the group through its individual members exercised a lasting influence upon Jewry in England. Schechter's zeal, vitality and knowledge of the Talmud and Jewish literature ignited the enthusiasm of the group. Here, also, Schechter tested his views, bearing down heavily on the views of the others. He denounced rationalism as leading to absurdity and an empty recital of word and doctrine. His contagious spirit, glowing faith, and extraordinary presence made him the recognized leader of the society.

Schechter also spent much time in the famous British libraries where he pored over the manuscripts day and night. He was at home in the manuscript rooms. His knowledge increased tremendously and he began to prepare publications to share his new insights. He had come to England without knowledge of the English language but soon mastered it to such an extent that his published works have been recognized as major contributions to English letters as well as to Jewish scholarship. Three years after his arrival, he published his first article, "The Study of the Talmud, An Analysis of the Life and Times of Jesus." He answered assertions made by a convert about Christianity and Jesus. This was the first of a series of many essays, many of which appeared in the *Jewish Quarterly Review* and were later collected and published in his *Some Aspects of Rabbinic Theology* and *Studies in Judaism,* first, second and third series. These essays brought to the world a clear understanding of Judaism, the Jewish attitude toward Truth, the Kingdom of God, the concept of Israel's selection, etc.

Two years later, after much painstaking research among the dusty manuscripts, Schechter gained international fame by publishing *Abot de Rabbi Nathan,* an exhaustive edition of an important and interesting Talmudic book of ethical content. He dedicated this great contribution to his friend Claude Montefiore. This was the first time a second version of the book was published. He discovered it in the manuscripts and he published it side by side with the well-known text. The publication placed Schechter in the front lines of scholarship and his fame spread quickly.

Inspired, he became even more prolific. He wrote about the Hasidim, the sect from which he derived, with broad humanity and sympathy. More recognition came. In 1890, Cambridge University appointed him lecturer in Talmudics and his influence widened. He served for 12 years, giving courses in rabbinical learnings, Mishna, Psalms, and post-Biblical Jewish literature. The small circle of friends he had earlier developed had to go on without him. Schechter became center of the distinguished academic world of Cambridge, taking his place with Sir James George Frazer, author of *The Golden Bough,* W. D. Buckland, Regius professor of law, Eiriker Magnussen, the great Icelandic scholar, F. C. Burkitt, the ecclesiastical scholar, Dr. Charles Taylor, Dr. Rendel Harris, the distinguished New Testament scholar, Professor Robertson Smith, and others. To them, he was not only a sage steeped in rabbinical lore but a scholar who had amassed an extensive knowledge of theology, German Biblical criticism, and English literature. There was a mutual magnetism, Schechter irresistibly drawn to the men of the circle and they to him. They admired his erudition and acumen and his gift for the sharp rejoinder. One tells of his response to a great non-Jewish authority on Semitics, "You Christians know Hebrew grammar. We know Hebrew." Another time he was visited by a member of the Society of Jesus. Schechter greeted him with, "I am a Jew, and you well understand that I hate Jesuits. Now let us be friends." Schechter never refrained from sharing his dynamic views about Judaism with his fellow scholars and advanced students.

Schechter was not a scholar to inhabit an ivory tower. Away from the university, Schechter and his wife were the center of a small Jewish community which gathered about them. His warm personality drew many to him, notably a group of Jewish professional men known as the Maccabean Club. Undergraduates looked to him as guide, rabbi and friend. A small group joined together and conducted services. The services were, as was to be expected from Schechter's early childhood and attachment, Hasidic in spirit and feeling. The group met regularly, especially on the Sabbath, to share their joy in the day—a practice which the master was to introduce years later when he was president of the Seminary.

Shortly after coming to Cambridge in 1893, Schechter took the first of three scholarly journeys. He had gained additional income by serving the Oriental section of the library as curator. When the opportunity to go to Italy to visit the Vatican libraries and study the manuscripts there arose, Schechter went eagerly. The sights of that eternal city moved him deeply. Its art, architecture, and sense of history strongly affected him. Said he: "If anything is eternal in the Eternal City, it is the little Jewish community in Rome."

The chief librarian of the Vatican said that Schechter was the most intent scholar ever to search the centuries-old documents. Indeed, Schechter pored over the fine old documents. He searched for new insights into the ethical tractate Abot. He dug for more information about the dating of the Hebrew Covenant of the Bible. Pleased with the results of his studies, he shared the knowledge he gained in articles and essays, most of which were later collated into his famed *Studies in Judaism*.

Schechter's second major journey was to America at the invitation of Judge Mayer Sulzberger and Dr. Solomon Solis-Cohen. He went to Philadelphia primarily to deliver a series of lectures on rabbinical theology. The subjects tell the story of his scholarship: "The Surprise of the Jewish Student at the Assertion of Christian Theology of the Remoteness of the Jewish God," "The Kingdom of God in Rabbinical Literature," "The Invisible Kingdom," "The Torah as Law," and "Sin." He was warmly received and his addresses highly regarded. He met many of the famous people of the time and was invited to many institutions. He also lectured at Johns Hopkins and Bryn Mawr. The seeds for his coming to America and the Seminary were being sowed. Venerable Dr. Sabato Morais, aged founder of the Seminary, discussed the matter with him, discussions which later bore fruit.

Schechter's third and most dramatic journey, the trip which more than any other experience was to record his name in the annals of Jewish and general scholarship, was his visit to Egypt. Here was the turning point of his career. On behalf of Cambridge University and with the financial aid of Dr. Charles Taylor, master of St. John's College, armed with credentials and proper introductions, Schechter set out for Cairo in December of 1896. He knew that treasures were hidden there. Fragments of old manuscripts had been finding their way into world libraries.

The impetus for the trip came from a visit soon after his return from America. Two women, Mrs. Agnes Lewis, widow of the Librarian of Corpus Christi College, and her sister, Mrs. Gibson, who had just returned from the East, showed him a few old Hebrew fragments.

Schechter's remarkable mind and memory immediately spotted familiar passages. He thought that one of the small, shriveled parchments contained a piece of the original Ben Sira (Ecclesiasticus), a document of ethics written the third or second century before the common era. The book was known but the original Hebrew had been considered lost. Only the Greek version was known. Ecclesiasticus, which strongly resembles the Book of Proverbs, was not part of the Hebrew Bible, nor of the Protestant version, but it was part of the Catholic version of the Bible. Excitement ran through his veins. He left the ladies, urging them not to say a word to anyone, and rushed to the library to examine the fragment. He soon verified his find, verification which was destined to stir the entire world. Here was a find of part of the Bible recognized by the Christian world and hitherto thought lost. The book, Wisdom of Ben Sira, part of a literature known as Apocrypha, was to Christianity transitional between the Old and New Testaments. To Judaism, the book formed a link between the Bible and the rabbinic writings. Its discovery and Schechter's analysis caused many a hypothesis of Biblical critics to be re-evaluated. He was able to show that neither the Book of Job nor Ecclesiastes nor any other part of the Hebrew Bible could be ascribed to the Maccabean Period.

The trip to Cairo was blessed with success. Schechter had known that Cairo contained one of the oldest Jewish communities outside of Palestine. He also knew that it was customary in Jewish circles not to destroy ancient documents, holy scrolls and books. Jewish tradition required that they be buried or hidden. In Cairo, in the Great Synagogue, hidden away in an area reachable only through the gallery of the synagogue annex, Schechter found the inexhaustible mine of literary treasures, the Genizah. Genizah means hidden. The Genizah had obviously been the final resting place for many an old and decaying book and manuscript. Fortunately, the Egyptian climate had helped preserve the documents. Schechter spent weeks in the dusty, stench-filled rooms. He wrote home about the almost unbearable odors of decaying paper and parchment. It was not physically possible to continue examination of the documents there, and Schechter used his charm and powers of persuasion to prevail upon the authorities to allow him to take the entire Genizah to England. Over 100,000 fragments were packed into 30 bags and removed to England. One of the well-known pictures of Solomon Schechter shows him sitting in rooms at Cambridge with boxes and boxes of delicate, dusty pieces of parchment piled all around, his head resting on his right fist as he ponders the contents. His job involved determining source, background, dates, and relationship to other works.

Upon his return, he set out at once to classify them. He went from fragment to fragment, taking the pieces, however small, and placing them in different boxes marked Bible, Talmud, Philosophy, History, Liturgy, Literature and Rabbinics. Each fragment was part of a puzzle which Schechter studied to begin the reconstruction of the fullness of Jewish life and thought. Others will be scrutinizing the treasure for generations to come.

> Looking over this enormous mass of fragments about me, in the sifting and examination of which I am now occupied, I cannot overcome a sad feeling stealing over me, that I shall hardly be worthy to see the results which the Genizah would add to our knowledge of Jews and Judaism. This work is not for one man and not for one generation. It will occupy many a specialist, and much longer than a lifetime. However, to use an old adage, "It is not thy duty to complete the work, but neither art thou free to desist from it."

It has been said that Schechter's brief visit to Egypt, Palestine and the East caused middle age to pass him by. He moved from youth to old age in physical appearance. Schechter modestly disclaimed credit for unearthing the great treasure. Said he: "I should like to correct a mistake which I often meet in books and articles, in which I am described as the discoverer of the Genizah. This is not correct. The Genizah practically discovered itself."

In addition, Schechter brought back to Cambridge the ancient Ark of the old synagogue in Cairo. The same Ark he later brought to America, and it became the Ark of the synagogue in the Seminary. It is probably the oldest piece of synagogue furniture in America.

Schechter's original excitement about the Ben Sira was justified. The find enlarged and deepened knowledge of the Jewish past, altering conceptions about conditions in Babylonia, Palestine and Egypt. It became the primary source of Jewish historical research. Publication after publication announcing facts of Jewish and general history continued to bring fame to Schechter. The entire collection, known as the Taylor-Schechter Collection, became quickly the basis of studies in Jewish history, theology and literature. The collection has led to a reconstruction of long periods of Jewish history. It has resulted in a clearer appreciation and understanding of the teachings of the different sects and rabbinic schools, and to a restoration of many literary monuments thought to be lost. Schechter published voluminously. Books like *The Document of the Zadokite Sect,* a code of a long forgotten group which, coming from Palestine, settled in Damascus in the early second century before the common era; *Saadyana,* writings of the Gaonim (rabbis), principally Saadya Gaon; *Documents of Jewish Sectaries, The Fragments of the Book of the Commandments* by Anan, founder of the Karaite Sect, and others, secured his fame in the world of scholarly creativity.

Schecter had reason to be happy at Cambridge. The University honored him with a degree. Here he was a scholar among scholars. But he was not completely content. He and his faithful wife, Matilda, whom he married in 1887, sensed a feeling of emptiness. He especially felt a void in his Jewish life, as scholar, father and Jew. He longed for a deeper Jewish experience and opportunity of expression, and his children were not growing up in a Jewish environment. Thus, when approaches were made to him to come to America, he looked kindly upon the idea. When Sabato Morais passed on, the pull was stronger. Finally at the insistence of many friends, including Dr. Cyrus Adler, he accepted the call to serve as president of the Jewish Theological Seminary of America. He had long felt drawn to America. Lincoln was one of his heroes. America was the land of the future for the Jew.

The year was 1902. Schechter took the country by storm. He had been awaited. Jewish life in America was growing but many were unhappy with the progress of Reform Judaism. Schechter—a conservative steeped in Jewish lore and experienced in modern scientific approaches to God, Torah, Talmud—was to represent the counter-reformation.

Upon his arrival he immediately selected an emblem for the Seminary —the Burning Bush. The Biblical account of Moses' first encounter with God says, "And the bush was not consumed," words which expressed Schechter's view that Judaism was a constantly growing plant, and tradition, like the bush, never ceases to develop and is never to be consumed. The Seminary would be the source of this doctrine, the source of Schechter's own blend of Torah, tradition, and the modern world. In addition, Jewish scholars must be trained. The time had come for Jewish scholars to speak authoritatively about Judaism. Jews had for too long a time allowed others, non-Jewish scholars, to be the authorities even on the Bible. The Jewish scholar had to come to the fore. A Bible commentary from the Jewish point of view needed to be prepared. Post-Biblical history was a world for Jewish scholarship to enter. The passage "Ayt laasot l'adonai—It is time to work for God" best described Schechter's passionate call. In his inaugural address on November 20, 1902, basing his goals upon scholarship and learning, he set forth the platform on which he would stand and the principles for which he would strive:

> The crown and climax of learning is research and the object of all learning is truth, the truth which gives unity to history and harmony to the phenomena of nature. The study of ancient manuscripts was not mere antiquarianism. Every discovery of an ancient document giving evidence of a bygone world, if undertaken in the right spirit, that is, for the honor of God and the truth, is an act of resurrection in miniature. . . .
>
> The religion in which the Jewish ministry should be trained must be specifically and purely Jewish, without any alloy or adulteration. Judaism must stand or fall by that which distinguishes it from other religions as well as by that which it has in common with them. Judaism is not a religion which does not oppose itself to anything in particular. Judaism is opposed to any number of things and says distinctly, "Thou shalt not." It permeates the whole of your life. It demands control over all your actions, and interferes even with your menu. It sanctifies the seasons, and regulates your history, both in the past and in the future. Above all, it teaches that disobedience is the strength of sin. It insists upon the observance both of the spirit and of the letter; spirit without letter belongs to the species known to the mystics as "nude souls," wandering about in the universe without balance and without consistency, the play of all possible currents and changes in the atmosphere. In a word, Judaism is absolutely incompatible with the abandonment of the Torah. . . .
>
> The past, with its long chain of events, with its woes and joys, with its tragedies and romances, with its customs and usages, and above all, with its bequest of the Torah, the great entail of the children of Israel, has become an integral and inalienable part of ourselves, bone of our bone and flesh of our flesh. We must make an end to these constant amputations if we do not wish to see the body of "Israel" bleed to death before our very eyes. We must leave off talking about Occidentalizing our religion. . . . There is no other Jewish religion but that taught by the Torah and

confirmed by history and tradition, and sunk into the conscience of Catholic Israel.

Later, he was more specific about the role the Seminary was to play in the scheme of Jewish life. It was:

... to connect Israel with its past, watch over Jewish institutions that they develop on historical lines, to preserve the chain of tradition which shall be continued by our children, and to restore the unity of Israel which shall be, as it always was, a union of doctrines, a union of precepts, and a union of promises.

He insisted on his view of Catholic Judaism, expounded the doctrine of historic Judaism, the Bible as God's word, and tradition as the method of interpreting and retaining the ties of the glorious past. He was the theologian of the historic school. To his office as president he devoted himself tirelessly and with boundless moral courage. His intensity of conviction, his extraordinary power of initiative and execution, his insistence on perfection, and his striking frankness, raised him to great heights as the new leader of Jews in America. To the students he was father, guide, counselor and friend. His sympathy and wisdom remained their guiding influences as they traversed the land after ordination.

He early recognized the need for training, not only rabbis but teachers.

... it is only when we have provided for the needs of the nine hundred and ninety-nine by well-equipped training schools for teachers and proper textbooks in the English language, fit to be put in the hands of the so-called laity, that the mission of the thousandth (that of the rabbi) will be accomplished.

In 1909, he organized the Teachers Institute and Professor Mordecai Kaplan, a recent graduate and later one of America's foremost original thinkers and founder of the Reconstructionist movement, was appointed its director.

Schechter set about to establish a leading seat of learning. He brought the greatest scholars to form the faculty. True to his scholarly inclination and love of books, he established one of the finest libraries in America. He also felt the need of an avenue to disseminate the fruits of Jewish learning and in 1913 called into being the United Synagogue of America.

The purpose of this organization, he intended to be:

1. To advance to the cause of Judaism in America and to maintain Jewish tradition in its historical continuity.

2. To assert and establish loyalty to the Torah and its historical exposition,

3. To further the observance of the Sabbath and the dietary laws,

4. To preserve in the service the reference to Israel's past and the hopes for Israel's restoration,

5. To maintain the traditional character of the liturgy, with Hebrew as the language of prayer,

6. To foster Jewish religious life in the home, as expressed in traditional observances,

7. To encourage the establishment of Jewish religious schools, in the curricula of which the study of the Hebrew language and literature shall be given a prominent place, both as the key to the true understanding of Judaism, and as a bond holding together the scattered communities of Israel throughout the world.

8. It shall be the aim of the United Synagogue of America, while not endorsing the innovations introduced by any of its constituent bodies, to embrace all elements essentially loyal to traditional Judaism and in sympathy with the purposes outlined above.

Of this creation he later wrote: "This will be the greatest bequest that I shall leave to American Israel."

The Seminary, the United Synagogue, his concerted efforts for the Jewish Publication Society of America as one of the editors of the Bible translation and chairman of the committee on the Series of Jewish Classics, and his numerous scholarly writings, kept him infinitely busy through the years.

When Harvard University awarded him the honorary degree of Doctor of Hebrew Letters in 1911, the first time a Jewish scholar was so honored, George Foot Moore, great Gentile scholar of rabbinics, was his sponsor. He was described as "expounder of his people's ancient law, the discoverer of lost records, tireless in amassing and generous in sharing his vast store of knowledge."

He was the symbol of the harmonious fusion of the old and the new, in Jewry and in American Jewry. More than anyone else he brought about a renaissance of Jewish culture and learning and a renaissance of traditional Jewish life in America. Almost single-handedly, yet working through students and lay leaders, he infused a whole generation with the beauty of the synthesis of Torah, tradition, and present-day living.

A very striking personality, Schechter looked like a Rembrandt rabbi or like the royal high priest of the temple. Always a dominant figure, he was erect, colorful, radiant, massive, overpowering. His physical appearance reflected his character. His views were firm and constant. Any task he undertook was engaged in with incomparable determination. He spoke with assurance and precision, and he wrote as he spoke. Of Catholic Judaism, Schechter's favorite theme, he said:

Its [the Historical School] theological position may perhaps be thus defined: it is not the mere revealed Bible that is of first importance to the Jew, but the Bible as it repeats itself in history, in other words, as it is interpreted by Tradition. . . . Since, then, the interpretation of Scriptures or the Secondary Meaning is mainly a product of changing historical influences, it follows that the center of authority is actually removed from the Bible and placed in some *living body,* which, by reason of its being in touch with the ideal aspirations and the religious needs of the age, is best able to determine the nature of the Secondary Meaning.

This living body [Scripture] is not represented by any section of the nation, or any corporate priesthood, but by the collective conscience of Catholic Israel as embodied in the Universal Synagogue. The Synagogue, "with its continuous cry after God for more than twenty-three centuries," with its unremitting activity in teaching and developing the word of God, with its uninterrupted succession of Prophets, Psalmists, Scribes, Assideaus, Rabbis, Patriarchs, Interpreters, Elucidators, Eminences, and Teachers, with its glorious record of saints, martyrs, sages, philosophers, scholars, and mystics; this Synagogue, the only true witness to the past, and forming in all ages the sublimest expression of Israel's religious life, must also retain its authority as the sole true guide for the present and the future. . . .

Another consequence of this conception of Tradition is that it is neither Scripture nor primitive Judaism, but general custom which forms the real rule of practice. Holy Writ as well as history, Zunz tells us, teaches that the Law of Moses was never fully and absolutely put into practice. Liberty was always given to the great teachers of every generation to make modifications and innovations in harmony with the spirit of existing institutions. Hence a return to Mosaism would be illegal, pernicious, and indeed impossible. The norm as well as the sanction of Judaism is the practice actually in vogue. Its consecration is the consecration of general use—or, in other words, of Catholic Israel.

Schechter viewed the synagogue with wonder and respect. The synagogue was a powerful force in history. It knew what to do, what to accept, what to reject, in order to maintain the universal bond of Judaism:

> It is one of the most interesting of religious phenomena to observe the essential unity that the Synagogue maintained, despite all antognistic influences. Dispersed among the nations, without a national center, without a synod to formulate its principles, or any secular power to enforce its decrees, the Synagogue found its home and harmony in the heart of a loyal and consecrated Israel. . . . The power of Judaism was manifested in its obliteration of all that was strange and objectionable in such accretions, so strong were its digestive powers. But equally, the Synagogue was manifested in what it eliminated and rejected as inconsistent with its existence. Whenever any influence, no matter by whom advanced or by whatever power maintained, developed a tendency that was contrary to a strict monotheism, or denied the binding character of the Torah, or aimed to destroy the unity and character and calling of Israel, although it may have gained currency for a time, the Synagogue finally succeeded in eliminating it as noxious to its very existence.

He vehemently opposed rationalism. His objection to it is based on his conviction that feeling and emotion are important in religious expression. It was not reason itself which he opposed; it was his feeling that reason was simply not enough. Religion needed more than rational thought. It needed a heart and feeling. It needed love above all. Indeed, mysticism, on which he was fed, had a significant part in his religious feelings. He says it firmly and forcefully in his *Studies in Judaism:*

> Mysticism, as a manifestation of the spiritual and as an expression of man's agonies in his struggle after communion with God, as well as his ineffable joy when he has received the assurance that he has found it, is not foreign to the spirit of old rabbinic Judaism. . . . Those who are at all familiar with the rabbinic literature hardly need to be told that the "sea of the Talmud" has also its Gulf-stream of Mysticism which, taking its origin in the moralizing portions, runs through the wide ocean of Jewish thought, constantly co-mingling with the icy waters of legalism, and unceasingly washing the desolate shores of an apparently meaningless ceremonialism, communicating to it life, warmth, and spirituality.

Just as Schechter was an advocate of Judaism with a heart, he was equally firm in his belief in the institutions of Judaism. One of his epigrams, "Man cannot live on oxygen alone," points this up. Judaism's institutions were its nourishment and life. Said he in an address at the seminary in 1909:

> Only a gypsy camp is possible without institutions, ceremonies, and symbols. The classic nations, the Greeks and Romans, had some sort of religion, but never formed a religious community. For me the Tephillin (Phylacteries) are my banner, the Sepher Torah (Scroll of the Law) our Magna Charta, the Synagogue our Parliament. The Dietary Laws are consequences of holiness. Greece aimed at manhood; we at saintliness and holiness. Judaism will always be best understood by Judaism, and not for foreign parallels.

To Schechter, observance of the Law was not to be construed as a burden. It is rather the supreme expression of spirituality, a great joy, as shown by the lives of the great Jewish teachers and saints, who were filled with love of God and His people.

Schechter was a vigorous proponent of Hebrew. It was an indisputable part of his doctrine.

> The Hebrew language is not merely a language, such as Latin and Greek to the student of classical languages, or French and German to the student of modern languages. To the Jew, it is a sacred monument of bygone times. Every word recalls to him great and glorious epochs in his history, when God had still converse with man, when the Prophets still admonished Israel with "thoughts that breathe and words that burn," when Psalms were still sung in the Temple. It is the language in which the nation poured out its grief and sorrow on the waters of Babylon, but in which also its joys and its hopes and its consolation found adequate expression, the Sanhedrin gave its verdicts, and the Sages taught their disciples all that was worth knowing, whether of a religious or of a civil kind. In brief, it is a Holy Language to the Jew because of its memories of the past and of its promises for the future.

When the issue of Zionism came to the fore, and controversy raged over it, Schechter at first hesitated to affiliate himself officially with its cause. Not that he was against Zionism. He could not be. But he felt that the leaders lacked religious loyalty. Leaders of Jews without faith meant to him people out of touch with Israel's very soul. Indeed, both

Jewish nationality and Jewish religion were inextricably bound up together; as he wrote in December 1898 to Herbert Bentwich, one of the leaders of *Hovevei Zion,* Lovers of Zion, in England:

> I have spent fifty years on the study of Jewish literature and Jewish history. I am deeply convinced that you cannot sever Jewish nationality from Jewish religion. The destruction of the latter will end in the destruction of the former. Zionism must begin at home if it really wishes to be a power for good.

Palestine had to be the spiritual center of the Jewish people. But Zionism must contain religious fervor and love, not mere nationalism. Moreover, it should espouse the observance of fundamental Jewish institutions.

He said further in a letter to Gottheil in November 1900:

> . . . I am not claiming to be a Zionist, but I mean to remain a Jew in religion and nationality, and I abhor all universalism, which must, in the end, land us in Paulinism.

Yet later, when he saw in Zionism a movement to stall the drive toward assimilation, he felt that no matter its deficiencies, he had to come out openly in its cause. He issued a paper entitled "Zionism: A Statement" (December 28, 1906), an expression of his forthright decision to align himself officially with the Zionist movement which stirred Jewish leaders throughout the country. For the head of Conservative Judaism to come forth for Zionism was of monumental importance. Here is how he stated his position regarding Zionism:

> To me personally, after long hesitation and careful watching, it recommended itself as the great bulwark against assimilation. . . . What I understand by assimilation is loss of identity, or that process of disintegration which, passing through various degrees of defiance of Jewish thought and of disloyalty to Israel's history and its mission, terminates variously in different lands. . . . It is this kind of assimilation that I dread most, even more than pogroms. Whatever faults may be found with its zeal or self-appointed leaders, Zionism forms an opposing force against the conception of the destiny of Israel and the interpretation of its mission. . . .
>
> History may, and to my belief will, repeat itself, and Israel will be the chosen instrument of God for the new and final mission; but then Israel must first effect its own redemption and live again its own life, and be Israel again, to accomplish its universal mission. . . .

His view of Zionism was described later more succinctly in a message to the Zionist Convention of America, in 1908. It is indeed his credo as a Zionist:

What Zionism hopes for is a Jewish polity hallowed by sacred memories, equipped with Jewish institutions, taught and propagated through the medium of the Holy Language. Mere nationalism of the brutal type, satisfying only the racial instincts and aspiring to nothing higher than a certain material prosperity, is not worth striving for. Indeed a nationality without its own historical language, without a sacred literature, without reverence for its ancient institutions, without love for its past, without devotion to its religion, is a mere gypsy camp, and will be of very little promise.

What Zionism may hope for is the restoration of the Jewish nationality in the Promised Land, accompanied by a renewal of Jewish life, vouchsafed by Scripture and tradition, and dreamed of and prayed for by prophets, sages and saints of our nation for numberless generations.

The force and vigor that were Solomon Schechter gave way on Sabbath eve, November 20, 1915. Man of the spirit, messenger of the Lord, true interpreter of the rabbis, Schechter left the spirit of Judaism ignited in the soul of American Jewry. He loved the past and stressed it as the basis for the present and the future. The greatness of the past, the thoughts of the sages, he sought to revivify. The documents he studied meant life to him and he sought to make them live for others. More effectively than others, he was able to blend the heritage of Israel, from Torah through Talmud, through Midrash, through Jewish history, through Jewish science and criticism, into the Judaism which has become Conservative Judaism in America. Though not appreciated by all as middle-of-the-road Judaism, Schechter's balancing has indeed become just that. The Judaism he spoke and fought for is linked indissolubly to its past, forming a chain to the present. Solomon Schechter deserved his recognition as a beloved giant of faith.

HENRY COHEN

Jewish Pastor for All Faiths

[1863-1952]

No rabbi was ever the property of a state. Except Henry Cohen. He belonged to Texas and Texas claimed him. No rabbi was ever known by the name of a state. Henry Cohen, giant of social justice, master servant of God and man, was always referred to as Henry Cohen of Texas. True, in days gone by, great rabbis' names often attached the city of their service. Famed Rabbi Elijah of Vilna was called the Vilner Gaon. Sainted Reb Levi Isaac of Berditchev was affectionately called Reb Levi Isaac Berditchever. But Henry Cohen belonged to the entire state of Texas. Woodrow Wilson called him the first citizen of Texas, and he had a heart as big as the great state. Indeed, he belonged to America. Stephen S. Wise called him Prime Minister of American Jewry.

Henry Cohen, however, the real Henry Cohen—rabbi, scholar, linguist, bibliophile, servant of mankind, striver for justice for the widow, the orphan, the needy, the helpless, Catholic, Protestant, Jew, American, European, African, Negro, white—belonged to time, not Texas. His peerless humanitarianism, devoted service, unconquerable compassion and boundless energy were legendary in his lifetime. He belonged to eternity and the immortal greats whose names stood out, like Abou ben Adhem, above all the rest in brotherhood and understanding. He was, as Lyndon Johnson said, living proof of the essential brotherhood of man. Henry Cohen lived Judaism as few others have. Henry Cohen lived Americanism as few others have. Henry Cohen lived humanitarianism as few others have. Indeed, Henry Cohen was like few others. Who else could have served so many so tirelessly, unceasingly, wholeheartedly? Henry Cohen was a rabbi's rabbi. He was the Jewish pastor for all faiths; a knight of mercy for all.

Legend often intertwines with fact. Perhaps both tell the dynamic story of this giant of faith who gave his life on the altar of service. The short, wiry Cohen seemed to be everywhere at the same time. What was impossible, he achieved. What could not be done, he did. What was needed in terms of help, he secured. If his requests for help were denied, he demanded it. Whatever the approach, thousands upon thousands of Americans who crossed his path are now safe, secure and successful in America because Henry Cohen lived.

There are stories which cannot and ought not be forgotten and which must forever stand out as symbols of dedication and profiles of courage. Such are the stories of this rabbi, as a man and servant of mankind.

One of the most dramatic stories in American history involves Cohen, a Russian stowaway, and William Howard Taft, President of the United States. Galveston is a port of human freedom, not only of freight. Hundreds and thousands of Jewish immigrants are escaping the persecutions and pogroms of Russia and are being diverted from the mass immigration port of New York so that new arrivals might be directed to parts of America other than the East Coast. Good Rabbi Cohen is contributing direction and enthusiasm. While ministering, he learns that one of the arrivals, a boiler maker who had stowed away to escape from Russia, is being held at the detention center. He is to be returned to Russia on the next boat. Rabbi Cohen contacts all the officials but their hands are tied. The stowaway must return. In the meantime, Rabbi Cohen learns that the man's family is in Russia and that he would certainly face the firing squad if he ever came back. Cohen is all the more determined. One life saved—a world saved, say the rabbis.

Since no success can be expected here in Galveston, he must go beyond the local scene; he will go to Washington. Early the next morning, he rides down the street on his trusty bicycle, borrows $100 on the way from a member of his congregation, and boards the train for Washington.

In the capital, he goes from department to department, from bureau to bureau, to no avail. The Russian had entered illegally; they could not violate the law nor foster unpleasantness with Russia. No matter how

much he pleads, Cohen can get nowhere. With the help of his Congress-
man, he manages to secure an audience with President Taft. The President listens carefully and sympathetically but expresses his regrets. The
matter is one for the Department of Labor to handle. Definite decisions
have been made. Hurt, disappointed, saddened, Rabbi Cohen begins to
take his leave. President Taft, touched by the rabbi's concern, says that
he is indeed sorry that he cannot do anything in the case. "I certainly
admire the way you Jews help each other out," he adds, "traveling all
the way up here from Galveston, Texas, when a member of your faith is
in trouble."

The little rabbi whirls to face the President: "Member of my faith!
No, Mr. President. This man is not a Jew. He is a Greek Catholic."

The President is stunned. This he cannot believe. "Do you mean to
say," he asks, "that you traveled all the way up here at your own expense
to help out a Greek Catholic?"

The beloved rabbi's response is typical of him: "He is in trouble. They
are going to deport him on the next ship and he will face a firing squad
when he gets back to Russia. He is a human being, Mr. President; a
human life is at stake. That is the way I see it."

More surprised than ever, the President acts quickly, asks Rabbi
Cohen to be seated, rings for his secretary, and then orders the secretary
to wire the chief inspector of immigration at Galveston. The message
to send: "Hold Demchuk in Galveston and release in the custody of
Rabbi Cohen on his return. Say they will hear further from the Department."

The same kind of feeling for human beings is mirrored in the classic
declaration which became a motto or creed of his: "There is no such
thing as Episcopalian scarlet fever, Catholic arthritis. Baptist domestic
troubles, Presbyterian poverty, Jewish mumps."

Gentle Henry Cohen could also thunder and issue ultimatums when
wrongs were being committed. He could storm into a newspaper office,
as he did, and demand to know why the editor wrote "Hebrew" next to
the merchant's name in a story of a fire in town. He could lock up a judge
in his chambers and—like sainted Reb Levi Isaac Berditchever who
stood up in the pulpit Kol Nidre Night and insisted that he would not
move until God promised to bring redemption to mankind and Israel—
demand that the judge release a young man on probation. "I won't open

that door until you agree to parole this boy," thundered the good rabbi.
"You are a fine one to refuse to give him a chance! We picked you out
of the gutter dozens of times, a confirmed drunkard. Yet, you reformed.
Here you are, in a position of responsibility in the state. How can you,
of all people, refuse this boy a chance to become a decent, self-respecting
citizen?"

Henry Cohen could do many things, and he did. The citizens of Galveston and Texas respected and revered him. His request they considered
almost a command. Stories about the rabbi's good works abound all
over America wherever social justice is talked about. The setting is
the city of Galveston where Henry Cohen served his congregation and
community for 62 years, from the days he came from Woodville, Mississippi, from Jamaica, and originally from England.

It was in England, land of his birth, that Henry Cohen learned to
devote his life to his people and humanity. An early life of intensive
Jewish education fed by a traditional Jewish home and an opportunity
to work on behalf of and for people for three traumatic years in his teens
combined to produce the American drama that became Henry Cohen.

When Henry was born April 7, 1862, son of Josephine and David
Cohen, he was introduced to an environment of traditional Jewish life.
David, Henry's father, was a devotee of his faith, studying, learning
daily the treasures of his heritage. Thus Henry absorbed the sound and
spirit of traditional lore and practice. Such was the source of his feelings
and perspectives for the first nine years of his life. The close family
ties of his childhood were reflected later in the large rabbinage (par-
sonage) which became the home for not only his own family but everyone's family at 1920 Broadway, Galveston. Security of home, in early
age, though without affluence, was transferred to his own home and
sensed by the many men and women who came in droves for help and
guidance.

At nine, Henry moved on to a boarding school. Traditional and secular
studies formed the curriculum at Jews' Hospital, so called because the
buildings originally housed a hospital and old people's home. At school
a child of benefactors, personally experiencing the broad charity of
wealthy Jews, Henry studied diligently and intensively. He also began
to understand here the meaning and value of charity applied universally.
For seven years he matriculated here, always eager to learn, blessed with

a remarkable memory and unusual skill in languages. Here he was Bar Mitzvah and here he developed habits destined to last a lifetime.

At fifteen, he was set on the path he was to follow for the rest of his life. Three years of service propelled him into this life. Legend has it that a traumatic experience at fifteen moved him to go to work to avoid taking more money from his father's hard-earned and limited funds. The story has it that by chance he placed his hand in that of his father. The shock of feeling the hard, tight calluses of a tinsmith stunned him. He vowed that he would never again accept financial help from his father. He would be on his own. Looking for work, he soon was engaged by the Board of Guardians, leading Jewish welfare agency in England. His job was to distribute bread tickets to those in need. He made visits. He saw people. He saw need. He was the avenue of help. Though young in years, he was already serving as a vehicle of good. He enjoyed the work he was doing, but he was not completely satisfied. He had goals in mind. He had an insatiable thirst for knowledge and a longing to become a rabbi. Accordingly, he matriculated at Jews' College, the center of Jewish learning in England, where for three years he imbibed the traditional studies of Bible, Talmud, and the other legal and literary sources of Judaism.

The studies were interrupted when, persuaded by his older brother Mark, he went to Africa where he spent two hectic and thrilling years. He had many experiences during those years which he kept alive by memory and repetition all his life. His dexterity in language served him well. He learned a number of dialects which earned for him a job as translator for England and later helped in his charitable work. He loved to tell the story of the Zulus who suddenly went on a rampage and how he, together with others, stood guard near the barracks. Suddenly he was knocked unconscious and retained a scar on his head as a permanent memento. During the two years he also continued his rabbinical studies in order not to forget. He had decided that for him Africa was a temporary experience and that he would complete his studies for ordination upon return. He did return to England in 1883, and the following year completed his course of study at Jews' College and received his ministerial diploma. Thus at 21 years of age he was ready to go out to minister to the people of his faith.

His first pulpit was in Kingston, Jamaica, to which he was sent by the Chief Rabbi of the British Empire, Dr. Herman Adler, probably as Assistant Reader, because of his familiarity with the Sephardic liturgy. Enthusiastic and determined, Henry Cohen was disappointed immediately on arrival. The congregation was not a unified one; it had recently been created from two factions of Jewish traditional thought, the Spanish-Portuguese (Sephardic) community and the German-Polish (Ashkenazic) group. Conflict in the congregation, snobbery on the part of some of its members, made the first year of Cohen's rabbinate a frustrating and unhappy one. He would not stay there and made plans to leave. He did, in fact, leave after the year, and came to New York en route to England for reassignment. By chance, he met a Rabbi Henry Jacobs, who told Henry that there was a pulpit open in Woodville, Mississippi, and that the members of the congregation were fine, gentle and charming people. In any case unhappy about returning to England, Henry went south to Woodville and became the rabbi of the small, cottonbelt Jewish community.

His arrival meant a marked change in the life of a community accustomed to American rabbis and heralded also a major change in Henry's life. He found himself rabbi of a reform temple. He was surprised but not entirely unhappy. He had long since begun to project changed views and practices and felt that he would succeed in this different arena of Jewish thought and practice. His inherent traditionalism, however, came to the fore almost immediately on acceptance of the pulpit when he learned that the members of his congregation were publicly desecrating the Sabbath by keeping their business establishments open. Fearlessly, young Henry demanded that the Sabbath be observed and properly. The businessmen in turn were shocked to hear the new young leader speak with such force and insistence. Rather than flout his commands, they commended him for his courage and agreed after consultation and mediation to keep the businesses closed until after service hours on the Sabbath, a practice which the non-Jewish community learned to respect and admire.

Cohen had made his mark. Full of zeal and enthusiasm, he immediately became active in the general community, joining in every civic endeavor and serving energetically all the town in the vicinity and beyond. The pattern of his life—his capacity to serve, his willingness to give of himself unstintingly—was being set. For three years, Henry

Cohen ministered to the needs of the small community. When he was called to Congregation B'nai Israel in Galveston in 1888, his congregants, while saddened at losing him, knew that opportunities were greater in this growing port of Texas with its 22,000 people and encouraged him to accept. He did, and remained with the congregation for the next 65 years, including Emeritus status, perhaps longer than any rabbi in America ever served.

The next 65 years were dramatic ones for the Jewish community of Texas, for Texas, and for America. America was forming and establishing firmly the American way of life. Jewry was destined to make of America its number one home. Jewish organizational life was in its embryonic stages, synagogue groups were being rooted, Jewish communities rising and flourishing. Among the reasons for the vigorous, historic years ahead was the energetic service of Henry Cohen, the rabbi with the detachable cuff, his daily notebook and diary. The years that then lay ahead are now part of history in fact and history in legend and folklore.

Henry Cohen lived a most productive life, a fruitful, gratifying adventure. His scholarly pursuits were legion: he created a large personal library by gathering a massive 12,000 volumes, including many rare editions; but his greatest scholastic contributions occurred during the first twelve years of his ministry in Galveston and the last decade of the 19th century. It was then that he published articles, studies, essays and books. He wrote prodigiously and vigorously. He edited and he translated, from both French and German. The range of his scholarly productions and pursuits was wide. He wrote of Judaism and he wrote of Americanism. He wrote of Jewish history and of American Jewish history, especially Jewish history of local color, in and around Texas. A partial list of his versatile publications during this decade tells the story:

Mathematics
Energy
Three Years in Africa
To the Late Emma Lazarus (poem)
Talmudic Sayings (translated from German)
Distribution of Alphabets

The list not only tells a tale of scholarship. It tells another story. It tells of the direction Henry Cohen was taking. He was preparing to live out his life in Texas and he was determined to know it thoroughly and completely. He quickly became part of Texas and captured its spirit. His involvement in the community was wholehearted and passionate. Not a civic endeavor was begun or considered without the advice, counsel, and active participation of Henry Cohen. He became not only the rabbi of the Jewish community, limiting his service to his own people. He became hero of the city, admired, sought after, respected. When the Great Flood hit Galveston in the first year of the 20th century and over 3000 lives were lost and many left homeless and destitute, Henry Cohen was in the forefront of the relief operation. He went everywhere, helping physically as well as spiritually, giving comfort, aid and hope to thousands who lost family and home. Every day, every hour, was devoted to help.

When Russian pogroms reached massive, frightening proportions and Jacob Schiff, great American philanthropist, and others, together with the cooperation of Israel Zangwill in England, wanted to help the distressed new arrivals find homes throughout the land, Galveston was selected as the port through which they would be admitted. It was Henry Cohen who in Galveston led the Movement, as it was called. It was he who met the ships on arrival. It was he who first met the unsure, bewildered, frightened immigrants when they docked. It was he who eased the tension of their uncertainties and doubts. He was their mouthpiece and their first warm welcome to America. He helped them begin to learn the language in the new land. He helped direct them to smaller towns and larger ones in the great Southwest, where they were destined to become the pioneers of newly rising Jewish communities in the thinly populated young states.

One of the most touching incidents in Cohen's life tells of his experience on the first day of the first ship's arrival. The immigrants were overwhelmed by kindness. The mayor of Galveston in the traditional American manner welcomed them. All was sweetness and light. Suddenly a husky Russian stepped forward, rolling up his shirt sleeve to reveal ugly, jagged scars. Then he said, slowly, haltingly, searching for words: "The knout was our greeting. You have clasped our hands. A time may come when your country will need us; we will not hesitate to serve you with our blood." Cohen was entrusted with a Herculean task and tirelessly, unstintingly he served.

He also helped administer relief programs when refugees poured into Galveston as a result of the United States-Mexican difficulties in 1914. The United States government placed $75,000 at the rabbi's disposal at that time. Every conceivable area of social justice came under the purview of Henry Cohen. Every phase of interfaith activity was his concern.

At the same time Cohen ministered to the needs of his own Jewish community, directing its religious and educational services with determined strength. Judaism had to be learned, taught, and expressed. Judaism was not only a religion of the heart. Judaism was not only the kind of faith and heritage to be contained within the body. It had to have external expression in daily living. Lip service was not enough. The preachments of the gentle yet dynamic prophets of Israel to aid and comfort the poor, the downtrodden, the sick, the widowed, the orphaned were very real to Henry Cohen. This was Judaism personified: Judaism on its highest level.

Prison reforms? Henry Cohen was an agitator, member and leader of the Texas Committee on Prisons and Prison Labor.

Rehabilitation of prisoners? Henry Cohen was in the forefront of the movement.

Social justice? Henry Cohen was in the vanguard.

Social critic? Henry Cohen was among the outspoken.

Bigotry? Henry Cohen was in the first line, fearlessly, unhesitatingly attacking and condemning it, especially its expression in the Ku Klux Klan.

Counselor? Henry Cohen was ahead of his day in technique and practice.

Teacher? Henry Cohen was gentle, direct, sincere, beloved.

Welfare worker? Henry Cohen was in the forefront.

Rabbi? Henry Cohen was the finest example of the profession.

Henry Cohen was in the forefront of Jewish and American life. In Galveston—together with the names of noted civic leaders, priests (especially his dear friend Father Kirwin, with whom he worked so closely), ministers—the name of Henry Cohen lives. Thousands owe their first warm welcome to America to the small, nimble, bespectacled rabbi of Texas who opened his heart to them. In the hearts of generations of Jews who grew up in the state of Texas, Henry Cohen was, and is, a source of profound inspiration. His spirit—lovable yet dynamic, delightful yet determined, reflected in the constant recollection of stories, events, even legends—lives today.

Among the many causes that absorbed him in his own community was that of preserving free speech and fostering free expression. Leaders of American thought occupied the Galveston Open Forum, which he headed. This was but one of numberless civic causes to which he gave his best efforts. He was President of the Lasker Home for Homeless Children. He was President of the Adove Seamen's Bethel. He was a founder of the Red Cross in Galveston, chairman of its Home Service Committee, and a member of the Galveston County Jewish Welfare Association and the Galveston Community Chest.

Henry Cohen was an American institution. He was a Jewish institution. Beloved by children and adults alike, he was ever abreast of every living situation; ready to move in whenever strong action was needed. When he learned during World War I that there were no arrangements made for Jewish men in the Navy to be served by Jewish chaplains, he immediately contacted Woodrow Wilson. Through the good offices of Senator Morris Sheppard, legislation corrected the situation. One of Cohen's prized possessions was the pen which Woodrow Wilson used to sign the bill into law and which the great President sent to him.

Hospital operations absorbed their share of Cohen's interest and concern. He even helped administer when necessary. He was a favorite and familiar figure in every hospital. When a gentle approach to a sensitive frightened patient was needed, the call went out for Henry Cohen.

Moreover, he helped many a medical student through school either personally or by serving as the agent through whom they secured loans.

When he thought a prisoner was being unduly held or bail had been set too high, he demanded release in his custody or a lowering of the bail. Jack Johnson, famous heavyweight boxing champion of the world, was one who benefited from his zeal.

When an American citizen named Richardson was sentenced to be shot by the Mexican government, Cohen's pressure and insistence secured his release.

He was outraged when he learned that the age of consent for girls was ten years. He cajoled, maneuvered and fought until the state legislature changed the age of consent to 18 years.

Rabbi Cohen lived his ideals. He lived his Judaism. Mirroring his own life he wrote once about the purpose and role of the rabbi:

The true rabbi serves and brings; he is not served, and he does not take. The moment of debate with himself as to the worldly wisdom of his choice of a profession is the criterion of his rabbinical fitness; the service of the sons of Kehath [the tribe of Levi from which the priests were chosen], willing bearers of the ark of the covenant—an earlier form of the term *noblesse oblige*—should be his only test. The rabbinate should not be used as a spade wherewith to dig, as the Talmud wisely says, or as a crown for self-aggrandizement, but as the very epitome and personification of the function of Israel—the priest people of God— designated by Isaiah, *Ebed Adonoy*—servant of the Lord. . . .

He [the Rabbi] molds the religious thought of his people. He makes social justice a factor in his community, and nothing human is alien to him. By his general attitude to the non-Jew he is a standing protest against intolerance—and he wins friends for his people and for all causes that he represents. It is in his power to make Judaism understood by those who do not see eye to eye with him, and, more than that, to make Israel's name honored. He gives freely of his spirit to all, and within human limits, he is at the call of all his fellow citizens. . . .

His communal activities redound to his credit; he has an ear and eye for the poor and the sick, and he ameliorates their condition either by actual contact or by his counsel; and in no way does he hide himself from his own flesh. His pulpit bears fruit, and his classes awaken a love for Judaism. Civic and general religious matters bespeak his active interest; energetic in all fields, social justice—the passion of Israel's prophets—

is his uppermost thought. The performance of any or all of these things brings him the appreciation of his fellow citizens; hence the respect in which he is held. . . .

There is so much real work to be done for the living God . . . .

In summing up the real accomplishments of a successful rabbi—for when all is said and done a successful ministry presupposes a successful rabbi—one who is thoroughly imbued with his work and inspired by vision, one who has a message for humanity and is by character and temperament fitted for the calling—upon whose altar of sacrifice the fire continually burns, one who defies discouragement and determines to make himself useful in his surroundings, the excellence of the congregation itself and the tone of the community is the supreme test. Working to this end is not labor in vain. What a splendid climax to the rabbi's work is the pride and dignity of a fine community whose social life is such that the rich and poor can meet on common ground, that his congregation influences the general public, that it raises Judaism in the estimation of his fellow citizens of other beliefs, that it cooperates with other Jewish congregations in the same city and with Christian congregations also, as well as with the general body of Jews in the United States. . . .

This was not only a platform that Henry Cohen set forth for the ideal rabbi. It was a precise reflection of the kind of rabbi Henry Cohen was. He served his community locally. He served his community nationally. He served his people locally. He served his people nationally. He was active in the Reform Movement, the Hebrew Union College, and was once reportedly considered as successor to the eminent Kaufmann Kohler. His modesty, however, prevented further pursuance of the discussion. He was active in the fraternal order of B'nai B'rith. Although he worked for the rebuilding of Jewish settlements in Palestine, he was a non-Zionist, accepting the thinking of the Reform Movement of those days. Judaism was to him a religion. He had come a long way from the days he was a member of the *Hovevei Zion,* Lovers of Zion, one of the earliest Zionist youth groups, when he was a young man. His attraction to Palestine was evident, however, in his service as a non-Zionist member of the Jewish Agency for Palestine.

Henry Cohen lived a long, full, useful and productive life, encompassing almost a century. His helpmate, Mollie Levy, whom he married in 1889, blessed his life with children, courage, and confidence. He loved doing, loved serving, loved ministering. The love he showered upon others through deeds came back to him primarily in the joy of the deed, but he was loved in return as well. Recognition and praise followed him throughout his lifetime. His service bore fruit. His accomplishments were applauded. When Stephen S. Wise penned a short list of the greatest religious leaders in America in 1930, only one rabbi was recorded—Henry Cohen.

The National Broadcasting Company's famous program, "Frontiers of Faith," televised the life of Henry Cohen in a program entitled "An American Ballad." The *Reader's Digest* sent Webb Waldron for a feature story and the resulting account, "The Busiest Man in Town," brought world fame and adulation to the little rabbi in Texas. Franklin Delano Roosevelt referred to his life as one of helpful activity in behalf of God and country and fellow man. The Bishop of Galveston described Cohen's life as one of "charity," as one of a friend and brother. Many poems and sonnets were written in his honor and to his memory. They have become part of the American dream and the American drama.

It was Henry Cohen who had the distinction of suggesting to the artist Blashfield the inscription to be placed on the rotunda of the central reading room of the Library of Congress. There is a figure there symbolizing Judea—typifying religion. The figure is seated, her hands upheld in prayer. On her lap rests a scroll; at her feet a censer and breastplate. To her right, on a tablet of stone there are carved in Hebrew letters the immortal words: "V'ahavtoh l're-acho komocho—Thou shalt love thy neighbor as thyself." Henry Cohen lived this commandment.

Heine said a long time ago, "To love and be loved—this on earth is the highest bliss." Henry Cohen, true servant of the Lord, self-sacrificing friend of man, symbol of democracy, pioneer of social justice, giant of faith, attained the highest bliss on earth.

BERNARD L. LEVINTHAL

Nestor of the American Orthodox Rabbinate

[1864-1952]

The year 1939 was a crucial one in history. The same year that saw Hitler attack Poland witnessed Great Britain, which by the Balfour Declaration of 1917 had "viewed with favor the establishment of a Jewish national home in Palestine," scuttle her solemn promise. Her White Paper on Palestine severely curtailed rights of the Jewish people in Palestine. Protests poured into world embassies. In Washington, meetings and conferences abounded. Here was Germany systematically destroying millions of Jews and the doors of Palestine were closed.

The government of the United States had to know what American Jews were feeling. A group of the most distinguished leaders of American Jewry met with Secretary of State Cordell Hull to urge him to intercede with Britain to rescind the vicious instrument. Among those present and representing Orthodox Jewry was Rabbi Bernard Levinthal, then 75 years old. The image of Socrates must have occurred to many as they regarded this venerable figure, whose white, curly hair formed a halo around a saintly countenance. Here sat the symbol of an ancient priestly people.

As the conference ended, to the astonishment of the entire assemblage, Secretary Hull approached the gentle sage and said: "Rabbi, please offer me your blessing." Rav Levinthal, as he was affectionately known, rose and pronounced the priestly benediction over the Secretary's bowed head.

Cordell Hull was not the only man who had sought the blessing of the dean of the Orthodox Rabbinate in America. For almost 60 years, from the moment Rabbi Levinthal landed in America, men and women had been drawn to him, seeking help and counsel and receiving his blessings. For the last ten years of the last century and the first half-century of this era, Rabbi Levinthal's Philadelphia home was a miniature city hall which drew rich and poor, rabbi and scholar, men and women, Americans and Europeans. It was a veritable Mecca for members of the Jewish literati and personages of such diverse types as Naphtali Herz Imber, author of "Hatikvah," Rabbi Jacob David, the Slutker Gaon, commentator of the Talmud. Thousands upon thousands walked the beaten path to the Levinthal home in Philadelphia. If you had a problem, you went to Rabbi Levinthal's home whether the need was for financial aid, marital counsel, or simply comfort and solace. Even in European lands, rabbis and leaders of Jewry advised potential immigrants: "Go to Rabbi Levinthal's home." From this home came forth happier people, better prepared to confront the trials of life.

Rabbi Levinthal presided over this home with his adored wife and four sons and a daughter—Rabbi Israel H. Levinthal, Judge Louis E. Levinthal, Abraham A. Levinthal, Esq., Cyrus Levinthal, Esq., and Lena L. Ehrlich. They observed to its fullest the exemplary Jewish tradition of Hachnasat Orchim, hospitality to guests. Always a dining room was in readiness, a table set with food and delicacies. Whoever was hungry was welcome to eat. No one was turned away, nor was any charge made. This was not his table but their table. It was everybody's table as he was everyone's Rav Levinthal.

Rabbi Levinthal was not always available to each and every person at the very moment of arrival. A loving grandson recaptures the feeling of Levinthal's home:

As I would enter the house through the living room which was always filled with waiting Jews, sitting and standing in small clusters, I would invariably hear the whispered murmur as eyes were turned in my direction—*Der Rov's einikle,* "the rabbi's grandchild."

Although grandpa lived in the house, and the house was in a residential section of Philadelphia, it had assumed the character of a public building—a small town city hall wherein a group might meet informally in one room and another group conduct an arbitration proceeding across the hall.

Adjacent to the living room was what once must have been the dining room. It was in this room that grandpa held court. Beyond this room was a slightly smaller room in which there was a large table covered with a cloth and on the table there was always a large salad bowl, bread and butter and condiments, including *chrane* (horseradish) for *gefulte* fish. It was here that Philadelphia could boast of a dining table that was open to all seven days a week. At least eight or ten chairs were set around the table, and everyone wishing to eat had but to seat himself and a rotund, good-natured cook named Mollie would emerge from the kitchen and inquire in Yiddish what she should serve.

This "open house" was probably never planned, but because of the open-heartedness of both grandpa and grandma, it just developed naturally. Grandpa had no office "appointments." If a Jew had a problem at noon, and if he were in the neighborhood, he would drop in. He would do his best to see grandpa, but if grandpa was too busy, he would *schmoos* [friendly discussion] with the other men in the house, and if lunch was being served, neither grandma nor grandpa were the type to go off by themselves to eat; they would invite all present to join them.

He would meet each person or group individually as he moved slowly from room to room. He met with representatives of every group of Judaism. He was busy greeting delegations from various parts of the world who came for advice on pressing problems facing the Jewish people. The problems were religious, ritualistic, financial. He was busy meeting with rabbis who had come for guidance in this new land with its opportunities for security in contrast with the pogroms and persecutions which were increasing elsewhere. He was busy conferring with representatives of synagogues which had conflicts in organization and personnel. He was busy counseling societies concerned with Jewish education. He was busy consoling the bereaved and encouraging the ambitious. He was busy meeting with leaders who were trying to establish a Jewish community in the city. He was busy guiding men who felt that an Orthodox seminary for the training of rabbis for America was necessary. He was busy talking with delegations involved in the Zionist movement. He moved from group to group, person to person, giving to each his undivided attention.

This was Rabbi Levinthal's life, a long, fruitful tenure on earth which brought countless blessings to the Jewish community growing up in Philadelphia. It was this warrior for God and Torah who molded like a potter the Jewish community, organized it, shaped it, and impressed upon it his stamp of devotion to Jewish ideals.

Who was this extraordinary man? Where did he come from? A younger contemporary and friend, Rabbi C. David Matt, was moved to write on Rav Levinthal's 70th birthday:

> Hail scion of a Torah-loving line
> And son of Aaron's priestly lineage!
> In thee the grace of sage and priest combine,
> Thy brow to crown with two-fold heritage.
>
> Thy ministry with joy, yet heart-ache fraught
> Beholds the triumphs of thy life's ideal;
> That countless sons the ancestral faith he taught
> And Torah,—endless fount of Israel's weal.
>
> Thy sapient counsel steered thy people's course
> And gladdened downcast heart and troubled mind;
> Yea, all who to thy guidance have recourse,
> In thee abundant wisdom ever find.
>
> God keep thee well, and save from envy, strife;
> Apportion thee contentment, peace, long life!

Rabbi Levinthal was born on Lag B'Omer, the Scholars' Festival, May 12, 1864, in Srednick, Kovno, Lithuania. He was named in Hebrew Dov Aryeh. Dov means bear. Aryeh means lion. If names can be said to play a role in determining character, these are fitting examples. His background lists like the Blue Book of rabbinic society, the first families of Judaism in terms of scholarship, stature and worldwide renown. The Hebrew term *Yichus,* status or stature, applies fully to the Levinthal heritage. The Hebrew title *Gaon* was appended to the title Rabbi of each of his forebears, as it was later attached to his name by his colleagues. His mother was Bath Sheba Lipshitz, daughter of Rabbi Chaim Gredniker Lipshitz, one of a famous family of rabbinical scholars. His father, Rabbi Abraham Levinthal, was one of the renowned scholars of the day. Both families could boast hundreds of years of fame in Jewish circles.

It was most natural that Bernard's education should be steeped in

Jewish traditions, as it indeed was. He was educated at the feet of Israel's greats and early recognized as an *Ilui*, meaning precocious and outstanding student of the Talmud. His reputation for brilliance and scholarship spread quickly. Rabbi Alexander Moshe Lapides, Rabbi Samuel Mohilever and Rabbi Isaac Elchanan Spector were his masters, the latter two officiating at his ordination in 1888. Their towering personalities left indelible impressions upon their esteemed student, Rabbi Isaac Elchanan bequeathing his religious spirit and fervor and Rabbi Mohilever, founder of the first Hovevei Zion Society in Warsaw, his love for Zion.

In 1885, he married Minna Kleinberg, daughter of another outstanding rabbinic family. Her father was the Dayan Rabbi Eliazar Kleinberg, judge or chief scholar of Vilna. In 1890, Rabbi Kleinberg was called by Chief Rabbi Jacob Joseph of New York to assume the pulpit of B'nai Abraham Congregation in Philadelphia. He served for only three years, until his death in 1891. Then the congregation, having heard of the distinguished young son-in-law of their rabbi, issued a call for him to fill the vacant pulpit. Actually, four congregations joined forces to extend the invitation. Thus it was that at the age of 27, Rabbi Levinthal assumed the pulpit that he was to serve with distinction until 1952, 61 productive years.

The history of a Jewish community is intertwined with the lives of its rabbis. They give it character and direction and establish its pattern of Jewish living. This is true of an established community when strong-minded rabbis come onto the scene. It is truer still of a community that is not yet organized and which has little unity. In such communities the rabbi does more than guide. He creates and molds. Like a potter who molds clay into a form, Rabbi Levinthal came into an embryo community in the last decade of the 19th century and shaped it enduringly throughout 60 years of devotion.

In 1934, Rabbi Levinthal reminisced:

I came to Philadelphia in 1891 as rabbi of the Jewish Community. I was young, full of enthusiasm and energy, eager to serve my people with all my heart. I wanted to dedicate myself to the enhancement of Judaism in America, make secure its existence here, and make my people part of the American community, to create new structures and to translate ideals quickly into reality. I found virgin territory here, plain, simple, undone.

Even the ground, as it were, was not prepared, not ready for sowing. I had to begin from scratch. I saw immediately on arrival that the road would not be smooth; nor would it be a bed of roses. There were obstacles en route, lying every which way, almost at each step. The road was strewn with mounts to hurdle. I was not, however, to be deterred. On the contrary, the confrontation gave me renewed strength and determination. I felt summoned. "Come what may, I shall do my duty and I shall do it with all my strength and complete faith. God will help."

With this prayer of faith in God's help, Bernard Levinthal proceeded to mold a Jewish community. There was no community to speak of when he came. True, a small settlement of Jews had come much earlier from Spain, Portugal and Germany, but these belonged to a vintage of Jews different from those Levinthal had known. There were few synagogues in Philadelphia in the 1880's when droves of Jews poured into America on the heels of Russian persecutions. The mere coming to America did not solve all problems for these people. Earning a livelihood was of primary concern to them. Jews began early in life working for a living. Few had real childhoods. Before ten years of age they sold newspapers, helped in little stores parents opened, carried loads of merchandise to customers, acted as barkers outside in bitter cold weather. Others started peddling, selling whatever merchandise they could secure on credit from jobbers—envelopes, hairpins, needles, pencils, shoelaces, etc. Many lived in what were called bandbox houses situated in filthy alleys, without water and other comforts. Nor were Jews harassed only by the forces of anti-Semitism. Poor immigrants often suffered at the hands of wealthier fellow Jews who had established an earlier beachhead in America. Synagogue influence upon the lives of Jewish people was limited to the confines of the synagogue. Jewish people were divided amongst themselves. Radical groups thrived, with socialistic views maintained by many. Their aggressive radicalism made itself felt as, dissatisfied with merely preaching their doctrines, they vigorously sought to put them into practice. Often such groups openly violated Jewish traditions. Public feasts on Yom Kippur were held and dances encouraged on the Sabbath. Division existed even among Orthodox Jews, who had come from different European lands and brought with them various customs and traditions which they were unwilling to relinquish. Obstacles to unity seemed

insurmountable. The rabbis themselves were helpless, their influence
limited to the synagogue. Even there their leadership was ineffective.
The hour called for firm action, which, alone, could bring order out of
chaos. It was as the psalmist had cried out: "Et laasot l'adonai." It
was a time to work and do for God.

Rabbi Levinthal accepted the call to work for God. As he surveyed
the task ahead, questions coursed through his mind. How does Jewish
education fare here? What of the Jewish future? Jewish traditions? Will
the Torah live and be vital here? The scion of great rabbis was touching
upon the essence of rabbinical service. He knew that if his influence was
limited to the four synagogues, his goals would not be attained. God
would not be served nor His people. His influence had to extend beyond
the walls of these synagogues, onto the streets, into the homes and
into the lives of the entire Jewish community. Only in this way could
a real community be established.

He immediately began his mighty effort to strengthen Torah and
spread its authority. There were objections. There were sneers. There
were cynics who said it could not be done. Such was the pessimism which
prevailed. But Rabbi Levinthal pressed fervently on.

Within the first decade of his arrival, the last of the 19th century,
he founded study groups in many synagogues in the city, not only in
those where he personally ministered. They were called *chevrahs*—
groups. He looked for leaders for the study groups and found them.
Whenever unable to produce a proper teacher, or if a synagogue was
unable to compensate for this service, he himself lectured and taught
until the congregation was able to assume the financial responsibility.
The Jewish public responded with enthusiasm to this adult education
program and rallied behind the rabbi. His effort spread throughout the
city and was blessed with success as congregation after congregation
instituted study groups. Thus, the first in the city to espouse adult
education on the level of Torah study, the rabbi created units which
would eventually comprise the larger community organization.

Convinced that the role of the rabbi ought not be confined to the
synagogue tower, Rabbi Levinthal worked for larger community participation. The rabbi must be concerned with every vital issue in life.
He must be an active part of the total society. He must be involved
in politics, so long as it does not militate against religion, just as he

must oppose any force in the community which undermines religion. Rabbi Levinthal used to say that in communal efforts the rabbi has to be above parties and special interests. Furthermore, though a rabbi be of one sect within Judaism, he must not close his eyes and ears to Jews of other views. He must be willing to listen to all parties and perspectives. A rabbi is a rabbi of all Israel, not merely of Orthodox, Conservative, or Reform. The liberalism of such a view stands out in the age in which Rabbi Levinthal served his people.

Allowing his broad views to be known, Rabbi Levinthal readily accepted invitations to meetings, conferences and gatherings of all kinds, religious, cultural, social and of all groups. The working classes, not always friendly to religion, were surprised to learn from his brilliant analyses that the principles of workers' rights—social justice and economic reform—came directly from the Bible. He showed them that the Talmud is deeply concerned with labor's rights. Gradually, Levinthal came to be sought after by many groups. Few meetings in the community involving Jewish causes were held without Rav Levinthal. He participated fully and with boundless enthusiasm. He was the rare type of student whose sense of practical realities inspired him to counsel magnanimously and advise sagaciously.

Rabbi Levinthal's ministrations for God and Torah were directly involved in the field of education. No communal educational program was available. Obstacles existed which have long since disappeared. Attendance in public schools meant not enough time for Hebrew school and Torah study. Private, itinerant teachers who depended on tutoring for their subsistence were opposed to any communal education program as a threat to their livelihood. Differences in Hebrew pronunciation, even among Orthodox Jews because of dialects in the countries from which they hailed, further hindered a communal school project. Levinthal, however, had a goal to achieve and he was not to be deterred. Problems there were—he would not deny them. There was something beyond them, however, that was more important, more significant. Early in his ministry in Philadelphia, in 1892, he succeeded in establishing the first Talmud Torah, Communal Hebrew School, forerunner of the present-day system of the United Hebrew Schools and Yeshivots.

Education on the elementary level had to be provided, too, and continued through the secondary level. Thus he created a Hebrew High School, which he served as principal. Still he was not satisfied. There had to be higher education available. In 1902 he organized the Yeshiva Mishkan Yisroel (Tabernacle of Israel), where he personally taught such Jewish subjects as Mishna, Talmud and Codes. He served as the guiding light of this seminary all his life. Again, he was not satisfied. A growing America would need Orthodox rabbis. They would have to have a seminary where they could prepare for ordination and for service in the American Jewish community. With others he helped found the Rabbi Isaac Elchanan Seminary, now Yeshiva University, in New York and recommended renowned Rabbi Bernard Revel to be its first president. He was for years chief examiner of the rabbinical department. Later, it was his recommendation that placed Rabbi Samuel Belkin at the helm of the world-famous institution.

Education to Levinthal was closely related to life and Jewish life in particular. Knowledge in a vacuum was valueless. Education must train the individual in the service of God. To the sage of Philadelphia, the deplorable situation regarding Kashruth, the observance of the dietary laws, called for vigorous action. Accordingly, after ten years of carefully laying the groundwork, working cautiously with each group, each synagogue involved, Rabbi Levinthal succeeded in bringing together 18 synagogues to organize the Vaad Hakashruth, the united body to direct the destiny of Kashruth in the city. It was a Herculean achievement—to create such unity out of stubborn disunity. It marked the commencement of Jewish communal life in Philadelphia and thus deserves recognition as an historic event. This does not mean that every difference suddenly disappeared into thin air, but it was the first breakthrough toward unity.

Disturbing experiences continued but their number decreased through the years. There is the well-known case of the "Chicago Meat Incident," in which doubts were cast on meats certified kosher for public consumption. Turmoil rent the community. The rabbi was offered a retainer of four figures to certify the Kashruth, so low had conditions sunk. But Rabbi Levinthal was not one to sell his soul. With renewed vigor and force, he labored incessantly to bring respect into the field. He was later instrumental in persuading the state legislature of

Pennsylvania to pass a law which made it a misdemeanor to sell *trefe* (non-kosher) meat as kosher.

A man as outspoken and fearless as Rabbi Levinthal was bound to have enemies. Truth was his criterion, not friendship. Friendship was subservient to the overriding principle of honesty and integrity. He was prepared for those who might seek to humiliate and embarrass him publicly.

The great organizer created more institutions which would be vehicles for service to Judaism and the Jewish community. He called into being the first *Chevra Kaddisha,* Free Burial Society. Many families were ill-prepared to expend large sums for funerals. They had to be helped. This was one of the great duties of Judaism. Rabbi Levinthal, once again, and early in his impressive career, stepped forward.

Group after group felt the force of his dynamic personality, his statesmanlike grasp of the needs of American, and of world Jewry. His impact was local and national. He founded the Council of Jewish Clubs in Philadelphia. He organized the first Philadelphia Lodge of the Independent Order of B'rith Sholom. He was vice-president of the Federation of American Zionists. He was chosen by Judge Mayer Sulzberger to be a member of the American Jewish Committee, one of five in Philadelphia. He was one of the founders of the American Jewish Congress and in 1919 attended the first Peace Conference at Versailles as representative of Orthodox Jewry.

In 1911, Rabbi and Mrs. Levinthal were invited to and attended the silver wedding anniversary of President and Mrs. William Howard Taft in the White House. During World War I, Rabbi Joseph Krauskopf, speaking for Reform Jews, and Archbishop Ryan, of the Catholic Archdiocese of Philadelphia, met in the rabbi's home to arrange for the sale of United States Liberty Bonds. During the same war, Rabbi Levinthal regularly visited railroad stations to offer his blessings and words of encouragement to the soldiers who were off to war.

Jewish life was intertwined with the Holy Land; Palestine was firmly rooted in the Jewish consciousness. It was part of Judaism to dream of Zion and seek a homeland for the Jewish people. There was, however, sharp disagreement as to how the ideal was to be achieved. Even among Orthodox rabbis the Zionist cause and movement was met with opposition, some feeling that the Messiah would bring about the Return in his own good time. Rabbi Levinthal was one of the eloquent pioneers of Zionism. History records him among the founders of the Federation of American Zionists. He participated in the World Zionist Congress at Basle, Switzerland by wiring a message of encouragement and hope. He inspired a whole generation of Zionists devoted to the Zionist cause, as he taught them how to serve with almost total abandonment of self the great cause of the revival of Zion and the renaissance of the Jewish people. Together with Theodor Herzl, Max Nordau, Israel Zangwill, and Menachem Ussishkin, he helped to found the Zionist movement. In America, two of the key founders were Dr. Richard Gottheil and Rabbi Bernard Levinthal. He was one of the founders of Mizrachi, the religious Zionist organization. Thus, on the ground floor of the historical movement which eventually led to the State of Israel, stands firmly and mightily the imposing figure of the sage of Philadelphia.

Judge Levinthal tells the story of his father's involvement in a major crisis which developed early and which could have split the Zionist movement in America had it not been for the sagacity and wisdom of Rabbi Levinthal.

Stephen S. Wise, then president of the United Palestine Appeal, and one of American Jewry's most dynamic and colorful figures, had made statements regarding Jewish acceptance of Jesus. Mizrachi, religious Zionists, demanded that Rabbi Wise resign his post. Louis Lipsky was chairman of a special emergency meeting in New York. Mizrachi threatened to withdraw from the United Palestine Appeal. Poale Zion, Labor Zionists, threatened from their side. The debate was bitter and a major crisis was developing.

Louis Lipsky then announced a recess, called Rabbi Israel H. Levinthal and Judge Levinthal who were present, and said, "Call your father in Philadelphia. Tell him what is going on and ask him what we ought to do. I will follow his advice."

The two Levinthals went to a telephone booth and called their father, Rabbi Levinthal, a dear friend and admirer of Rabbi Wise. He advised that it would be a serious error to force Rabbi Wise, friend of Zionism, to resign. It was all a mistake, true, and all people make mistakes. Force him out and we turn away a devoted friend and servant of his people.

The Levinthals reported to Lipsky and when the meeting was resumed Lipsky announced what he had done. The Mizrachi were divided,
but a majority agreed to listen to Rabbi Levinthal's advice. A belligerent
minority insisted that the matter be taken to a vote. The vote was
taken and the minority soundly defeated.

Thus, even the Mizrachi people sided with the wisdom of Rabbi
Levinthal and thus, perhaps unknown to many, Rav Levinthal was
instrumental in resolving a potential breach which could have seriously
hurt the Zionist cause.

To Chaim Weizmann, first President of Israel, "Rabbi Levinthal has
long been a source of inspiration and an untiring tribune . . . a great
spiritual figure."

To Chief Rabbi of Israel Isaac Halevi Herzog, Rabbi Levinthal was
a ". . . venerable spiritual head . . . who for more than half a century
has lent the weight and support of his authority to the world-wide
movement for the restoration of Israel, which, thank God, has now
been consummated, and who at the same time adorned the religious
wing of the movement, the Mizrachi. . . ."

Over the years, between thought and fulfillment, the spirit of
Palestine saturated the Levinthal home. Representatives from religious
and charitable institutions needing help made their way to Philadelphia.
The Rav had intimate knowledge of each group, each Yeshivah, and to
each he gave time, effort and money. Many an institution now in Israel
owes its very existence to him.

Perhaps the image of this venerable leader remains most vivid in
the memory of his appearance on the podium. The sight, especially on
the High Holy Days, of the white-clothed, white-haired figure, so strik-
ingly spiritual, was enchanting. One thrilled at this embodiment of
the Jewish spirit bringing home the eternal message of the ages and
making it live and throb. His sermons drew hundreds and often lasted
for hours. Yet the audiences did not tire—these listeners who came from
every strata of Jewish society. They were scholars, rabbis, religionists,
atheists, conformists and nonconformists. For 60 years he preached, his
oratorical genius growing with the years. His exhortations were at once
impassioned, profound and logical. When moved, he moved his listeners
to feel as he felt. Levinthal wept when he told of the massacres in the
Kishenev pogrom and his audience wept with him. When President

William McKinley was assassinated in 1901, the powerful master of the rostrum broke down and with him his people. America had been hurt to the core, his America, their America, his land of liberty, their land of freedom. When Theodor Herzl died, Levinthal felt a sense of personal loss. Though Herzl was not Orthodox, he was Levinthal's spiritual father.

In addition to being a man of strong feelings, Levinthal was a deep and original thinker. Moreover, he had the rare ability to simplify his ideas so that all could understand. He spoke on every issue of life, but he always returned to his Torah texts, directing his message in the light of the Torah. His speech was a living, vital Yiddish, rich in literary allusions. When especially moved he broke into chants, which stirred his listeners to *feel* as well as *know* his meaning. Often he spoke in beautiful and modern Hebrew, especially at celebrations, national conventions and institutional affairs. And although he understandably retained an accent, his English was faultless. He spoke English with colleagues and leaders of the community, Jewish and non-Jewish, with ease and comfort.

He spoke whenever called, so long as he could deliver a message, teach Torah. He preached to citizens, guests, and new arrivals. To immigrants who had come to learn English at Touro Hall, the center founded by Isaac Leeser in the middle of the century from an endowment of Judah Touro, the New Orleans philanthropist, he emphasized the compatability of Judaism and Americanism, urging them to become part of their adopted land and give their best to it. He was a father of the now accepted late Friday evening lecture, walking long distances week after week to deliver weekly Sabbath discourses. Hundreds, young and old, attended regularly.

To his own colleagues, Rabbi Levinthal was a rabbi's rabbi. It was he to whom they turned with their problems. He kept pace with every phase of American life to know better which rabbi could serve better where. He thoroughly educated himself in American history, economics and sociology, the better to appreciate the land of his adoption. Recognizing that the Orthodox rabbinate needed unity to be effective, he was one of the guiding spirits in founding the Agudath Harabonim, the Union of Orthodox Rabbis of the United States and Canada. For more than 40 years he was its moving force and hence spokesman in the councils of Orthodoxy and beyond. Secure in his position of eminence, he helped rabbis coming from Europe to relocate. He founded *Ezras Torah,* meaning help of the Torah, an organization designed to assist needy rabbis and scholars. He sought pulpits all over America for promising rabbis, guiding many an American Jewish community through its growing pains. His wisdom and example invariably inspired harmony and understanding.

His personal life was interwoven with his life of service. He adored his family. His four sons all became lawyers and dedicated leaders in American Jewish life. As devoted husband, father and grandfather, he knew no equal.

He left an ethical will, a century-old practice in Jewish scholarly circles, in which he shared with his family the hope that they would live by the principles of Torah. He urged them to cherish dearly the family name, associated as it had been with rabbis for generations.

Be careful not to participate in and waste your efforts in movements which are not to the advantage of traditional Torah, or on activities which go counter to efforts which I—with the help of God, blessed be His name—have made and to achievements for the strengthening of Torah and observance which I have nurtured and fostered with a sense of dedication rising from the very depths of my soul and for which I have sacrificed my very life.

In 1934, he wrote his memoirs. There had been hard times throughout the years. It had not been easy to make a living for a large and growing family, but he had never faltered or lost his nerve. Especially the five-year period between 1929 and 1933 had been difficult. He had lost both his beloved partner in life and his only daughter. Yet faith had carried him through. He had now reached the age of 69. He compared the events of these years to the destruction of the Holy Temple in Jerusalem. Friends had tried to assuage his hurt and urged him to reduce his heavy schedule. He refused:

It is often the duty of Jewish leaders and teachers to withdraw individual interest and concern in favor of communal needs. It has never been my nature or temperament to avoid any work or service which must be performed. Nor am I one to rest on past laurels. Nor do I desire that my dear friends, deeply concerned about me, press me to refrain from doing this or that. I do not want to lessen my load or any kind of work which must be performed. I do not want to become a weak link in the chain of service to my people. I must remain a strong, firm link. "He who refreshes the tired and the weary" will provide me with fortitude.

A man of strength, optimism, patience, and determination to carry on his work and to continue to lead his people through whatever wilderness they may be called upon to traverse, could not stop. The driving force within him would not permit him to relax.

Family devotion to him may be seen in the words of tribute spoken publicly to him by his son, Israel H. Levinthal, at the celebration of Rabbi Levinthal's 50th anniversary in the rabbinate, in Philadelphia, February 1, 1942.

When I think of his influence on our lives, I am reminded of an interesting comment by our ancient Rabbis regarding the scene portrayed in the Bible in which God called to Moses from the burning bush. "How did that Voice appear? How did it sound?" the rabbis ask. And they answer: *Nigleh Olov Be'kolo Shel Aviv,* "God revealed Himself unto him in the voice of his own father!" . . . In a more modest way, we, the children, can proudly say that the *Shekhina* [divine spirit] has always spoken to us in the voice of our father, that whenever his lips spoke to us we felt that the *Shekhina* itself was addressing us. That is the real secret of his unbounded influence in our lives . . . .

Were I to evaluate his success as father, I could do it in no better way than by referring to a beautiful and touching comment of our ancient sages. In the Bible passage that describes the meeting between Jacob and Laban, when the former was on his way home to Canaan, we read that "Jacob said *L'echov,* to his brothers, gather ye stones." The Rabbis, studying these words, were puzzled, and they ask: *"Brothers?* How many brothers did Jacob have? Did he not have only one?" One of them replied: *Echov Elu Banav,* "These were his children to whom he spoke, *She-hu Koreh Oton Belashon Hakodesh Echov,* and speaking to them in the *sacred tongue,* he addressed them as *Echov,* brothers."

When he spoke to his children he addressed them in that sacred, tender, loving fashion as brothers, comrades, pals! He never looked down upon them from on high. Rather, he raised them up and made them feel that they were his equals, his companions in life. When I analyze the relationship between our dear father and us, his children, and ask myself how it is that he succeeded in leading us in his way, I find answer in this comment about Jacob. . . . In all the years of our life, I can truthfully say, not once do I recall our father regarding us as children—his was the attitude of comrade calling to comrade, pals, companions, in all the tasks and problems that faced us. . . .

In an earlier address, January 1925, Israel Levinthal said:

He is primarily and above all a student of the Torah, versed in all that remarkable literature which has come to us from the ages. But he is not the Rabbi who is confined within the "four ells of the *Halakha* (Jewish law)." He is *Hamelitz Benosum,* "the interpreter between them," interpreting to the old the philosophy of the new age, as well as to the young the teachings of the days gone by. . . . He never regarded himself as the Rabbi who must seek the welfare of only a certain group or certain party in Israel; he has ever regarded himself as belonging to Catholic Israel. Like the High Priest of old, this priest of today has borne the names of all the tribes of Israel upon his breast. Not of the pious alone, not of the orthodox alone, but to be the steward of all Jews, seeking the welfare of *all Jews*—that was his mission in life. And he has not only borne their names and interests upon his heart, but again, like the High Priest of old, he has borne the names of all the tribes in Israel upon his shoulders. He has not only thought of his people, but has labored for them; no burden was too great for him to bear as long as it served the interests of the Jewish people. . . .

Many deserving honors poured in on him during the last three or four decades of his life. He had made his mark on Judaism, on Jewish people, on America. He had made his impress on the community. His name was spoken with reverence, respect, appreciation. Organizations vied to do him honor and offer public recognition for his massive contributions. Yeshiva University in 1942 bestowed upon him an honorary Doctor of Divinity degree. The words of the citation are significant and descriptive:

As candidate for the first Honorary Degree of Doctor of Divinity to be conferred by Yeshiva College, I have the honor to present Rabbi Dov Aryeh Hakohane Levinthal, Dean of the American Orthodox Rabbinate.

For half a century he ministered with wisdom and understanding in the City of Brotherly Love. There he founded institutions of learning and of mercy, and there he won admiration not only for his Talmudic knowledge, but also for his sagacity in the affairs of men. Indeed, he came to be recognized as the uncrowned head of the Jewish community of Philadelphia.

The choicest blessing of his rich and fruitful career is the gift of *banim i'vnay banim oskim batorah,* children, aye, and grandchildren, who in the pulpit, on the bench of justice, in public affairs and within our own Yeshiva, are occupied with Torah and the performance of great deeds. For the continuation of this blessing he has our prayerful wishes.

For the Yeshiva he bears a two-fold significance. First, he was ordained in the rabbinate in the year 1888 by the saint and sage Rabbi Isaac Elchanan, for whom our rabbinic school is named. Secondly, he helped to bring to our institution our late and immortal president Dr. Bernard Revel, for whom he felt the love of a father and from whom he received the devotion of a son.

Having worn for fifty years the Keser Torah [Crown of Torah], having been born to the Keser Torah and having earned the crown of Shem Tov [Good Name], I present him now to you for yet an additional crown, that of Doctor of Divinity from Yeshiva College, *honoris causa.*

In 1948, the Jewish Institute of Religion, headed by Rabbi Stephen S. Wise, dear friend of Rabbi Levinthal, brother in Zionism and love for the land of Israel, awarded him the Doctor of Letters degree. In Israel 15,000 trees, planted in his honor under the name Yaar Levinthal; remain as a living memorial, testifying eternally to his devotion to the Holy Land.

Rabbi Levinthal's 50th, 60th and 70th birthdays were communal celebrations, but he did not allow his 80th birthday to be publicly noted. The spirit of the times—a nation at war and one saddened by the sudden passing of Franklin Delano Roosevelt—precluded for him any festive observance.

At his 70th birthday celebration, a special Jubilee volume in Hebrew was issued in his honor. In addition to literary contributions, rabbis from all over the world hurried to send their tribute. A roll call of Judaism's great is found here. To each of the world's Talmudic and Hebraic scholars, Rabbi Levinthal was known as *Morenu,* Our Teacher, Master; or *HaGaon,* the Illustrious, terms and titles reserved for a few of a generation. An outpouring of messages of this kind has not been duplicated. He was indeed *Morenu,* and *HaGaon*—a sage whose impact on American Jewish history is indelible. Militant leader of his faith, uncompromising advocate of traditional Judaism, Bernard Levinthal was one of the giants of faith in American Jewish history.

STEPHEN S. WISE

Indomitable Defender of the Faith and the People

[1874-1949]

The year is 1947. The city is Philadelphia, cradle of American liberty. Thousands have braved the inclement weather to gather in the massive auditorium of the Academy of Music to hear the latest report on the struggle for a national home for the Jewish people. Zionism is reaching a climax. The days are charged with tension and anxiety. Delegates to the United Nations are deliberating the proposal to establish a State of Israel. Behind-the-scenes maneuvering and lobbying must be going on. The assemblage is not really there to hear reports. These are communicated by radio, television, and other media. They have come, rather, to hear reassuring words that the centuries-old hope is nearing victory in the council of nations. They are desperately in need of encouragement to continue the effort. They seek inspiration.

Leaders of the Jewish community are seated on the stage. In its center sits a tall, distinguished figure, his arms folded, his head slightly bowed, his eyes closed. It appears that he is sleeping. He is. Yet, nothing really escapes him. He is capturing a few moments of precious rest after long grueling sessions in and out of the United Nations, embassies and consulates, and with leaders of American and Jewish life.

Speaker after speaker is presented. Each shares his views and feelings. The audience is heartened. The chairman is now reading a long list of accomplishments and the name Stephen S. Wise is announced. Thousands rise spontaneously and applaud vigorously. Stephen S. Wise opens his eyes, rises, and slowly walks to the rostrum amid the thunderous ovation.

He is a stately figure of a man, wearing his favorite Prince Albert cloak. His large square face suggests determination, earnestness, steel nerves. The steady gaze, now fixed upon the audience, has been leveled at statesmen the world over as he demanded action for the good of man.

Like the great American eagle, stretching her wings protectively, Wise slowly raises his long, mighty arms, and in a deep, resonant voice, thunders: "Let my people go! Let my people go!" The crowd is electrified. "Let my people go," he repeats. "We have pledged!" he continues. "We have pleaded! We now call upon the United Nations to solemnly honor the pledges and establish a haven for our people in the land of our fathers." Wise inspires himself as his own tensions are released and he senses the responsive feelings of the crowd. His incomparable voice easily reaches the hearts of the assembled as he roars to his climax: "We will win! The Jewish people will have a home!"

Thousands have once again listened to Stephen S. Wise, leader of his people, rabbi, reformer, orator extraordinary, militant advocate of justice. All over America, in every city, town and village, in the stark realization that 6,000,000 Jews had been destroyed, thousands had come during the crucial days following World War II to hear the story of the battle for freedom. Everywhere Wise had captivated audiences, Jew and gentile, as he had been doing for 40 years. Everywhere the response was inspiring. Everywhere people looked to Wise as protector, guide, counselor. Everywhere, it was "*my* people." The strong, fatherly Wise had, like the zealously protective eagle, taken the Jewish people under his wing. Fearless, dauntless, aggressive, Stephen S. Wise had all his days lived the life of the challenger, confronting statesman, diplomat, politician, Jew or Christian, whenever a challenge needed to be issued. Truth must out, justice must be done.

The year is 1933. Hitler has taken over Germany. Few have the foresight to anticipate the future. Wise pleads with leaders to plan ahead; do something now. He foresees destruction, annihilation, and horror. But they do not listen. Not even all Jewish leaders agree with him. Wise is determined to alert the world to the danger that lies ahead. Urged to remain silent by statesmen and diplomats, he is not deterred. A massive march and meeting is scheduled for Madison Square Garden in New York where 20,000 people will raise their voices in protest. Wise announces it and the dramatic event is carried out.

John Haynes Holmes, minister of the Community Church of New York and Wise's dear friend for half a century, describes the event:

> I shall never forget that day of demonstration against iniquity. What a meeting that was, and what a parade! Thousands of men, women, and even children, mostly from the poorer classes, the slum-dwellers of the East Side. Most of them, in their working clothes, unwashed, yet strangely clean. Their footbeats on the pavements were keeping time—block after block. The silence echoed the lamentations that the heart alone could sing. Nor were there uniforms, unless we count the garb of the ancient rabbis, with their towering hats, their sweeping beards, their black robes trailing the ground, and here and there the scrolls of the sacred law. Of wordly banners there were none, save only the nation's flag hanging limp on its staff, as though mourning for Israel on this tragic day. What a multitude this was—like a great river rolling on to the sea! And at its head one solitary figure who, by his mere presence, suffused the whole with dignity and power.
>
> There was something in Wise's appearance that day which marked him for attention. There was the mighty stride which bore him beyond the easy compass of other men to follow. There was his bared head with its black mane of hair rolling back from his noble brow. As usual, his large black felt hat was in his hand, to be lifted in response to some silent salute from the crowds of spectators on either side. Wise's clothing was unchanged—the same black suit, with its long and heavy folds in Prince Albert style which had long since become familiar. He was getting dusty as his feet tramped on, and obviously tired from this exhausting day. Even his giant-like frame could not indefinitely endure without fatigue. But he moved undaunted, and could have gone miles further had duty called. His face that day was stern and terrible. It was molded as of a block of granite, and knew not a single smile.

And so on, back through the years, from the very beginning of his ministry, Stephen S. Wise was in the forefront of history in the making. Ever watchful for attack against the young, unprotected, downtrodden and weak, Stephen S. Wise bestrode half a century of American and Jewish history, everywhere making his mark as a giant of faith, giant of social justice, prophet of God and man. From 1900 to 1949, American history, economics and government is intertwined with the life and deeds of Stephen S. Wise as is Jewish life of the same half-century. Without him, Jewish and American history would be very different.

Without him, who knows whether the oppressed worker in America would have risen to his present status. Without him, who knows whether labor legislation would have moved so dramatically to protect the masses. Without him, who knows whether social justice and civil liberties would not be years behind their present positions. Without him, who knows whether England would have announced the Balfour Declaration in 1917, offering a national homeland to the Jewish people in Palestine. Without him, who knows whether Israel would have been a nation among the council of nations today. Without him, who knows whether rabbis in America would have freedom of the pulpit, for which principle he sacrificed and labored all his life. Without Stephen S. Wise, the world, Jewish and non-Jewish, would be vastly different.

The character traits which distinguished this commanding American Jewish figure were early visible. He was born in Budapest, Hungary, on March 17, 1874, to Rabbi Aaron and Sabine Weisz. The Weisz family possessed a famed rabbinical heritage. Stephen's paternal grandfather was a distinguished chief rabbi of Hungary, Rabbi Joseph Hirsch Weisz, renowned for his piety and liberalism. His maternal grandfather, a success in the artistic world, was granted by Emperor Franz Joseph II the rank of Baron. When Stephen was 16 months old, his parents brought the entire family to America, his father becoming rabbi of Temple Rodeph Sholom in New York where he served until the end of his days.

One of seven children, Stephen, guided by an adoring father and loving mother, early determined to enter the ministry. His seriousness, earnestness and eagerness to learn and excel assured him success. Each course of study was attacked with equal vehemence. He treated each subject as a challenge—a trait which became his dominant characteristic. He was to be the great challenger; the great confronter. Under his father's personal tutelage, he studied the sources of Jewish tradition, which he studied as well under the guidance of other distinguished rabbis in New York. At the same time he mastered secular studies, including Latin, Greek, and the great literary masters. He was preparing for his destined role in American Jewish life and history.

Not satisfied with being graduated from New York's City College in 1891, young Stephen Wise went abroad. He studied under Chief

Rabbi of Vienna Jellinek, from whom he received rabbinical ordination, and continued his advanced studies at Oxford University.

When he returned to New York, he became assistant to Rabbi Henry Jacobs at Temple B'nai Jeshurun in New York, better known as the Madison Avenue Synagogue. Within the year, Rabbi Jacobs died, and young Stephen Wise at only 21 years of age was selected spiritual leader. The future leader of American Jewry served the congregation for only four years, 1895 to 1899. They were years which set the foundation and pattern for his future career. During this period major events altered the course of his life and hence the life of the American and Jewish community. First, his revered father, who had inspired within him a deep love for the traditions of his people, passed away suddenly. Bereft, Stephen Wise became the head of the household. Second, the Jewish world was suddenly overwhelmed and deeply pained by the wave of persecution against Jews in Russia and the infamous Dreyfus Trial in France. Stephen Wise saw how much work had to be done for liberty and freedom. Third, Theodor Herzl, founder of political Zionism, emerged on the scene of Jewish history and Stephen Wise rallied to his support. To the everlasting blessing of his memory, Stephen Wise, almost alone, turned the tide toward the cause of Zion. He moved quickly to action, establishing the first Zionist Federation in New York, significantly on Independence Day, July 4, 1897. One year later he joined world Jewish leaders, attending the Second Zionist Congress in Basle, Switzerland. Not only did he become a close friend of the great Theodor Herzl, but his future with Israel, his people, was then and there carved out. Fourth, Stephen Wise met Louise Waterman, his future beloved wife and companion, partner in the service of God and man.

These events having impressed themselves deeply on him, Wise, after much soul-searching, left the pulpit in New York, and accepted the call to serve Temple Beth Israel in Portland, Oregon. Far from being isolated there on the northwestern coast of the United States, he served with conspicuous distinction. From his outpost in Oregon, in but seven years, he became one of the country's foremost rabbinical leaders. Not only his own congregation did he serve, but all people whatever their race, creed or color. He became a protector of the human being and of American principles, engaging in any controversy wherever human beings were involved and their lot needed improvement. He lashed out against vice and corruption. He inveighed from platform and pulpit against crime and social injustice. He did not care that certain affluent members of his congregation might prefer that he limit himself to Judaism or religion. To Wise all human beings were the concern of Judaism. His role as rabbi was all-encompassing. He traveled from city to city, speaking before Jews and non-Jews, the first such rabbi many Americans saw. To Wise must be credited the beginnings of the interfaith movement in America. He has been called unofficial Ambassador to the Gentiles, Apostle to the Gentiles, God's Angry Prophet. The names are meaningless unless by them is conjured a man who fearlessly indicted evil and called men to action on behalf of morality, justice, civil liberties, and civil rights. Everywhere he drew tremendous, eager crowds. They respected his boldness and honesty and rallied to his support, even changing political administrations and local governments as a result of his message.

Recognition came quickly as leaders of movements for better government realized the champion they had in Stephen Wise. In 1903, he was appointed commissioner of child labor for the State of Oregon. His family also was completed here, for his son James Waterman Wise and his daughter Justine, now Judge Justine Wise Polier, were born in the great Northwest.

Such a voice, however, could not be limited to service away from the center of Jewish and civic life, New York City. In 1905, when he was 31, famed Emanu-El Temple of New York, known as the "Cathedral Synagogue of the Country" invited Wise to deliver a series of trial sermons. With some misgivings he came, completely conquering the membership and officers. A committee consisting of leaders of American Jewish life and masters of industry—Louis Marshall, James Seligman, M. H. Moses, Daniel Guggenheim and Isaac Spielberg—called upon Wise and offered him the pulpit. The scene must have been an interesting one—to see these distinguished, affluent leaders of men asking this young, dynamic rabbi to lead them. Stephen Wise, never one to be overawed by names, but impressed only by ideals and principles, spoke forthrightly: "You are calling me to be the rabbi of Emanu-El. I am not a preacher or scholar of note, but you have heard that I have gained for my temple, Beth Israel, my people throughout Oregon, and their rabbi, the respect and, for the most part, the good will of the entire Northwest community. If I have achieved that, it has been because in my inaugural sermon at Beth Israel, September, 1900, I declared, "The pulpit must be free."

Louis Marshall, himself a towering Jewish figure, of whom it had been said that "Temple Emanu-El lives under Marshall Law," responded: "Dr. Wise, I must say to you at once that such condition cannot be complied with; the pulpit of Emanu-El has always been and is subject to and under the control of the board of trustees."

Wise retorted with aplomb: "If that be true, gentlemen, there is nothing more to say."

While the interview continued, the die had been cast. Wise's firm stand was expressed brilliantly and with unparalleled frankness and honesty. Few others would have dared to speak with such candor. When asked what he meant by a free pulpit, Wise declared: "I have in Oregon been among the leaders of a civic reform movement in my community. Mr. Moses, if it be true, as I have heard it rumored, that your nephew, Mr. Herman, is to be a Tammany Hall candidate for a Supreme Court judgeship, I would, if I were Emanu-El's rabbi, oppose his candidacy in and out of my pulpit. . . . Mr. Guggenheim, as a member of the child labor commission of the State of Oregon, I must say to you that if it ever came to be known that children were being employed in your mines, I would cry out against such wrong. Mr. Marshall, the press stated that you and your firm are to be counsel for Mr. Hyde of the Equitable Life Assurance Society. That may or may not be true, but, knowing that Charles Evans Hughes' investigation of insurance companies in New York has been a very great service, I would in and out of my pulpit speak in condemnation of the crimes committed by the insurance thieves."

Members of the board continued to visit with Wise during the following week, seeking to dissuade him from his adamant position, but to no avail. His mind was made up and he was blessed with the encouragement of his noble wife, who said simply, "You had no other choice."

The entire matter had not ended, however. Wise was yet to have the last word in an unprecedented pronouncement. News of the experience preceded Wise back to Portland, and he unhesitatingly revealed the entire incident to his congregation. The contents of his address were telegraphed to New York and Louis Marshall felt moved to deny on a technicality that an offer had been made to Wise. The youthful preacher in response poured his heart and soul into an open letter which has become a classic declaration of principles:

I write to you because I believe that a question of supereminent importance has been raised, the question whether the pulpit shall be free or whether the pulpit shall not be free, and by reason of its loss of freedom, reft of its power for good. The whole position of the churches is involved in this question, for the steadily waning influence of church and synagogue is due in no small part, I hold, to the widespread belief that the pulpit is not free. . . .

The chief office of the minister, I take it, is not to represent the views of the congregation, but to proclaim the truth as he sees it. How can he serve a congregation as a teacher save as he quickens the minds of his hearers by the vitality and independence of his utterances? But how can a man be vital and independent and helpful if he be tethered and muzzled? A free pulpit, worthily filled, must command respect and influence; a pulpit that is not free, howsoever filled, is sure to be without potency and honor. A free pulpit will sometimes stumble into error; a pulpit that is not free can never powerfully plead for truth and righteousness. In the pursuit of the duties of his office, the minister may from time to time be under the necessity of giving expression to views at variance with the views of some, or even many, members of the congregation. Far from such difference proving the pulpit to be in the wrong, it may be, and ofttimes is, found to signify that the pulpit has done its duty in calling evil evil and good good, in abhorring the moral wrong of putting light for darkness and darkness for light, and in scorning to limit itself to the utterance of what the prophet has styled "smooth things," lest variance of views arise. Too great a dread there may be of secession on the part of some members of the congregation, for, after all, difference and disquiet, even schism at the worst, are not so much to be feared as that attitude of the pulpit which never provokes dissent because it is cautious rather than courageous, peace-loving rather than prophetic, time-serving rather than right-serving. The minister is not to be the spokesman of the congregation, not the message-bearer *of* the congregation, but the bearer of a message *to* the congregation. What the contents of that message shall be must be left to the conscience and understanding and loyalty of him in whom a congregation places sufficient confidence to elect him to minister to it. . . .

The Jewish minister, I repeat, does not speak ex cathedra, and his views are not supposed to have a binding force upon the congregation to which he ministers. He is to express his convictions on any subject that comes within the purview of religion and ethics, but these convictions do not purport to constitute a creed or dogma to which a congregation must in whole or in part subscribe. . . .

While Stephen Wise did not accept the call to Emanu-El, destiny had already carved him out for ministrations in New York City. Prior to going to New York, he had expressed the hope that the time would come when he would call into being a Free Synagogue which would reflect his passionate thinking and feeling about Judaism and allow him without hindrance or stifling to speak his mind and conscience as he saw fit. His very nature would demand such a pulpit. Accordingly, in 1906, much to the unhappiness of his congregation in Portland, which had in the meantime offered him a lifetime contract at an unprecedented salary, the call back East asserted itself and drew him. He resigned, returned to New York, and with a few adherents and friends founded the Free Synagogue. Services were at first held in the Hudson Theater near Times Square, and later in Carnegie Hall. The organization of such an institution did not sit well with all rabbis or religious groups in the city. Both left and right inveighed against him. Wise, however, true to his principles and firm in his determination, persevered. The Free Synagogue idea was not known or understood, and Wise was moved to explain:

> I made clear beyond all doubt that the Free Synagogue would never become a retreat or asylum for faint-hearted and pusillanimous Jews, that it was to be wholly, unequivocably, a Jewish adventure, that it would be deeply, unreservedly, and even rejoicingly Jewish.

His first address told the story of his idea. He had long felt that Judaism was becoming pulseless and lifeless; attendance at Sabbath morning services meager; knowledge of, and concern for, the Zionist cause minimal. He sought to revitalize the Synagogue in terms of his own feelings and views. The Free Synagogue was to be:

> . . . a Jewish society, for I am a Jew, a Jewish teacher. The Free Synagogue is not to be an indirect or circuitous avenue of approach to Unitarianism; it is not to be a society for the gradual conversion of Jewish men or women to any form of Christianity. We mean to be vitally, in-

tensely, unequivocally Jewish. Jews who would not be Jews will find no place in the Free Synagogue, for we, its founders, wish to be not less Jewish but more Jewish in the highest and noblest sense of the term.

The guiding principles for the Free Synagogue were named as the following:

1. Freedom of the pulpit.
   "A pulpit that is not free is without moral and spiritual meaning."
2. Democratic management and equal privileges of all members.
   "The synagogue must again become democratically managed and there could be no synagogue democracy as long as the pews and dues system obtained."
3. Inward freedom of the synagogue.
   "The synagogue must be inwardly free, free in its innermost ideals and aspirations, free to follow the high tradition of its prophetic genius. This was the beginning of my never ending revolt against that reform which had become formal and lifeless, which, after having long fought orthodoxy, had with the years become no less unvital than orthodoxy, without evoking the loyalty that the rich and traditional beauty of the synagogue at its best was still capable of commanding."
4. The synagogue's participation in the social service of the community.
   "I had felt from the beginning that a synagogue should be more than a gathering of divine worshippers and that within the synagogue's life, worship should be translated into collective and organized human service."
5. The complete indentification of the synagogue with Judaism, its faith and Israel's fate and future.

Once established, the Free Synagogue and its social division grew in stature and recognition throughout the land and world. Every area of human service became part of the division's efforts. Medical assistance, mental hygiene, employment guidance, were all part of this unique venture by a synagogue in America. Wise had pioneered an ideal into a reality and was ever its driving force. The credo of the social service division is best understood in the sensitive words of one of its leaders and benefactors, famed philanthropist Jacob Schiff, who said:

The word of God heard in the Synagogue becomes of value only if it is carried into everyday life. This is so well understood that it sounds like a commonplace to repeat it. And still how few in daily life practice this! How few stop to consider how egotistical are their lives, and that most of their acts, unknown to themselves, are done for their own personal comfort.

There is, perhaps, no more cruel principle, even though it be inexorable, than that upon which, as Herbert Spencer has expressed it, the world rests, "the survival of the fittest." Because of this we should feel that duty calls us to step in and be of help to those who are left behind in the race by reason of this inexorable rule. These we meet everywhere —in our families, among our acquaintances, in the pursuit of our daily vocations, and we so often pass them without taking notice.

In this large community how many need us, to how many can we be useful! It need not only be the sick and the needy, who perhaps more readily excite our compassion, to whom service can be rendered in many forms. To every one of our fellow-citizens, through work for the municipality, to the dependent classes, through cooperation in movements for the benefit of the dwellers in tenements, to the immigrant, to the delinquent, to numberless others who need us and to whom we can become of service.

Social Service is service to the very society of which we form an integral part, to which we owe a constant duty and in rendering service of value to society, we bestow the greatest benefit upon ourselves. It is in this spirit of benefiting all who need you that I wish you Godspeed in the work of Social Service which you are about to inaugurate. If you achieve success therein, as I doubt not you will, you will only the more largely increase the claim for recognition of the movement which your self-sacrificing leader has taken up with so much inspiring enthusiasm.

Many thousands were destined to be beneficiaries of that social service division. When it was founded and its pattern of service established, demands rose to organize branches in other areas of the city. Stephen Wise responded by establishing the Downtown East Side Free Synagogue. There, too, the response was inspiring. The Free Synagogue had become an institution. It continued to expand over the years, reaching a high point when Mrs. Stephen Wise established a child adoption center. Another pressing need had been met.

The Free Synagogue was Stephen Wise's platform for half a century, years during which there was no bolder analyst of American and Jewish affairs, no more thrilling orator. From this platform, Wise pleaded his causes, some of which were won, some of which were lost from the out-

set. But no cause, however popular or unpopular, escaped his scrutiny.
Civil rights, religious rights, protection of the weak and indigent—he
had time for all. Here, in this pulpit, Stephen Wise functioned as the
apostle of freedom for all men. And when he spoke, people listened
and newspaper reporters filed stories.

Fame came and grew as in every arena of life, Wise became a commanding figure. Jew and Christian alike looked to him for guidance and
counsel. He withheld his efforts from no just cause, from no drive
which needed support. For Judaism, for America, for the world and
humanity, Wise gave his heart and vitality.

Unlike other rabbis of the day and probably most of this day,
Stephen Wise felt deeply that the rabbi ought to be involved in politics.
He searched his soul time and again; should he or should he not enter
politics. It was unheard of then for a minister to be allied with any
political cause. Religion was religion, and there it belonged. It had
no welcome in the fields of political maneuvering. Wise—creative,
original, fearless, driven by a profound sense of justice—felt differently.
Politics was what it was because religion had withheld its spirit:

> I felt very early in my ministry the necessity and advantages of the min-
> ister going into politics. To me neither religion nor politics was remote
> or sequestered from life. Religion is a vision or ideal of life. Politics is a
> method, or *modus vivendi*. To say that the minister should not go into
> politics is to imply that ideal and reality are twain and alien. Politics is
> what it is because religion keeps out of it.
>
> I am persuaded that the minister can go into politics without partisan-
> ship, without compromise. And most important, he must seek nothing for
> himself or his church, and accept nothing. Convinced that the ideals
> of religion, separated from their day-to-day application, were meaningless,
> I early entered into one area of controversy after another that many might
> call political, and which I recognized as part of the socio-political life
> of America. There were many state, national, and international issues
> in which I felt that as a minister of religion I had a place.
>
> Throughout my life it seemed to me that all ministers of religion were
> for justice in principle, but too ready to be silent about injustices in
> practice. One of the dangers of all of us is that we are willing to fight
> for justice for ourselves alone, forgetting that justice will be for all or
> none. For me the supreme declaration of our Hebrew Bible was and
> remains: "Justice, Justice, shalt thou pursue" whether it be easy or hard,
> whether it be justice to white or black, Jew or Christian.

Convinced of these views, Stephen Wise engaged wholeheartedly in the world of politics. Thus he came into contact with the great political leaders of the century, becoming friend and guide of Presidents, who looked upon him as spokesman for the Jewish people. Friend of Wilson, Hoover, Roosevelt and Truman, Stephen Wise came to be regarded as the unofficial representative of American Jewry. He crossed political lines whenever and wherever justice demanded. He was a Theodore Roosevelt Republican but swung over to Wilson when convinced that the country could be better served by the latter. He did not hesitate to attack political evil and leadership, never fearing to mention names and places, and more than once he was responsible for the sidetracking of political aspirants and toppling of corrupt administrators.

His involvement in politics provided him with an enviable vantage point from which to perform human service. He was one of the leading supporters in the battle for voting rights and full citizenship for women in America. He encouraged bills and commissions to investigate legislation designed to benefit the old, the sick, and the unemployed. "These measures became part of my work as a minister of religion," he said. He used the pulpit to challenge the insidious work of the Ku Klux Klan and religious discrimination against a Roman Catholic candidate for the Presidency in the Hoover-Smith election of 1928.

During the presidential campaign of 1928, when Al Smith opposed Herbert Hoover, the politicians did not leave religion in the churches or to the pulpits. Religion became the central issue despite high-sounding denials by some candidates. Instead of discussion of national problems, the forum of the national election became nothing more than a nationwide whispering gallery. The foulest of methods were used by those prepared to do anything short of lawlessness in order to prevent a son of the Roman Catholic Communion from becoming President of the United States. The Klan seemed to be revived in spirit without having been brought back to life in letter.

Here was an issue, both religious and ethical, to challenge every pulpit. Too many church leaders were silent, and some men who deplored the intense bigotry that came to the surface took the position that the Democratic candidate should have been wise enough not to accept the nomination lest the church issue be injected into the campaign. This position was all but identical with the counsel too often urged upon Jews, sometimes from without and usually from within the household of Israel, that they must not do this or that, even though it be right, lest the

Jewish question be dragged into the foreground. Such counsel I had always spurned for my own people because it violated the dignity and self-respect of Jews as men and as citizens of America. It was equally abhorrent to me when applied to Al Smith. Perhaps, because I had experienced the hurt to my people of such counsel, I felt a special obligation to speak out when it was addressed to another minority group.

Where discrimination raised its ugly head, Wise was invariably vehement. He was at the forefront of every movement dedicated to its erasure. He was among the founders of the National Association for the Advancement of Colored People. He fought economic discrimination, struggled against anti-Semitism in all its ugly aspects, pleaded for a permanent Fair Employment Practices Commission, and fought the introduction of religion into the public schools.

Labor, too, found a devoted friend in Wise. He fought for better working conditions, spoke out against child labor, attacked those who abused human life by not providing safety measures for workers, strove for higher wages. He encouraged the organization of the steel workers, as he did of workingmen in other industries. He lost much support for his beloved Free Synagogue and retarded its building program by speaking thus, knowing that some of his wealthy members were guilty of injustices. But he believed firmly in this approach, basing it on the Biblical account of Nathan the Prophet who went to King David's chambers and unhesitatingly pointed, saying, "Thou art the man." When Wise was accused of sensationalism he retorted thusly:

> There are things which are absurd and sensational and vulgar in the pulpit, but that is no reason for confusing the vulgarian in the pulpit with the man who makes people think and feel aright. I for my part have found that the term sensationalist or sensation monger is oftenest applied to the men in the pulpit by those of their colleagues who have a peculiar genius for leaving their congregations undisturbed in their weekly church or synagogue slumber.
>
> Startling is another name for or an interchangeable term with sensational. Do not men need to startle? Are there not times men require to be roused, when they must be awakened out of the depths of their slumber? It was said of Tolstoy that he stabbed men awake. There are times when men need to be dynamited into wakefulness.
>
> I have never felt the need of defending myself against the charge of

sensationalism for I have known my own motives. In a world of shame, the truth bravely uttered is bound to sound sensational. I have sought the truth and aimed to further the sovereignty of righteousness among men. Within my limited powers, I have proposed to magnify the ideal of justice, and I have spoken and speak for the sake of these things and only for them.

He worked with many of the great labor and human rights leaders: Sidney Hillman, Senator Borah, Lillian Wald, Frances Perkins, Al Smith, Samuel Gompers, in halls of legislatures, local, state and federal. Early successful efforts on labor's part can be traced back directly to the devotion of this great rabbi who worked in its cause. He prided himself on his invitation from the New York Chamber of Commerce offered in 1911. He knew that many of the captains of industry would be present, and indeed they were: Andrew Carnegie, James J. Hill, J. P. Morgan, Charles Schwab, George Baker. He searched his soul. What should he do? How shall he speak? Shall he say what they want to hear, or shall he speak the truth as he sees it? "I could ingratiate myself with this august assembly and lose my soul; I could displease them and keep it." The magnificent credo itself gave him the answer. He spoke, kept his soul, and was never invited again:

When I have read from time to time of religious noonday meetings in shops and factories for the wage-earners, I have ventured to observe that the important thing is not so much to bring religious ministration to the daily toilers—the soldiers of the common good—as to bring it to the captains of industry, and commerce, which you are. For the con-science of the nation, after all, will be that which you make it,—yours is the high and solemn duty not only of registering, but in large part of determining the character of the conscience of the nation. . . .

Not only ought the barter or trade side of business be completely moralized, but we need to ethicize what might be called the processes of creating and production, of distribution and consumption. No business order is just nor can it long endure if it be bound up with the evil of un-employment on the one hand and over-employment on the other, the evil of a man's under-wage and a child's toil, and all those social malad-justments incidental to our order which we lump together under the name of poverty. Let us not imagine that we can shift to the shoulders of overworked charity the burdens that can be borne only by the strength of underworked justice. Yes, the stricken ask not the occasional tonic of charity, but the daily meat and substance of justice. We are never to forget that ours is a democracy, that a democracy, in the words of a high servant of the commonwealth, means "the use of all the resources of nature by all the faculties of man for the good of all the people. . . ."

The conscience of the nation is not real unless the nation safeguard the workingman, safeguard him from the peril of overwork, as well as from the occasional accidents of industry. The conscience of the nation is not vital unless we protect women and children in industry, and protect them with half the thoroughness and generosity with which, for many decades, we have protected infant industries. We have not the right to speak of the importance of conserving the opportunity for initiative on the part of the individual as long as masses of individuals are suffered to perish without the opportunity of real life. The aim of democracy is not to be the production of efficient, machine-like men in industry. The first business of democracy is to be the industry of turning out completely effective, because completely free and self-determining, citizens.

Whatever may have been Stephen Wise's heavy involvement and massive contributions to every arena of human endeavor, home base was still his people and faith. That was the rock from which Wise was hewn and from which he drew his strength.

Together with other great names in American Jewish history—Justice Louis Brandeis, Julian Mack, Felix Frankfurter, Pinchas Rutenberg, Louis Lipsky, Bernard Richards, and Nathan Straus—Stephen Wise felt that the time had come when a democratically elected body of Jewish representatives ought to be spokesmen for the Jewish people. No persons, or groups, they felt, had the right to speak *for* American Jews unless they were prepared to speak *with* American Jews. The World War was going on. There would be need for conferences after the war to protect rights of Jewish people among the councils of nations. The protection of these rights could come only from democratically elected representatives. Thus, Wise was in the forefront in the battle for Jewish democracy. A preliminary conference was held in Philadelphia on March 26, 1916, and Stephen Wise delivered the keynote address in which he said:

This day is destined to be memorable in the annals of Israel—the more because we are thinking not of ourselves alone, nor for ourselves, but after the Jewish manner, of and for all Israel. . . .

We again solemnly aver that a people is not worthy of respect which does not insist on the right to be heard touching its own affairs, but surrenders the right of judgment and decision to a company of men, however wise and benevolent, who substitute their own opinions and wishes for the convictions and determinations of the whole Jewish people. . . .

The world cannot be expected to assent to any program touching Israel's future as long as Israel does not unitedly deliberate and speak. Secrecy, always futile as a curative method, has proven disastrous in prolonging and intensifying Jewish woes. We now freely discuss our will where aforetime we furtively listened to the edict of others. A Congress means deliberation not agitation, discussion not division, enlightenment not secrecy. . . .

The only program acceptable to the men in control of our affairs has been a program of palliation, as if nothing more than temporary relief could be hoped for Israel, wounded and oppressed. Relief, alas, is at times sorely needed, was never more needed than today. But relief is not to be exalted as the policy or program of a people unless these be hopeless beggars and that people adopt a program of relief as the only way out. Not relief but redress, not palliation but prevention, not charity but justice . . . is the only program worthy of a great and proud people.

One year later, June 10, 1917, 335,000 Jewish men and women went to the polls to choose their representatives to the first American Jewish Congress, which met in Philadelphia on December 15, 1918. The Congress adopted programs for submission to the peace conference in Versailles, sent delegates to represent the Jewish people, and began a series of major undertakings and programs destined over the years to bring security to Jewish life, aid in the struggle for the establishment of a Jewish national home and give meaning to the realization of American democracy.

The Congress has played a consistently important role in the shaping of American affairs and in the constant battle for justice and equality for all races and peoples in America. Stephen Wise was its president throughout his life.

Home base meant more. He was for many years unhappy with the development of the various movements in Judaism at the beginning of the century. Each of the three groups, and the seminaries which represented them, he felt had deficiencies which had to be corrected. He was especially concerned because Zionism, which to him was interchangeable with Judaism, was not being explicitly emphasized. Moreover, he felt that rabbinical students ought to have adequate college education before concentrating on theological studies. He wanted to train rabbis to carry on the work he had begun, especially in the social service field. Accordingly, he took steps to found the Jewish Institute of Religion in 1922, bringing to it an impressive faculty which included Dr. George Alexander Kohut, Dr. Alexander Kohut, Dr. Ismar Elbogen, Dr. Israel Abrahams, and Rabbi Harry Lewis. Modesty prevented Wise from accepting the presidency and for years he served as acting president. He stated his views in the founding of this new seminary to train rabbis for service in the rabbinate, for contributing to Jewish learning, and for community service, leaving the faculty and student body free, not merely in the matter of ritual observance, but intellectually and spiritually free in accordance with undogmatic liberalism, which to him was the heart and genius of Judaism. He wrote:

> It had come to be recognized—in any event by us, the founders of the Jewish Institute of Religion—that the old differences and quarrels and even battles over creed were of little moment by the side of the consciousness of the deepening need of Jewishness. For us, Jewishness meant and means a sense of oneness with our Jewish brothers in all lands and times, whatever their circumstances, their so-called faith or unfaith. Jewishness meant loyalty to historic Jewish ideals—spiritual, moral, social, intellectual. Jewishness could only be perpetuated through understanding and appreciation of the best that has been thought and said and done throughout thirty centuries and more of Jewish history. This Jewishness of life and loyalty was the bond that linked us alike with the storied centuries of the past and with our people's deathless hopes and dreams for the future.

The new seminary was "animated by the purpose to welcome within its walls teachers and students who would alike be free, in teaching and learning. . . ." It "required no commitment of teacher or disciple save to communicate and master the fundamental and historic truths of Jewish life and letters. It welcomed students from all groups within Jewish life and trained rabbis for service in Reform, Orthodox and Conservative congregations."

The Jewish Institute of Religion continued to exist until 1948, when, at long last, Wise's dream of Israel reborn had been fulfilled. It was merged at that time with the Hebrew Union College, but not until Wise had made certain that the basic principles of J. I. R. would always be retained and respected.

Over the years, many students entered the portals of the unique institution, drew inspiration from the fiery flame of Stephen Wise's burning soul, and, spread throughout the land in pulpits, ignited the flame in other hearts. The flame continues to burn as rabbis share knowledge gained from masters, which included also Professors Chaim Tchernowitz, Henry Slonimsky, Harry A. Wolfson, David Yellin, Adolph Gressman, Charles Torrey, Charles Albright, Gershon Sholem, Rabbi Joshua Loth Liebman, Reverend Doctor James Parkes, and many other great thinkers, philosophers, and scholars.

His magnificent words to the last commencement class tell of his faith and reflect the warmth and love he felt for his students:

> I have been thinking of a new way of translating that phrase I love, the words of the second chapter of the Prophet Ezekiel: "Son of man, stand upon thine own feet and I will speak not with thee, *but through thee.*" Remember, you must strengthen the infirm, you must reassure the timid, you must rebuke the cowardly. Remember, you are teachers in Israel; you have not only the right to speak frankly, simply, sincerely to those who hear you in your congregations, but you must speak as men to your fellow Americans of Christian faith. When they deserve your praise, praise them, but when you must speak harshly and bitterly, be not afraid. Sometimes it is more important to utter the clearest dispraise of that which is wrong than to speak in terms of praise, even when that praise is deserved.
>
> This be my last word to you if we never meet again. God speak not to you chiefly or alone, but through you to your congregation, to your people, to American Israel. I part with you in sorrow but with limitless hope and with a deep affection for you, my dear boys. And I pray that the God of our fathers may bless you, bless you now and always.

Two previous paragraphs of this message tell of Stephen Wise's historic, eternal, everlasting contribution to the Jewish people—his blessed leadership in the cause of restoring the Jewish people to Zion. In this cause he ranks alongside Herzl, Nordau, Sokolow, Weizmann, Lipsky, Ben Zvi, Ben Gurion.

Laugh at those who speak of dual loyalties and divided allegiance. We have an allegiance to the spiritual heritage of a great and imperishable people. We have another allegiance to the people of our great country, of whom we are a part. There is no divided allegiance. There is a transcending allegiance crowning and glorifying both.

If men say to you, ask of you, "Are you a citizen of the State of Israel?" or "Are you a citizen of the American Republic and teacher of its people?" answer them, "The memories, the traditions, the hopes, the dreams, the sufferings, the sorrows of four thousand years have not sundered me from the blood and the race of the people of Israel. I am one of them. As a citizen I belong wholly to America. America is my country and I have none other. To it I give the utmost of my loyalty, the deepest of my love, the truest of my service."

"I am one of them," said Wise—a simple, dramatic assertion, as pregnant with meaning and feeling as Jonah's "I am a Hebrew and I fear the Lord," or Joseph's "I seek my brethren" and "I am Joseph!" Stephen Wise, one of the few Reform rabbis at the beginning of the century to espouse the cause of Zionism, worked tirelessly behind the scenes with Zionist leaders, British statesmen, and American Presidents and diplomats. The story of Zionism reborn and Israel restored is the story of Wise, Herzl, Nordau, Weizmann, Lipsky, and Sokolow. It is the story of Wise, Lord Balfour, and Ben Gurion. It is the story of Wise, Woodrow Wilson, Franklin Roosevelt, Louis D. Brandeis. It is the story of Wise and Harry S. Truman, whose name especially stands out, since it was he who proclaimed America's recognition of the State of Israel in May of 1948, less than fifteen minutes after Israel declared herself a state. The story of Zionism is the story of Stephen S. Wise. Long, long will the shadow of Stephen S. Wise be cast over the greatest event in Jewish history since the destruction of the Holy Temple in 70 C. E.

His "I am one of them" dates back to his earliest days. Memories of his pious grandmother, who insisted on going to the Holy Land to die, are among the roots of his love for Israel. She wrote:

I must go to the Holy Land. I go not to live there but to die there. There I wish to pray; and there to die, to be laid to rest amid the sacred dust of Jerusalem; to be buried on the slope facing the Holy of Holies.

In his father's rabbinical home he heard night after night stories of the suffering endured by his people, how they were tortured, how they sought escape to America, how they longed for a haven of refuge.

My Zionism I owed chiefly to my father. It may have been in my blood, but it was the tide of his devotion which bore it to the heart of my being. My father, without being strictly Orthodox as was his father, was an ardent Zionist, and his Zionism is one of the earliest and sweetest memories of my life. As very young children in our home, we got our first lesson in saving and giving in connection with the humble ambassadors from the land of Israel, into whose little tin cups we placed our scant savings, that these, in turn, might be given to satisfy needs in the Holy Land.

He attended the Second Zionist Congress in Basle, Switzerland in August, 1898, and was at once completely enraptured by the towering personality of Theodor Herzl, founder of modern Zionism. "He stood like a man before kings and he looked like a king among men," Wise said. He describes the experience of his service as a delegate. He is 24 years of age.

At Basle I made a twofold discovery. Joseph, the Bible relates, said, "I seek my brothers." Without seeking, I yet found my brothers. It may be that I should qualify the words "without seeking" for I, a Zionist, consciously and with the utmost deliberation, had chosen to be a delegate. To that extent, it might be said that I sought my brothers out. Whether or not I sought them out, I found my brothers. I found not simply a collection of Jews bent on the high ends of Zionism but an assemblage of fellow Jews united by a single and exalted purpose—and my brothers.

Before meeting them, I barely knew that they existed save as a name, as a group with whom I had become closely associated under the impact of the Zionist movement. Not only did I find my brothers, but by the same token I found myself. . . .

I journeyed to Basle merely as a delegate to a conference. I returned home a lifetime servant of the cause in the name and for the sake of which the Congress was assembled. I caught the first glimpse of my people as a people, gathered from many lands, one and undivided, not in creed but in their human faith. This faith was that the tragic dispersal of Israel must end, that the miraculous survival of the Jewish people did not forever guarantee survival in an increasingly hostile world, and that the ancient home of Palestine could and must be rebuilt. We were united by the faith that despite partial dispersion in many parts of the world the survival of the Jewish people and the revival of its creative genius could only come to pass in the land of ancient glory, which needed to be awakened from its centuries-old and enfeebling slumber. This newly gained conviction became and remained the lodestar of my life.

Indeed it did. It was the beginning of the great adventure of his life. Enemies of Zionism were legion. Many were his close friends—leaders of the Jewish community, philanthropists, affluent supporters. He cared not. The principle was far more important than any offense he might give. The inspiration of Theodor Herzl, who became a close friend and correspondent, inflamed him. Herzl prophetically had said to Wise in 1904: "I shall not live to see the Jewish State. But you, Wise, are a young man. You will live to see the Jewish State."

One can almost picture the scene. The stately black-bearded journalist, who had emerged as Zionism's brightest star in centuries, as he looks out a window into the future and says to the young rising star in his Viennese accent, "You will see the land of Israel." How Wise must have been moved and thrilled!

His youth and vitality carried him all over America to tell Jewish and Christian audiences the dramatic story of Zionism. His first trip to Palestine in 1913 kept the flame burning as he saw with his own eyes the beginning of fulfillment. He founded the first Zionist organization, becoming one of its prime movers. He was a friend of Woodrow Wilson and of Louis D. Brandeis, both of whom were significantly involved in the planning and execution of the now famed Balfour Declaration, issued in November of 1917, in which Britain announced that it viewed with favor the establishment of a Jewish national home in Palestine. The declaration was two years in the making, a period in which Wise's astute diplomacy was instrumental in bringing it to glorious fruition. Stephen Wise, Chaim Weizmann and Justice Brandeis played leading roles, as did Dr. Gaster of the Spanish-Portuguese Synagogue in London, Woodrow Wilson, and Prime Minister David Lloyd George.

I had taken occasion to give to President Wilson, even before his inauguration, a rather full outline of Zionism. From the very beginning of his administration, Brandeis and I knew that in Wilson we had and would always have understanding sympathy with the Zionist program and purpose. I have always felt that his sympathetic attitude grew in large part out of filial reverence for his parson father, the Reverend

Thomas Wilson, in the manse of whose Staunton, Virginia, pastorate Woodrow was born. I recall a word of his which made clear that he felt and acted herein at times as his father's son. As I urged him one day to cooperate with the British government re the hope of the Balfour Declaration, he was touched, and soliloquized aloud, "To think that I, son of the manse, should be able to help restore the Holy Land to its people. . . ."

Toward the end of June, 1917, when I went to see the President concerning plans to convene the first session of the American Jewish Congress, we again discussed Zionism. He said at that time, "You know of my deep interest in Zionism. . . ." He then said, "Whenever the time comes, and you and Justice Brandeis feel that the time is ripe for me to speak and act, I shall be ready."

In October of 1917, Wilson received the Balfour Declaration for final approval. The British government, before making the manifesto public, had stipulated that Wilson give his assent. The President sent it to Justice Brandeis who in turn forwarded it to Wise. Wise and Jacob DeHaas suggested a change in the document from "national home for Jews" to "national home for the Jewish people." Colonel House agreed. The declaration was ready to make and change the course of history.

Stephen S. Wise was the vehicle through which President Woodrow Wilson publicly announced his support of the Balfour Declaration. The means selected was the advent of the Jewish New Year. The Rosh Hashanah message would reflect Wilson's and American agreement to the pronouncement and incorporate almost exactly the words of the Declaration. Here is the letter Woodrow Wilson sent:

August 31, 1918

My dear Rabbi Wise:

I have watched with deep and sincere interest the reconstruction work which the Weizmann Commission has done in Palestine at the instance of the British Government and I welcome an opportunity to express the satisfaction I have felt in the progress of the Zionist movement in the United States and in the Allied countries since the declaration of Mr. Balfour on behalf of the British Government, of Great Britain's approval of the establishment in Palestine of a national home for the Jewish people, and his promise that the British government would use its best endeavors to facilitate the achievement of that object, with the understanding that nothing would be done to prejudice the civil and religious rights

of non-Jewish people in Palestine or the rights and political status enjoyed
by Jews in other countries. I think that all America will be deeply moved
by the report that even in this time of stress the Weizmann Commission
has been able to lay the foundation of the Hebrew University of Jerusalem
with the promise that that bears of spiritual rebirth.

Cordially and sincerely,
WOODROW WILSON

The announcement brought limitless joy and happiness to all Jewry.
There were, however, objectors, and Wise, hearing of planned protest
meetings and complaints on the part of well-known Jews, made haste
to meet with Wilson and assure him of the correctness of his position
and its acceptance by the vast majority of the Jewish people. With obvious delight he relates a behind-the-scenes story of opposition to the
Balfour Declaration in England and how the Prime Minister handled it:

Sir Charles Henry told me, in December, 1918, the story of Lloyd
George's bidding Lady Henry, "Julia, get together at breakfast the Jewish
members of both Houses of Parliament who are opposed to my Zionist
position that I may convince them of the rightfulness of it and the wrong
of their own." She did just that. A *minyan* (Jewish religious quorum of
ten) was assembled at breakfast to meet the Prime Minister. After bidding
Julia, "Bring me a Bible," which happily was to be found, he thumbed
its pages, reading passage after passage from the Hebrew Prophets,
prophesying the restoration of Zion to the Jewish people and of the Jewish
people to Zion. Triumphantly, he closed with these words to the Jewish
members of Parliament, "Now, gentlemen, you know what your Bible
says. That closes the matter."

But Wise drove on, realizing that the task had just begun. The statement was just an announcement of principle. It had to be implemented.
Many more years of concerted labor and effort—political maneuverings,
behind-the-scenes lobbying, personal conferences with great statesmen
of the day—lay ahead. Wise introduced Chaim Weizmann to Woodrow
Wilson in Paris. When the San Remo Conference awarded the Palestine
Mandate to Britain, Stephen Wise wrote to the President:

My first impulse upon learning of the consummation of our hope is to
write to you and to express to you the deep and abiding gratitude of the
Jewish people, for whom I speak, for all you have done to make this great
consummation possible.

Jewish history, which is the history not of a day but of centuries, will never fail to make mention of the great and generous service which you were ever ready to render to the cause of a national homeland for the Jewish people.

The American Jewish Congress lent its wholehearted support to Zionism. While dedicated to the protection of Jewish rights, the Congress delegations knew that Zionism stood for the safety and security of Jewish people. As president, Wise forcefully led the many conferences which were held, especially those conducted in European lands. Leaders of Jewish thought and great Jewish statesmen met, and Wise was there.

The arrival of Hitler on the scene of history in the early '30's brought out in Wise even more fervent devotion to the causes of Jewish relief and Zionism. He was among the first, and the few, to foresee the magnitude of the evil which was to spread. For 20 long, hellish years, Wise dealt with Hitlerism. His foresight impelled him to act. He once said of those who did not accept his analysis of the forthcoming tragedy: "The penalty of foresight is always inflicted upon the foreseeing by the blind, whom foresight reproaches and exacerbates but never teaches."

When the famous Madison Square Garden demonstration in March, 1933, described in the early pages of this chapter, was announced, many pleaded with Wise not to pressure Germany by an open display of this kind. Even the German embassy in Washington telephoned Wise, urging him not to go through with the plans. Wise, resolved to go forward, nevertheless consulted Justice Brandeis, who unhesitatingly responded: "Go ahead and make the protest as good as you can."

Wise also lent support to the massive boycott of German goods, as he did to every endeavor of resistance to Hitlerism, leading the American Jewish Congress into ways of uniting the Jewish people against Hitlerism.

In one of the addresses he made when he returned from Europe and saw what was happening and what would happen, he roared:

. . . When will American civilization challenge Hitlerism? My answer, the answer not of a Jew but of an American is: America will and ought to challenge Hitlerism, not with guns, not with arms, not by enmity, but by the voice of the President of the United States. It is a mighty voice, a magic voice, it is the one most potent voice in the whole world. God give it that for the sake of civilization, for his own sake, the President's mighty voice may yet be raised in one of the critically decisive hours of human need in human history. Up to this time America has not yet ranged itself alongside of the forces of civilization. It cannot, it does not and it will not sympathize with Hitlerism and all that Hitlerism means. Some day, it may be soon, that voice *must* be lifted in no uncertain terms. And after it shall have been, with a new faith, and a new loyalty, we shall thank God for America, our country, and for its leader, our President.

Franklin Roosevelt did speak out and the world heard the President's magnetic voice intone words which Stephen Wise had prepared and written to him. On January 15, 1937, just before Roosevelt's second inauguration, Wise wrote to F.D.R.:

As a result of your great leadership, our country did not forget those whom economic breakdown left without means—twenty to forty million people whom you refused to permit America to forget and to forsake. Oh! that you might say one word, dear Chief, on Wednesday to the effect that, wide as are the boundaries of our land, there is no room for forgotten men. Every American citizen is the subject of his country's interest and concern. Nor will the American Democracy ever hold any faithful and law-abiding group within its borders to be superfluous.

That, after all, is your conviction, and you have lived and led by virtue of that faith. I beg this of you because your words next Wednesday will, of course, be listened to by the whole world and will serve as the inaugural of what I know will be an administration of worldwide influence for justice and for peace throughout the world.

On January 23, 1937, the President wrote to Wise:

Dear Stephen Wise:
Yours of January fifteenth came just in the nick of time—i.e., when I was going over the final draft of the Inaugural speech. Your sentence, as you will have noticed, was included verbatim!

As ever yours,
FRANKLIN DELANO ROOSEVELT

Wise frequently spoke and counseled with Franklin Delano Roosevelt, to whose White House office he had almost free access, seeking help for his brethren in Germany and in countries which one by one fell under the trampling feet of the Nazi regime, ever tireless in his efforts to find ways of saving Jewish people from crematoria and concentration camps.

One of the bitterest experiences of his life was contained in his attempt to save Jewish lives in Poland. In 1943, word reached him that some 70,000 Jews in France and Rumania could be saved and some Polish Jews moved into Hungary. The condition: money. Money would have to be deposited in the names of Nazi officials in Switzerland to be available to them after the war. Wise went to Roosevelt to discuss the matter. It was a daring plan, and he hesitated to bring it to the President's attention. But he did, assuring Roosevelt that the Nazi mercenaries would never benefit from the money. The President's immediate reply is classic: "Stephen, why don't you go ahead and do it?"

When Wise explained that he did not feel secure in broaching the plan to Secretary of the Treasury Henry Morgenthau, F.D.R. quickly telephoned Morgenthau and said: "This is a very fair proposal which Stephen makes about ransoming Jews out of Poland into Hungary."

Secretary of State Hull also knew about it, and the Treasury approved the plan. Five months—long, hard months—were to elapse before foreign funds licenses were finally issued. Wise always felt that thousands of lives could have been saved and the Jewish catastrophe partially averted had action been taken at once. It was always a sore hurt to him.

Unfalteringly, however, Wise held aloft the banner of Zionism. Nor did he refrain from speaking out against Britain when she began to backtrack on the Balfour Declaration and scuttle Zionism by the issuance of the infamous White Paper. He met often with leaders of Britain, in the company of Ben Gurion and Weizmann. There was to be no compromise with the fundamental principle of Jewish peoplehood and the re-establishment of a Jewish commonwealth in Palestine. He insisted on the fullest implementation of the Mandate and the Balfour Declaration, keeping watch at all times to safeguard the democratic character of the Zionist movement.

Happily, Stephen S. Wise lived to see the establishment of the State of Israel. He sent to President Harry S. Truman a detailed memorandum, outlining the reasons for United States recognition to be made swiftly and surely. Like Moses he was not, however, destined to set foot on it as a Jewish state. Nevertheless, his dream had been fulfilled. He had labored with all his heart and soul for Zion, and his cup of joy must have been filled to overflowing on that fateful November 29, 1947, when delegates to the United Nations voted for the establishment of the State of Israel.

Shortly thereafter, in April of 1948, at the convention of the American Jewish Congress, Stephen Wise, tribune of his people, summoned his people:

Thus we go forth and forward together. We go forward to battle for the survival of Israel and the revival of its faith. We go forward in order to build a Jewish homeland in Eretz Israel. We go forward to deepen and strengthen the foundations of American democracy. We go forward to build the foundations of world peace.

When he reached his 75th birthday, all the world, Christian and Jew, rich and poor, acknowledged his greatness as they paid tribute to him for his massive contribution to Judaism and to mankind. His adoring wife died in December of 1947, and Stephen Wise joined her one and a half years later.

Though he was not rabbi of a parish congregation, Wise, more than any other rabbi, raised the spirit of the Jew and showed him how to speak out for the right and not to be afraid so long as he was on the side of justice and righteousness and morality.

His memory, engraved in history, will endure as long as the Jewish people live. His memory will go on forever, as long as prophets preach the principles of justice and righteousness. His memory will be blessed so long as the democratic principles upon which America is based are taught and practiced. The man who wrote with fervor, "I want to speak the truth, but it must be my truth, my deepest, truest truth—almost my ultimate truth," must live on, and will. The great humanitarian who wrote with spirit: "No man hates the wrong and shall hit it harder than I do," must live on and will.

Stephen Wise was honored time and time again. Tributes flowed to him. Honorary doctorates were offered, and France bestowed membership in the coveted Legion of Honor upon him. Perhaps the greatest tributes paid to him are mentioned in his writings to his dearly beloved wife, to whom he poured out his greatest love and to whom he constantly looked for inspiration and sustenance. There were two incidents which particularly impressed him. One concerned a poor little Jewish newsboy who came up to him in Philadelphia in 1919 and said, "I know who you are and what you have done for the Jews. God keep you alive for the sake of our people." The second concerned Melville Elijah Stone, founder of the Chicago *Daily News,* who said of him at a luncheon, "Dr. Wise does not belong to the Free Synagogue; he belongs to the nation. We Christians have an equal right to him."

In Israel, thousands upon thousands of fruit trees stand as a tribute to his mighty stature. A village named Gan Shmuel (*Gan* means garden and Shmuel was Stephen's Hebrew name) honors his unparalleled service and devotion to Zion's cause.

His last letter, written to his children, which they saw only after his passing, reveals the deepest feelings and sentiments of the man—the loving husband, adoring father, devoted grandfather, faithful friend and servant of God:

> I am not tearful or maudlin as I write this, but I am so wretched that I would be insensitive and stupid not to write as I do. When something happens to me, Ed knows about the things I prefer for the Service [Edward Klein was then associate, later rabbi, of the Free Synagogue].
>
> Ed, of course, is to have charge of the Service, whether at the Synagogue House or in Carnegie Hall, where I preached for thirty years and with which I became associated during the stronger years of my life—or, best of all, in the new building.
>
> In view of the large part which the [American Jewish] Congress and Zionism have had in my life, I think that, just as in the case of Mummie, I would like Dave [Petegorsky] to speak the word of farewell if he were equal to it. Dave [executive director of the Congress] has grown very dear to me. He knows what it is that I most deeply care for: the State of Israel and freedom and justice for Jews everywhere. If an address is to be made, it shall be made by Dave. He has become very dear to me and he is a loyal and faithful comrade.
>
> I would like a prayer or the reading of a poem by my beloved friend, Holmes.
>
> You won't see this while I am alive. When you do see it, I beg you to understand that my release, whenever it comes, is a great mercy. I am far from well and comfortable. As you know, I hate to leave you both and Shad and Helen and my precious grandchildren, but I feel time is drawing very near for me to go Home. If God will, it will mean the reunion of my spirit with that of Mummie's, and you know that I want my dust to be placed in the niche wherein she lies.

All love forever to you who have taken such wonderful care of me and will do so, I know, to my end, whenever it is to be. You will love and care for each other always.

Into the Hand of God I commend my spirit. May He continue to vouchsafe me His grace and mercy.

SAUL SILBER

Gentle Fighter of the West

[1881-1946]

Behold him, with Knowledge stored abundantly within his soul.
The Law speaks loud through him, the deep toned words,
Leaving an impress of authority.
His lips are steeped in wisdom handed down
In golden links, unbroke from sire to son,—
Long-treasured race traditions, still to live,
And living, pass through ages yet unborn.
So with his glowing words of metaphor
Grows green the Old Faith's beauty.

The words are from a folio of the Talmud
recorded almost 2000 years ago. The language is English, the everyday
tongue of our country. Both the old and the new combine to tell the story
of the little giant of faith who in his lifetime fought strenuously, persistently and self-sacrificingly to blend the old and the new. There was
to be no erasure of the old. The Torah, as taught by Judaism throughout
time, was to remain inviolate. Its teaching was immutable. But it needed
to be brought into clearer focus and perspective. American civilization
had to be dealt with constructively and blended into the traditional
Judaism of the ages. The Torah was to remain the canvas on which
American Jewish life was to be superimposed. However, both could be
synthesized for the American Jew, whose strength as well as his future
lay in the melting of the two into a unifying force. So held Saul Silber,

the dynamic spirit of Orthodox Judaism at the beginning of the 20th century in America's growing Midwest.

His passport describes him as five feet seven in height; complexion, light; eyes, brown; hair, dark brown. His passport picture suggests firmness tempered by gentleness. His dark, penetrating eyes beneath bushy brows communicate understanding and deep feeling. A neatly trimmed beard barely covers a strong chin.

Silber was a new type of Orthodox rabbi. His perception of American Jewish life, his understanding of American ideals, and his knowledge of American thought, gained him entrance into every sphere of life, non-Jewish as well as Jewish. He moved easily in every circle, professional, business, political; the lawyer's office, judge's chambers, factory and store. With equal dexterity he communicated with scholar or businessman; tradesman or worker, mingling freely with the Orthodox and Reform. Doors opened for him that had previously been closed to Orthodoxy's representatives. His pungent humor and delicate irony found their mark as he criticized constructively, whether employing the written or spoken word. Having deserved the respect of all in his position as spokesman for Orthodox Judaism in Chicago and the great Midwest, Silber transformed the image of the Orthodox rabbi, thus serving to glorify Israel. Contributors to Orthodox Judaism were impressed by this new symbol of the ancient faith, and Saul Silber took advantage of the respect he won so easily for his people's good as he drew unto him an ever increasing circle of businessmen who theretofore had little or no association with traditional Judaism. They became the financial backbone of the traditional Yeshivah he came to lead as president and of many newly organized Jewish charitable institutions and movements. Judaism is being served today through the hundreds of students who have been graduated with traditional ordination and who function throughout the length and breadth of America carrying on the traditional faith. Thus Saul Silber lives on through his students.

Family environment and early intensive Yeshivah training molded the mind, heart, and future destiny of Saul Silber. Life began for this matchless champion of the Torah on March 15, 1881, in the little village of Alexandronsky, near Mariampol, Kovno, Lithuania. His parents were simple working folk, but their religious fervor, love of learning and devout observance of the traditions brushed off on Saul. As it was for other young boys of his day, his Jewish education was intense and complete. His quick, eager mind conquered Torah study easily and moved on to master Talmudic lore. At ten, his family having moved to Dvinsk earlier, he entered the Yeshivah of that city and studied under renowned Rabbis Yom Tov Lipman and Nahum Fefferman. Fortunate for American Judaism and Jewry was the unique seminary environment in which Saul studied. In other seminaries, the Talmud was studied to the almost complete exclusion of Biblical and other literature. The emphasis was on the legalistic, Halachic aspects of Talmud. Saul's education differed. It included Midrash or folkloristic and homiletical aspects as well. Thus, his background, combined with his own qualities of sensitivity and attraction to the poetic and fanciful, provided for him a wider frame than that of most of his contemporaries for the accumulation of knowledge.

When he was 16 years old, in 1897, he matriculated at the Yeshivah at Lida. This Yeshivah, unlike most others, included Biblical and literary studies. Saul quickly submitted to the influence of one of the greatest sages of the generation, Rabbi Jacob Reines, founder of Mizrachi, the religious Zionist organization. That year was marked by spirited activity among Jews throughout the world. Zionism, with Herzl leading, was sweeping the world. Rabbi Reines, founder of the Yeshivah in Lida, was sympathetic with the Zionist cause but felt that religion must be intertwined with the new movement. A nationalistic Zionism as propounded by the Zionist leaders did not go deep enough, he felt. His point of view made an indelible impression on young Saul Silber, who in later years became one of the foremost leaders of Mizrachi. The Yeshivah orientation, with its emphasis on Bible as well as Talmud and on the need to be aware of current thinking, became Silber's perspective. He lived it and acted it out in his lifetime of service.

At the age of 19, Saul Silber came to America, destined to carry out the influences of home, Yeshivah, and his experiences of the world. He married in 1904 and then occupied pulpits in both Youngstown and Columbus. His six years of rabbinical work in these two cities were years of preparation during which he mastered English and studied American history and literature in depth. His real contribution to American Judaism began in 1910 when he was called to the pulpit of the newly merged Anshe Sholom congregation in Chicago, one of the major Orthodox synagogues in America. Here he served for 35 years, dividing his time between his congregation, the Hebrew Theological College of Chicago, and the Jewish community. The word "divide" is misleading here, for he created a unity of the three and served them all as he served each.

His arrival in Chicago heralded a new era for Judaism. Chicago Jewry soon felt his impact. Orthodox Jews numbered some 75,000 of an approximate 100,000 Jews in 1910. There were about forty synagogues and more were rapidly springing up. But there was little Jewish organization, and Jewish communal life was either disorganized or not organized. Anarchy and turmoil prevailed, even though the synagogue and Talmud Torah (Hebrew School) played significant roles in daily life. Saul Silber's methodical far-sighted mind went to work. Jewish life had to be unified. Reform Judaism had made great strides in Chicago. Saul Silber became the first Orthodox rabbi to challenge its leadership. Moreover, he was the first Orthodox rabbi in Chicago to bring world culture into the synagogue. His vigor, singleness of purpose, incisive mind, almost prophetic insight, ingratiating personality, and devotion to God and Torah enabled him to bring about a revolution in Chicago's Jewish population. Within a decade this eloquent guardian of Torah had made his indelible mark on Judaism in Chicago, center of America's Midwest, and hence on American Judaism. With inspiring orations, combining the best of American literature and Talmudic and Midrashic lore, he recaptured and won over a languishing generation. He called for organization and unity in Jewish life. But he did not confine his efforts to preaching. He personally led the campaign to help organize and unify the community. Every phase of Jewish life required direction and Saul Silber was at the helm of them all.

The movements that were established in this crucial decade have remained throughout the years. Silber was involved heart and soul in the organization of the Consumptive Relief Society of Denver, the Central Relief Committee of the Joint Distribution Committee, the Keren Hayesod Zionist campaigns, the Jewish National Fund, the Marks Nathan Orphan Home, the Old People's Home, the Jewish Charities, the Jewish Historical Society, the American Jewish Congress and various hospitals and orphanages everywhere in the world. Silber also found time to solicit financial aid for seminaries around the globe.

He was a key figure in the establishment of Mount Sinai Hospital in Chicago, succeeding in his insistence that the hospital be maintained on a kosher basis. As a leading advocate of the Zionist cause, he served as a national vice-president of Mizrachi and later on the organizational committee. He attended World Zionist congresses where he was a recognized world leader. Chaim Weizmann, later Israel's first President, had called for him.

His administrative ability coupled with rare good judgment resulted in his being offered the presidency of the Hebrew Theological College of Chicago, which he turned into the largest seminary in America west of New York as he gathered to it highly qualified teachers and exceptional rabbinical scholars. Relationships were developed with synagogues and Jewish communities throughout America in order to provide pulpits for the college's graduates. Students were attracted from far and wide by the eclectic program Silber established, a program similar to that of his own experience in Lithuania. Rabbis in America must be fully acquainted with the culture and surroundings in which they were to serve, according to Silber, a position which often earned him the wrath of his seniors. He engaged in frequent debate with those who sought only a Talmudical education for the students, but his courage and fortitude carried the day and the policy. Silber also foresaw the rise of the day school movement in America, and time has vindicated him in his ardent efforts in its behalf.

To the students who flocked to hear him, Saul Silber was an inspiring leader. As he explained a difficult Talmudic passage, generously sprinkling his oratory with references to such literary greats as Spencer and Emerson, he opened ever widening horizons to his hearers. His warm personality and his kindly concern for every student in the seminary endeared him to all. He was their president but he was also their sincere, wise counselor. To the hundred who lived in the college dormitories Silber was like a father to whom they could freely come to discuss their problems. His advice was eagerly sought, and he had time for all.

Silber's contribution to Chicago Jewry endures, a tribute to his vision and powerful personality. He was not only concerned with the younger generation of his time. Future generations yet unborn beckoned him and his devotion. His restlessness drove him on. He developed not only a large number of rabbis who lead Jewish communities throughout the

world, but what is equally important, a generation of Jewish communal
leaders. An intelligent, interested lay leadership was as important to
him as able rabbinical leadership. He taught members of his congregation the meaning of communal responsibility and persuaded them
and others to give to Jewish philanthropic, religious and cultural causes.

At home, Silber was not the rabbi of the pulpit or council table. He
was always the father, loving, loved, adoring, adored, by wife, children
and grandchildren. He was able to cast off the mantle of leadership
when he crossed the portals of his hospitable home. Leaders from all
walks of life—world scholars, political leaders, industrialists, judges,
governors, Zionist leaders such as Nahum Sokolow, Shmaryahu Levin,
Chaim Weizmann, Rabbi Meyer Berlin—all felt blessed as they shared
his table on Sabbath, Passover, Sukkos and the other holidays. The
dynamo of Jewish communal life in Chicago became simply the father
and host at home. The transformation was easy.

In the pulpit Saul Silber was a master orator and wit. His inexhaustible
fund of humorous stories and parables was a source of wonder to his
hearers, who frequently quoted him to those not privileged to have
been there. He believed in teaching from the pulpit. He was a teacher
of Israel primarily and his podium was his vehicle, but his services
were attended by non-Jews as well as Jews. His audiences departed
with renewed hope, full of the sense of having listened to a giant of
faith.

His Yiddish and English were fluent and devoid of pedantry. He
spoke with his audience, not down to them, in a sort of unilateral dialogue. Often his sermon was an I-Thou, or I-Du, interchange with
God. The gentle message penetrated painlessly. A sample of his rhetoric
follows:

> I speak to you now of freedom.
> My words may sound strange and perhaps even incongruous to you;
> like the echo of a wild storm that laid cities waste, uprooted forests,
> destroyed fields, and planted numberless graves beneath their endless ruin.
> To speak *now* of freedom!
> The world lies bleeding. In many lands the infernos are still smoldering.
> Huge burning coals are still glowing as though winking to mankind and
> saying: "See what your brutality has done. You had the devil's craftiness
> and the strength of wild beasts to kindle this fire. But now you are help-

less. You have lost your mind entirely, and now you know not how to quench this fire nor even to control it."

Freedom you say? . . .

And yet, behind the dark heavy clouds of smoke, I see thin, pale rays, couriers of a new era, a better and brighter one, an era in which man will not lose his freedom—if only he will have learned how to cherish and guard his freedom and not sell it for a mess of pottage, and if only he will understand the true meaning of this great word. . . .

Freedom is a holy word. I believe that the Creator implanted the law of freedom in the entire cosmos. The urge for freedom, for self-revelation, is at the very core of the universe. It reveals itself everywhere and in all objects—in the leaves of trees, as well as in buds of flowers, which break through "heavy walls" in order to attain their freedom. . . .

He who is blessed with eyes that see, and who can look deeply into the wonders of nature, will readily see that the urge for self-revelation and freedom is to be found everywhere.

I hope that my few words will convince you that freedom can never be obliterated. If it sometimes falls upon sad days, and tyrants try to destroy it, it will ultimately be resurrected and will live again just like the grass which has withered away—apparently dead—and yet it blooms once again. That which is Godly is eternal, and freedom is eternal.

Like Russell Conwell, who delivered his remarkable "Acres of Diamonds" thousands of times and electrified his audience at every presentation, so, too, Saul Silber repeated his dramatic and magnificent address, "And We Still Thank Thee, O God" many times. Audience after audience thrilled to its delivery and hearing it once or twice was not enough. It was as inspiring at its fifth hearing as it had been at the first. One could not help looking forward as he listened. The present may be dark, but faith could transform the future. A portion of the address follows:

Night was preparing to end her course and to roll up the black cover over the heavens. A few pious stars are tardily twinkling their silent prayers and whispering to each other the hidden secrets of the coming dawn.

At the twilight hour *he* (this heavenly messenger) came to me. Treading softly, he approached the spot where I was lying. He placed his tender hand, which was as soft as a newly clipped wing of an angel, upon my head. In a gentle, trembling voice he said to me: "Awake! Come with me.

We must traverse many wildernesses. We shall witness many terrifying scenes. But we shall also hear much that is heartening. . . .

"Remember," he said to me in a deep, earnest voice, "remember that every word you will hear will have imponderable meanings. For every word is written with Jewish blood and every psalm is conceived in external pain. Moreover, the worshipers you will see are not ordinary, everyday Jews—they are martyrs."

The drama continues. In scene after scene we follow the path of the old man and the boy as they portray the trials and events of Jewish history. The boy asks. The old man answers. In their dialogue the listener has spread before him the entire panorama of the Jewish experience. The drama ends on a note of promise. As always, Silber's words breathe life and hope.

The easy flow of words, no matter the profundity of the subject, disarmed the listener. The message always came home and touched off a positive response. He often illustrated his message by drawing on the lives and contributions of outstanding Jews. Whether it be the Gaon of Rogatchov or Louis D. Brandeis, the approach was fundamentally the same.

He said of Supreme Court Justice Brandeis:

A prophetic heart decrying the wrongs of society, protesting against the groups that "plunder the poor and crush the needy," a spark kindling itself into a blazing torch, reached its ultimate goal incarnate in a frail body. By sheer chance it was born in Kentucky and transfigured into a person whose name was Louis D. Brandeis.

Often when one writes of another he describes himself. Saul Silber's immense love of Brandeis reflects his devotion to and love of people:

Brandeis was not contented with merely delivering speeches about the duties which the wealthier should exercise toward their poorer brethren. In his later years he realized that his moral urge was due to the call of his kindred, the heritage bequeathed him by his own people. He accepted the mission by right of next-of-kin. Brandeis was thus transformed into a champion of human rights; the work he so deeply cherished became bone of his bone and flesh of his flesh, and in the course of time he was crowned with the title "the people's servant."

When Saul Silber accepted the mission of rabbinical duty he was likewise transformed into a champion of Jewish rights as well as a champion of traditional Judaism and fighter for Torah. The work he so deeply cherished became bone of his bone and flesh of his flesh, and now, in the course of time, he is crowned with the title Giant of Faith.

Saul Silber, fighter for God, would not stop. A serious heart condition could not deter him from his work. He brushed aside any suggestion for allowing others to carry on his efforts with a characteristic: "Some day I will have a good, long rest."

On the day Saul Silber breathed his last, the press, as it announced his passing, carried a passage from Samuel. When King David learned that his general, Abner, had fallen, he exclaimed: "Sar gadol nafal hayom hazeh b'yisrael—A prince and a great man fell this day in Israel."

Saul Silber, captain of the ship of Orthodoxy in Chicago for 35 years, dynamic molder of Judaism in America, was a prince in Israel and together with a select few, a giant of faith.

BERNARD REVEL

Intrepid Sculptor of American Orthodox Judaism

[1885-1940]

In Hebrew, the words *hah-cho-layim* and *hah-lo-chayim* sound almost alike, suggesting similar definitions. Their meanings however are vastly different. The first means dreamer and the second, warrior, reflecting opposites in temperament and goals. It would seem unlikely, if not impossible, for the characteristics implied by both terms to be found coexisting in one individual. Yet Bernard Revel, pioneer in the field of traditional Jewish education in America, could be appropriately called dreamer and warrior of Israel. East European rabbi, Talmudic genius and American scholar, the dreamer became the warrior.

Bernard Revel saw the compelling need to interweave the traditions of his people into the vital culture of America, else Judaism would wither away. He sought to make Orthodox Judaism a living vibrant faith in a new land and environment where competing philosophies were deflecting faith from the ancient heritage of Judaism. He challenged the right and the left, the right-winged Orthodox and the left-winged Reform, and was bitterly challenged by them. And although obstacles were strewn in his path, he confronted them head on and surmounted all hurdles.

The fruits of his efforts were manifold: the massive Torah empire of Orthodox Judaism presided over by towering Yeshiva University, Rabbi Isaac Elchanan Theological Seminary, and 12 other schools at Amsterdam and 186th Street, New York City. Few men at 50 have achieved such rich, fruitful realizations of their dreams. At the half-century mark, Bernard Revel had already made his impress indelible on the course of American Jewish history. His dreams were, almost all of them, fought through and fulfilled when death snatched him in the prime of life.

The name of the institution which stands majestically as his eternal monument, Yeshiva University, itself mirrors the union of forces which Bernard Revel embraced within him. *Yeshiva* means seminary or academy and refers to the traditional institution which has as its prime purpose the intensive study of Talmud, Codes, and authoritative commentaries of the ages. *University* refers to a secular institution where the sciences, humanities and wisdom of the ages are taught and imbibed. The two form a whole: a union of two worlds and two civilizations. Bernard Revel, driven by an inner compulsion to provide an academic center where Jewish young men would gain knowledge of both worlds, created a new concept in Jewish life, fought indefatigably for it, and brought it into being. While the goals for each were dissimilar, Dr. Revel was certain that combining secular with spiritual would make for the ultimate in viable education preparation of rabbis and intelligent lay leaders for America. These men would be serving in a new land and they had to know and understand it. The students had to see America as it was, how it lived, how it thought, how it felt. Yet the study would be under the roof of Torah. While both the religious and the secular would be autonomous and independent, the unity established would be a fusion under Torah. The graduation key of Yeshiva University contains two Hebrew words—*Dat* (religion) and *Da-aht* (secular knowledge)—thus merging the two worlds.

Born on September 17, 1885, Bernard Revel was a scion of one of Israel's greatest rabbinical families. The city of his birth was Kovno, Lithuania: more precisely, a small nearby town, Pren. His father was Rabbi Nahum Shrage Revel, one of the generation's sages and close friend of Rabbi Isaac Elchanan Spector, the rabbinic master in whose memory the New York Torah Tower was later to be named.

Revel's brilliance was seen early in life. His sainted father recognized the tremendous potentialities of his young son and personally taught him. The boy's grasp was immediate and his perception keen and sharp. Father and son and teacher and pupil became one and the same relationship. At the age of six, Bernard's phenomenal mind astounded Talmudic scholars as he quoted lengthy Talmudic passages and explained them. Rabbi Revel, however, was not privileged to see his son's meteoric rise to greatness. At 12, Bernard was orphaned and on his own.

As he developed, Bernard's searching, restless mind led him to one Yeshivah after another, at each of which his knowledge and acumen amazed teacher and peer. And the more he studied, the more knowledge he amassed, the deeper became his love for Torah and the traditions of his people. He became known as the *Prener Ilui,* meaning the genius or prodigy of Pren, name of his birthplace. It was customary to assign the name of the town of birth to a brilliant son of Torah. Unlike many other Yeshivah contemporaries, Bernard Revel also studied at the gymnasium (secular high school) and became thoroughly versed in the Haskalah, studying the Hebrew language and literature and Jewish history, subjects which were not taught in the Yeshivah.

At 21, Bernard Revel came to America, firmly determined that Torah teaching would be his life's work. Three years later, in 1909, he married Sarah Rabinowitz Travis of Marietta, Ohio, whose family became consistent supporters of their renowned son-in-law in his service to his people.

Bernard Revel early came to the conviction that knowledge of the ancient codes, Talmud, commentaries, and Hebraic and Judaic studies were not enough to sustain Judaism in America. On the contrary, such limitation spelled the ruination and destruction of Judaism. It was sheer blindness and obstinacy to fail to note the trends of American life. One had to be sensitive to the disturbing forces enticing many young Jewish men and women away from their faith.

Encouraged also by great American rabbis, such as Rabbi B. L. Levinthal of Philadelphia, who were impressed by his unusual combination of Jewish and general learning and his sterling character, Bernard Revel sought a complete secular education. He received his Master of Arts degree from New York University and his Doctor of Philosophy degree from Dropsie College for Hebrew and Cognate Learning in 1912. In 1915, at the age of 30, he was invited by New York rabbinical leaders to assume the presidency of the floundering Rabbi Isaac Elchanan Theological Seminary, a coveted title, but a position which demanded superhuman strength and exacting effort. Bernard Revel accepted the challenge and a new era began for American Judaism and Jewish education.

It devolved on his shoulders to reorganize the Seminary. Actually, he almost had to start all over again and build a new foundation, surer and more secure. The Seminary was drying up. It had been called into being in 1896 and merged with a preparatory Yeshivah known as Etz Chaim (Tree of Life) which had been organized in 1886 upon the great exodus of Jewry from Russia and the desire to transplant its heritage in American soil without change. The spirit and environment of the Seminary was European in character and spirit. There was little or no recognition of American influence. It self-containment did not allow the new world to penetrate. The general feeling of the Seminary leadership was that a Yeshivah or a Talmudic academy in America could not reflect the new age. America to them was a country concerned only with material success. This narrowness discouraged the small student body. The Seminary was rapidly disintegrating. A strong mind, a strong hand, a man of vision and optimism was called for.

The new president boldly revealed his plan of a united Orthodoxy: a Yeshiva University which would train rabbis, teachers and intelligent lay leaders for service in America. He stated his purpose as:

> To fuse the teachings of Judaism with the knowledge of the ages for the development of the complete personality, the enrichment of the life of the Jewish community, and the advancement of our beloved country.

Toward this goal, the students and potential leaders would be required, in addition to mastering Judaism and all its branches of learning, to attain a deep knowledge and understanding of America, its past and present. Of course they must be imbued with Judaism and develop an uncompromising love for justice and truth. But at the same time they needed a secular training which would serve as the tools by which to bring their ideals to realization. His Yeshiva would thus be the central arsenal of Orthodox Judaism in America. This was the way—no other. He had thought through his plan carefully, and the more he calculated, the more convinced he became that his position was right.

As he thoughtfully elaborated his plans, he had but one concern—how would his idea be accepted. Would there be cooperation? Or would a major conflict ensue? He must chance it, he decided. Even if a major crisis in Jewish life arose and Jewish leadership opposed, he would have to fight with all his heart and soul.

Once firm and certain, he moved into action. He organized in 1915 the first Yeshiva High School in America in which the Yeshiva part would teach traditional subjects and the high school part would offer the secular courses of the public high school. The merger of religious and secular, his life-long work, was thus begun at the threshhold of his ministry to God. He was 30 years old and he was ready to confront the giants of the age who would soon attack.

The Orthodox had never heard of such heresy. This was assimilation. Bringing secular studies into the sacred institution was defilement. Their myopia astounded the young president and inspired him with greater courage in struggling for his goal. He would not step aside. The Reform attacked him for withdrawing young men from the public school system and persuading them to study under only Jewish sponsorship. But this man of iron will and steel nerves would yield to pressure from neither, though it must have hurt him deeply to watch Orthodox leaders, lay and rabbinic, withdraw support from the institution or reduce their cooperation to mere lip service. He was left with almost no loyal support. Still he went doggedly on from place to place, office and home, seeking financial help.

In 1922, he reached out and absorbed into the new Torah structure the Mizrachi Teachers Institute which had been organized five years earlier for

> . . . men who should be imbued with the genuine Jewish spirit, filled with love for our past, and idealism for the future, thoroughly trained in Hebrew, Talmud, the Bible and the commentaries, and Jewish history and at the same time possess a sufficient secular education,

and which had been successful in sending trained teachers throughout the land. Student enrollment increased. Dr. Revel's efforts were paying off. Inadequate accommodations and facilities caused the institution to move time and again.

The dream had not yet ended. There were finer aspects of education to be concerned with and developed. Dr. Revel labored diligently through the years to bring to the Yeshiva High School, Teachers Institute and his Yeshiva itself the finest, most erudite scholars in the world. He had to prove his dream valid. The institution needed stature and stature is attained primarily by a renowned faculty. Developments in a period in which the two new phases of Yeshiva received emphasis and concentration brought recognition to the new center of learning. Then Dr. Revel set his visionary gaze beyond the high school level and saw all too little interlinking between Yeshiva itself and the great secular institutions of metropolitan New York. There was no inter-relation between the vast knowledge contained within the universities and colleges in the area and the Talmudic and Hebraic studies of Yeshiva. True, students could matriculate at those institutions and ac-quire secular training, but this was not in keeping with Dr. Revel's over-all concept of unity, the union of the religious and secular under one umbrella, as he had effected earlier in the high school. Another revolu-tionary step forward was in the making. It would be bolder than be-fore and invite fiercer criticism, but his goal, Judaism in America, depended on it and it had to be achieved. In 1928, Dr. Revel organized Yeshiva College. The secular and the religious (Talmudic) for the first time in history came within the domain of Torah.

Criticism was immediate and violent. The critics feared that Torah and the traditional system of Yeshivah study would now be given second place. Torah would be reduced in dignity and position. Supremacy would go to the secular. Assimilation, integration, annihilation of the eternal truth of Torah—these would overtake the Yeshivah and portend the end in time of the Yeshivah itself. It was a *Chilul Hashem,* profana-tion of God's name. But Dr. Revel, inveterate optimist that he was, looked beyond the present. The future told him that he was right and he foresaw success. This was the only way to build a real American Yeshivah, with both words emphasized and with all aspects intertwined, as in American life. So he moved ever onward, often disappointed and frustrated by the lack of cooperation of ostensible friends and supporters, but never flinching—so sure was he of the firmness of his ground and logic of his hope.

The institution as it was now constituted was unsatisfactory also in terms of location. Room for growth and expansion was needed. Ac-cordingly, in December of 1924, a group of 125 men attended a dinner at the Hotel Astor and pledged almost $1,000,000 for new facilities. One tenth that amount would have been adjudged sufficient. One year later, a second million was raised at a $1000-a-plate dinner. The vision of a beautiful modern structure was unfolding and being translated into reality.

The dreamer guided Yeshiva to new quarters on Washington Heights, away from East Broadway. The year was 1929, one year after the founding of Yeshiva College. The same year witnessed the historic financial crash which shook America to its very foundations and reverberated around the world. The difficulties of building the new institution, compounded as they were by the newness of the idea itself, were staggering, even though one building had already been erected. The president feverishly sought ways and means not only to save but to continue to erect the institution of Torah. As usual, his will prevailed.

Through the years Yeshiva College grew in stature and esteem. The world's greatest scholars became associated with Yeshiva. Rabbi Solomon Polachek, internationally renowned Talmudic master, headed the Yeshiva teaching staff from 1920 to 1928. Rabbi S. Shkop served for two years and Rabbi Moses Soloveitchik came in 1930. The most illustrious rabbinic scholars of the day gladly delivered discourses to the student body and faculty members. Their names suggest a veritable galaxy of Talmudic greats: Rabbis Abraham I. Kook, Chief Rabbi of Palestine, Abraham D. Kahane-Shapiro, Moshe Mordecai Epstein, Baruch Ber Leibovitz, Meir Don Plotski, Meir Shapiro, A. I. Block, Aaron Kotler and Isaac Sher.

Gradually many of the earlier critics retreated as they saw the magnificent growth of Yeshiva and its position of centrality for Orthodox Judaism. Yeshivot K'tanot (Preparatory Academies) sprang up all over America. Many communities sought aid and counsel from Dr. Revel. His guiding genius encouraged and inspired them. He and they understood well that from these preparatory schools the Yeshiva would gain students and potential Orthodox rabbis and teachers. The schools were to be a continuing source of students to the Yeshiva, thus ensuring the rising structure of Orthodox Judaism in America.

Dr. Revel, unfailingly alert and sensitive, dreamed on. Time was helping him dream. He looked ahead of the years of matriculation at Yeshiva College. Graduates sought further knowledge and higher education, entering universities and other colleges in the city.

Dr. Revel's goal had not yet been reached. Here was another group which could be served. He sprang into action and in 1935 founded the

Graduate School for Jewish Studies where graduates could take courses in Jewish history, Semitic languages and related studies in Yeshiva itself. The curriculum could lead the student to the Doctor of Hebrew Literature degree. Again, the studies could be incorporated under the banner of Torah. The Graduate School is now named Revel Graduate School, an appropriate honor to a mighty man of Israel.

The following year, 1936, was a glorious year for Yeshiva and Rabbi Revel. It marked the jubilee of the founding of the Yeshiva—that is, Yeshiva Etz Chaim in 1886 and the Rabbi Isaac Elchanan Theological Seminary, which combined with it in 1896—and also the 50th birthday of the dynamic president. Almost gone were the harsh vilifiers of the past. Almost gone were the pessimists, even among the Orthodox, who could not and would not share the vision. Recognition replaced criticism. Yeshiva was now renowned, standing at the apex of a massive empire of religious and educational institutions and casting its spiritual shadows far and wide.

From scholar and sage, Jew and non-Jew, poured encomiums to Dr. Bernard Revel, who was described variously as High Priest in God's Sanctuary, Diadem of the House of Torah, Profound Interpreter of Traditional Judaism, Rare Talmudic Genius and Halachah (law) master, Harmonious Blender of Intellectualism and Faith, Man of Prophetic Insight and Vision. The salutations reflected the unified thinking of the Jewish and non-Jewish world. In his honor and in honor of the Jubilee Year, a special literary volume called *Hedenu* (Our Echo) was issued by the students' organization—a rare tribute to a man only 50 years of age, one usually reserved for men of 60 or 70. The Talmud says that the age of 50 is for giving counsel. Dr. Bernard Revel had become the Great Counselor and Guide for American Orthodox Judaism and appreciated as such at his Jubilee Year.

The great dream was fulfilled, a superhuman task accomplished, but the man who single-handedly executed it was only human. His indefatigable labor and self-sacrifice had taken its toll; the fragile frame was weakening, albeit still fighting. Time was running out on earth for him. Yet he refused to heed his physicians who urged the lessening of his burdens. Many were depending on him and he would not let them down. Students had to be taught, policies continually evaluated and executed, more dreams realized.

His last two Shiurim (Talmudic discourses) mirrored his blessed spirit and determination. His students filed sedately into his study which was lined with thousands of volumes of all sizes and vintages. Talmudic folios were opened on the cluttered desk. In his presence students always experienced the spiritual delight and joy which comes only from contact with the truly great. The power of his imagination, the example of his sacrifice, the inspiration of his supreme idealism, always enriched their lives. They were surprised to see Mrs. Revel there. The master, seated in his chair, appeared weak and tired. He spoke haltingly with eyes closed, as if to help him unfold the intricacies of the theme. He paused as he lectured, obviously in pain but fighting it, as he had fought so many times for his institution. His eyes were giving way and he could not read the books. When he concluded, his head sank to the table and rested on his arms. Mrs. Revel explained that he had been forbidden to conduct this lecture but he did not want to disappoint his students.

His final session with them told the story of his life as he himself saw it. Following the lecture itself, delivered with difficulty as it was, he spoke directly to "my boys":

> I have never sought material success. You, my students, know that this institution has cost me much toil. I have hardly enjoyed of this world. My life's work, my life is Yeshiva. You, and all who came before you and those who shall come after you, are my life.

He spoke on, portraying the problems of the Jewish people in Europe, 1940, under Nazi domination. He noted with despair the dimming of Torah in Europe and the disappearance of hope for life there. You students, he said, must carry on. You must be the beacon lights to shine for Orthodox Judaism. He concluded: "Even if someone would want to deter you from the task I have set before you, tell him in my name that you must continue. The Yeshiva is yours to build."

In his name Yeshiva is still building, still growing. As it expands, so does his name become emblazoned ever deeper on the historical scene of American Judaism. Yeshiva stands as his monument—stately, dignified, secure. It is magnificent living testimony to the man who built it and gave it his life.

The life he gave was a full life, and complete, though short. In his

Stephen S. Wise

Bernard L. Levinthal   *Henry Cohen*

Saul Silber

Bernard Revel

limited span he won the admiration of Jew and Gentile, Orthodox and Reform Jew. The drive of the sainted leader of American Orthodox Judaism was expressed in other areas of service and devotion to God and Torah. Many historical, religious and literary journals contain his creative efforts. The *Jewish Quarterly Review, Forum, Otzar Yisrael,* (Treasury of Israel), *Yagdil Torah* (Elevation of Torah) and others are studded with his essays and articles.

His field of interest was vast and limitless. He wrote of the Sources of Karaite Halachah and of the Epistle of Saadya Recently Found. He wrote biographies of historical figures, past and present, and of renowned cities. He wrote of ethics; he wrote of Lincoln. Education and philosophy captivated him. Talmudic discourses and ingenious new analyses and approaches enlisted his interest and the results brought him esteem in rabbinic circles. He wrote in clear, finished English as he did in impeccable Hebrew. His style could be popular or classic, depending upon the audience. From the time he assumed the presidency of the Seminary, hardly a year passed without publication of a number of essays and articles in scholarly journals and magazines.

His painstaking efforts for Orthodox Judaism carried his name far and wide. Requests for guidance in establishing schools came from all parts of the world. He answered letters also from American cities where dedicated Jews sought to found preparatory academies. Ever watchful of the trends and tendencies of history, Jewish life and movement, Dr. Revel saw in the destruction of European Jewry by the Nazi holocaust the imperative to build anew and quickly here in America. He sought to transplant the spirit of the traditional faith onto the shores of America and imbue it with the climate of the civilization here. To this he dedicated his life.

His love for America was passionate. In his deep conviction that a good Jew makes a better American, he persistently forwarded the view that the Jew can serve America best by promoting, elevating and holding high the standard of Judaism. The educated Jew, he maintained, living by the tenets and principles of Torah, has no equal as a desirable instrument in the elevation of American and democratic institutions. His love for God was faithful and reverent. His love for Torah was uncompromising. His love for America was intense and fiery. His love for

Israel was abiding and contagious. A forest, known as Yaar Revel, pays tribute to him in the land of Israel.

Dr. Revel's last written words tell the story. Indeed, his legacy is here:

Ours are ominous and fateful days, days of apocalyptic cataclysm. Dark and heavy are the clouds that hang over the human horizon; a hurricane of hate is raging over three continents and is threatening to extinguish the light of human reason; Satan appears to be triumphant, and democracy, the free, inquiring and aspiring spirit of man, is humbled and is fighting for its life.

A large portion of mankind has repudiated the sovereignty of God and of human conscience and has returned to the savagery of the jungle. It proclaims as its aim the destruction of human culture and idealism, of the belief in the universal and eternal God of Justice and Mercy, and the deification of brute force and conquest.

The great heart of America feels most keenly the indignity and sorrow of outraged humanity. The stronghold of human freedom reared by the Founding Fathers, men of prophetic vision, founded upon the realities of a living and creative faith, upon the spirit of the Bible, stands today, more than ever, as a guide and inspiration to all mankind. "American democracy has grown out of the spiritual soil of the Bible." The Bible was the cornerstone upon which was reared the enduring structure of our national life, the guide and inspiration of the sturdy and steadfast settlers of the land and of their followers who made it truly free.

The heritage of Judaism, through its tragic and triumphant millennial history, is of continuous and basic significance to the life and progress of mankind. Its spiritual strain is civilization's source of strength in its struggle for survival and ascendancy.

Democracy, love of freedom and justice, is the great affirmation of Judaism, its most cherished ideal and quenchless aspiration. For our passion for freedom, peace and righteousness, we have been hated and persecuted by enemies and misunderstood by friends. But love of light, learning and liberty will remain our sacred burden until it becomes the heritage of all mankind.

Israel, eternal companion of history, the barometer of man's humaneness, is once again in many lands the chosen martyr of inhumanity. Distressingly tragic is the fate of millions of refugees in blood-drenched Europe, innocent victims of blind hatred, of Satan let loose! Appalling is the sudden homelessness of the millennial soul of our people there!

Our sanctuaries of living faith, tradition and idealism, and of steadfast spirituality, have been destroyed by the new enemies of God and man.

It has ever been the strength and glory of Israel that comparatively few of its children were spiritually illiterate. "Vechol banayich limudei Hashem—All your children shall be taught of the Lord"—is our great ideal; "Umalah haaretz deah eth Hashem kamayim layam mechasim— And the earth shall be full of knowledge of God as the waters cover the sea"—is our Messianic hope.

The outstanding eras in our history during which we have made our greatest contributions to human progress were ages of intensive Torah-Loyalty. Every lesson of our millenial history teaches us that every attempt to transfer the center of gravity in Jewish life from Torah to empty rationalism, to secular nationalism or internationalism must end in disaster. A Torahless Jewish life is a childless life which dooms itself to ultimate disintegration and disappearance.

American Jewry has resolutely set its course on the road of constructive endeavor and is squarely facing its supreme problem, that of the education of its youth in Jewish loyalty and idealism. We are beginning to recognize that, important as are the synagogue and charity as expressions of Torah life, the structure of the House of Israel is neither complete nor safe without Torah, without the spiritual education of the growing generation. The creation of a sound system of Jewish education and the enrichment of Jewish learning and culture constitute our supreme problem. We must call a halt to the complete secularization of Jewish life, even of our sanctuaries, and stem the tide of spiritual illiteracy. The source of the living stream of Jewish tradition and idealism and spiritual strength is in the Jewish school, conceived and conducted in the true spirit of the Torah. The stream of Jewish creative life can at no time rise to a higher level than this source of Jewish spiritual life. We must learn to distinguish between substance and shadow in Jewish education. A secular Jewish nationalism with a world culture or a so-called civilization as its goal, cannot and will not maintain Jewish life. An understanding knowledge of the Torah, its message and meaning, a knowledge of our vital and continuous contributions to the spiritual unfoldment of mankind, of the essential unity of Israel of all ages and climes and of our unique history and destiny, is our strength and hope; without it there can be no continuity of Jewish life.

We behold the guiding hand of the Hashgaha [Divine Providence] in the fact that, before the spiritual sun of Israel has set in Europe a sanctuary of the eternal soul of Israel has been established on this continent.

A sound system of Jewish education culminates in the Yeshiva. The Yeshiva brings to the Jewish community a vision of a more intensive Jewish life. It helps us to recognize that there is but one power that can lead to the solution of the problem of spiritual survival—the intense cultivation of the study of the Torah in its most comprehensive sense. In a spiritually integrated Jewish laity, a fuller understanding of our faith and ideals and of the millennial aspirations of the Jewish soul, is the hope of our survival.

The Yeshiva is the successor to the sanctuaries of the Torah of all ages, a link in the lighthouses of learning on the stormy seas of our millennial history, uniting Israel in aspiration and loyalty to the God of our fathers, lighting the way to creative faith and steadfastness. Yeshiva and Yeshiva College were conceived in the spirit of steadfastness to the spiritual certainties and abiding values of the Bible and historic Jewish idealism which, in ages of transition, of shifting standards and changing values, stand torch-like, pointing the way to human freedom and dignity, to the spiritual ascendancy of man. Devoted to the ideals, aspirations, teachings and traditions of millennial Israel, the Yeshiva takes its place in this land commensurate with the unique responsibilities of American Jewry in our tragic days.

The lofty ideals of our Torah of truth, of everlasting life and light, of divine and human love and loyalty, will again manifest themselves as a living and creative force, helping to shape the cause of human progress in its ever upward march.

The blessed spirit of the Nestor of Orthodox Judaism in America lives and throbs in the magnificent will. The words tell of the man himself and describe clearly how he was able to persuade and influence. They reveal the gigantic personality of this giant of faith who drew to the product of his toil some of America's greats, who, in turn, became one with history. They share with the reader the reasons he could bring glory to Yeshiva through the many masters who became honorary sons of the citadel of learning. To Albert Einstein, who in 1934 eagerly and graciously accepted an honorary degree, he was able to say as he read the citation:

Albert Einstein, seer and reinterpreter of the cosmos; lover and beloved of nature and men, voice of the enlightened conscience of striving humanity, and devoted champion of the cause of your people. The cosmos is your sphere of contemplation and your vision penetrates into mankind's

highest day. Cosmic understanding, embodied in searching theories, opening new frontiers of knowledge and giving new impetus and direction to
man's eternal quest of ultimate unity and reality; cosmic beauty, the majesty
and the mighty mystery of measureless space and the music of the spheres,
expressed in art and in the glory of the ideal life; great moral passion and
human compassion are harmoniously fused within your being. Within your
lifetime you have become to all men the symbol of the supremacy and
the sanctity of the free human spirit; of man's ever searching, ever
unfolding and all embracing mind; of prophetical zeal for justice and
peace.

To Supreme Court Justice Benjamin N. Cardozo, who in 1935 ap-
preciatively accepted an honorary degree, he was able to say:

Benjamin Cardozo, scion of a distinguished family, searching student
of the foundations of the law and torch-bearer of Justice; patriot, statesman and humanist; serene and chosen spirit of true humility; acknowledged
master in the domain of Jurisprudence and discerning servant of man's
highest aspirations; master of self-mastery; philosopher in law; artist
in letters, your classical style of crystalline clarity and rare charm symbolizes
you and your life. For a generation you have been the glory of the bar and
the bench, and have been signally honored by your fellow-men and by
many of our great lighthouses of learning. Richer in spirit are they who
have come within the sphere of your comprehending influence. Yeshiva
College, dedicated to sound scholarship, to the spirituality and service
of man and his free spirit, rejoices in honoring you.

To Herbert H. Lehman, one of the greatest American Jews of the
century, and to many college presidents and intellectual giants, Dr.
Revel, through the medium of honorary degrees conferred upon them,
was able to say and did: "This is the composite of the very best of
Judaism, distilled and crystallized, and the very best of America, purified and sanctified." Audiences agreed, seeing a joyous servant of God
and a zealous guardian of tradition and human liberty.

The depth of thought of this creative scholar was thrilling to contemplate. His analytical mind was able to take in the total world picture.
With breathless fervor and imaginative insight he spoke these words of
wisdom to his last graduating class in 1940:

Mankind is in the grasp of a nightmare come true. The ghosts of the
darkest ages are casting their sinister shadows over a mankind dismembered

and at war with itself. The free spirit of man is humbled. Every day catastrophe is mounting and the tragedy of human destruction and degradation is reaching new depths. The terrible trap that is now Europe is ablaze with the passion of hate and destruction and is facing the end of the moral order it has been living by. The fate of Western civilization hangs in the balance.

As we witness the cataclysmic tragedy and behold the gathering momentum of intellectual nihilism and spiritual anarchy, we ask ourselves where is this unprecedented crisis in the history of man and his spirit, this world of conflagration, to stop? Are there any fundamental concepts, sanctions, and judgments, any abiding bases of the true human spirit which shall remain inviolate and unshaken? Or do these values and the inspiration of the noble human types, seers and servants of mankind of all ages, belong, as many contend, to a passing age? What are the dykes mankind can erect against the flood of hate and brute force, against the demon in man bent upon the extinction of the light of human reason, upon destruction and eventual self-annihilation? Is this agony of the vast majority of civilized humanity, this deluge of fire that has swept over mankind, all in vain? Mankind is groping in the dark, seeking a new way, clearer guidance, and is yearning for farsighted and fearless leadership, capable of comprehending the causes and the implications of the cataclysm, of dealing comprehensively with the basic forces of this titanic struggle, and of giving new direction to a civilization that has lost its way.

The tragic state of mankind today is largely the disastrous consequence of an attitude of detachment and spiritual isolation; of our long tolerance of evil; of indifference to wrong and suffering born of a static concept of democracy and of human history and destiny, of an interpretation of human liberty in the light of self-interest, as the right to be free from unpleasant responsibilities—from being our brother's keeper—with a resultant indifference to the rise of power-mad men and nations, contemptuous of their fellow-men, who aspire to the vestments of the Supreme Being to order the course of human history according to their evil will, to mould human society in their image.

A sense of futility is gnawing at the very vitals of humanity. A large portion of mankind is adrift and retreats before despots and brute force, and permits itself to be led by men "who do not believe in man," because of the weakened faith in the high purpose of human life and the unique destiny of man.

The answer to the challenge of the embattled forces of blind hate can come only from faith in human destiny and men and women who place the spiritual and cultural ascendency of man above a promised security of slavery.

The issue we are facing is basically that of the spirit. We are face to face with the cardinal problem of the meaning and purpose of human life and history, of the validity of the values that transcend the physical and temporal, of the moral and spiritual concepts and judgments that are the core of human progress for which mankind has striven and bled during millennia. Do we truly believe that there are basic ideals and causes, views and ways of life worth living for and sacrificing for; that there are ways of life inherently evil, intolerable and degrading, cults of hate and conquest, of worship of force, of supermen and super-races, and the deification of the state, worth fighting against and sacrificing to hold against them the standard of life of free men?

Only in the light of our answer to these searching questions does the full meaning of the present terrible struggle and the role of every one of us in it become clear to us. It was said long ago that man does not live by bread alone, and that without vision he will perish. The ultimate fact upon which the outcome of our days depends is the ability of the adherents of the free spirit of man to abandon themselves, with a supreme measure of devotion, to its cause in this hour of trial. Can the belief in the free, inquiring and aspiring spirit of man, in the supremacy and sanctity of human personality and reason, in the divine origin and the high and unique destiny of man, and in the reality of spiritual life and experience, sanctify and summon a death-defying allegiance, man's capacity for self-sacrificial devotion to a supreme cause? Is democracy to fail where the enemies of the free spirit of man have succeeded in capturing and holding, for their gospel of hate, of dark and destructive doctrines, this human capacity for joyous sacrifice? In a new vision of human destiny, in a return to a dynamic, creative democracy, in a reinterpretation of the ideals of human freedom and fellowship in the spirit of the seers of Israel and mankind and of the sturdy and steadfast settlers of our land, as man's most sacred cause and possession, is our salvation. In this way only can we move toward the glory and the goal of truly free men. Without such rededication, all efforts at preparedness against the enemies of human freedom, dignity and happiness, must be of no avail.

Man must return to the great affirmations of Judaism concerning the meaning of life, to the divine optimism and promise of the seers of Israel, to their passion for humanity, peace and justice, to their spiritual interpretations of human existence, and their insistence upon a new, a purified heart, a heart of greater compassion and discernment. American democracy, as a creative way and philosophy of life, must reforge its spiritual and moral weapons. It must regain the courage and vision, imagination and initiative, the heroic qualities which have characterized the founders of our great democracy, the only remaining light in the darkness that is closing in about us.

Man's deepest need today, if he is to free himself from the slavery of fear and hate and from the growing sense of futility and frustration, is a revitalizing and fortifying faith in his Creator and in himself, in the reality and basic validity of his cherished aspirations, in the ageless striving of the human soul. Only such renewed faith, expressed in sacrifice, will see us through the new dark age—the extent of which no one can tell—with our spiritual, moral and cultural standards untarnished and held high. Through the heavy clouds which cover the human horizons is discernible the eternal light of the human spirit, ever reaching for the Infinite; for truth, justice, love, and spiritual harmony.

If history has any meaning, if it is not a blind alley, the modern transvaluation of all values, child of pagan materialism, which underlies the new crusading politico-economic faiths and threatens to destroy liberty and democracy, is but a tragic snare and delusion, doomed to destruction on the eternal rock of the true spirit of man.

The true meaning of human destiny, its eternal law and purpose, is ever greater human liberty, the ever greater spiritual and cultural unfoldment of the individual in the human fellowship, in humble cooperation with his Maker. Real are the forces deeply rooted in the human soul, yearning for truth and justice, for beauty and brotherhood, great forces to be released, to cleanse and bless mankind. They assure ultimate victory against the dark forces in man. These "invisible allies" of light and loyalty have ever been a source of strength to men and women of all ages who beheld great visions and achieved mightily, whose lives and enduring influence are mileposts in the highway of human progress. It is of them that Elisha spoke to a Gehazi who was frightened by the overwhelming physical power of the enemy: "Fear not, for they that are with us are more than they who are with them."

The voice of the deeper nature of man, the spirit of the Infinite within him, and the collective and cumulative conscience of mankind will reassert themselves in a life purified of the present-day iniquities and unrealities, in a life more free and happy, more creative and purposeful. This is the faith that gives meaning, zest and abiding value to life, upon which human life must be reconstructed, through which mankind will be saved.

Creative scientific thought is gradually freeing itself from the tyranny of the mechanistic interpretation of life and is growing more cognizant of a purposeful universe guided and directed by an Infinite Intelligence, and of man as a rational and responsible being. Science is restoring to us the vision of a meaningful universe. The more profound the insight of the scientist into the phenomena of nature, the more intensive and refined his scientific experience and his intuitive understanding, the more attuned his soul becomes to the voice of the Infinite, the more harmonious his knowledge and his faith. With the Psalmist, the scientist stands in awe and reverence before the mighty majesty and mystery of the unmeasured cosmos constantly unfolding before us, before the ordered harmony of myriads of spheres, and life of the spirit.

This growing recognition of the need for and the validity of spiritual experience will give new direction to man's quest of ultimate reality and unity, wherever the spirit of man is free. In this search mankind is coming once more increasingly to rely upon the basic concepts and affirmations of historic Judaism; upon the essentially constructive spiritual message of its seers and sages.

In such an intelligent faith leading to the firm resolve to uphold reason and the free spirit of man, to strengthen human solidarity and brotherhood, and to reintegrate the shattered spiritual and cultural forces, is the hope of man. This is the supreme adventure on which free man will stake his all. . . .

For a quarter of a century, perhaps the most crucial 25 years for American Jewry, Dr. Revel stood at the helm, directing the course of Jewish history for generations to come. He foresaw the increasingly important role America was to play in the activities of world Jewry. He was determined to prove that it was possible to practice Orthodox Judaism in the midst of Western civilization. All Jewish life could be based on the Torah as the hub from which all knowledge would radiate, with scientific knowledge as one of the spokes. Furthermore, a dynamic and creative Torah life, clothed in the habiliments of science and humanistic learning, could prevent the slow dereligionization of the Orthodox Jewish community by a mechanistic scientific environment. He worked under intense pressure always, now lecturing, now soliciting funds, now examining his students for Semicha, now guiding the policies of a new concept in Jewish history, now visiting with educators, now meeting with academicians. He moved from one realm to another with ease and confidence, always sure of his goals and willing to fight militantly for them.

His fighting spirit was the same as the fighting spirit of the Founding Fathers of America. He was the Founding Father of Orthodox Judaism in America. He described the meaning of spiritual heritage at his last graduation ceremony:

> You have learned the meaning of values, to be measured not in terms of practicability and gainful success, but in terms of human happiness, of spiritual and cultural aspirations and fulfillment. We look to you, sons of Torah and its true home—the Yeshiva, loyal children of our blessed land, "conceived in liberty" and forever sanctified by its dedication to the "proposition that all men are created free and equal," to hold high the torch of human progress and idealism in the spirit of our Torah of life and light. This is your spiritual heritage. The ability gladly to sacrifice for one's convictions, honestly and painfully arrived at, is the measure of the mature man; in it is the full meaning of life.

Dr. Bernard Revel, dreamer and warrior for God, was the mature man. He knew and lived the full meaning of life. Judaism in America will ever be grateful for his blessed stubbornness and sainted life. The historian of the future will write a glorious chapter on this sage and prophet who in the 20th century, like Ezra of ancient days, helped restore the crown of Jewish knowledge to our generation.

ABRAHAM E. HALPERN

Messenger of the Lord

[1891-1962]

In the beautiful quadrangle of the towering Jewish Theological Seminary of America in New York, fountainhead of Conservative Judaism, an impressive historic ceremony takes place one Sunday every June. Before hundreds of renowned scholars, faculty members and parents, young men having pursued many years of intensive study are ordained rabbis in Israel. The Sunday afternoon of June, 1953, was somewhat different. An annoying drizzle had transferred the ceremonies to the Juilliard School of Music across the street. The exercises were conducted with simple dignity and a proper sense of history. Distinguished Chancellor Louis Finkelstein called each young man, conferred certification, and bestowed the title, Rabbi, Teacher and Preacher in Israel.

Parents, with understandable pride, felt deeply the spiritual significance of the hour. It is the thrill of a lifetime to see a son become a rabbi of his people, destined to carry on the torch of Judaism.

Among the privileged parents sits a man whose pride in his son is mixed with tender recollection, for 36 years before, in 1917, he himself had walked slowly to the president of the Seminary, Dr. Cyrus Adler, stood before him, and received the same cherished title.

The ceremonies proceed. The commencement remarks are charges to the new rabbis, exhorting them to lead with courage and firm determination. They are bidden to accept the sacred obligation to serve God, country and man. Rabbis, new and old, and assemblage listen with rapt attention. History is being formulated here.

The hour has come to recognize those who have served Judaism with unswerving faith. The name of Abraham E. Halpern is called. The man who has just watched his son ordained steps forward. The toga representing an honorary degree is placed over his head and on his shoulders. The chancellor speaks:

On behalf of the Board of Directors, Board of Overseers and Faculties of this Seminary, it is my privilege to present for the honorary degree of Doctor of Divinity, Rabbi Abraham E. Halpern and Congregation B'nai Amoona of St. Louis, Missouri, and a graduate of this Seminary of the year 1917. Rabbi Halpern is one of the graduates of the Seminary to whom all of us are indebted for the preservation and survival of our faith in the Middle West. Called to his present congregation immediately upon his graduation from the Seminary, he has led the community from strength to strength, until it is now one of the foremost congregations not only in that region, but in the country. Throughout his life he has been dedicated to the principles and ideals taught in this Seminary, and has remained a staunch and indefatigable laborer for the preservation and advancement of Torah in this land. His great qualities of human affection and leadership have won him the admiration and love of his own community and of numerous disciples in other communities. He has today the great joy of seeing his son, who follows in his footsteps, being admitted to the ranks of the American Jewish Rabbinate. I am privileged to present Rabbi Abraham E. Halpern as a candidate for the honorary degree of Doctor of Divinity in this Seminary.

As Rabbi Halpern comes forward, the Chancellor addresses the distinguished, pioneering rabbi of America's Middle West:

Rabbi Halpern, your great devotion and dedication to our faith and to our people have stirred in all of us profound emotions of affection, respect, and admiration for you. Grateful to God for the inspiration He has given you, and desiring to express our love for you, the Faculty of the Seminary has voted, and the Board of Directors and Board of Overseers have approved, that you be admitted to an honorary degree in this Seminary; and by virtue of the authority vested in the Board of Directors of this Seminary by the State of New York, and by them in me, I hereby confer on you the degree of Doctor of Divinity, *honoris causa,* in this Seminary and confer on you all the rights, privileges and immunities thereunto pertaining.

Then they stand together, father and son, the literal picture of Israel's hope to convey the faith of father to son. It is the great object lesson, two rabbis in Israel, one who had carved his mark deep on the American Jewish community and the second beginning his life's tour of rabbinic duty. Pride and exhilaration sweep through the audience. The words of the psalmist surge: "This is the day the Lord hath made; let us rejoice and be glad in it." God is being served, his people assured of guidance and leadership. The father to son sequence is the symbol of thriving Judaism.

The theme of father and son, basic to Jewish ideology and hope, and expressed in this emotional event, went back to include Rabbi Abraham Halpern's father, also a rabbi in Israel. The elder Rabbi Halpern, Isaac, together with thousands of immigrants who sought freedom from European harassment and persecution, fled his native land, Austria, in 1888, arriving in America with his wife, Faige, and three children. New York was the first stop but the stay there was brief. Rabbi Isaac moved his family to Toronto, Canada, and there founded and served the Shomray Shabbos Synagogue.

Three years later, 1891, Abraham was born and was early destined to follow in his father's footsteps, even as his son after him pursued his path. A rabbinical home provided the natural environment for acquiring a love of learning and tradition. Rabbi Isaac, adhering to the traditional injunction to begin education early, studied with his son daily for a minimum of three hours. Perseverance, determination and a keen mind were the ingredients of his thorough Jewish education. One by one, the traditional sacred books were studied. Interest mounted and swelled in the eager youth. Many times Rabbi Isaac was compelled to urge his son to rest with: "It is enough for tonight."

The foundation of Jewish knowledge was thus carefully laid, the boy early recognizing that Judaism was synonymous with beauty and holiness. Indeed, this understanding was so deeply ingrained that the words became bywords in his later years' messages. Hardly a sermon or address was preached or article written that did not contain these terms in some context. His mind, heart and soul had been completely saturated with the beauty and holiness of Judaism; so much so that an outlet in a life of service was a foregone conclusion: this, however, not until he had acquired a secular education in Toronto schools and McMasters College, University of Toronto.

His early training and spirituality directed him, at the age of 21 in

1913, to enter the rabbinical school of the Jewish Theological Seminary. For four years he studied diligently, as he had at his father's feet and table, gaining recognition for his brilliance of mind, depth of perception, and indomitable spirit. It was perhaps this combination of characteristics that led him out to the then Wild West in 1917.

Colleagues in the rabbinical school were skeptical about the future of Judaism in the West. Only two graduates from the Seminary had by this time dared venture beyond the Mississippi. But Rabbi Halpern's pioneering spirit was dauntless. He saw an unconquered land for Judaism out there. In Cincinnati five reform congregations were flourishing and young Halpern felt deeply the need to insinuate traditional Judaism into the hitherto unoccupied areas. Fiery, vigorous, full of ambition, the student-rabbi visited St. Louis on the Passover of 1917, delivered four powerful sermons, and totally captivated the congregation. His first sermon dealt with the hope inspired for the 6,000,000 Jews in Russia (how ironic the figure), now that the Russian Revolution of 1917 had brought freedom from Czarism. On the second day of Passover he pushed hard the theme that Judaism was a way of life and concerned with every phase of living.

> Judaism is not just a religion of observance without concern for the ethical and moral ideals. . . . Ethical ideals alone are not enough to give body and content to Jewish living. Both are necessary if the Jew is to live a full and rich life.

On the seventh day of Passover, he preached on the Song of Moses and the universalistic theme of Judaism, stressing the concept of the brotherhood of man and the sacredness of human life. Freedom, he insisted, is the ideal of Passover, not the downfall of Egypt as in the Exodus account. His sermon on the last day of Passover, at Yizkor (Memorial) Services, more than the others, struck home. The congregation fully felt the dynamic force of the young rabbi from the East.

> On the last day of Pesach, at Yizkor, the little Shule was packed. I was anxious to arouse the congregation to the beauty of Judaism as the religion of life rather than, what I called at that time, a Yizkor Religion. In my eagerness to emphasize this thought, I pointed out how many of our people turned to religion only in time of sorrow, when in truth it was in time of joy that the Jew should fortify his life to be able to meet the hours

of stress and sadness that confront all of us from time to time. I introduced my sermon mildly with an interpretation of life and death, at least as I understood it, and then minced no words when I said, "Unfortunately, our religion has become a religion of the dead; a *kaddish* and *yizkor* religion." And to dramatize it a bit, I said, "To many Jews the House of God is a cemetery." I didn't say undertaker's chapel, as I never saw one before in my day—all funerals were from the home. I added, The holy ark is the coffin, and *tachrichim* or shroud is the *Tallis*. The *Ner Tamid* is the light kindled around the casket; the sermon is the funeral address, and the prayer is the *Kaddish*. The entire religion of some Jews was the religion associated with death and full of superstitious beliefs. I compared this to the religion of the Egyptian whose sacred book was known as the Book of the Dead. The dead body was regarded as holy, so every means was taken to preserve it. But I made it clear, at least I thought I did, that our Torah was opposed to this because to the Jew the dead was unclean, and all who touched it had to cleanse themselves. Our Torah was the *Etz Chayim*—"The book of life."

He then portrayed the real purpose of a synagogue, what it should be and do, the purpose and functions of a modern school, and responsibilities of the parents. "Whether I remain as your rabbi or not," he concluded, "I hope that my words will not have been in vain. May you start life anew and be ever conscious that you are Jews and should live as Jews."

The entire philosophy of Rabbi Abraham Halpern was contained, in essence, in this trial sermon experience. His life of service amplified and deepened the words sounded on that fateful Passover. Judaism is alive, vigorous, full of joy and happiness. It is more: it is beautiful and holy and must so be lived. For 45 years he hammered away at this theme.

His last statement to the congregation was also significant. On Sunday afternoon a committee came to offer him the pulpit. He often recalled the thrill of excitement he felt when the three distinguished officials, all older than he, arose respectfully when he came into the room and graciously asked him to become their rabbi.

He returned to the Seminary for his last two months of study and found his colleagues chiding him for accepting the call of the wild. The months passed rapidly. When he was preparing to travel the 34-hour trip, his classmates, who had learned to love their piano-playing, charming, warm friend, gave him as a parting gift a bow and arrows with which to defend himself against marauding Indians. But instead of aiming arrows at Indians, he sent shafts sharply and swiftly across the plains for the Judaism of tradition. His aim was accurate, and many were the souls he won to his cause. His credo:

> Concern for all the Jews in the world.
> Insistence on observance of the traditions and ceremonies.
> Universalism of Judaism as a basic ideal.
> Spiritual and cultural well-being of Jewish people.

The credo, while shifting in emphasis, remained his guide throughout his career. Although he created new forms and used new approaches, he retained the sacred, time-hallowed traditions.

In the fall of 1917, just in time for the High Holiday season, Rabbi Abraham Halpern arrived in St. Louis. He alighted from the train with luggage, skates, tennis racket and golf bag. His serious concerns had always been tempered by a love of fun and a belief in the values of physical fitness. Indeed, he had been an avid sports fan and hoped that his pulpit would allow him time to continue his interests. Such was not to be the case—then or ever.

The synagogue to which he had dedicated his life was small. More room was needed and more attractive surroundings for the expanding congregation. He was determined to fulfill the words the Seminary registrar had written to the congregation when he was elected, "I am confident that in securing the services of Rabbi Halpern you will have a man who will place your congregation in the foreground." It took courage for a new rabbi at the first High Holy Day services to call upon his congregation to build not only a new synagogue but a firmer foundation for Jewish life in St. Louis. But in less than a year the cornerstone for the new synagogue was laid, and the next year work was completed. Years later, the congregation again followed the suggestion of their rabbi and moved further out. The synagogue must be placed strategically to accommodate a continuously developing new community. That was a great year for St. Louis Jewry as it was for Rabbi Halpern himself, for this was the year that he married the sister of his classmate, Rabbi Louis Feinberg, Bessie, who was to bear him three children.

Knowledge of Rabbi Halpern's phenomenal success spread rapidly. The Jewish community and larger community quickly took note of his ability to get things done, and he was sought out by organizations, civic and Jewish. The Young Men's Hebrew Association needed a spirited leader to direct the destinies of young men fired with Zionist and Jewish ideals. A group called Hashomrim had been called into being. Rabbi Halpern, an ardent life-long Zionist, was asked to head the group. Testimony to his brilliant leadership is to be found in the fact that many Hashomrim members attained national renown in Jewish service and life.

St. Louis was sharply divided between a strong Reform group, which in the main stemmed from German-Jewish immigration, and a strong Orthodox community, members of which in the main came from Russia and Poland. The division was deep, culturally, religiously and economically. Unity, if not uniformity, was needed. Young Rabbi Halpern moved in. A new Jewish community had to be formed. Rabbi Halpern's drive led to the organization of the Jewish Federation of St. Louis, in which for the first time all Jewish groups joined forces. The Federation served as the base from which Rabbi Halpern's communal service stemmed. In 1926, when the Federation was planning a new building for the Jewish Hospital, Rabbi Halpern, still a fierce exponent of traditional Judaism and one of its staunchest guardians, fought for the establishment of a kosher kitchen in the hospital. After much persuasion, he achieved his aim and willingly assumed the responsibility of supervising the project, a labor of love he maintained all his days.

Throughout his life, Rabbi Halpern's love for Palestine was intense. The feeling had been instilled early in life in his father's home, where he had been initiated into the practice of soliciting funds for Palestine. He later would recall often with a touch of nostalgia and hint of a smile the youthful adventure of packing pennies, nickels and dimes into little packages to send to Palestine. As early as 1918, one of his earliest articles, "Palestine Restored," written for *The Jewish Voice,* St. Louis, tells of his hopes for Zion and its effect on Judaism:

> With unflinching faith in the future of Israel has the Jew clung to his ideals and to his religion. With unwavering hope has Israel been able to retain its identity amidst the nations of the world. Although scattered over the entire world, yet the Jewish heart has beat in unison. The soul of the Jew was not dead even though his body was dismembered. And now has he been given the greater hope of a restored Israel to be his own home.

The effect that this hope will have, and, even already has, has stirred the hearts of even those Jews who were indifferent in their attitude towards things Jewish. It has put new life into them; it has rekindled the spark that lay dormant within their breasts; it has awakened them to a realization that Israel has a brighter future and that the suffering of the past two thousand years has not been in vain. . . .

Would we not benefit, yes, all the Jews outside of the Jews in Palestine, if a home were established in Palestine, not even for political reasons, but that the Jews in Palestine who would live in a Jewish environment, would not have the obstacles with which we have to contend here? Would not Jewish scholarship have a normal growth where the atmosphere is truly Jewish? In Palestine the Jew would not have the difficulties of proper observance of his religion that naturally confront the Jew in America or in any other country. And with so many obstacles removed, would it not be so much easier to grow and develop? Up to now we have had to strain every energy at least to conserve and preserve our heritage; but in our own home we should be able to progress and grow as well as conserve. Progress is possible only under a normal life, and where could the Jew live a better normal life than in Palestine? Would he not then be giving to the world more than he has been doing in these long years of exile? Would he not then be the true missionary and carry on his mission from Zion? And would not the hope of Isaiah and Micah be fulfilled when they said that "from Zion shall go forth the Laws, and the Word of the Lord from Jerusalem"? . . .

The restoration of the Jewish home does not necessarily mean that all the Jews of the world desire to go back to Palestine. All the Jews of the world never lived in Palestine, for it is not large enough even if all should desire to go back. But would we not all benefit spiritually and culturally from the developed Jewish State? We would be nourished from the land of our fathers, for it would give a new impetus to live as Jews in all the lands where we are now scattered. We would get courage and gain strength to continue our separate existence, if the source of our heritage were again to rise as the spring of living waters for a famished people.

When Dr. Chaim Weizmann came to America in 1923 to seek funds for the Zionist cause, Rabbi Halpern issued an ardent plea in the semiweekly magazine for unity and help:

It would be interesting indeed if those Jews who are so bitterly opposed to the Zionist movement would at least come forward with some constructive suggestion that might in some way give hope to a heartsick people. It would at least show that they are concerned, it would be evidence that they are moved by the wretchedness of the Jewish people. If they are opposed to the political program of the Zionist, they might support the cultural and spiritual upbuilding of Palestine. If they refuse to affiliate themselves with the nationalist, they might lend their support to the other groups that are doing something for the rehabilitation of our people. But no such thing; their entire attitude is absolute indifference to our people struggling on a storm-tossed sea, thrown hither and thither, spat upon and despised, rejected and excluded. They have withdrawn into their shell and call that the "mission" of Israel. Let Louis Marshall speak to them, perhaps they may awaken to the responsibility that rests on the shoulders of EVERY Jew, irrespective of his previous disposition. "It is a solemn, a sacred duty to step to the side of Dr. Weizmann and to help him to bring about the solution of one of the greatest problems that has ever been placed before human beings; and to help him shoulder a burden which requires a man of gigantic mold to carry. You must all, regardless of any past preconceptions, stand at his side, hold up his hands, wish him God-speed, and put money into the treasury. It is for you who are Zionists and for us who are non-Zionists to work shoulder to shoulder for the purpose of redeeming the land of Israel."

Jewish leaders spoke out for Zion and Rabbi Halpern was among them. He believed that the social ideals of the great prophets of Israel could be translated from the pages of the Bible into reality in Palestine. He believed that Palestine ought to be developed educationally and culturally toward that end. Long before others, he called for the consecration of a Hebrew University, an institution of higher learning on the sacred soil of the Holy Land. These words were written in 1923:

When the momentous declaration of Balfour was made to the world, every Jew with a true spark of sincerity rejoiced. Crushed as he was by the years of war, he seemed to forget for the moment all his troubles and sorrows. His eyes sparkled and his pulse began to beat faster when his ray of hope came through the clouds of darkness. And, at this moment, when he should have turned to the economic question of Eretz Yisrael, and which would have been the most natural course to follow, Israel's SOUL responded to the ray of hope that was given him. Instead of setting out to build factories of steel and iron, instead of fortifying himself with ammunitions of war, and it might have been more practical, the FIRST step of the Jew was to LAY THE FOUNDATION STONE OF A GREAT SEAT OF LEARNING.

For thousands of years, the Jew has been accused of materialism. He has been called the financier, the man without ideals, the beast without a soul. And this creature without ideals and without a soul begins the new era, not with crushing others, not with pogroms, BUT WITH THE BUILDING OF A UNIVERSITY. What a reply to the rest of the world; what an answer to the accusing mob.

The Jew started out on his journey in the wilderness, after leaving Egypt, with the greatest gift that man has possessed, HIS TORAH. The Torah has been called the "ETZ CHAYIM," the tree of life, because it was to give him life as long as he used it as his guide. Nor was it written as a guide-book for his own day, but for ALL times. And it is as important today as it was three thousand years ago and it will be NEW ten thousand years hence. Because the Torah was the everbubbling spring was the Jew able to survive the ages. Others have disappeared; nations have been conquered; empires have passed into oblivion; kings and princes are no more. Systems of philosophy and ethics have been much heralded and are things of the past. A new psychology and sociology are introduced by every new thinker, but the TORAH still remains the basis of them all. Nor has the Torah become stereotyped and cold, but has retained the same fire with which it was given to Israel. . . .

The seats of learning have shifted from time to time. . . . The great question for us today is: "WHERE SHALL THE NEXT CENTER BE?" To this, there is but one answer. We must return to the original seat of learning in Eretz Yisrael. The most appropriate place for the Jewish intellectual center is Palestine, with the Hebrew University as the hub of Jewish learning and intellect. It would stand out as a LIGHTHOUSE and its rays would penetrate the ends of the earth. The Jews in the diaspora would be nourished and strengthened by the source of Jewish life. We have been called a parasite people by our enemies. We have been accused of always receiving and never contributing. This, in spite of our contributions throughout the ages. It is quite natural because no matter what contribution the Jew has ever made, he has never been given credit for that contribution. Attempts have been made to depreciate our greatest contribution, the BIBLE. Our great men have been claimed by the countries in which they have lived; the rogues have been left for us.

Not speaking of the thousands of intellects and geniuses of the past, who give us credit for Bergson, Cohen, Michaelson, Einstein, Aaronson? How are we credited with our men and women who have enriched the fields of medicine, science, literature and music? But how different it would be if these shining lights had made their contributions through the Hebrew University. Many of them have promised to attach themselves. . . . The only logical center of Jewish learning MUST be Eretz Yisrael. We shall not, then, be at the mercy of a capricious government and a fanatical people. The Jews of the world would benefit by the "MEKOR MAYIM CHAYIM," the spring of living waters. The Jew WILL REVENGE THE WRONGS OF THE WORLD AGAINST HIM, but the revenge will NOT be with the sword and cannon. He will not celebrate his victory by pogroms and bloodshed. The Jew will conquer by the power that gave him life, for "NOT BY STRENGTH AND NOT BY MIGHT, BUT WITH MY SPIRIT, SAITH THE LORD OF HOSTS."

There on Mount Olive will burn the TORCH of light, as a brilliant star to be welcomed by all.

He foresaw the fulfillment of the Zionist dream a decade before its creation when he visited the land in 1937:

My Zionism is the inspiration of my father's teaching and my Jewish home life. I have seen the land of my forefathers and I believe that some day soon it will be the free nation of my fellow Jews.

The arrival of World War II found Rabbi Halpern preaching courage to his countrymen. He held out the hope that freedom would prevail. He clung to the view that Americans, who understood the meaning and blessing of freedom, would lead the way:

We in America know what freedom means. We know what democracy means. We know what liberty means. We know what to do, but must all be courageous enough to do it. The church [meaning organized religion] must begin to teach with courage. The layman must be willing to listen to the word of God, for the word of God is concerned not only with dogma and forms but also with justice and righteousness, with love and brotherhood, with decency and integrity. The church leader and the industrialist must sit down together to plan the economic, the social, the moral, and the cultural life of the American people. Together the American people will carry on, and we need not fear Fascism, Nazism, or Communism. But liberty and the pursuit of happiness must be the opportunity for all, and not merely a suggestion without the possibility of fulfillment. America will stand as the great fortress for democracy only when every American will be able to enjoy a decent part of the blessing that God has bestowed upon us. I would say to the layman, "Watch the writing on the wall," and when the time comes, let it not be said that he has been weighed and found wanting. We Jews are part of this great democracy and may it never be said that we failed in any attempt to help adjust the ills of our country. God bless and preserve our beloved land. May she rise to the occasion as a beacon of light to guide the way of mankind.

In word and deed, he called upon members of all faiths to guard zealously the freedom which was theirs. Political freedom had to be coupled with religious freedom, and these fundamental freedoms should be joined with freedom from want and fear. All were entitled to full and complete freedom. And from pulpit and platform he asserted: We are all Americans, Jews differ only in religious views and the expression of those views:

It is important that we always bear in mind that we are not a separate unit in America but an integral part of the whole. It is only in religious concepts that we are different and it is also well to know that the Bill of Rights grants that privilege to Americans of all faiths. Thank God there is no state religion so that in all religious matters every group can live in its own way without regulation or interference by the state. We should cherish this great ideal in American life because wherever there is a state religion or where religious privileges are given to one religious group in preference to another the minority group is restricted and a limitation is placed on the freedom of religion. . . . We are living here and thank God, again, we are free to live our religious life as Jews. We should never underestimate this freedom. We should hold it dear to our hearts and oppose any attempt that might in any way lessen the separation of state and religion. This is a fundamental ideal that makes America really free. It is the standard that we hope all peoples of the world will adopt as the basis of democracy.

To Rabbi Halpern, though America offered the world's fullest expression of freedom, universal enjoyment of human rights was to be sought as a primary goal. Each human being deserves all God's blessings, and no law, nation, religion or individual has the right to undermine any man's enjoyment of these blessings. Indeed, it is the sacred duty of society and government to protect the individual and give him the opportunity to live securely and well.

The brotherhood of man means just that. Anything less hinders the progress of man and deters the establishment of God's Kingdom on earth. We must always proclaim and act in the knowledge that *man is a person and not a thing.* . . .

We must become ever conscious of the rightful needs of others. Honesty must prevail in the industrial and economic world, and decency must be the watchword of all human endeavor. There must be the religious urge to do good and the inner conviction that we are all God's children and have a right to the opportunity of God's gifts to the world. Human and social interests must be the result of a religious conviction, otherwise the artificial application regulated even by an honest and decent government can only be temporary. True religion must function in the heart of man. It must be the inspiration of our daily life and I underscore true religion because too often religion has been known more by ritual observed than by morality and justice practiced. The real happiness of humanity must be stimulated not merely by a minimum of wages and a minimum of employment but by the maximum. A minimum wage scale of fourteen dollars a week [the year is 1934] for a family of five still ignores human rights and human dignity. This does not represent the ideal of life and no man with a bit of self-respect should be satisfied until a further adjustment is made. For after all, what happiness can there be if we know way down in our hearts that there are millions of our fellow men just existing without one bit of opportunity to enjoy that life? What happiness can there be if the human family is torn by strife and struggle as if we were living in a great jungle where brute force commands the day? Real contentment can come only if we live as human beings with the spark of the Divine recognizing our duty to our fellow men. We must give of ourselves graciously so that others might live with dignity and joy as well. . . .

No shifting of responsibility will solve the problem, no hiding will effect a change of heart. A man's job must be secure for the morrow if he is to participate as a normal citizen in the welfare of the land. Greater opportunities for the greatest number will bring rest and repose. As long as mankind will have the simple comforts of life and bread there will be no need to fear the spectre of unrest and disturbances.

We, the more fortunate ones, do not know what it is to be without bread. We have not experienced the wretchedness of the millions who live in hovels, and we do not fully appreciate the horror of it and what it can lead to if the status of these millions is not changed. These are not mere empty words. It is the cry of the millions who still rest in the hope that the future will give them the opportunity of work by which to earn their living. . . .

With deep love for human beings he spoke, this preacher to and of the people. His language is simple and direct—yet it enflames, stirs. No flowery phrase mars the sharpness of his thought and feeling. No ornate facade covers the meaning he seeks to convey. His message is unmistakable; it cannot be misunderstood or distorted. The down-to-earth style reflects the character of a down-to-earth human being who understood people, their drives and needs, who sought to encourage and bolster them, who craved to instill within them the principles of justice, mercy and righteousness. Nor did he confine his utterances to the classical concerns of religion. If justice had to be done, that was the concern of religion. If human beings needed help, this was the concern of religion. If fearless outcry was called for, this was the role of religion. All of life was religion in that it was *holy* and could be *beautiful,* to recall Rabbi Halpern's favorite terms. Said he:

As for the Talmud, it is replete and full of understanding of what true religion is. The rabbis made no distinction between one phase of life and another. All life was included in their concept of religion. That is why we have whole sections which ordinarily are not generally regarded as religion. Imagine including the *Seder Zeroim* [a section of the Talmud], which deals with agriculture, in our religious literature. Or take *Seder Nezikin,* which deals with civil and criminal law and is not ordinarily included in any religious system, but it *is* part of our Talmud and religious law because civil and criminal law concerns the relationship between man and man, and between nation and nation, and it is not beyond the sphere of religion. . . .

The pulpit will have to become the forum of true religion and not merely the exponent of some theology. The pulpit can no longer afford to stand by while the burning social problems are confronting the human family, and the church [meaning religion] can no longer be blind to the upheaval that is shaking the very foundation of society. . . . The church cannot teach religion by remaining indifferent to the cries of hungry souls. Nor will the church inspire respect for religion merely by the singing of hymns, or the shaking of the censer, and we Jews will not inspire admiration for our faith simply by the blowing of the Shofar or fasting. . . . Let it [religion] condemn all forms of oppression and let it plead the cause of the downtrodden and weak. Let it not be afraid to speak against ruler

or prince, against industrial magnate and blind financier. Let the peace
and welfare of the entire human family be its greatest concern, and
religious inspiration will once again find response in the hearts of man.
This is the only way to teach religion, for then the church and the
synagogue will stand as great beacons to light the way of mankind and
bring peace and spiritual repose to the human family.

While he spoke to all men and for all to hear and understand, Rabbi
Halpern reserved his concentration for his own people—teaching them,
imbuing them with the beauty, joy and feeling of Judaism, explaining
how they in turn might lead their children in the paths of positive Jewish
living. He established rapport as he spoke, not with pompous admonition, but as a father who knew and loved them.

My admonition to you is because I love you and want you to have
the spiritual satisfaction that I find in my living as a Jew. I want you
to have "nachas" through your children in knowing that they are willing
and ready to carry on the program of the Jew through Judaism in all its
manifestations. If I call on you for intensifying your religious life, it is
because Judaism, if it is to be soul-satisfying, must have a maximum goal
and not a minimum. . . .

Our program of traditional observances is the tangible means through
which we express our religious yearnings and through which we, as Jews,
have maintained our identity. These have added color and beauty to our
Jewish way of living, religiously, but at no time were they to be an
end in themselves, but rather a means to a higher end. Too often do
some forget that the objectives of our Torah are the great moral, ethical,
and social ideals that are woven into our historic fabric like a golden
thread. . . .

When we pray we stand before a God who listens. When we cry
we know that God cries with us. When we sing, God rejoices, and when
we are in trouble God reaches down to help us even through the valley of
the shadow of death. This is my God—a personal God. . . .

We mustn't be afraid to stand on a still starlit night and repeat the
words of David, "The heavens declare the glory of God," and as we stand
in awe, we should try to absorb the full significance of those words.
We must feel the majesty of God's handiwork and have faith that it is the
handiwork of a God who is personal and to whom we can turn in a
spirit of closeness and declare without limitations and without reservations,
"We are Thy children and Thou art our Father."

... It is this feeling of closeness that we need to experience. It will not come just by wishing it today or tomorrow. It will come through a continual yearning to feel the presence of God, and by a continual desire to walk humbly with God. It is just in this hour of possible devastating terror and cruel cynicism that we must find our way back to God. It will not be by limiting God's powers to man's limitations. It will come when we think of God as the supreme power, yet ready to take hold of our hands to walk with Him and to speak to Him in the relationship of father and child. This is my God—a personal God. "The soul is Thine and my body is Thine." We belong to God body and soul together. God waits for His children to return to Him, not as cringing slaves but as children returning to a loving father who weeps with his children when they are in pain and rejoices with them when they rejoice. "This is my God and I shall glorify Him." This is my God—a personal God.

The inviting feeling of closeness with members of his congregation was ever expressed in this way. This intimate touch was his trademark in the pulpit: "Parents and children in one House of God" was a favorite phrase of his. He spoke to parents of the great debt they owed to the Jewish people—proper training of their children in the ways of God. They must not be indifferent, he insisted. Children are instinctively religious. Parents must use that instinct, develop it, and instill in their children the love for their people. Be realistic, he exhorted. The external environment is not a Jewish one. Parents must make their home the basic environment. From the home the children must come forth—intelligently, securely, rejoicingly Jewish. It was the duty of parents, and more, their burden; but a good burden for all that, a burden borne for God and people. Parents could not but be moved by this gentle pleading. They knew he was right. Set the example, he urged, a plea many a rabbi has issued; and many were inspired to comply. He thus saved lives and souls for Judaism and posterity.

The soft-spoken rabbi turned also to the younger people. He understood them well and the pressures pushing and pulling them in the world beyond the home and synagogue. He urged them not to discard a tradition or an observance simply because they did not comprehend it. It was not the fault of the ceremony or rite, he suggested. Give it time, give yourselves time. These ceremonies are not intended to be ends in themselves. They are means to higher, nobler goals. Certainly, he cajoled, you have no objections against higher, more worthy ideals.

Every ceremony in Jewish life has a value and a religious significance and it is your duty to learn, as it is the duty of your parents to teach. You must study your religion if you want to know it and live by it. When you want to be an engineer you study engineering; if you want to be a physician you study medicine; and if you want to be a Jew you must study Judaism and all that pertains to it. It is an easy thing to follow the line of least resistance. There is no valor in throwing aside everything merely because it does not appeal to you at first or because you find it difficult to observe under certain conditions. Nothing more is expected of you by Judaism than that you do your best sincerely and conscientiously. You must remember that you are the Jews of the future, and on you depends the future of Judaism. If it will be a Jewish life, Judaism will again become the religion of life. . . .

One of the most beautiful passages to come from his facile pen is the selection taken from his magnificent sermon delivered on Yom Kippur 1947 entitled, "Cramming for Finals," in which he compares living Jewishly to studying for final examinations. He gently develops the theme that it is everyday living as it is everyday studying which produces the best results:

The rare visits to the synagogue remind me of the two youngsters who noticed that their grandmother was busily engaged in reading some book and one said to the other: "What is grandmother doing reading so much?" and the other answered, "She is reading the Bible. She is cramming for finals." I take it that most of you know what the answer implies. But just as the best results can only be attained by daily study, so that when the final examinations come around we have only to review, so can the best results be attained in our spiritual life by daily living our religious program. We cannot cram everything into a few days and we certainly can't wait until the finals approach when we are to be tested as Jews.

Sincerely and consciensciously he preached and practiced what he preached, this dedicated rabbi of the West. To children and parents, to Jew and non-Jew, to an entire community, he spoke energetically on every theme of life for almost half a century. He became the oracle of Judaism, spokesman of the faith, representative of his people. He championed cause after cause. He was a seeker after truth and its uncompromising exponent. His love for Judaism was contagious; he made his listeners proud of their Jewishness and sacred traditions. Moreover, he captured the hearts of all citizens, who respected him for his arresting views and passionate defense of human rights.

A partial list of his sermon titles illustrates the range of thought and feeling he shared in his lifetime of consecration to God and people:

How Not to Teach Religion
The Religion of Little Men
Man's Quest for God
Afraid of Religion
A Hundred Million Miracles
The Lord's Week-end
Labor Looks to Religion
Survival through Design
Man Is a Person—Not a Thing
Gilt-edge Investments
Instant Judaism
Watchman—What of Tomorrow
The Hunger Fighters
Peace of Mind—Is It Good or Bad?
Lengthen Your Cords—But Strenghthen Your Stakes
Why Every Family Needs Rituals
Business Ethics, Government Ethics and Ethics of Judaism
I Am an American—A Catholic or a Protestant or a Jew
Are the Ten Commandments Unconstitutional?
We Should Investigate the Prophets
What Makes America Great
Slaughter for Sale

His family shared many honors conferred upon him. Three children, one a son, comprised the family. Jewish and non-Jewish leaders rejoiced when the son of the beloved rabbi and leader was ordained a rabbi; thus establishing the three-fold cord of which it is said: it will never be torn asunder. Three generations in America, serving the land and Judaism, first Canada, then Missouri, and now in 1955, Michigan, when Rabbi Halpern was called to Oak Park to install into God's service his own son.

The scene must have been impressively touching. Two rabbis, father and son, stand on the same pulpit, as both had two years earlier before the chancellor of the Seminary, the son to receive ordination and the father an honorary Doctor of Divinity degree. It is Chanukah, the Feast of Lights, and the rabbi of 38 years of service delivers the charge to both congregation and rabbi-son. His message contains his philosophy of life and Judaism. He speaks of the synagogue, describing it as a symphony of steel. The steel structure is the backbone of the beautiful synagogue, as Jewish traditions are the backbone of the ancient, majestic faith:

It is when they are welded together that they produce the symphony of Judaism. One piece of steel, no matter how large, doesn't make the structure of a synagogue, and not even two or three. It requires hundreds of smaller beams and plates in addition to the ten ton girders, and while larger girders are supports for the entire structure, yet they could not stand without the hundreds of smaller beams that hold the entire structure together.

In our [the] synagogue the Commandments and the ark stand between these two massive girders, but while the Commandments are the foundation of our entire religious structure, yet they are held together by our whole program of positive Jewish living. Every phase of Judaism dovetails and fits in with the entire structure and each lends support to the other. And altogether they make up the citadel of traditional Jewish living.

The rabbi-father forcefully speaks about social justice and moral law as he discusses the significant roles of the long procession of spiritual giants who had inspired throughout time. "The world is in need of spiritual builders," he says, and continues:

We have always revolted against injustice and every wrong perpetrated by man against his fellow man. Our Torah is a revolt against the enslavement of man. Our prophets are the spokesmen for the oppressed. Fearless and with courage, they turned upon king and people alike and chastized them with stinging words because they forgot the widow and the orphan, the needy and the stranger; because they forgot the moral law of God. . . . We must be sensitive to all indecencies and injustices in life, and being sensitive we must do everything to arouse decent men to establish justice in our own land if we are to exert our influence elsewhere. We must come to the world with clean hands, if we expect them to be interested in our pattern of living. . . .

To the congregation he speaks as a wise father and successful rabbi:

I would counsel you, too, that your pulpit be a free pulpit, where your rabbi is not inhibited, and where he may preach and teach Judaism as he understands it; let him be free with his pronouncements on the great social problems that confront mankind, because too often organized religion has been too timid to arise as did our prophets of old to demand of all men that they live in accord with the laws of social justice of our Torah and our prophets.

Then he turns to his son in the presence of the entire congregation and says, his heart beating with pride:

Chazak veamatz—"Be strong, be courageous, and be humble before God." You have a tremendous opportunity to build the lives of your very fine congregation. They, too, are young and enthusiastic and are ready, I am sure, to work with you, but they look to you to guide them and inspire them in the traditions of our people. You will have moments of disappointment but you will overcome these moments through mutual understanding of the problems that face all of us. We are living in a world of confusion, and it will be your task to help your people adjust to a world that is wavering but which can regain its balance by its spiritual leaders who still speak with conviction in the fearlessness of our prophets.

May God bless you and your people with a determination to build and to live through the heritage of our people. May your years be filled with accomplishment and achievement that will redound to the glory of God.

The life of Rabbi Abraham Halpern was studded with achievement and accomplishment. It redounded and still redounds to the glory of God. This sensitive spiritual leader passed away on March 26, 1962, but his memory lives on, for in his message and example he re-echoed the message and example of the prophets of old. His creed that of Conservative Judaism, he was ever true to the traditional ritual and ceremonial observances of the ancient faith. He sensed beauty and holiness in all that had been bequeathed by past generations. He turned the hearts of the sons he taught to their fathers, educating the growing American generation to a knowledge and appreciation of the faith that had sustained their parents and grandparents. Thus this uncompromising giant of faith built in America's Midwest a veritable stronghold of Judaism; a landmark for Conservative Judaism in America.

His last sermon, as earlier ones, always searching and delving into the heritage, was significantly entitled, "If the Prophets Spoke Today." He reviewed his life and service, as though he knew it to be his ethical will and legacy consigned to history and time:

The prophet will not overlook America. He will say to her that she, too, will be punished if she does not awaken in time and keep sacred the promise of her Constitution and the Bill of Rights that were to grant all equal opportunity to share in the prosperity and culture of America, irrespective of race, color, or creed. He will say to America: "I brought you from the lands of oppression. I gave you a land, indeed, flowing with milk and honey. You have grown fat and at times forgotten your God. You have regarded the oil of Arabia more important than the dignity of men. You have permitted your schools to close because of the color of a child's skin. You have failed to demand equality of consideration from peoples who have shut their door to citizens because they are Jews. You did all this because oil was more precious than justice. I give you warning only because of so much good that you have done in the past, and in the words of one of my earlier prophets I say to you, "You have I known of all the peoples of the earth. I gave you this land of plenty. I made your children rich. I caused the rain to fall and the dew to water your meadows. Because of this I shall punish you unless you turn again to the words of the founding fathers and make them the source of your living. Have courage to defend the weak everywhere, not for profit, but because it is just and right to do so. Demand justice for all peoples who may be enslaved. Share your bounty with the needy of the world. Open up your granaries and feed the hungry in far-off lands. Do not raise your voice only when a small nation appears to do some wrong. Raise your voice against the big powers when they crush the weak and steal their lands and make them their slaves. If you will do all this I shall again turn to you and bless you as I promised your fathers who founded this blessed land." My prophet Isaiah again speaks to you and he says: "I care not for all your churches and synagogues and cathedrals unless there is justice and decency in the land. Of what value are the number of your prayers if your hands are not cleansed of hatred and selfishness and greed and hypocrisy? Cleanse yourself, make you clean, put away the evil of your doings. Learn to do well, seek justice, relieve the oppressed, judge the father less and plead for the widows. Establish absolute equality in the land. If you honestly do all these then though your sins be as scarlet, they shall be as white as snow; though they be red like crimson, they shall be as wool. If you be willing and obedient ye shall eat the good of the land. For America will be redeemed through justice and all the world will look to her for inspiration and courage."

Thus he spoke, this man of faith, whose memory is carried forth in many a mind and heart as his service to America and Judaism is recalled. In his memory, a huge Educational Foundation has been established. It will translate for generations to come the Jewish way of life in which he persevered and which he encouraged in a crucial era of American Jewish history.

*Abraham E.
Halpern*

Aaron Kotler

Milton Steinberg

Solomon Goldman

Alexander D. Goode

AARON KOTLER

Patriarch of the Twentieth Century

[1892-1962]

On Sunday, December 2, 1962, over 50,000 Jews, rabbis, students, disciples, gathered on the East Side of New York City to mourn the passing of Reb Aaron Kotler. Thousands drove in the procession to the airport, for the remains of this blessed mentor of Jewry were destined for the Holy Land, Israel. Thousands more greeted the bier as the plane put down at Lydda Airport, Israel. The following afternoon over 100,000 attended services in Jerusalem and accompanied the coffin to Har Menuchot, where he rests eternally.

It was a funeral accorded presidents, princes, kings. Reb Aaron Kotler was a Prince of Israel and mighty captain of Orthodox Judaism in America. The figure of this short, angelic, black-garbed patriarch is impressed on the minds and hearts of millions. His whole life of 71 years was geared to God and Torah. God was the loving Father. Torah meant not only the Bible, Talmud, and their authoritative interpretations during the centuries, but the whole gamut of traditional Judaism—all its codes as set down by the sages of yesteryear. It was the sum total of Jewish spiritual culture. There was but one road from the Bible and that was the path of tradition. Reb Aaron Kotler, perhaps more than any other of his time, fought for the absolute retention of traditional Judaism. He countenanced no compromise. To him, no arbitration was possible in religion. There was but one way; any other was destructive and annihilating. He would brook no dilution of Torah in its sacred march through time.

Gaon in Hebrew means *illustrious*. It is a title reserved for those few rabbinical greats who are recognized for their intellectual prowess. Reb Aaron Kotler was known as Gaon of Gaonim—Most Illustrious.

Rabbi in Hebrew means teacher. It is, of course, a title bestowed upon those who pursue the study of the heritage and are ordained leaders of the faith. Reb Aaron was rarely called by this formal title. He was accorded the loving, familiar *Reb*. And it was always *Reb Aaron,* the first name rather than the more formal last name.

Tzaddik in Hebrew means righteous. It is a rare title and only a blessed few earn it. Reb Aaron Kotler was called a Tzaddik.

Kodosh in Hebrew means holy. Only one or two in an entire generation are thought of as being Kodosh. Reb Aaron was everywhere thought of as Kodosh. His sainted soul and blessed spirit illumined the path of Torah. He was the shining star of the 20th century.

Yeshivah in Hebrew means a seminary or academy. It refers to the institution dedicated to Talmudic studies almost exclusively or primarily. Attendance is limited to those who can absorb the Biblical and Talmudic interpretations of the ages. The atmosphere of Yeshivah living and experience is wholly Orthodox in spirit, learning and practice. Rosh Yeshivah in Hebrew means Head or Head Master of the Seminary. Reb Aaron was since early manhood recognized as the Rosh Yeshivah above all others.

Shiur in Hebrew means lecture or discourse. In a Yeshivah it means much more. It refers to a discourse based on previously studied materials, basic sources. The methodology intertwines text, assumptions, legal difficulties, references to the sources and cross references, and the eventual arrival at solutions which are the results of original thinking and creative intellect. It is always oral, never written. The Shiur is the vehicle of many student discussions and becomes part of their mine of information. It is often repeated, reviewed and shared with younger students, thus suggesting the ongoing process of Talmudic teaching and tradition. Reb Aaron was admittedly the master teacher and lecturer, whose keen insights deepened and broadened the knowledge of the earlier masters of Talmud and Codes and brought indescribable delight to listeners who could grasp his brilliant perceptions.

Reb Aaron Kotler was early marked to be patriarch of the generation. His birth in 1892 into prestigious, aristocratic rabbinical families who had provided leadership in Europe for centuries marked him for accomplishment. His father was Rabbi Shneur Zalman Pines, graduate of the Voloshin Yeshivah and grandson of the Gaon Reb Moshe Pines of Minsk, rabbi of the town of Svislovitz. According to custom, his earliest education was directed by his father, who studied with him daily and shared with him the knowledge he had himself amassed. It has been said that at the age of five, Reb Aaron knew the entire Bible by heart and could quote it verbatim in the original Hebrew. Knowledge of his brilliance spread throughout the scholarly world. At the age of ten he was sent by his father to Kerensky to study at the feet of famed Gaon Sender Shapiro. A colleague at whose home young Reb Aaron was guest revealed that when the two came home for the first time, the host's mother asked, "Who is this youngster? It seems that the *Shekhina* (Divine Presence) rests upon him."

Reb Aaron's brilliance generated the need for deeper knowledge and more intensive study. He matriculated at Yeshiva Keneseth Israel in Slabodka, whose Rosh Yeshivah was renowned Reb Moshe Mordecai Epstein and whose dean was Reb Nasan Tzvi Finkel, affectionately known as "The Old One." Reb Aaron was quickly referred to as the *Ilui* (intellectual genius) of Svislovitz. A prevailing custom related a brilliant mind with the name of its possessor's home town. The Old One, impressed with the intellectual prodigy, once said, "I have not seen or met such a heaven-born genius in 40 years." Another legendary figure in the rabbinical world, Reb Chaim Ozer, was visited by young Reb Aaron. The interview lasted longer than expected and a visitor, Rabbi Tzvi Eisenstadt, was kept waiting in the reception room. Coming out of his study after the session, Reb Chaim Ozer said to his next visitor prophetically, "Forgive me for the delay. The young man who was in my office is Reb Aaron Kotler; he is the Gaon of the next generation."

The Yeshivah's officials and teachers expressed deep pride in Reb Aaron, pointing to him as an example for others to follow. The young student was also unsurpassed in piety and observance. Thus it was that Reb Aaron's fame continued to spread. Peers, colleagues, even older rabbis began to quote him—his interpretations and new insights. "Reb Aaron said this, Reb Aaron interpreted the Biblical passage in this way. What does Reb Aaron think of this question?"

In 1913, he married the daughter of famed Rabbi Isar Zalman

Meltzer of Slutsk, who was also the director of the Yeshivah there. At 22, Reb Aaron became the Rosh Yeshivah there, the Academy gaining world renown under his careful guidance. But a peaceful life of study was not meant to be his lot. The world was in a state of turmoil and tension. War clouds hung heavily over Europe, soon to burst into World War I. The city of Slutsk was in a uniquely vulnerable position, located as it was on the Russian-Polish border. But Reb Aaron's complete devotion to his Seminary did not allow deviation from study even while shells rained over the city. It has been said that his father-in-law once asserted that Reb Aaron's concentrative faculties were so astounding that he could persist in studying while sitting on a sharp-edged sword. And so he continued in his work, striving also in communal areas of service, even as the Russian Revolution was bringing the Yeshivah to the point of destruction. Anti-Semitic outbreaks were constantly threatening the Yeshivah. Reb Isar Zalman himself was arrested many times by the Russians. Still Reb Aaron held his ground, and for a number of years succeeded in keeping the Yeshivah intact. In 1921, however, Reb Isar Zalman decided that the time had come to move the Yeshivah and students to more secure and stable surroundings. Half were transferred to Kletsk, Poland. He himself did not want to leave the city he had served for so many years, and so the entire responsibility for the transfer and establishment of a new Yeshivah in another locality fell upon the shoulders of the 29-year-old Reb Aaron.

The transfer of a number of the Yeshivah students from Slutsk was accomplished and there began all over again the process of building a Yeshivah. Poland was not the most inviting homeland. The country was in a state of virtual economic ruin. It had borne the brunt of war. Soldiers had overrun the land, ruined the crops, and laid waste everywhere. Socialism as a doctrine and religion was sweeping the country. Nationalism was rampant. The new ideologies were attracting the young, who were seduced by their easy answers. In addition, Reb Aaron had brought many of the young men to the Yeshivah through illegal means, thus compounding the difficulties which confronted him. Yet he remained untroubled. His faith sustained him. Brilliant leadership qualities came to light quickly as he took up the task of building an institution of learning. He had come with empty hands, a young man known only in the world of the intellect and learned societies. But he had also come with an iron will and determination to build Torah.

The citizens of the community were stimulated by this champion of Torah. They marveled at his passion and ardor and responded to his call for help. Students needed food and clothes. They were brought. Students needed friendship. The community offered friendship and homes. Students needed encouragement to study Torah. They were encouraged and inspired. The community appreciated the blessing that had been brought them with Reb Aaron's arrival on the scene and they responded with alacrity and eagerness.

The Yeshivah of Kletsk began to grow and develop, becoming one of the foremost in the world. Reb Aaron created a towering Torah academy whose beacon light shone the world over. Students from many lands sought admission. To become a student was a high honor. To sit at the feet of Reb Aaron, Great Teacher of Torah, was a coveted privilege. His lectures were enormously popular. Not only his mental genius, but his fatherly mien, his concern for his students, drew students to the Yeshivah.

In the city of Kletsk he became recognized as the watchman of the Torah and all it stood for. He was like a seismograph, listening everywhere for the infractions of Jewish tradition which quickly brought down his wrath. The community knew exactly where he stood and respected him for his undeviating position.

Reb Aaron's leadership qualities soon established roads from, as well as to, his Yeshivah. A warrior of God cannot long remain within the confines of his own environment. There was work to be done for God and Torah all over the world, and Reb Aaron was beckoned. The work of directing a Yeshivah, lecturing and carrying the entire responsibility, may have been enough for one man to carry. Not for Reb Aaron. Judiasm existed everywhere. Problems arose everywhere which needed attention and solutions. The Yeshivah at Kletsk gradually became home base for an overwhelming effort. Reb Aaron broadened the scope of his service. He was involved in the establishment of a Beth Jacob School. He waged bitter wars against foreign influences which threatened to undermine the traditions of Judaism. He could not sit back while secularism was beginning to insinuate itself. It had to be rooted out. Not a matter of Jewish concern arose which did not call for and have his attention. It has been said that if he heard that a father had withdrawn his child from Cheder [literally "room" but referring to Hebrew School] in favor of the so-called "cultural" schools, Reb Aaron personally contacted the father, admonishing and cajoling until he succeeded in returning the child to the Cheder. Every child was important. Every child was a world and carried a potential world of God's truth within him. He became the guardian of Torah, protecting the traditions with all the vigor of his being.

Meanwhile destiny moved him into still larger realms. Communal matters in Poland required thought and direction. Conferences were called and he attended. Slowly he began to lead as he spoke up with fervor and fiery conviction. Although he was the youngest Rosh Yeshivah in attendance, the older rabbis viewed him as equal in stature.

Reb Aaron's affiliation with Agudath Israel, the international right-wing Orthodox movement which aims to solve all the problems of the Jewish people in the spirit of Torah and under the concept of Torah authority, was lifelong and thorough. He played every significant role in the widespread organization. The group was not Zionist-oriented. It was rather vehemently opposed to the Zionist concept, declaring that Zionism summoned the nation of Herzl rather than the Nation of the Torah. It held that to conquer Eretz Israel (the land of Israel) for the life-giving and life-ruling Torah is not only one of the 613 Mitzvos (commandments or duties), but fulfillment of the historic ideals of the entity of Land, People and Torah. If Agudism summons the Nation of the Torah as such, it cannot do it without at the same time directing the eyes of the Nation of the Torah towards the Land of the Torah.

His first participation with Agudath Israel brought protests from the city fathers where his Yeshivah was established. Kletsk was Zionistic. The Zionist press of Warsaw openly warned him that his activity in Agudath Israel would not be advantageous to the existence and furtherance of his school. It would seriously affect his campaign for funds, it was suggested. They misunderstood Reb Aaron. He was not one to frighten easily. They should have known that once convinced he was immovable. He had seen in Agudath Israel an educational force for Judaism and to him this was enough. He poured his heart and soul into the movement, even organizing a branch in the city of Kletsk and impressing his students with a consciousness of the Agudath, its principles and importance in Jewish life.

Conventions were one thing. There was much else to be done, and Reb Aaron traveled all over the country. Warsaw, Vilna, and European lands other than Poland summoned him for help and counsel. When the government threatened to close the Hebrew schools, Reb Aaron interceded. He agitated an entire Jewish population, particularly mobilizing Orthodox forces, until the law was nullified.

This was the first time Reb Aaron was the great mobilizer. He was destined to utilize the same technique on a much larger scale in America and Israel. But it was here at an early age that Reb Aaron became the Great Agitator for Torah. It was here that it was demonstrated that people and governments would have to listen to Orthodox Judaism when it spoke as one voice.

It was natural for traditional Torah education to become Reb Aaron's primary interest and concern and to it he devoted almost all his vigorous energy. The quarter million Jewish children who attended a vast network of Hebrew Schools organized by Agudath Israel had his devoted attention. He was called often to plan new methods and seek ways and means of broadening their scope and perspective.

At the same time public issues affecting Jewish life demanded his thought and action. When Poland tried to abrogate the Jewish laws of ritual slaughter, it was Reb Aaron who again became the Great Agitator, gathering forces, maneuvering strategically and pressing relentlessly until the government backed down. The powerful force of Reb Aaron and a united Orthodox front had again moved a government.

In 1937, at the Third International Conference of Agudath Israel, he was one of the leading keynoters and policy makers. His measured yet flaming words hit their mark, and the aged masters of Israel sat up and took notice.

Reb Aaron made his first visit to America in 1936—his purpose to solicit funds for his Kletsk Yeshivah. Conditions in Poland, as throughout Europe, were disintegrating. But while in America, Reb Aaron did not limit his concern to his own Yeshivah. He utilized his long awaited visit to influence Orthodox Judaism and Torah study. He carried with him the spirit of the European Yeshivah with its devotion to study and entrenchment in the ancient traditions. The European approach was thus reborn in American higher institutions of learning. He persuaded Rabbi Shrage Feivel Mendelovitz, dean of Yeshiva Torah V'Daas, to strive for fuller concentration on Torah study. At his suggestion, Reb Shrage Feivel established the Beth Midrash Elyon, Academy of Higher Learning, in

Spring Valley, New York, thus founding a new institution and laying the groundwork for a new generation of Torah students the likes of which America had not yet known. Study of Talmud, Codes, and other basic sources were to comprise the entire curriculum. The course of study was not to have set hours but to run virtually from sunrise to sunset. In addition, Reb Aaron encouraged individual brilliant students to study in European Yeshivot. Thus he planted the seeds for a renaissance of Talmudic learning and a new era of Yeshivah study which he was later to nurture directly. He seemed to sense that the time would come when America would become the center of Yeshivah study and Europe would fade into history. He foresaw that the golden age of Talmud in Europe was drawing to an end.

Two days after Hitler drove into Poland, the Russians occupied eastern Poland. One day after Rosh Hashanah, Soviet Union forces marched into Kletsk. Reb Aaron, however, did not suspend study and his students stood by him. But conditions deteriorated rapidly. Financial aid, of course, quickly dropped, and his treasury was soon depleted. Still his faith held, the same faith which had supported and driven him all of his days. Inspired by his example, his students did not falter, studying with ever-increasing diligence and fervor. This, he taught, was the supreme test of faith, the test of devotion to Torah and abiding love of God. Once again, the Jewish people of the city, stirred by this demonstration of faith, came to his aid, supplying the needs of the Yeshivah out of their own meager possessions. To them, the Yeshivah was a stronghold of faith, the visible emblem of trust and security.

But the war intensified. Study had to give way ultimately. Reluctantly, Reb Aaron began to allow reality to assert itself. He knew well what the Russians were capable of doing. He remembered Slutsk. Under Russian domination, a Yeshivah could not possibly exist. The day after Sukkos, Feast of Tabernacles, 1939, he journeyed to Vilna to consult with the great rabbis there. Closing a world-renowned citadel of learning was no easy task; such an institution was not a private establishment. It belonged to all Jewry. The great rabbis, after serious, earnest consideration and evaluation, concluded that the Yeshivah should be moved to Vilna, long known as the Jerusalem of Poland. There the possibility of its continuation would be more certain.

Thus, the Yeshivah of Kletsk went into exile. It was Reb Aaron's second major move in the face of a rising threat of violence. It was not to be the last. He was soon to make one more drastic move, from Europe to America.

As he was preparing to evacuate, Reb Aaron received word from his father-in-law, Rabbi Isar Zalman, who by this time had settled in the Holy Land, urging him not to move the Yeshivah to Vilna, but rather to come to Israel (then Palestine). Reb Aaron was neither prepared to dissolve his Yeshivah nor to flee. He succeeded in bring his Yeshivah to Vilna, where studies were resumed.

The Yeshivah restored, Reb Aaron shifted his sights to a new area which required his leadership talents, the rescue of lives. Many students, rabbis included, had been captured. Jews were being taken as hostages and assembled for the crematoria. *Rescue, save* became the themes and goals of conferences and surreptitious meetings. The handwriting on the wall was clear and sharp. While study at the Yeshivah continued unabated, Reb Aaron now knew that its official days were numbered. It was now a question of arranging for its secret existence and saving its students. He divided the Yeshivah into three sections and located them in three different towns, continuing to keep careful watch over his beloved students.

In Kovno and Vilna the great men of Israel met again—like the Passover Haggadah of five scholars who sat at B'nai Brak ostensibly studying Torah but really mapping a campaign for liberty and freedom—to match wits against a government which had already summoned Reb Aaron before its Secret Police, NKVD, for questioning and torture. Details of these meetings may never be known or revealed, but many visas were arranged as the leaders worked feverishly against time. They had to secure visas which would take their bearers across the wide expanse of Russia to Japan and then to the United States or South America. Travel through Western Europe was impossible with Hitler running rampant.

Meanwhile, here in America knowledge of the great danger brought immediate action from Orthodox Jewry. The urgent call to save Reb Aaron and Yeshivah students, together with the call to save Jews in Europe, began to be heard. President Franklin Delano Roosevelt himself granted Reb Aaron a special visa to the United States.

Reb Aaron believed that from a place in America he could alert

Jewry to the crisis and succeed in rescuing hundreds and thousands of students. He began his long, arduous trek across Russia in February, 1941. Meanwhile, as a result of the groundwork laid by the great rabbis in Kovno, over a hundred Yeshivah students also began traveling across the plains of Russia with visas on their persons. One month after he had started out, Reb Aaron arrived in Japan, where the students, too, gradually began to turn up. The latters' visas, however, allowed them to travel no further, while Reb Aaron's destination was America.

Once here, Reb Aaron redoubled his rescue operations. He made contact with American rabbis and officials; he lodged in consulates and visited persons of eminence. He pleaded, cajoled and exhorted. Through his efforts, hundreds of students were evacuated from Europe in the nick of time.

April, 1941, will be regarded by generations to come as a historic month for American Judaism. This was the month and the year that Reb Aaron arrived in America and, accordingly, the month and year when the format of American Jewry began to change. The move to the more traditional, perceptible in some areas only at present, commenced. The story may not be told for many years to come. History will have to evaluate and note, but signs are already visible. Judaism in America began the shift back to its ancient glory with Reb Aaron's arrival in America. His contagious love of his faith was caught by thousands who had long sought leadership. Man of the spirit, man of action, Reb Aaron inflamed the hearts of many Orthodox Jews who had already given up hope for the future of Orthodoxy in America. His first words on arrival were a call to American Jewry to help save the Jews of Europe. *Rescue* was his life's motto. Rescue Torah and rescue lives—both were the same.

Significantly and coincidentally, he landed in San Francisco on the eve of Passover, festival of freedom, for *rescue* and *freedom* were favored themes throughout his life and especially in those first moments.

On the day after Passover he arrived in New York, welcomed at Pennsylvania Station by thousands of admirers. His first question was compelling: "Has something already been done to save lives and secure visas?" He stood on the train platform and said:

> For myself, I would not have come! I have come here to help rescue, through you American Jews, the century-old religious centers of Jewish life in Europe. . . . Do not rest! Work! Work! Do not rest, work, work to save.

To the officers of Agudath Israel, he said:

> I thank you for the honor you pay to the Torah and I hope you will not rest one moment until all Jews are saved. . . . America is now the only country which has the power to save and rescue. See to it that the road to America, only channel of rescue, becomes wider and broader. See to it that America allows more Jews to come in!

This was Reb Aaron Kotler. At the railroad station, tired from his long journey, already calling on America to save; save Jews from the vale of tears. At the same time, he thrilled many thousands of Orthodox Jews and formed them into a solid union when he proclaimed: "Torah has a future in America."

Orthodox Jewry immediately rallied around Reb Aaron and conferences were called. Policies had to be formulated, plans laid. There was work to be done. Reb Aaron set his goals high. Rescue work began. The Vaad Hatzalah, Committee for Rescue, became the agency through which he labored. Though it had been organized before his arrival, he instilled a new spirit and faith into the group, teaching the lesson that God's help is commensurate with man's effort.

Rescue of life was related to rescue of Torah. And this meant study, study, and more study, in the fashion of the traditional European Yeshivah. A year after his arrival, 1942, and following his suggestion to Rabbi Shrage Feivel in 1937 regarding the Yeshivah in Spring Valley, Reb Aaron organized the Beth Midrash Govoha, Academy of Higher Learning, in Lakewood, New Jersey (since April 1964 known as Rabbi Aaron Kotler Institute for Advanced Learning). A seminary of this kind, he was convinced, must be removed from the distractions and tumult of the metropolitan city. Ten students, formerly of Yeshivos from Europe, comprised the first class.

The Yeshivah grew steadily under Reb Aaron's careful supervision. He drew there the brilliant young minds, infused the spirit of Torah in them, and established the Yeshivah as the center of traditional study in America. In time, hundreds of students made their way to Lakewood to study at the feet of the master. Hundreds were graduated, steeped in the ancient codes, saturated with the brilliance of the greatest rabbinic minds of the ages. They in turn established other Yeshivos, academies, parochial schools and day schools and became teachers in religious and other institutions.

His Yeshivah also became the mother of other seminaries: in Philadelphia, St. Louis, Vineland, New Jersey, Boston, and New Haven. The seeds planted were being nurtured. The fruit was sure to be rich.

Reb Aaron's consecration to education, as in earlier days, drew him to other educational institutions. He became the guiding light of Torah u-Masorah—literally, Torah and Tradition—an organization sponsoring a network of preparatory Talmudic academies which would in time feed the Yeshivot. Thus over 50,000 students ultimately came under his powerful influence. His flaming enthusiasm changed the curriculum contour of these preparatory schools and further affected Yeshivah study in America.

All this naturally swept him into circles of Orthodox leadership, lay and rabbinical. He became active in Agudath Harabonim, Union of Orthodox Rabbis of America and Canada, and soon was elected member of its presidium—this in but a few short years after his arrival. From this position, he stood guard over Orthodox principles. Unhesitatingly he reprimanded Orthodox rabbis for mingling with Conservative and Reform rabbis. He led the drive against acceptance of the new Ketubah (marriage contract) adopted by the Conservative Rabbinical Assembly, He inveighed against the Synagogue Council of America and New York Board of Rabbis where Orthodox rabbis worked closely with rabbis of other groups within Judaism. He would countenance no other brand of Judaism save Orthodoxy, and he minced no words if he saw the ancient faith threatened.

Reb Aaron's world-wide perspective took in problems of his people in the Holy Land. He visited Israel in 1946, before it officially became the State of Israel, and attended the Third International Conference of Agudath Israel. He visited every Torah institution in the land, wanting to see personally the status of each school and how it was faring. In this way, he gained a total picture and became part of the fabric of Torah education in Israel.

New immigrants were arriving constantly in the Holy Land. They had to have places to stay before rehabilitation programs could begin. He helped the newcomers circulate throughout the land and was involved in the establishment of welcome centers for them and religious settlements. His trip to Israel convinced him that Israel was destined to become a center of Jewish life.

He visited Israel again in 1950 and gave tremendous impetus to the flourishing Torah institutions and Yeshivot. The more he moved from school to school, the more his influence was felt. The pious, tender spirit was caught by the thousands of children and young adults who looked to him as their teacher and captain of the ship of Torah. Thus in Israel also Reb Aaron inspired a generation of Jews to become devotees of traditional Judaism.

While in Israel Reb Aaron learned that only 5000 children were attending Zerem R'viee, fourth of the four educational systems in Israel, directed by the Agudath Israel. He was stunned. Only 5000? In all Israel? How was this possible? Where would the leaders come from? What of the future of Torah in Israel? He immediately summoned a conference and proclaimed: "Thousands and thousands of children are waiting and we can win them for Torah. Every day is a loss. We must not hesitate. We must not desist. We must work, work, work!"

New buildings were necessary, facilities had to be trebled, quadrupled and more. He insisted that within a matter of one year, 30 buildings were necessary. His impassioned call was a command to the assemblage. There was to be no discussion. It was a categorical imperative. The response was overwhelming. World Jewry answered with astonishing alacrity. In two years, 40 Talmud Torahs were created and the 5000 enrollment jumped to 20,000. Reb Aaron was again proven right. It could be done. Unity and spirited action could perform miracles for Torah and education.

Later, in 1954, Israel revamped the entire educational system, creating two out of the four existent systems. The budgets of educational systems which did not submit to government control would be curtailed. To Reb Aaron, the division into religious and secular schools was destructive. It meant that Torah education as he conceived it would be subject to and dependent upon the government. Torah education had to be supervised by Torah leaders, men steeped in the traditions of the ages. He would not allow the religious schools he had fought so hard to create and foster to submit. He would not allow the state to control the hundreds of schools of Agudath Israel, which meant the lives and futures of 40,000 youngsters. It meant liquidation of his principles.

He sprang into action, called world Jewry together, fiercely led the organization of Chinuch Atzmahi, Torah Schools for Israel, and undertook the staggering financial responsibility for all the schools. It was fantastic to assume such a responsibility, but Reb Aaron would not relent. It was a holy campaign, a continuing drive for God and Torah. Again he set Orthodox Jewry astir, and again he succeeded. The result was that there are still 40,000 students in these schools. Reb Aaron had once more amassed Jews and finances for Torah.

The Great Agitator for Torah mobilized Jewry time and again. When the Yemenite immigration crisis, Magic Carpet, developed in 1952, Reb Aaron learned that the religious Jews coming into the country were being herded into settlements where their religious rights were being violated. The Mapai government was accused by religious Jewry of forcibly enrolling the new immigrants in nonreligious camps, removing their religious dress, and deterring them from observing their traditional faith. Reb Aaron again leaped into action, calling conferences, mobilizing forces. Religious Jews had an inherent right to practice their religion as they saw fit. It was improper, even illegal, to coerce them to violate their religious principles. The irrepressible power of Reb Aaron and the pressure he exerted was effective. The government backed down to review and re-evaluate its position.

Orthodox Jewry in America began to realize that it was a mighty and influential movement. It was Reb Aaron who brought this recognition to the fore. In the short span of two decades in America, he altered the course of the mainstream of Jewish life and left his indelible imprint on the American Jewish scene. Repeatedly, he spoke out fearlessly. What belonged to Torah was his concern, no matter the obstacle or person. Yet, whatever the major problem to be met head-on, Reb Aaron's underlying principle was study and more study, according to the Talmudic dictum, *Talmud Torah k'neged kulam,* "The study of Torah is equal to and balances all the other commandments."

In 1954, when the Fourth International Conference of Agudath Israel was convened, Reb Aaron was no longer *one* of the leaders; he was the keynoter, *the* leader—recognized, admired, respected. He had risen to the highest position in Judaism and Jewry. He became president of the Moetzet Gedolai Hatorah, the Supreme Rabbinical Council or Council of Torah Authorities of Agudath Israel, and thus watchman over Israel.

Time began to take its toll. The spirit was driving on, but the body was weakening. Reb Aaron had been too busy to be concerned for his own health, and the daily interviews, travels, correspondence, Yeshivah schedule and lectures were draining. But though illness came, there was no complaint. There was still work to do for Torah.

His devoted disciples stood by and with him during his illnesses, reciting psalms and praying. Though under the influence of drugs, he exhorted his disciples to listen carefully while he recited the prayers and blessings lest he fall asleep and not finish one, which would mean that a blessing had been recited in vain.

On the morning of his last day, after a massive heart attack, with the same fervor and piety which had sustained him throughout his long and fruitful life, Reb Aaron recited the Shema and confession prayers and gently expired, taking his place alongside the saints and martyrs of Israel.

The patriarch of the 20th century was dead, but his legacy was secure. He had sowed, and the seeds had taken root. Legends multiply as recollections are brought to light and repeated. For generations to come, it will be: "Reb Aaron said this," or "Reb Aaron said that," or "Reb Aaron would have done this," or "Reb Aaron would have explained it in this way."

As a teacher and lecturer, he was unexcelled. Scholars of the day marveled at his acumen and extraordinary ability to build a system of thought into a monumental structure. He encompassed his subject completely, never losing sight of his central theme. And though he engaged in detailed analysis, he never sacrificed his broadness of scope. On the other hand he grasped the essence of a problem without losing sight of the most insignificant detail or implication. His Shiurim (discourses) inspired thousands. It was spiritually and mentally edifying to an extraordinary degree to be present on these occasions. He would walk into the central study hall, where each student sat at his own small "stander" (pulpit), kiss the Holy Ark, turn to his lectern and begin. His eyes would brighten slowly as he softly began. He was, after all, teaching—not lecturing. Gently he stated the text. General principles and assumptions followed, supported by proofs from related codes or interpretations of masters of another day. On these foundations he would gradually build a complete structure of thought, his incisive thinking eliciting an answering glow in the eyes of his students as his own eyes brightened. It appeared so simple, so obvious.

Suddenly, the whole structure crumbles, destroyed by contrary laws, differing views and interpretations. A law has been overlooked, an authoritative interpretation forgotten. The careful mental structure he had created is disturbed. Reb Aaron notes the answering disturbance among his listeners. After all this? After a pause he begins again. Leading his listeners, he looks at the meaning of the text and the context in which it had been stated. As he takes it apart and explains it, a light of comprehension appears on the faces of some of the students. They understand the relation to the original structure. They are a bit ahead of the master. He does not let on. Everyone must understand. He moves back to the initial structure and with calculated care explains, relates and intertwines, becoming more fluent as he approaches his conclusion. Now everyone is with him. How easy it is. Let us go over it to make sure that we retain this new approach to the problem the original text posed.

Reb Aaron's concern for his people, for humanity, is as legendary as his creative genius in the world of Talmud. He leaned over backward not to hurt feelings. Hurting feelings is degrading, a lessening of man's divinity, he maintained. Examples abound. While driving on a turnpike or expressway and approaching toll booths, he would always insist that the driver pay the attendant rather than deposit the coin in the automatic container, saying, "It is not dignified for a human being to see himself degraded. A man who watches a machine doing his duty must certainly feel hurt."

It was also his custom to demand that the driver pick up hitch-hikers on the road. Disregarding one who stands with arm outstretched he considered cruel. Jews especially, he used to say, ought to be more sensitive to a pleading arm. To his students and friends who warned him of the dangers involved in such a practice he would respond, "There are more of us in the car than the one hitch-hiker."

On Sabbath and holiday eves he would dine with his students and disciples. Upon entering the dining hall and before joining his students, he would go directly to the kitchen and greet the cooks with the traditional Good Sabbath or Good Holiday.

"The really great on earth are the simple," Heinrich Heine once said. Indeed, Reb Aaron was one of the great. The leader of all Orthodox Jewry never allowed his stationery to read other than the two words of his name, Aaron Kotler. No title, no decorations must appear. To himself he was simply Aaron Kotler, servant of God. To a world he was a giant of faith, Israel's patriarch of the 20th century.

SOLOMON GOLDMAN

Eloquent Zealot for People and Culture

[1893-1953]

Every Sunday morning for years, hundreds of people, Jews and non-Jews, beat a path to Chicago's impressive Anshe Emet Synagogue to listen to Dr. Solomon Goldman, one of America's most influential Conservative rabbis. It was not the handsomeness of the prematurely white-haired, rimless-spectacled, dignified rabbi which attracted them. Rather it was the original thinking, stimulating insight and unorthodox approaches of this leading American rabbi and Biblical scholar that drew the faithful crowds. Listening to Rabbi Goldman's lectures was habit-forming, sought after eagerly week after week.

The subjects were as varied as life itself, the themes as vital as life. As one listened history lived, religion lived, Judaism lived. "I shall live and speak and think," he once said, "as a free man. The most beautiful thing in the world, old Diogenes believed, was freedom of speech. This thing of beauty, of dignity, of very life, the seal of humanity, I shall not yield."

He lived up to this credo. It made little difference to him what or who the object was, he was not one to mince words. The discourse was not directed to ingratiate himself with those of a certain view or party. Truth and honesty were primary, not people, whoever they may be. As few others, Solomon Goldman took stock of Judaism, analyzing it, sifting, distilling, and seeking ways of reconstructing it. And he could call out for the reconstruction of Judaism and of the synagogue in words which aroused and moved:

The reconstruction of Judaism must begin with the reconstruction of the synagogue. Ventilate it, renationalize it, beautify it, make it alive to the needs of the Jewish people today. Let membership in the synagogue express a loyalty to the group, an anxiety to continue its life-process, rather than presuppose the acceptance of certain unalterable dogmas and fixed views of the cosmos. Make room there for men of divergent belief and challenging skepticism. To thousands of men and women, and particularly to young people, it will take on a new sense of value which all will recognize.

Some people did not understand. Others called out "Bravo." But all sat up, listened, and were moved to thought. Solomon Goldman called upon all to accept the proposition that Judaism is not a religion, pure and simple. It was more, he asserted forcefully. It was a nationality. It was "the personality of a people."

The nationhood of Israel is an ineluctable fact. . . . the Jew will learn that he must assume the responsibility of nationhood. He may be unable to accept the ideology of this nation, but he cannot dissolve it in a religious union. That a man's mother is his mother cannot be disputed, but that the son must accept all of the mother's philosophy is naturally open to question. We accept the nationhood of Israel as axiomatic and in our program we must seek to carry out the implications of this fundamental axiom. . . .

Nationalism seldom came to mean to the Jew a desire for conquest. It is only a stubborn refusal to dissolve his own identity; it was the manifestation of a stupendous elan vital. Unlike the Greek, Jewish nationality or the Jewish nation never grew weary, never lost "verve."

. . . If he wishes to continue the memories of the past and his Jewish personality, the Jew must assume the obligations incumbent on the members of a national group. He must learn its language and literature, interest himself in the upbuilding of his home, and seek to adjust its traditions and folkways and its religious concepts to the progress of human thought. Only in this way can the Jew maintain and perpetuate the Jewish personality.

Goldman was inveighing against Reform and right-wing Orthodoxy in 1930, a time when Zionism was not as popular as it later became. Zionism was in the air but had not been brought down to earth. Many Reform rabbis were vehemently anti-Zionist and attacked mercilessly. The right-wing Orthodox could not look with favor upon secular, non-religious Zionists as proper leaders of the Jewish people's return to the Holy Land. Goldman lashed out against both and all who mistakenly saw in the term "nationality" a chauvinism which precluded hope of the restoration of the Jewish homeland. He called up the words and stands of Brandeis and Einstein to demonstrate the compatibility between Zionism and Americanism. "Let no American think that Zionism is inconsistent with patriotism," Justice Louis D. Brandeis had written, "Multiple loyalties are objectionable only if they are inconsistent." In greater exposition of his position, Brandeis wrote:

A man is a better citizen of the United States for being also a loyal citizen of his State, and of his city; for being loyal to his family, and to his profession or trade; for being loyal to his college or his lodge. Every Irish American who contributed towards advancing home rule was a better man and a better American for the sacrifice he made. Every American Jew who aids in the advancing of the Jewish settlement in Palestine, though he feels that neither he nor his descendants will ever live there will likewise be a better Jew and a better American for doing so.

Goldman echoed the sentiments of Albert Einstein thusly:

The German Jew who works for the Jewish people and for the Jewish home in Palestine no more ceases to be a German than the Jew who becomes baptized and changes his name ceases to be a Jew. The two attachments are grounded in realities of different kinds. The antithesis is not between Jew and German, but between honesty and lack of character. He who remains true to his origin, race, and tradition will also remain loyal to the State of which he is a subject. He who is faithless to the one will also be faithless to the other.

The same Solomon Goldman who referred to the "personality of a people" as the definition of nationality did not refrain from frankness when it would arouse reproach and hostility. This is how he felt and understood and he would unhesitatingly state it.

Blasphemous and perverted as it may sound to some, it is nevertheless factually true that Israel has lived for Israel's sake. . . . It neither suffered nor fought for God—for an abstract, uniform God-idea. . . . For the Jews' martyrdom was for the continuity of Israel, for the God of Abraham, Isaac and Jacob. The martyr's affirmation was Hear, O *Israel*, the Eternal *our* God is One.

He went further:

> It is rather difficult to maintain, as some would have it, that it is theology, or the God-idea that holds Jewry together.

At the same time, he condemned the traditional view of history which to him was "not only the antithesis to common sense, intelligence and the modern spirit, but invalidates the very uniqueness—the selection concept it posits." He insisted rather on the theory of dynamic history, meaning a groping, blundering, willing-to-live Israel. To Goldman, a consciousness of kin created in the Jew an awareness of his Jewish personality.

> We must study the past not only reverentially but critically as well. We cannot assume that all the accounts which have come down to us from the past are literally true. We must not hesitate to separate the grain from the chaff. The interpretation of history found in sacred and learned literature need not be considered as final. On the contrary, we often are today in a better position to understand the movements and events of the days of long ago than were those who preceded us by centuries. Jewish history is certainly no exception. . . . It is clear that we are as much in need of a science of Jewish history as we are of a science of Jewish religion.
>
> What was it that kept the Jew together? What was it that wove through the fabric of his history? A consciousness of kin. This was the awareness which ever stood in the forefront of his mind and was translated in his deeds and actions. It is this vague feeling of oneness, this consciousness of kin that can constitute the only basis for Jewish unity. The Jew who senses it, professes it and is anxious for its continuity is a Jew. Devout theism and ethical monotheism alone no more make a man a Jew than nonresistance and naturalism imply that a man is a Hindu.

This consciousness of kin included the Hebrew language, which Goldman saw as the thread which kept the people together. Not the language alone, to be sure, but its literature and culture, the history of the people as they traveled from period to period—now peaceful, now less so, now fraught with fear, now sensing less danger, now subject to martyrdom, now enjoying closeness with political leaders, and so on. Language to Goldman was the index to the people's soul and the only way by which to become intimately acquainted with that soul.

> Style may be the man, but language is the people. . . . We need hardly add that a language without literature is mere dialect. When we speak

of the Hebrew language we have in mind the great literature that the Jew produced in this language. Of old, even as today, we know no better way of bringing the much abused younger generation nearer to the Jewish people than by acquainting it with the tremendous achievement in Jewish literature. From the Bible to Chaim Nachman Bialik [the great Hebrew poet of the last generation] what genuine beauty, what a glorious heritage.

Glorious is the word which is appropriate to describe the heights to which this powerful rabbi could rise, especially when he contemplated his people and their needs. His eyes would blaze with feeling as he reflected on the history of his people and told their story. He was proud of them and wanted all to know about it and be proud with him. He thrilled to the meaning that his people's history had for the world, for Christianity, for mankind, and he wanted all to know about it. He could cry for his people's hurt and shame, and he could rejoice in their achievements and success.

What sentiment he could generate, and did, as he stood before his audience, his eyes narrowing as he reflected on the movements of history, and made that history live again:

> The inward, continued struggle of Israel for its distinctive personality now appears to be unparalleled in the annals of man. The stubborn conviction of the spiritual import of our history still remains a singular phenomenon in the records of people. . . .
>
> It is not mere ideology that has kept us going. It is a lusty appetite for life, a zeal for the maintenance and perpetuation of our "ego," of our total life process, that makes us bear undefeated the burden of existence. . . .
>
> Hounded, persecuted, he was driven from shore to shore, from land to land, nowhere finding peace; everywhere was he treated with discrimination, suspicion, and, aye, worst of all, even with fear. Centuries, millennia rolled by; empires rose and fell; civilizations flourished and crumbled to the dust. Egyptian charioteer, Greek hoplite, Roman legion, cross and crescent, all dug their steel into the Jew's flesh, but undaunted, unswerving, immovable, he remained loyal to his ideals—aye, if you please—to his illusions. By all standards of history he should have long ago perished or at least should have become a straggling, despondent vagabond; his morale should have corroded centuries ago, but he refused to submit to an inexorable fate. He fought gloom, despair, pessimism. He doggedly retained his faith in an idea, in truth, in the supremacy of the inner life. He was confident of ultimate victory. He survived. . . .

It has profound esthetic appeal to the Jew himself and to the world. It is glorious to live, to roll up years, decades, centuries, millennia. It is thrilling to look back on vistas of time; there I was—then I was. . . .

Here is the Jew—roll back the book of history; you are almost at its very beginning. Abraham was there to exchange compliments with Hammurabi. Turn a leaf; here is Rameses, well, he had his difficulties with the God of the Hebrew. Rameses, as we now know, was the scion of a great people, but he is, after all, only a mummy. But even as a mummy, because it is so very old and has so admirably defied time, Rameses has attained a commendable reputation; but Moses, mind you, is no mummy and his burning bush is not yet consumed.

Continue to turn the pages; new names, new cultures, new countries, new habits, customs. The Jew, the Jew, he is yet there. You are at the end of ancient times. The whole world is at the feet of mighty Rome. The Jew, amongst many others, is battling for his life; Rome scores a victory.

Some three years ago [1927] a collector of coins brought to my study a number of coins of Jewish interest. One of them brought tears to my eyes. It was a coin that was minted between 69 and 70 A.D. at the request of Titus. There was stamped on it a crouching Jew, symbolizing Judea, and it bore the inscription, "Judea Capta, Judea Devicta."

I held the coin in my hand and mused with a pain at my heart. Suddenly I recalled that the firebrand which set the Temple on fire and reduced it to ashes 1,859 years ago was hurled by one of Titus' soldiers from Mount Scopus. At the very same moment it occurred to me that the University of Jerusalem was being built on the very mountain and that the world's greatest intellect, "The Tip Topper" of our age, as Bertrand Russell put it to me, Albert Einstein, emerged from his laboratory to campaign for funds in order to assure its existence and growth. I turned to the other face of the coin; there was Titus with his helmet and all his imperial Roman dignity. "Perhaps you are best remembered," I reflected, "because of your accursed deed, because you linked your name with an undying people."

In social as in biological problems, time is the sole real creator and the sole great destroyer. It is time that has made mountains with grains of sand and raised the obscure cell of geological eras to human dignity. Time has made the Jew. Time has thought him thus far desirable. Time alone will have to prove him undesirable.

Not only from pulpit, platform and podium did Solomon Goldman stimulate and excite. The spoken word was but one avenue for reaching the minds and hearts of people. Another was the written word. Solomon Goldman dug deep into his phenomenal mind where he had amassed encyclopedic knowledge and information of all literature, history, philosophy—Hebrew and secular—and brought forth many volumes, thus becoming the rabbi as teacher, first and primary role of a minister of Israel. Rabbi indeed means teacher. He taught the Bible through careful analyses—how it was born, developed and came to pulsate with vitality; who evaluated, who sought to undermine and who to defend; how to protect, and how to understand. The whole inexplicable vastness of Biblical scholarship through the ages, in all its depth and meaning, lay before the reader. His massive knowledge joined forces with an incisive mind to sway thousands of readers just as he moved more thousands with the eloquence of his utterances. But it is through the written word, Hebrew and English, that he lives on to inspire coming generations.

A mere cataloguing of his offices is suggestive of the influence he wielded above and beyond the range of his pastorate and writings:

President, Zionist Organization of America

Chairman, National Emergency Commission for Palestine

Co-chairman, United Palestine Appeal

Co-chairman, United Jewish Appeal

Member, National Hillel Commission

President, National Hebrew Association

President, Histadruth Ivrith

Vice-president, American Jewish Congress

Vice-president, World Zionist Congress

Board Member, Joint Distribution Committee, Jewish National Fund, American Friends of the Hebrew University, Palestine Hebrew Culture Fund, Jewish Publication Society of America, United Synagogue of America, *Menorah Journal,* Jewish Theological Seminary of America

Nor is this list complete. There was membership in many an intellectual society, and active membership was the demand of joining. How did he do all this? The answer lay in his remarkable powers of concentration and the iron self-discipline which characterized him all his life.

It was precisely this self-discipline and the projection of goals it implied which early marked Solomon Goldman for leadership in American Judaism. A glance at his heritage throws light on the development of such character and high purpose, a heritage which had given to Jewish people eleven continuous generations of rabbis. Rabbi Goldman's mother, when he was born in Kozin, Russia, on August 14, 1893, hoped that her son Solomon would be the twelfth generation in the rabbinical line. She began early to make sure that his knowledge was deep and intense. The home environment vibrated with the spirit of Judaism and Solomon readily absorbed the passion for tradition in the atmosphere. Zionism was an ingredient of this passion.

"I was born into Zionism," Dr. Goldman said on the day he was installed as president of the Zionist Organization of America, and he embarked on vivid recollections of his grandfather, Rabbi Joshua Grossman of Kishineff, who had slept for 40 years using a stone for a pillow as a mark of mourning over the destruction of the Temple.

Solomon came to America as a youth and studied diligently at the Rabbi Isaac Elchanan Yeshiva in New York. His grounding in Talmudic studies under the tutelage of his uncle, Mendel, was complete and intensive. Indeed, his education was limited to Hebraic studies. He was aware, however, that this training was not preparing him for contribution and service to the American Jewish scene. Blessed as he was with striking self-discipline, Solomon at the age of 16 established his own curriculum and pursued it relentlessly. The course of study included Latin, French, German, algebra and geometry, and he allowed himself two years to complete it. Coming as it did long before Dr. Robert Maynard Hutchins's famous accelerated study program, Solomon Goldman's crash curriculum amazed and bewildered his teachers. In but one and a quarter years, he completed the program and was graduated from high school.

He continued his studies at the Yeshiva for a while and then transferred to the Jewish Theological Seminary where he was ordained in 1918, having enjoyed favored status with the sainted Solomon Schechter and the great Professor Louis Ginzberg. In the meantime, he also attended New York University and was graduated in 1917. All this time, Goldman had to work to support himself. Labor at buttonholes in pants shops and tutoring sustained him and helped him work his way through school.

Ever the restless seeker after knowledge, Goldman took post-graduate work at Columbia University where destiny brought him under the influence of powerful teachers. During all of the formative years of college study he was fortunate in his teachers. There were Professor Charles G. Shaw of New York University, Dr. Solomon Schechter, Dr. Israel Friedlander, Dr. Louis Ginzberg and Professor John Dewey, each leaving indelible impressions on Goldman's receptive mind and transmitting to him his intellectual fervor and dynamic approach to learning.

The call to serve a Jewish community came quickly. His first pulpit was B'nai Israel Congregation in Brooklyn in 1917, and his recollections of his first meeting with the congregation are filled with human warmth. His father had been concerned about his son's first pulpit. Though he had been ordained he did not look the part of a rabbi. He had been known to friends and classmates as "Swede" because of his blond complexion and slimness. Dashing was another adjective applied to him. It was not wise to send such an Aryan in appearance to meet the congregation, his father mused. He therefore took his son with him on rounds of all the second-hand clothing stores, with the result that when Rabbi Solomon Goldman presented himself to his new congregation, he was impeccably attired in Prince Albert, wing collar and tall hat. A striking sight!

He served his first congregation for two years and then was called to Cleveland, Ohio, where he directed the destinies of two congregations, B'nai Jeshurun from 1918 to 1922, and the Jewish Center from 1922 to 1929. The eleven years in Cleveland were devoted to his synagogues, problems of his constituents and the community. They were, more significantly, years of preparation. Beyond the duties of rabbi and pastor, Solomon Goldman was casting his sights toward the larger community, directing his goals to the national and international scene. This he did by meticulously watching the turbulent events of the day, especially as they applied to his people. At the same time, he began amassing fantastically large files on the Bible. Every reference to the Bible he could secure became part of his library. His first loves, his people and the Bible, were constantly on his mind. His enlarging perspective was rooted securely in Bible, language and culture. His views of America, the world and Zionism, were interwoven with the knowledge he was storing. A time of crisis in America was coming. Crises were also approaching for his people. In intellectual circles scientific and political thought were bringing intellectual crises. All kinds of worlds were shaky.

The many years of dogged preparation ended when Goldman was called to Anshe Emet of Chicago. One of the largest Conservative synagogues in America, Anshe Emet became home base for Goldman's final quarter of a century of activity and service and impressive contribution to the development of American Judaism.

"The most dynamic human being that the American-Jewish scene ever produced, combining wonderful graciousness and innate kindness with a great advocacy of liberal ideals and prophetic zeal," as Stephen S. Wise described him, was ready to act. He became known nationally and internationally for his scholarship and altruism. Book after book rolled off the press, bringing to the larger audience the pregnant views and incisive thought of the great scholar. Speech after speech left thousands convinced and uplifted.

His first book in 1931, *A Rabbi Takes Stock*, brought quick acclaim. With characteristic forthrightness, Goldman had something to say and said it. "It will hurt only those who fear frankness," said one reviewer. "One of the most powerful books I ever read," agreed Clarence Darrow. All groups within Judaism were taken to task as he sought to infuse meaning and purpose into Jewish life. The synagogue has to be a more vital force, he asserted. It must become a laboratory of the spirit. He examined the motives of the unaffiliated, urging them into the synagogue. He scanned newspapers and magazines for attacks against his people, Hebrew and Zionism and came out fiercely in their defense. He spoke of nationalism and universalism, God and Israel, Palestine and the Jewish Home, the Civilized Jew and the Uncivilized Jew. The renaissance of the Hebrew spirit fascinated him. He delved into history for proof of the claim to Palestine as the Jewish Home. Nor did he write simply emotionally or sentimentally, but always provided copious notes, and precise sources.

On every scholarly front he became increasingly active, editing a series of texts for students of modern Hebrew and an annotated anthology of Hebrew literature. Other books came off the press, one after another. In 1936 his *The Jew and the Universe* offered a study of Jewish thought. By 1938 he had written *The Golden Chain* and

Crisis and Decision, the latter a volume of challenging essays. His views on Zionism were already set by this time, the year before he was elected president of the Zionist Organization of America. He wrote of the place of the Jew in the modern world, the relationship of Jew and Christian, the duty of rabbis, religion and change, leadership in America and throughout the world. Albert Einstein, reading the essay, "Is Einstein Religious," was moved to comment, "I might never have believed that one man could look into the inside of another so deeply." The book reaches a climax in an essay entitled "The Romance of a People," a prose poetry creation which was the basis for a magnificent dramatic production held at the Chicago's World's Fair in 1933. At Soldiers' Field, capable of housing over 100,000 guests, Jewish people of all ages, representing every Jewish organization in Chicago, were part of the massive performance directed by Meyer Weisgal. Out in the amphitheater, the drama of Jewish history unfolded proudly, with thousands participating in dance and song.

The words he wrote carried motion and driving activity, propelling a people and an idea through history:

A thick, fleecy, unfathomable darkness fills the stage, the very inside of darkness, shrouding chaos. . . . A tremor flitters across the stage. The Voice has spoken: Let there be Light . . . light effulgent, resplendent, dashing and speeding and warming Nature to life and action. . . . The robust, firm, dexterous frame of man, the delicate, velvety, ravishing figure of woman, arise. . . .

He raises his eyes to the heavens, to the sun, the moon, the stars, to all that lies beyond his reason and comprehension, imploring help, searching for a friendly spirit. . . .

Trek, trek, trek. Over the glittering sands of the Arabian desert, slowly trudges a caravan. . . . In the unbroken stillness of the desert, in its simplicity and austerity, the patriarch catches a glimpse of things undreamt . . . did not one God make them all? Is not the whole of Nature one? Is not man and child the handiwork of God? Why fear?

Trek, trek, trek. . . . Oh Egypt, warm, luscious sin, Memphis and Thebes, fleshpots of civilization. . . . The seed of Abraham too is part of the melting pot; it has bent its back to drudgery, it is building treasure cities for

Egypt's kings and gods. Stinging is the master's whip, maddening is the gathering of straw. . . . Freedom is forgotten, forgotten are the ancient memories of the desert, of Abraham, of God, of Justice, in the anguish of spirit and the cruel bondage. . . .

I am that I am. This slavery shall not be. The blood of Abraham will not rest. It gathers up all its latent energy and vigor in the man Moses, the Liberator, the lawgiver, the molder of a people. "Pharoah, let my people go! Israelites rebel, strike off your chains! The one God, the God of Abraham, the God of Justice is commanding your service; to man, to idols, to injustice, bend not your backs. There are prophets in your flesh, martyrs in your bones. . . ."

Hearken to the strident, triumphant voices of victory. . . . Yonder looms Sinai. A Torah, men, tablets of the Law, God's own words, Egypt's slaves, wake up. Seed of Abraham, you are witnessing a new, a greater creation. The desert quivers, the heavens are rent asunder. . . . Hear the clap of thunderings, the flash of lightnings . . . loud clangor of the Shofar . . . Heaven's trumpet—the very voice of God.

I am the Lord thy God, thou shalt have no other gods before me. Those graven images of Egypt are inanities. Remember the Sabbath day, understand life's end is leisure and contemplation. Thou shalt not—Thou shalt not—Thou shalt not. A Torah. A Law. A Discipline. Onward God's people. There lies the land of Canaan, your father's patrimony. Prepare to build a new civilization.

Naase v'nishma. We shall do; we shall hearken.

. . . A strange silence engulfs the scene. Where is the sound of God's words? How fleeting is the moment. Dare I trust the divine message to this miraculous moment of revelation? The words must be transmitted to generations yet unborn. . . .

Patience, Moses, thy people need decades, scores of years, ay, centuries. Heroes, judges, priests and prophets will be martyrs ere thy people shall know God and His Torah. . . .

S'oo shearim rasheichem v'hinas'oo pit'hei olam, v'yavo melech h'kavod—
Lift your heads, O ye gates! even lift them up ye everlasting doors: and

the King of Glory shall come in. *Kadosh, kadosh, kadosh, adonoy z'vaot* —Holy, Holy, Holy, is the God of hosts. . . .

Sharp, broken, plaintive blasts of the trumpet, reminiscent of Sinai's Shofar, summon a free people to the worship of the One God. . . . Levites ply the lyre, the harp, the gittith, the instrument of ten strings. . . .

O give thanks unto the Lord for He is good,
For His mercy endureth forever.
So let Israel now say,
For His mercy endureth forever.

David's psalms, priests and Levites and people intone. The Torah. The Sopher reads the Torah. Remember your high destiny. Fight the beast, fight the slave within you. The thundering voice of prophecy, the threatening, chastizing, instructing—withal comforting voices of Amos, Micah, Isaiah, Jeremiah, echo and re-echo. Serve ye God, the one God, the merciful, the just, Father of the fatherless, the widow, the stranger. Walk humbly with your God. . . .

The golden eagle glitters. The flags flutter. Rome, Rome. Its mighty legions tramp, tramp. . . . Judah's sons fight like lions. . . . God's hosts will not yield . . . they die but do not surrender. The flames devour post and pillar. A heap of ruins crashes to the ground. . . . Glory has departed. Rome, haughty Rome, grants a favor. Contemptuously it yields the townlet of Yabneh to ben Zakkai. Brave spirits gather about the master; the voice of Torah is heard in the new academy. Jerusalem lies waste but Yabneh, Titus, Yabneh and its scholars, Yabneh and its devotees of Torah, thou canst not subdue. . . .

Darkness over the horizon. A people in mourning, wailing, wandering, heartless, driven from shore to shore, from land to land, nowhere finding rest, everywhere denied peace. Restrictions, persecutions, libels, calumny are its lot. . . . But the spirit remains unbroken, the will to live unimpaired, hope unextinguished. . . .

How long will there be wailing in Zion? How long my martyrdom, Oh God! Spain and its inquisition . . . 1492! Behold the glittering light . . . a discovery, a new land—America. The Jew helps open it to the world. . . . The Renaissance dawns. . . . He helps usher in the Renaissance. . . .

O Eternal Wanderer, your misery is not yet at an end. Suffering is still your badge—your yellow badge! . . .

Another glimmer. More hope. The French Revolution. Napoleon. Emancipation for the Jew. . . . Ding-dong, ding-dong, America ring loud the bell, clang, clang, let its form burst with the echoes of its message. America, land of the free and brave, to thee my refugees flee. . . . Here their bleeding feet find rest, their aching hearts solace. Here indeed is hope. Upon these glorious shores of religious freedom we find our haven of refuge. . . .

The Russian hell, the new anti-Semitism, racial anti-Semitism, darkness, darkness. May laws, Dreyfus, Mendel Beilis—will they ever let us live? Will we ever be free?

Emancipation is not a gift, O Israel. It springs from within. Free men free themselves. The land of your fathers lies waste, its milk and honey are dried up. The land that yielded you prophets and martyrs and Maccabees —rehabilitate it. Become a people once again. If you will it, it is not a dream. Eastward, eastward, to the Burning Bush, to the wells of prophecy. . . . On Mt. Scopus, whence Titus' soldiers hurled the firebrand, erect the Hebrew University. . . .

For out of Zion shall go forth the Law
And the word of the Lord from Jerusalem.

Trum, trum, beat your swords to plowshares. Bend your spears into pruning hooks. Yonder see the vision. See the peoples of the earth! Black, white, yellow. Ascend the Mountain of the Lord. They are all masters, they are all servants. The lion and the lamb, child and serpent, crouch and play together. My Messiah's work is not yet done, but ay he straighteneth. See the Shofar in his fettered hand, it is the old Shofar of Sinai. He shall sound it yet again, in the end of days when hatred will be no more, when humanity will be redeemed, when the earth will be filled with the knowledge of God as the waters cover the seas.

Solomon Goldman holds the distinction of being the first man elected to the presidency of the Zionist Organization by the popular vote of delegates to a convention. He quickly became the idol and hero of the Zionist masses. As the brilliant interpreter of the democratic ideal of Jewish nationalism, he became the favorite of the people. He was only

44 at that time, but his dignified, white-haired appearance belied his youth. The year was 1940 that the convention in Detroit selected this popular leader to lead them through the crucial years of Germany's calculated destruction of European Jewish communities, years which made the need for a Jewish homeland in Palestine so immediately pressing.

His views brought the concept of the ideal of Jewish nationality— i.e., the Jewish personality—to hitherto unknown heights. Zionism was to him the very highest expression of the Jewish renaissance, and he was as instrumental as any in giving life to its cause. He wanted not merely an aggregation of passive dues-payers, but a band of lovers of Israel and the Hebrew world. In June, 1939, speaking before the Forty-First Annual Convention of the Zionist Organization of America, his first as President, he said:

> Once and for all we must restate that which was known to Yehuda Halevi, to Abraham, to Rabbi Loew of Prague as well as to Achad Haam, namely, that there is a Jewish ethos incorporated in a religion, a culture, a civilization and a nationality which can find only one homeland—Palestine. Only there can it achieve its supreme expression, unfold its highest character, acquire its clearest individuality.

Three masterful addresses delivered during the two years of his incumbency were collected in a volume significantly entitled *Undefeated*. Solomon Goldman was ever undefeated and the Jewish people were, and are, undefeated.

Now let us complete the human picture by recalling that not only does Palestine bear the deathless imprint of the Jew, but that the Jew bears about him the deathless imprint of Palestine. Jews remained in Palestine to testify ceaselessly to the Jewish claim; but the Jews who were outside Palestine did not relinquish it either. From the moment recorded in Genesis, when God promises the land to Abraham, down to the last page, then beyond the Bible through Midrashim, the Talmudim, further on through the prayerbook and up to the last song of the Halutz, the theme is there. Palestine has never disappeared from the literature and folklore of the Jew. There is not a book in the Bible in which the beauty of the land, and the love of the Jews for it, are not given emphasis. Poets, historians, and romances dwelt with passionate longing on mountain and valley, tree and sky of Palestine. Again and again we are reminded that it is the land which the Lord thy God hath promised unto thy ancestors. . . .

Zionism is not the ideology of a party and Eretz Israel is not the shibboleth of zealots. Zionism is Jewish history. It is the Jewish people. The negation of Zionism is the denial of the Jewish past. A people that denies its past destroys its future. . . .

The courageous president summoned his hearers to more zealous effort in the Zionist cause:

> We Zionists must restore courage to the weak, strength to the exhausted. We must not permit ourselves to be distracted for a single moment from our historic purpose. We reaffirm that there is only one solution to the Jewish problem the world over, and that is the rehabilitation of the Jewish national homeland. . . .

In another address, delivered in October, 1939, before the Twenty-Fifth Annual Convention of Hadassah, he pressed hard his convictions and called for courage:

> I am impatient with Zionists who, at the sight of every precipice and at the blast of every hurricane, become bleary-eyed with confusion, relax their hands in weariness, and cry, "Whither!" Zionism is not a tedious exercise in ever new formulations. It does not shoot its aims annually like the leaves or change color at every autumn frost. It is not the lichen of Jewish experience. It is the trunk and roots of our whole history. The Zionist heart may be sensitive to disappointment, but it remains impervious to despair. . . .
>
> Will American Jewry, I ask, rise to its full stature, or will this giant among the Jewries of the world fetter its own hands and feet? A timid Jewry in America is no asset to world Jewry. What if we extend charity but offer no leadership? What if we give bread but inspire no hope? Will that heal the wounded heart, comfort the broken spirit or sustain the frustrated will to live? On the contrary, an inarticulate American Jewry, a timid American Jewry, will by its sheer weight blast whatever hope there is in the House of Israel. . . . We are becoming habituated to defeat, whispering, begging. It is not ours to beg for tolerance. We must demand justice. . . .

In his last address to the Forty-Second convention as president delivered in July 1940 he brought almost the entire delegation to its feet as he thundered:

I charge you! Do not in this hour of gigantic world trial retreat one step from the demand for Zion and do not mitigate by a hair's breadth the wonder and the value of our achievements in that country. Do not say: Because vaster issues have arisen and gigantic forces have been set loose, we must forget. Far from it. If we, a small people with a small demand, permit ourselves to be bullied by the mere size of events, what becomes of the hope of the world? I plead with you, do not tremble before the mass of incident or before the tramp of millions. It is too late for the Jew to become a coward. It is our right, it is our duty, it is a necessity with us, it is part of our bargain with the world that we shall obstinately repeat, until full liberation has come to us, the evidences of our achievement in Palestine. . . .

Ours is the responsibility to assume the guardianship of the Jewish spirit and of the Jewish homeland. We have become, under the fierce pressure of history, the guarantors of the continuity and the coherence of our people. We are answerable before the Judgment Throne for its destiny. What shall we say in this day? We shall say: The burden is great but it is not greater than we can bear. We shall offer ourselves in new resolve. We shall not be satisfied with word offerings, with speeches and mass meetings and resolutions, with sighs of pity and with crumbs of charity. We will take the multiple burden upon ourselves. We shall forego comforts and forget pleasure. We shall live modestly and labor in thoughtfulness. All that we love, all that we value, that gives life meaning and dignity, threatens to become a heap of ruins. It shall not come to pass as long as there is a spark of life in us.

In the crisis year 1940, Solomon Goldman's words came as soothing balm to depressed hearts. The British White Paper on Palestine had in effect scuttled the aim and intent of the Balfour Declaration of 1917. Britain was closing the doors to Palestine. Incidents on the high seas of refugee Jews in dangerously inadequate ships seeking safety and home brought more hurt and pain as country after country closed its eyes and doors. Hitler's systematic extermination of Jews in Europe was proceeding on schedule. The picture for the Jew looked black indeed. It was easy to slide into despondency and despair. In this distraught Jewish world, Solomon Goldman rose up to rekindle the spirit of hope and courage. From his high post in the Zionist movement, his words carried weight, for when such an official demands courage and fortitude, the people must respond. Many on the periphery of lost hopes were snatched back to hope and to the determination to fight harder for the goal of the centuries. Thus, Solomon Goldman stands in the forefront of those fiery Jeremiahs whose exhortations and example stir renewed fervor. The words ignite the flaming torch of hope so that it may be carried forward from one to another until all is bright once more and the last vestige of gloom has disappeared. "We Will Build," he entitled his last address as president, and to this goal he set his sights.

Solomon Goldman's dedicated efforts for Zionism continued even away from the official presidency. He persisted, merging international service with congregational duties and leading his synagogue to distinguished primacy. The synagogue he ever regarded not only as a house of worship but as a complete cultural center. It was the laboratory of the Jewish spirit; the place where the entire heritage of the Jew finds expression. In turn, the culture is wholly suffused with the religious spirit. This religious feeling is not an abstract—it is the tangible affirmation of the Jewish national personality. The American Jewish congregation was not to be a center of superficial activities but an instrument for actuating the Jewish spirit. To this end, Anshe Emet was a workshop for Jewish living. An example of his approach is found in the manner in which the new synagogue annex and school building were dedicated. Instead of the usual ceremonies, an evening of Jewish folk music, a Jewish art exhibit, and an address by his great friend, Dr. A. H. Friedlander, who spoke on Hebrew literature, made up the observances.

When the synagogue was secure within the framework of his concept, and his efforts for Zionism and Palestine were bearing fruit, Dr. Goldman turned his mind and thoughts to a theme which had been building up within him all his life, a commentary on the Bible. Through the years he had amassed thousands and thousands of references relating to all phases of Biblical study. Those Biblical critics who had been undermining the authenticity of the Bible has long disturbed him. He wanted to restore the Book of Books to the Western man of today, to see a confused generation turn again to the Book and find meaning in it for them. So began the monumental project, *The Book of Human Destiny* in 13 volumes. Unfortunately, Rabbi Goldman did not live to fulfill his dream. Three have been published, only the first of two of which Goldman saw in print. The first was *The Book of Books: An Introduction* which was dedicated to Professor Alexander Marks on the occasion of his 70th birthday. The second, *In the Beginning*, encompassing the Book of Genesis, was published in 1949 and was dedicated to Professor Mordecai M. Kaplan, founder of Reconstructionism, with the comment, "determined and undaunted wrestler with God and men." Solomon Goldman might have been describing himself. The third volume, published posthumously in 1958 and entitled *From Slavery to Freedom,* encompasses the Book of Exodus. In 1956, an excerpt of the third volume entitled *The Ten Commandments* was published, edited by Maurice Samuel.

Dr. Goldman's intention was not that of the interpreter so much as the compiler. "Echoes and Allusions" he called his undertaking, for his goal was to assemble the thoughts and ideas expressed through the ages on each chapter and verse of the Bible. But he interpreted and translated as well, for he conceived of his commentary as a means by which he could point up the relevance of the Bible to modern life.

Another motive of Goldman's undertaking was his desire to answer exponents of the so-called "higher criticism," a theological phenomenon of the 19th century. These critics felt that the Bible was a patchwork of odds and ends deriving from endless sources. It was not divine, said they, but put together by different people in different ages. Goldman was not opposed to honest analyses of Biblical sources. He was not a fundamentalist in any sense. He was, however, outraged by the insinuation of prejudice and anti-Semitism into the "higher criticism." When he noted that the great Biblical critics, Wellhausen in particular, showed a hostile spirit, he felt counterattack was indicated. As Maurice Samuel put it, "Behind the secular and the religious reduction of the Bible to a commonplace he perceives a grudging and hostile spirit which has nothing to do with pure intellectual evaluation." Thus Dr. Goldman became the defender of the Bible, searching the minds of the human beings who sought to undermine its efficacy. Their motivations disturbed him. It was difficult for him to believe that a collection of shreds, such as the critics were making out the Pentateuch to be, could have for untold ages impressed mankind with its unity or individuality. It was permissible to dissect the Bible but if the surgery were mingled with outright anti-Semitism, Goldman struck out with outraged justice. He was always and acutely conscious of what Solomon Schechter called the "higher anti-Semitism."

And after cautious, careful scrutiny, weighing varied theories and balancing them, he concludes that there is nothing to contradict the traditional belief in the Mosaic authorship of the Ten Commandments or Decalogue.

Fate did not allow the dream of the commentary to be fulfilled. In the midst of preparing the monumental work, Solomon Goldman passed away in May of 1953.

Chaim Nachman Bialik, the great Hebrew poet, had words for his friend:

> There was a man,
>   And behold he is no more . . .
> Before his time he passed away,
> And the song of his life
>   was interrupted. . . .

Yet the song lives on in the brilliance and glory of his memory. Though he, the twelfth generation of rabbis, was the last of his line, generations of the future will honor his name through their response to the message of his works and example.

His large capacity to love was nowhere more evident than in the intimate phases of his personal life. His devotion to his aged mother was in keeping with the best spirit of the command, "Honor thy father and thy mother." The great love and devotion showered on his beloved wife and helpmate, his children and grandchildren, brothers and sisters, testified to the great, loving heart he possessed.

To Jews of America, Solomon Goldman for generations to come will be remembered as a spirited, fiery leader. To all Americans, Goldman will be remembered for his deep feeling for the land of his adoption:

We Americans are different. Ours is from the very beginning the sweet land of liberty, and our fathers bled for it. We are not a flock of goats, and we are constitutionally incapable of following a Führer. Our spiritual men were not always exiled or despised poets. We did occasionally send them to jail, but we sent Washington, Jefferson, and Lincoln to the White House. We did burn our hearts out over the woes of others. We did more. Thousands gave their blood to free our black-skinned brethren from slavery. "Fondly we hope—fervently do we pray—that this mighty scourge of war may speedily pass away. Yet if God wills that it continue until all the wealth piled by the bondsman's two hundred and fifty years of unrequited toil shall be sunk, and until every drop of blood drawn with a lash shall be paid by another drawn with a sword, as was said three thousand years ago, so still it must be said: The judgments of the Lord are true and righteous altogether." This is not from Isaiah or Amos. It is a quotation from a state paper.

Ours is not a tradition of uniformity. We have come here from many climes and many stocks to experiment in democracy, i.e., in the freedom of the individual. We regard self-realization as the noblest fulfillment of citizenship. It is in our Constitution. It is in our life's blood. . . . The Statue of Liberty, blazing forth a message of freedom unto all the inhabitants of the land, is the symbol of the true and the permanent in American life.

His open expressions of Americanism led to an invitation by the State Department to tour South America as part of a good will mission. President Harry Truman appointed him to the executive commission to plan the Mid-Century White House Conference on Children and Youth.

To the rank and file of American Jewry who needed inspiring hope in an era of despair and depression, Solomon Goldman will be remembered long—he wanted so avidly to make American Jews sensitive to the prophetic word, responsive to every opportunity for the deepening of their Jewish knowledge.

Of young Joseph in the Bible, the Midrash says that when Pharoah first saw him he exclaimed, "I see in him the bearing of royalty." From early days at the Seminary, which in later years gave him its highest recognition, the Louis Ginzberg Award, the bearing of royalty was seen in Solomon Goldman.

MILTON STEINBERG

Adventurer in Mind and Heart

[1903-1950]

When Pharoah of Egypt was impressed with Joseph's interpretations of his dreams, he took off his signet ring, handed it over to Joseph, arrayed him in regal garb, and placed him in the second royal chariot. Runners preceded the chariot calling out *Abrech.*

Abrech probably has related meaning to the Hebrew word for bending the knee. The rabbis of the Midrash, however, add more significance to the term. They suggest that it is a composite of two words—*Ahv* meaning father, and *Rahch* meaning tender. They amplify: *Ahv b'chochma v'rahch b'shanim*—meaning "father of wisdom though tender of years." Joseph, the dreamer and saint, who had turned out to an eminent degree to be a man of practical affairs though tender of years, was a father of wisdom.

Abrech in both the sense of summoning his presence and describing his person may well apply to Milton Steinberg, the youthful, colorful sage in Israel who lived but a half a century in time but compressed centuries of thought and creativity into his brief span.

The great mind and heart of this distinguished, beloved rabbi came to life on November 24, 1903, in Rochester, New York. Son of Samuel Steinberg, Milton was one of three children, and the only son. The fact that he was the son of Samuel Steinberg determined the direction he would take in life. Talmudic student of the famed Voloshin Yeshivah, Samuel Steinberg was highly regarded for his knowledge and learning. Moreover, his immersion in Talmudic lore was combined with an insatiable thirst for the secular. He read voraciously, often ensconced behind the massive folios of the Talmud, the writings of Abraham Mapu, Mordecai Zeev Feierberg, Sholem Aleichem, Mendele Mocher Seforim and Yehuda Leib Peretz—the forbidden Hebrew writings banned to Talmudic students. Long before he arrived in America, the elder Steinberg had stepped away from strict Orthodoxy, a direction which persisted as he confronted living conditions for Jews in Rochester when he arrived there in 1898. He saw that his own people were not respected citizens in the community, these new immigrants trying hard to establish a beachhead in America, laboring long hours in the garment industry. Even their Jewish employers, who had come earlier to America and hence were of a higher social stratum, were exacting and demanding and hardly acted with greater kindness and compassion toward their fellow Jews than did the Gentiles. Employers and employees were just that, religious and cultural ties notwithstanding. Many disillusioned immigrants were thus drawn to unionism and socialism, Samuel Steinberg among them. Soon an active member of the new group of leaders and reformers, the Talmud student of the Voloshin had now superimposed upon his old and basic knowledge the new world's secularism and tinge of radicalism. This did not mean at all that the former was wiped out. Indeed, it always served as the basis of his life and actions and that of his family. Observance of the holidays, the Jewish spirit within the home, was a living reality of their lives. Thus in an atmosphere of traditionalism tempered with secularism, Milton Steinberg grew toward manhood, early evincing the sensitivity and brilliance which would point him toward a rabbinical career.

In 1919, fortuitous circumstances helped assure the direction Milton's life was to take. The entire family moved to New York. The transfer was occasioned by an unusual event. Milton's sister Florence, a talented singer, had strongly impressed the world-renowned cantor, Yosele Rosenblatt, who encouraged her to study in New York where opportunities were infinitely greater. Florence went with her mother to the great metropolis to continue her voice training and the family came soon thereafter.

Milton's preparation for a career of the mind, established firmly in the first 16 years of life, was continued in the city. His direction was the same except that his curiosity intensified and sought greater challenges. Matriculating at DeWitt Clinton High School, one of the finest experimental secondary schools in New York, he repeatedly amazed his teachers. Arthur A. Cohen's excellent biography of Steinberg, in *Anatomy of Faith,* reveals that "Steinberg's English teacher was so overwhelmed by his skill and proficiency that he gave him at term's end the ridiculous grade of 105."

Steinberg's thirst for knowledge drove him on. He studied, debated, wrote, tutored. He had no time for anything save preparation for the future. Still, he did not limit himself to school studies. The family had settled in uptown Manhattan, in a Jewish community where synagogues of course existed, many of them distinguished. While the family led by Samuel had drifted away in some measure from the strict traditions of the faith, the feeling of Jewishness remained secure. Synagogue affiliation was a must. To be sure, it was not the Orthodox synagogue to which they turned. Milton's mother at first tried a Reform temple but was dissatisfied. The Conservative synagogue, Ansche Chesed, presided over by eloquent, aggressive Rabbi Jacob Kohn, was chosen and there Milton's love of religion and Judaism found an outlet. He quickly came under the dynamic influence of Rabbi Kohn. Indeed, his thinking throughout his life was reflective of this first major rabbinical guide.

Ever the student, ever the quester after knowledge and truth, Milton began to read and study Jewish materials in earnest—history, Hebrew, literature. His readings, coupled with the love for his people instilled within the home, developed an undying love and compassion for his people. He began to appreciate the miracle of their survival.

And then it was time to leave De Witt Clinton behind and embark upon a new period of study and development. At City College the youth met the illustrious Morris R. Cohen, then assistant professor of philosophy. The sparks flew at this encounter. Here was the great logician, who pursued every argument and proposition to its logical conclusion coldly, relentlessly. And here was Steinberg, who could not accept logic as the sole guide of thought. To the latter, reason must be directed by the heart if the goal were to achieve meaningful truth.

Steinberg's thought processes are succinctly described by his admiring disciple Arthur A. Cohen:

> Essentially Rabbi Kohn sought to take the first principles of the metaphysicians and logicians and turn them to the service of theism. Every philosophic argument is pressed to that point at which an axiomatic prin-

ciple is affirmed, a first and final premise articulated. Such first principles are principles to which logic assents without proof. If, indeed, logic and science must bow to principles which reason cannot demonstrate, where then is the unreasonableness of theism? Theism insists only that there is a more ultimate cause for the unfolding and display of life: a supreme intelligence who is God. Beyond this, what greater sanction for the order and beauty of life than to hold that this intelligence is also moral, that it obeys the law it makes? And lastly, what greater tradition can there be than that which worships that moral intelligence, which seeks to bring man into closeness and rapport with such a God?

The argument undoubtedly took this form in the early 1920's. It is preserved and extended by Steinberg throughout his writings; it is the groundwork upon which his religion rests. It was, above all things, a rational faith.

In September, 1923, Milton entered the Jewish Theological Seminary of America, fountainhead of Conservative Judaism. The rabbinate had special meaning for him. It did not mean mere acquisition of knowledge and conveyance of same. It meant continuous questioning, reflection and evaluation. Here, he quickly came under the influence of many great masters of Hebraic, Talmudic and Judaic lore: Professors Louis Ginzberg, Jacob Hoschander, Morris Levine, Alexander Marx, Moses Hyamson, Israel Davidson and Mordecai Kaplan. It was the last, founder of Reconstructionism, who influenced him the most. Kaplan's thought best fitted the developing shape of the budding rabbi's. The youth did not flinch when Kaplan announced the death of the concept of supernaturalism, nor when he renounced the doctrine of the chosen people, nor when he projected an untraditional concept of God. Indeed, Steinberg drew ever closer to his mentor, though in later years he found himself differing in some essentials from the doctrines then projected.

Milton attended the Seminary for five years and in May, 1928, was graduated and ordained. He won every prize available. He had the same year been awarded his Master's degree from Columbia University. After one year at the Seminary, he had been graduated from City College of New York *summa cum laude* and awarded Phi Beta Kappa. His first pulpit was in Indianapolis, Indiana. He had officiated there as a student rabbi on the High Holy Days and was urged by the congregation to occupy their pulpit upon ordination. For five years he served in Indianapolis with vigor and distinction, participating in every civic and humanitarian endeavor.

In 1933, the Park Avenue Synagogue of New York, one of the leading Conservative congregations in America, invited Milton Steinberg to fill its pulpit. Here the young rabbi could really shine. Soon he published the first of his many books, *The Making of the Modern Jew*. Despite the vast scope of his rabbinic duties, the book was finished in slightly more than six weeks.

Dedicated to his charming wife, Edith, who while he was writing was pregnant with their first child Jonathan, the book posed the "riddle" of Jewish survival:

> By every rule of reason his very memory should have been obliterated. No people should have desired life under such circumstances. And yet, stubbornly, uncannily, he persisted and survived. Like truth crushed to earth, he rose again at the first relaxation of pressure. He not only survived but lived joyously, and, within the limits of his own culture, creatively. What could mere logic make of such a phenomenon—a people whose very survival was a contradiction in terms? The medieval mind hypothesized its bewilderment in a legend in which the irrational immortality of the Wandering Jew mirrored the more baffling deathlessness of the Jew of flesh and blood.
>
> The myth is gone; the mystery persists. Israel still runs true to form as a riddle among the nations of the earth. The world still does not understand how the Jewish people contrived to maintain itself and its highly individual culture.

Meanwhile, Professor Mordecai M. Kaplan was readying his monumental *Judaism as a Civilization* for publication. The essence of Reconstructionist thinking is to be found in this volume. Steinberg was attracted to the new thought and readily assented when his former teacher invited him in 1934 to join in the founding of the Reconstructionist movement. For more than 15 years Steinberg worked closely with Kaplan. Only later did he depart from complete acceptance of Kaplan's thinking and theology.

The ever alert, questing mind of Milton Steinberg urged him on. He had formulated his philosophy in his first successful publishing venture. Now he would turn to fiction. With the devoted collaboration of his wife, he embarked on the writing of a historical novel. The result was *As a Driven Leaf*, published in 1939. Like the first book, the masterful novel was dedicated with even deeper feeling to his partner in life "in tribute to her love, in gratitude for her collaboration." The novel, one of the most moving, dramatic, intensely Jewish works of the age, revealed Milton Steinberg in all his questionings and strivings for a rational faith. It reflects as well the perturbed, confused Jew who seeks a faith and wants to adjust it to the world in which he lives. *As a Driven Leaf* thus mirrors Steinberg as it does the Jew he is trying to reach, to offer spiritual substance. The story is that of Elisha ben Abuyah, who in the 1st century of the era was a rabbinic sage, a recognized and respected member of the Sanhedrin, the Jewish High Court, and who defected to Rome in the early part of the 2nd century when Rome sealed the fate of the Jewish nation. In Jewish tradition, Elisha is referred to as *Achayr,* another, or the other. He was excommunicated and no mention of his name allowed. Around the life of this great rabbi, who had reached the pinnacle of esteem, but whose dissatisfaction escorted him away from the traditional faith, Steinberg skillfully builds the story of the perplexity of the age. Here is the skeptic who is driven to know and understand, who seeks meanings and knowledge, whether it be of Jewish or Greek or Roman origin. Not only Elisha seeks: the reader joins in the quest. The reader is an insider, who, together with Elisha, experiences the search for knowledge and truth.

Elisha's experimentations with alien philosophies lead him inexorably back to the faith of his fathers, and herein lies the message for the modern disaffected Jew. Unlike the real Elisha whom history excoriates as a traitor, Steinberg's Elisha is elevated to heroism, treated as an honest skeptic whose quest was rewarded. Through Elisha's final musings to his friend Meir, Steinberg paints a picture of the reborn Jew in words which are suggestive of his own personal spiritual odyssey:

> Is it not clear why I blundered so horribly in arriving at my decision? In my eyes the pagan world was the seat of science and philosophy, hence as I supposed, mankind's sole opportunity of ever attaining certainty in belief and action. What other course was open to me except to give it my absolute loyalty? I did not see then what I perceive now with such fearful clarity, that no society, no matter how great the achievements of its scholars, can be an instrument of human redemption if it despises justice and mercy.
>
> Aye, that was my great error—this reverence for the intellect, this overweaning reliance on it. It led me to condone the sins of Rome, it induced me to dismiss as blind emotion the impulses of loyalty and love for

my people. Only when it was too late did I come to understand that the processes of life overflow the vessels of reason, that the most meaningful elements in human experience, sensitivity to beauty, devotion to one's kind, are not matters to be determined by syllogisms. . . .

Do you remember, Meir, that epigram quoted in the name of Rabbi Johanan ben Zaccai: "There is no truth unless there be a faith on which it may rest"? Ironically enough, the only sure principle I have achieved is this which I have known almost all my life. And it is so. For all truth rests ultimately on some act of faith, geometry on axioms, the sciences on the assumptions of the objective existence and orderliness of the world of nature. In every realm one must lay down postulates or he shall have nothing at all. So with morality and religion. Faith and reason are not antagonists. On the contrary, salvation is through the commingling of the two, the former to establish first premises, the latter to purify them out of confusion and to draw the fullness of their implications. It is not certainty which one acquires so, only plausibility, but that is the best we can hope for.

Sometimes I have thought of myself as unique among men. As one who has been compelled to live apart because his only was a restlessness of spirit. But it is not so. In all men there is a relentless drive to know and understand. My destiny becomes then one episode in the eternal drama. In generations to come, others will desert the beliefs of their fathers and go seeking what I sought, others will put their trust in the intellect and strive to build philosophies and moralities after the fashion of the geometry book. If only I could discover some way of bequeathing to them my hard-won conclusion, that the light of man's logic is too frail, unaided, to prevail against the enveloping darkness, that to reason a faith is a prerequisite— then my career should not have been unavailing.

As a Driven Leaf is a document of our times. It was born out of the inner struggles of a passionate lover of his people who sought to guide seekers of truth in religion and Judaism into channels of fruitful reflection and ultimate understanding.

Novel completed and acclaimed, Milton Steinberg continued his pastoral ministrations, capturing more and more disciples. He also accepted more responsibilities of leadership in the Jewish community, becoming increasingly active in the Reconstructionist movement, the Rabbinical Assembly and its Commission on Social Justice. The outset of World War II found Steinberg disturbed and hurt as he viewed the persecution and torture of his people in European lands. He sought to serve in the corps of chaplains but was rejected on grounds of a slight heart impairment. Instead, the Jewish Welfare Board assigned him the task of serving as its representative to various army posts where Jewish personnel sought inspiration, guidance and counsel. Though not an official chaplain, he soon was known as a chaplain's chaplain, as he had been esteemed as a rabbi's rabbi.

It was on one of these tours in Texas that fate struck a devastating blow. On the first anniversary of Pearl Harbor Day, December 7, 1942, Milton suffered a severe heart attack and was confined in a hospital for many months. One of his most magnificent odes to God and nature came from this experience as he in a later sermon (published post-humously in *A Believing Jew*) described his feelings when he first walked out of that Texas hospital and what the sudden sight of the sunlight meant to him. It is a dramatic appeal to mankind to pause during the rush of life and appreciate God's blessings which surround us unnoticed. Entitled "To Hold with Open Arms," his message was a comforting one:

It is a sound convention which requires that a sermon begin with a text —some verse from Scripture, or from Rabbinic literature, which summarizes the theme. But it is well to understand that a text is, after all, only the soul-experience of some man boiled down to the size of an epigram. At some time in the past a prophet or a saint met God, wrestled with good or evil, tasted of life and found it bitter or sweet, contemplated death, and then distilled the adventure into a single line, for those that would come after him. That is a text.

But it is not only the great, the saints, the prophets, and the heroes who contemplate God, life, and death. We, too, the plainer folk of the world, live, love, laugh, and suffer, and by no means always on the surface. We, too, catch glimpses of eternity and the things that people do. Not only of Moses, but of us, too, it may be said, as Lowell put it:

> *Daily with souls that cringe and plot*
> *We Sinais climb and know it not.*

There are texts in us, too, in our commonplace experiences, if only we are wise enough to discern them.

One such experience, a *textual* experience, so to speak, fell to my lot not so long ago. There was nothing dramatic about its setting nor unusual in its circumstances. And yet to me it was a moment of discovery, almost of revelation.

Let me recount it very briefly, as befits a text. After a long illness, I was permitted for the first time to step out of doors. And, as I crossed the threshold, sunlight greeted me. This is my experience—all there is to it. And yet, so long as I live, I shall never forget that moment. It was mid-January—a time of cold and storm up north, but in Texas, where I happened to be, a season much like our spring. The sky overhead was very blue, very clear, and very, very high. Not, I thought, the *shamayim*, heaven, but *shemei shamayim*, a heaven of heavens. A faint wind blew from off the western plains, cool and yet somehow tinged with warmth—like a dry chilled wine. And everywhere in the firmament above me, in the great vault between earth and sky, on the pavements, the buildings—the golden glow of the sunlight. It touched me, too, with friendship, with warmth, with blessing. And as I basked in its glory there ran through my mind those wonderful words of the prophet about the sun which someday shall rise with healing on its wings.

In that instant I looked about me to see whether anyone else showed on his face the joy, almost the beatitude, I felt. But no, there they walked —men and women and children, in the glory of a golden flood, and so far as I could detect, there was none to give it heed. And then I remembered how often, I, too, had been indifferent to sunlight, how often, pre-occupied with petty and sometimes mean concerns, I had disregarded it. And I said to myself—how precious is the sunlight but, alas, how care-less of it are men. How precious—how careless. This has been a refrain sounding in me ever since.

It rang in my spirit when I entered my own home again after months of absence, when I heard from a nearby room the excited voices of my children at play; when I looked once more on the dear faces of some of my friends; when I was able for the first time to speak again from my pulpit in the name of our faith and tradition, to join in worship of the God who gives us so much of which we are so careless.

And a resolution crystallized within me. I said to myself that at the very first opportunity I would speak of this. I knew full well that it is a common-place truth, that there is nothing clever about my private rediscovery of it, nothing ingenious about my way of putting it. But I was not interested in being original or clever or ingenious. I wanted only to remind my listeners, as I was reminded, to spend life wisely, not to squander it.

I wanted to say to the husbands and wives who love one another, "How precious is your lot in that it is one of love. Do not be, even for a moment, casual with your good fortune. Love one another while yet you may."

And to parents: "How precious is the gift of your children. Never, never be too busy for the wonder and miracle of them. They will be grown up soon enough and grown away, too."

We human beings, we frail reeds who are yet, as Pascal said, thinking reeds, feeling reeds, how precious are our endowments—minds to know, eyes to see, ears to listen, hearts to stir with pity, and to dream of justice and of a perfected world. How often are we indifferent to all these!

And we who are Jews and Americans, heirs of two great traditions, how fortunate our lot in both, and how blind we are to our double good fortune.

This is what struggled in me for utterance—as it struggled in Edna St. Vincent Millay when she cried out: "O world, I cannot hold thee close enough!"

I want to urge myself and all others to hold the world tight—to embrace life with all our hearts and all our souls and all our might. For it is precious, ineffably precious, and we are careless, wantonly careless of it. And yet, when I first resolved to express all this, I knew that it was only a half truth.

Could I have retained the sunlight no matter how hard I tried? Could I have prevented the sun from setting? Could I have kept even my own eyes from becoming satiated and bored with the glory of the day? That moment had to slip away. And had I tried to hold on to it, what would I have achieved? It would have gone from me in any case. And I would have been left disconsolate, embittered, convinced that I had been cheated.

But it is not only the sunlight that must slip away—our youth goes also, our years, our children, our senses, our lives. This is the nature of things, an inevitability. And the sooner we make our peace with it the better. Did I urge myself a moment ago to hold on? I would have done better, it now begins to appear, to have preached the opposite doctrine of letting go— the doctrine of Socrates who called life a *peisithanatos*—a persuader of death, a teacher of the art of relinquishing. It was the doctrine of Goethe who said: *Entsagen sollst, du sollst entsagen*—Thou shalt renounce. And it was the doctrine of the ancient rabbis who despite their love of life said: He who would die let him hold on to life.

It is a sound doctrine.

First because, as we have just seen, it makes peace with inevitability. And the inevitable is something with which everyone should be at peace.

Second, because nothing can be more grotesque and more undignified than a futile attempt to hold on.

Let us think of the men and women who cannot grow old gracefully because they cling too hard to a youth that is escaping them; of the parents who cannot let their children go free to live their own lives; of the people who in times of general calamity have only themselves in mind.

What is it that drives people to such unseemly conduct, to such flagrant selfishness except the attitude which I have just commended—a vigorous holding on to life? Besides, are there not times when one ought hold life cheap, as something to be lightly surrendered? In defense of one's country, for example, in the service of truth, justice, and mercy, in the advancement of mankind? This, then, is the great truth of human existence. One must not hold life too precious. One must always be prepared to let it go.

And now we are indeed confused. First we learn that life is a privilege —cling to it! Then we are instructed: Thou shalt renounce!

A paradox, and a self-contradiction! But neither the paradox nor the contradiction are of my making. They are a law written into the scheme of things—that a man must hold his existence dear and cheap at the same time.

Is it not, then, an impossible assignment to which destiny has set us? It does not ask of us that we hold life dear at one moment, and cheap at the next, but that we do both simultaneously. Now I can grasp something in my fist or let my hand lie open. I can clasp it to my breast or hold it at arm's length. I can embrace it, enfolding it in my arms, or let my arms hang loose. But how can I be expected to do both at once?

To which the answer is: With your body, of course not. But with your spirit, why not?

Is one not forever doing paradoxical and mutually contradictory things in his soul?

One wears his mind out in study, and yet has more mind with which to study. One gives away his heart in love and yet has more heart to give away. One perishes out of pity for a suffering world, and is the stronger therefor.

So, too, it is possible at one and the same time to hold on to life and let it go provided—well, let me put it this way:

We are involved in a tug of war: Here on the left is the necessity to renounce life and all it contains. Here on the right, the yearning to affirm it and its experiences. And between these two is a terrible tension, for they pull in opposite directions.

But suppose that here in the center I introduce a third force, one that lifts upward. My two irreconcilables now swing together, both pulling down against the new element. And the harder they pull, the closer together they come. God is the third element, that new force that resolves the terrible contradiction, the intolerable tension of life.

And for this purpose it does not especially matter how we conceive God. I have been a great zealot for a mature idea of God. I have urged again and again that we think through our theology, not limping along on a child's notion of God as an old man in the sky. But for my immediate purpose, all of this is irrelevant. What is relevant is this: that so soon as a man believes in God, so soon indeed as he wills to believe in Him, the terrible strain is eased; nay, it disappears, and that for two reasons.

In the first place, because a new and higher purpose is introduced into life, the purpose of doing the will of God—to put it in Jewish terms, of performing the *Mitzvoth*. This now becomes the reason for our existence. We are soldiers whose commander has stationed them at a post. How we like our assignment, whether we feel inclined to cling to it, or to let it go, is an irrelevant issue. Our hands are too busy with our duties to be either embracing the world or pushing it away.

That is why it is written: "Make thy will conform to His, then His will be thine, and all things will be as thou desirest."

But that, it might be urged, only evades the problem.

By concentrating on duty we forget the conflicting drives within ourselves. The truth is, however, that, given God, the problem is solved not only by evasion but directly; that it is solved, curiously enough, by being made more intense. For, given God, everything becomes more precious, more to be loved, and clung to, more embraceable, and yet at the same time easier to give up.

Given God, everything becomes more precious.

That sunshine in Dallas was not a chance effect, a lucky accident. It was an effect created by a great Artist, the Master Painter of Eternity. And because it came from God's brush it is more valuable even than I had at first conceived.

And the laughter of children, precious in itself, becomes infinitely more precious because the joy of the cosmos is in it.

And the sweetness of our friends' faces is dearer because these are fragments of an infinite sweetness.

All of life is the more treasurable because a great and Holy Spirit is in it.

And yet, it is easier for me to let go.

For these things are not and never have been mine. They belong to the Universe and the God who stands behind it. True, I have been privileged to enjoy them for an hour but they were always a loan due to be recalled.

And I let go of them the more easily because I know that as parts of the divine economy, they will not be lost. The sunset, the bird's song, the baby's smile, the thunder of music, the surge of great poetry, the dreams of the heart, and my own being, dear to me as every man's is to him, all these I can well trust to Him who made them. There is poignancy and regret about giving them up, but not anxiety. When they slip from my hands they will pass to hands better, stronger, and wiser than mine.

This then is the insight which came to me as I stood some months ago in a blaze of sunlight: Life is dear, let us then hold it tight while we yet may, but we must hold it loosely also!

And only with God can we ease the intolerable tension of our existence. For only when He is given, can we hold life at once infinitely precious and yet as a thing lightly to be surrendered. Only because of Him is it made possible for us to clasp the world, but with relaxed hands: to embrace it, but with open arms.

The words are suggestive of the short time left to the rabbi and his realization of this probability. In point of fact, the years ahead were but seven, few indeed for a man with so much to give and do. Officials of his synagogue insisted that he reduce his heavy schedule of rabbinical ministration. Assistants were appointed to perform the tasks he would normally execute: Rabbi Morris Kertzer and Rabbi Simon Noveck. But though official duties lessened, Steinberg's inner compulsion to learn, seek and teach was not diminished. "The securest person is the one who does not fortify himself but who exposes himself completely to all things," he once said. He was grateful for more time and turned his sights to other spheres, such as the Zionist movement. He set aside time for younger men who were thinking through with him world problems, Jewish problems, theological and philosophical problems. And he turned to his writing with renewed fervor.

In 1945 *A Partisan Guide to the Jewish Problem* was published, in which he continued the theme developed in *The Making of the Modern Jew,* broadening and enlarging its scope. Once again the work was dedicated to his courageous wife Edith, with the simple, "In Tribute." She was his ever encouraging companion, painfully aware of what awaited in the inevitable rush of time. The writing was more mature, tighter, more forceful—the style recognizable as were the themes. The messages of his earlier books wound through this sincere, scholarly, open-minded analysis of the Jew, his faith, and his relationship with himself and with the world about him. The book received high acclaim upon publication. John Haynes Holmes in the October 27, 1945, issue of the *Saturday Review of Literature* reported that the book "calls not for blame at any point, but for high praise and gratitude. There is no more pitiful and poignant, or more difficult, problem in the world today than anti-Semitism. It wrings the heart, and outrages the mind. Insofar as there can be a sure guide through this labyrinth of torture, this book is it. Let the Gentile read one chapter ("Warning to Gentiles") and the Jew one chapter ("An Exhortation to Jews), and together they will understand their debt to Rabbi Steinberg."

Not only is anti-Semitism astutely analyzed, the book also evaluates the strands and strains of Judaism, especially Reconstructionism. In addition, Steinberg here pens a credo, calling it, "a declaration of the faith of a Jewish survivalist."

What do I get out of my Jewishness to justify the expenditure of time and energy upon it? How am I the better off for my adherence to it?

From the Jewish heritage, I derive my world outlook, a God-centered interpretation of reality in the light of which man the individual is clothed with dignity, and the career of humanity with cosmic meaning and hope; a humane morality, elevated in its aspirations yet sensibly realistic; a system of rituals that interpenetrates my daily routines and invests them with poetry and intimations of the divine. To be sure. . . . I have had to do some tinkering on the traditional apparatus. Despite this, it is a goodly patrimony I have received, goodly in faith, in ethic and in folkway.

. . . Like all historic religions, Judaism has a character of its own. Its uniqueness—and the word carries no implications of superiority—consists of many special features peculiar to it. For example, it assigns an extraordinarily large role to study as a religious exercise, and to understanding as a key to salvation. Again, salvation is conceived as an objective not for the individual only but for society as well. Still again, Judaism, in contrast with most Christian confessions, is unconcerned with matters of creed. It is less interested in that Jews shall believe alike than they shall strive to realize the same ideal objectives . . .

In brief, though I share with liberal Christians large areas of affirmation, mine is a special position, which simultaneously satisfies me and serves also as a foil, goad and stimulant to other persuasions. Besides, the materials of Judaism lie at hand, ready for me to use. It would be uneconomical not to exploit them. Finally, I have observed that those Jews who do not acquire their religion from the tradition of their group quite generally do not get it elsewhere. American civilization, be it remembered, is in itself largely secular. Such Jews then, as often as not, simply go through life without a sustained *Weltanschauung,* an organic ethical code, and patterns of ritual.

Beyond this, my life is enriched by the accumulated treasures of over three millennia of Jewish history—a large literature in which I read extensively, not as an outsider but with a sense of belonging; music for me to sing, art for me to enjoy. I have the privilege of companionship with the great personalities of Jewish history. At my disposal is a second fund of folklore when I spin tales to my children. Mine literally is a double past—the American and the Jewish. My horizons are distant, not in one direction but in two. I am twice anchored in tradition, and hence twice secured against the peril of being rootless and "unpossessed."

And because my Jewishness is something positive, anti-Semitism looms less large in my life than in that of many of my fellows. . . . I am furthermore quite confident that by virtue of my attitude, I am less susceptible than escapist Jews to infection by self-contempt . . . .

Let it be recalled that I acknowledge only one political allegiance—to America; just as I profess only one religion—the Jewish. Here there is certainly no cause for conflict. Beyond that, I have two heritages—the American and the Hebraic. English is my language and that of my children. I was educated in the public schools of my community. The history of America is my history. But Hebrew is my tongue too, and Jewish history my background also. Lincoln and Jefferson are my heroes together with Moses, Akiba and Maimonides. They all get along in my imagination most companionably. When I read Van Wyck Brooks on New England in its flowering and autumn it is in my own literary past that I am being instructed. I have studied Spiegel's *Hebrew Reborn* with the same sense of identification. I sing Negro spirituals, American ballads and Hasidic or Palestinian folk songs wth equal ardor. On the Fourth of July, I set off fireworks and attempt to transmit to my children an appreciation of the significance of the occasion. With equal earnestness I kindle the Hanukkah lights and discuss with them the meaning of that festival. At no time am I conscious of the strain between the two worlds. I move from one to the other with such naturalness that I am scarcely aware of the change in spiritual locale.

The process is immensely facilitated by the essential sympathy in spirit between the two traditions. Both are democratic. Both emphasize the worth of the individual and his right to freedom. In both there is passionate devotion to the ideal of social justice. And the vision of the more abundant life is a secularized parallel of the ancient Jewish dream of the Kingdom of God on earth. . . .

But I am not fair to either Judaism or Americanism when I say of them only that they are mutually compatible. In my Jewishness, by very virtue of its differential quality, indeed in all the diversities religious and cultural exhibited by American life, I see a breath-taking promise, a unique and unparalleled opportunity.

Though time was running out, Steinberg was to produce one more volume, *Basic Judaism,* published in 1947. Intended for believing Jews to strengthen and encourage them in their faith, for indifferent Jews to show them the significance of Jewish tradition in modern life, and for non-Jews curious about Judaism, *Basic Judaism* offered a brief, clear exposition of the Jewish religion, its beliefs, ideals and practices. It is dedicated to his parents and his children—he being the recipient from the former, transmitter to the latter. Thus he dedicated his major literary life's efforts to family—wife, parents, children. In the preface he asserts: "I am a professional Jew whose faith is a matter of heart as well as head, of ardor no less than conviction. Of this enthusiasm I could not make a secret if I would: I would not if I could."

Three years were left for Steinberg and he devoted them almost completely to contemplation, study and discussion. He produced article after article for many a learned journal, and in 1949 before the Rabbinical Assembly Convention delivered a long presentation entitled "Theological Problems of the Hour," which Will Herberg called "epoch-making in the history of American Jewish religious thought." It comprised 64 pages of the 1949 *Rabbinical Assembly Proceedings* and is included also in his *Anatomy of Faith*. Soon thereafter, Steinberg delivered a series of four lectures at his own synagogue—his last public presentations.

In 1948, in recognition and appreciation, the Jewish Theological Seminary bestowed upon its learned son a Doctor of Hebrew Letters degree, *honoris causa*.

On March 20, 1950, Milton Steinberg died, and was mourned deeply by colleagues and disciples. His memory lives on in the brilliant works he left behind. This is how great men achieve immortality. Thus the man who said, "A faith cannot be inherited, it must be won," won his faith for himself and for many after him who have, and will, like their mentor, personally seek and win theirs.

ALEXANDER D. GOODE

Supreme Man of Faith

[1911-1943]

Near the center of the city of Philadelphia, in the heart of Temple University, stands an old stone-towered church known as the Baptist Temple founded by Russell Conwell of "Acres of Diamonds" fame. Above the north tower door are a cross and Star of David, the latter mounted above a decalogue. They tell of what is contained within the structure below street level, the Chapel of Four Chaplains. Built to spread the message of brotherhood, the chapel was named for four men of God—two Protestant, one Roman Catholic and one Jew.

Above the entrance burns an eternal light, and chiseled into the stone is this prayer:

> Chapel of Four Chaplains
> An Interfaith Shrine
> Here is Sanctuary for Brotherhood
> Let it never be violated.

One enters the chapel by either the north and the south tower, the one to the north containing the main entrance. The chapel is approximately 30 by 60 feet, with a raised end adding another 20 feet in length. Two to three hundred people can be seated at one time. On each side of the chapel is an arcade of five stone arches supported on massive stone columns with ornamental carved stone caps. The center arch on the west side frames the bronze memorial tablets dedicated to those who lost their lives in the sinking of the S. S. *Dorchester*. In front of these tablets stands the Book of Remembrance containing the names of servicemen who lost their lives in World War II, registered by friends or relatives. The center arch on the east aisle faces a mural showing the sinking of the S. S. *Dorchester,* with the four chaplains, hands clasped, in an attitude of prayer as the dominating theme.

The south end of the chapel features a large ornamental stone arch framing a turntable on which stand three altars—Catholic, Jewish and Protestant. The table revolves slowly at the push of a button. As each altar comes into view, one is reminded that while there are three faiths acknowledged, there is only one God.

The effort to create the Interfaith Memorial began in 1943, championed by Dr. Daniel A. Poling, minister of the church and father of one of the chaplains. It was dedicated by President Harry S. Truman eight years later, February 3, 1951, to the memories of Reverend George L. Fox, Protestant; Reverend Clark V. Poling, Protestant; Father John P. Washington, Roman Catholic; and Rabbi Alexander D. Goode, Jewish. The President said on that occasion:

> We must never forget that this country was founded by men who came to these shores to worship God as they pleased. Catholics, Jews and Protestants, all came here for this great purpose. They did not come here to do as they pleased, but to worship God as they pleased, and that is an important distinction. The unity of our country comes from this fact. The unity of our country is a unity under God. It is a unity of freedom, for the service of God is perfect freedom. If we remember our faith in God, if we live by it as our forefathers did, we need have no fear of the future.

Two years later, on the Sabbath closest to the tenth annniversary of a mighty act of faith, January 30, 1953, under the auspices of B'nai B'rith and its National Service Committee for the Armed Forces and Veterans and Philadelphia B'nai B'rith Councils of Men and Women, the writer was privileged to conduct the service of dedication, consecrating the Jewish altar to the blessed memory of Alexander D. Goode.

A rough, turbulent, icy ocean turned into a sea of glory as it brought down and together four men of God. Brought together by destiny, they died together as they had prayed together and worked together.

Alexander David Goode was the Jewish representative on this rendezvous with destiny! Determined to serve, motivated by a burning ideal born out of fierce loyalty to the land he loved, Alex Goode entered the chaplaincy in July, 1942, and was assigned to active duty in August. Less than six months later his period of duty was over and he was assigned to eternity.

The life of Alexander Goode began in Brooklyn, New York, on May 10, 1911. The first son of a rabbi, he grew up in the environment of a traditional Jewish home. The traditions and customs, which always remained vividly in his mind, instilled in him a deep love for his people and for human beings in general. From his pious father and gentle mother, he absorbed an abiding faith which strengthened him throughout his life. Steeped in Jewish ideals, blessed with keenness of mind and sensibilities, he drew heavily on the knowledge of the past and the Bible that was passed on to him by his father and teachers. But study, no matter how important, was not the only maturing agent of his early years. Sports and activities of the outdoors drew him as well. Here, as in all things, he was driven by a compulsion to succeed, a drive which remained a part of his being all his life.

The elder Rabbi Goode moved his family to Washington, D. C., when Alex was yet a boy, accepting the call of a Georgetown synagogue. For Alex the transition was difficult to make, as such changes always must be for children accustomed to one locality.

School experiences of the average American boy were in store for Alex. He grew up in an area of the nation's capital that was not devoid of gang rumbles and street fighting. A number of times he and his brother literally fought their way to school after being set upon by gangs of boys who sought money or who merely needed to express hostility against a society which was not providing equal opportunity for all races and colors. Such events can be instructive to a sensitive boy, and Alex was deeply sensitive. He had learned at first hand something of the basic conflicts inherent in this society and devoted much energy later toward the amelioration of the causes for such experiences as he had had to face.

Alex's scholarship and athletic prowess brought early recognition from his peers. He was the all-American boy of legend. First, he was a keen, serious student. He was, in addition, the finest boxer and track man in the school, and an accomplished wrestler and tennis player. All this does not mean that his life was a completely happy, serene, complacent one. He was a thinking youngster who constantly re-evaluated his life, his religion, his people, mankind. Often he was disturbed by what he saw in the world about him, by the gap between the ideal and reality. He saw in America the great promise of freedom and liberty, but when he looked around and beheld evidences of inequality of opportunity, the deplorable living conditions of both Negroes and whites, he was appalled. His emotion urged him to deeper thought and to the seeking of ways to better the lot of his fellow-men.

One of the most significant experiences of his life was his attendance at the ceremony of the Unknown Soldier consecration on November 11, 1921, when he was only ten years old. He had made his way on foot to Arlington, where the great leaders of America, the great diplomats of all nations, had assembled to do honor to the Unknown Soldier. Who that Unknown Soldier was, no one of course knew, and it was to the everlasting credit of America that it made no difference. He might be Jew or Christian. He might be white or Negro. No matter! Here Alex perceived suddenly and deeply the unity of America, and he never forgot the lesson this experience taught. In a sense, his entire life was devoted to serving the Unknown Soldier, meaning Anyone or Everyone who needed help, no matter what race, color or creed.

This vision he held before him throughout his high school years, as he prepared himself for the day he could really do something concrete to help his fellows. In these early years, he met Theresa Flax, niece of Al Jolson, who became his shining light and later his dedicated partner in life. Always, he gave the best that was in him—whether to friend, study or sport. His schedule was a busy one. Besides conducting a newspaper route, he began his service in the National Guard.

Upon his completion of high school, the sisterhood of a Washington congregation provided a scholarship for Alex to matriculate at the Hebrew Union College in Cincinnati. The rabbinate called.

Studies at the University of Cincinnati and the Hebrew Union College opened up new vistas for him. Here in a world of the intellect, Alex Goode was at home. He had an inextinguishable thirst for Jewish knowledge. History became his favorite subject. At every opportunity he devoured volume upon volume of Jewish history, literature and sociology. But studies did not consume him utterly. After his first year he married his childhood sweetheart.

Alex continued his vigorous interest in history, and it was this field that drew his first literary efforts. His *A History of Jewish Philanthropy in America until the Civil War* won for him the Rosenberg-Schottenfels Memorial Prize. From there he moved into the realm of economics with *A History of Jewish Economic Life from 1830-1860.* "The Exilarchate in Babylon during the Talmudic Period" and other long essays delighted his teachers, who marveled at their clarity, discipline and logic.

His rabbinical thesis, an overpowering title, is considered a primary source for historians: *A Critical Analysis of the Book of Yosippon as Compared to Josephus and Other Sources with a Discussion of the Literary Problem of Its Composition and Style.* The theme is indicative of the depth and range of the youthful scholar. He did not, however, limit himself to historical themes. He was alive to Jewish experience and sensitive to its subtleties. He had his hand on the pulse of the people. Rooted in a traditional upbringing, he was ever aware of changes and modifications in Jewish living. He perceived the rising trend of Reform Judaism and foresaw its course of development. Three months before his ordination in 1937, his article "Reform Comes Home" appeared in the March issue of the *National Jewish Monthly:*

> The often heard truism that the liberal movement of one generation is the conservative movement of the following generation is nowhere more applicable than in the case of the Reform wing of Judaism. The generation of Emil G. Hirsch, Joseph Krauskopf, Henry Berkowitz, Max Heller, and David Philipson set the pace in radically liberalizing the Judaism of their day, making it conform to the American scene. That generation of crusading liberals has now been replaced by a generation of rabbis whose virtually unanimous aim is to return Reform to the observance of those traditional ceremonials and customs which their predecessors so violently "liberalized."
>
> What are the facts underlying this return of Reform to its home? The Reform Jews of the last generation, like the Reform rabbis of that day, deliberately abolished many rites.
>
> The present generation of Reform, free of the heady spirits of "liberalism," early became conscious of the rapidly growing neglect of the temple. Once discarded ceremonies are resuming their rightful position in the temple and home. The Kiddush ceremony on the Sabbath and on

festivals; a congregational ceremony of kindling the candles on the Sabbath and Chanukah; a congregational Succah for Succoth; a communal Seder on Passover—all are once more filling many Reform homes and temples with their warmth. Other ceremonials which have been reintroduced into the temple are the memorial service on the last day of Passover and the traditional ceremony of Simhat Torah, observed on Shemini Aretz. The response of the Reform Jews to the return of these observances has been immediate and salutary, for temple attendance is pleasingly augmented, at least on such occasions. From the temple the rites are thus being reintroduced in an ever larger number of Reform Jewish homes.

According to the latest information on file at the headquarters of the Union of American Hebrew Congregations in Cincinnati, about 20% of the large congregations and 15% of the smaller ones have reintroduced the Kiddush. That the number is growing is apparent from the fact that several congregations have very recently inaugurated the custom. Some congregations have special social gatherings in honor of the Sabbath and the Kiddush cups are now found in every fifth home of Reform Jews.

The return of Reform to the ceremonies and traditions still retained by Orthodoxy is most marked in its new manner of Sabbath observance. Says Rabbi Jacob D. Schwarz of the Union of American Hebrew Congregations: "While it is a matter of common knowledge that there has been a revival of certain customs and practices in connection with the Friday evening service, it is astonishing how widespread this has become within recent years." Besides the Kiddush, traditional Sabbath melodies are sung in many temples by the cantor, who is now becoming a feature in an increasing number of congregations. The "Lechah Dodi" and other melodies formerly only to be heard in Orthodox synagogues are now sung in many temples.

The kindling of the Sabbath candles has also been reintroduced. A ritual for the lighting of these candles, either by the rabbi or a member of the Sisterhood, has been incorporated in the new experimental Friday Evening Service prepared by the Central Conference of American Rabbis. Sabbath candlesticks and Chanukah menorahs are now to be found in every other home of temple members. The study of Jewish ceremonials is now part of the curriculum of many Reform religious schools and institutes of adult Jewish studies, such as B'nai B'rith is now sponsoring in several cities. Emphasis is being placed by Reform lay leaders as well as rabbis upon the importance of fostering Jewish customs and ceremonies in the home. Jewish ceremonial objects are exhibited in the religious schools for this purpose. Almost half the homes of Reform Jews have a Mezuzah on display, while a like number have a Jewish calendar available. . . .

The returning emphasis on traditional Jewish values is further evident from the type of sermons being delivered by Reform rabbis in their temples. Most of them are outspoken in their opinion of the undesirability of the book-review type of sermon. The rabbis who preach on the Sabbath, using a Jewish text, represent congregations whose members are interested in traditional Jewish techniques and customs. They base their sermons, therefore, on the traditional literature; on the Bible, on Jewish history, on the Midrash, Talmud, and Commentaries of the great medieval rabbis on the Bible. All but a trifling percentage of Reform rabbis concern themselves mainly with Jewish problems in their sermons.

The temple, like the synagogue, is still the Beth-Ha-tefillah and the Beth ha-Midrash. Not only is the use of Hebrew in the principal prayers retained but Hebrew as the subject of instruction is becoming increasingly important. . . .

That there is a strong movement in the ranks of Reform temples to recapture the spirit of the traditional ceremonies of Judaism cannot be denied. . . .

More responsible for the return to tradition perhaps are the efforts of those Jewish leaders who early recognized Reform's loss when it dropped certain ceremonials. For by no means is the return to be considered as of recent origin. As far back as 1918, Rabbi Henry Berkowitz, "The Beloved Rabbi," wrote about a colleague who made it his practice to have two of his confirmants at his own table for Kiddush each week. The rabbis not only preached the charm of the traditional Jewish home but illustrated it by their personal example. From the same period is to be dated the reinstitution of the Seder and observance of Chanukah. Not only have Reform rabbis initiated the rapidly accelerating movement back to the observance of the traditional forms but the Central Conference of American Rabbis and the Union of American Hebrew Congregations have contributed greatly to its progress by publication of the beautiful Union Haggadah, of educational material for the teaching of ritual and ceremonial, of special holiday rituals and other important aids for the return of Jewish observances in home and synagogue. B'nai B'rith, through the A.Z.A. and Hillel Foundations, has surely contributed to the growth of knowledge of Judaism among our youth and thus have aided in this return of Reform.

Ordained rabbi, he accepted a pulpit in 1937 at York, Pennsylvania. His arrival in York and his involvement in the manifold activities of the community transformed the city. The citizenry had never seen such an aggressive, concerned, active rabbi. Every communal endeavor was of interest and importance to him. He became the leader of the inter-faith forces. He helped organize a library of books for children, books which would teach them the ideals of their blessed country and how to live with all people. He was concerned with developing tolerance in children—their understanding of the principles of Americanism and American brotherhood.

Where there is intolerance and bigotry in our midst let us take steps to enlighten the uninformed. The best cure against religious hatred is information. Let us know one another better and thus learn to appreciate the good inherent in every man.

He practiced the words of the Declaration. He preached the ever fresh pronouncement of the prophet Malachi:

> Have we not all one father?
> Hath not one God created us?
> Why do we deal treacherously every man
>   against his brother,
> Profaning the covenant of our fathers?

Scout work aroused his interest. However, he refused to organize a Scout troop in his synagogue unless children of all denominations were welcome. He also served his people in the Jewish Organized Charities, B'nai B'rith, the Board of the Jewish Community Center and United Jewish Appeal. He belonged to the Social Service Club and the University Club. To each and every one he gave generously of his time, effort and thought. He was not a mere joiner; he was an active officer in each. But despite his full schedule, he was not satisfied. His questing mind, his searching soul, demanded more and more. He wanted more knowledge, for one thing. In spite of his overwhelming schedule of activities in the community and in his synagogue, he found time to pursue a course of study at Johns Hopkins University which culminated in 1940 in his being awarded the Ph.D. degree. His thesis, again in the field of history, was *The Jewish Exilarchate during the Arabic Period, 640-1258*. He was 28 years old at the time. Judging by his accomplishments thus far, greatness seemed assured for the gifted young rabbi.

Meanwhile, World War II was rushing on from climax to climax. Country after country lined up against the forces of darkness. Persecution of Jews was intensifying, as Hitler brought the practice of genocide to a terrifying perfection. Concentration camps were readying thousands of Jews for the furnaces. Here, young men were either enlisting in the services or receiving Greetings from the President. America was clearly on the move, preparing to defend her principles. Alex Goode preached the American ideal as he went from community to community, from one civic organization to another. He spoke of Judaism and the democratic ideal, everywhere warmly greeted as audiences thrilled to his presentations.

We are fighting for the new age of brotherhood, the age of brotherhood that will usher in at the same time the world democracy we all want, the age when men will admire the freedom and responsibility of the common man in American democracy. Our methods will be imitated and improved upon. Our spirit of tolerance will spread. Systems of coinage, trade products, scientific discoveries, inventions useful in commerce, new tools of useful living, will find a world-wide distribution and use.

Justice and righteousness as dreamed by the prophet who gave the world the democratic spirit will cover the earth as a torrent. Men the world over will have enough to eat, clothes to wear, opportunity for improvement through education and full employment. Tyranny will no longer be possible in a united world because before it can gain power, the forces of justice speeded through space by the airplane will have overwhelmed it. Protests against injustice will be heard in every capital of the world the moment it occurs and redress granted at once.

What has seemed like civilization up to this point is but a crude effort compared to the era that lies just before us. The new world will be the goal of the cavalcade of democracy through the ages. Toward this new world the cavalcade of democracy marches on, heralding the century of humanity.

He poured his deep feelings, his heart and soul, into his writings, moved by the tragedy of his people and of war. His hope shone through the horrors of the day like a beacon light and gave courage to the despairing. The new persecutors in Europe would not succeed in crushing the Jewish spirit, he asserted.

Writing in the *National Jewish Monthly* in 1941, he used the long history of European persecution of the Jew as background for his article entitled "Ghettos Will Fail":

The world has been horrified by the news that the Nazis in Poland have built an eight-foot wall enclosing 100 squares of Warsaw. There 500,000 Jews are forced to dwell. The wall will facilitate the studied, cold progrom whereby Jews are forbidden to buy clothing, food, milk; to use the radio, bomb shelters, street-cars, and streets; to engage in business or to have rights before the law; curfew, yellow badge, and jim crow street-cars are the symbols of the new ghetto. Its purpose is to demoralize, degrade, and crush Jewish self-respect and dignity.

The new ghetto will fail. The medieval ghetto it imitates could not destroy the Jewish heritage and spirit in 300 years. Like Hitler today, Pope Paul IV in the 16th century sought to isolate the Jews from the rest of the world by a walled district, named ghetto for a nearby iron foundry. He forced 400 to live in one house, 10,000 in a small area, in Rome. The ghetto was instituted in all lands under the Pope's influence. Yet despite the desecration of Jewish cemeteries, despite the shame of being forced to allow houses of ill-repute within their walls, despite the indignity of being chained in nightly, the medieval Jews did not despair, but strengthened their Jewish institutions; the public bath, the synagogue, the communal center, the hospital, the school, the charities. Forbidden to build new synagogues or to make the old ones higher than the church, they made more room by building beneath the ground. They still found means to support the synagogue despite exorbitant and discriminatory taxes. The bearers of the badge of shame had to endure false accusations of ritual murder, charges of desecration of the host, the stones and clods thrown by ruffians, the diatribes of priests seeking to convert them, the indignity of taking the oath on a swineskin. Yet nothing could destroy the fibre of the Jew.

As steam under pressure generates power, so the Jewish heritage under the pressure of persecution became an effective instrument of survival. The chains of the ghetto only made the Bible, the ethics, the ideals, the philanthropy, and the scholarship of the Jew more precious to him. The Jewish heritage was the mortar that kept the Jewish edifice intact. It was to be seen in all aspects of Jewish life.

The Jewish home was established on the solid foundation of loving family life. The father was a good provider, faithful husband, sober spouse, loving his children. The mother was an equal when the rest of the world regarded women as chattels; wife-beating was sanctioned by the Church but forbidden by the rabbis; her knowledge of things Jewish and practical made her the adviser of her husband; her piety and industry were proverbial. The child stood in the presence of the father, never sat in his seat, never entered or left before him, stood by his pew when called to the Torah. The home shone with sanctity; marriage was a holy bond not sullied by divorce, though divorce was rampant outside the ghetto. Public morals were degraded but Jewish morals were exalted. Every act was hallowed: before every meal the 23rd Psalm was said; the pious were buried in coffins made of the wood from the table at which they had studied Jewish lore and fed the needy. The world lived in filth and squalor while the Jew lived in dignity and cleanliness. The English philosopher Locke praised their unique custom of bathing weekly and commended this practice to the unwashed Christians; the Jew washed before every meal and used a finger bowl after it and a napkin at it. The table was regarded as an altar of the Lord, honored by fine table manners, lofty talk, marked by hymns and learning. Scorned for introducing the handkerchief, for keeping their windows open to sun and air the year around, the Jews thus avoided the full effects of the black plagues.

In business the word of the Jew was his bond. He was guided by the vast ethical literature, based on the principles of Judaism, that was so popular during his day. Cheating was forbidden. The Church forbade positions of public trust to the Jew, but kings broke that prohibition because the Jews were loyal and trustworthy. The prevalent practice of clipping the coinage was unknown among the Jews. Canon law allowed dealing in stolen goods, but Jewish law forbade it. Forced into usury by the Church, the Jews charged only 18% interest when the legal rate was 300%. The populace of France wept when the Jews were exiled in 1306 because they knew the fair-dealing Jews would be replaced by the exorbitant non-Jewish traders. The fictional story of Shylock is the very reverse of an actual incident in which a Jew, Samson Cesena, was sued for a pound of flesh by an Italian, Paolo Secchi. No greater tribute to the integrity of the medieval Jew can be found than that of Bishop Rudiger of Speyer, who wrote: "Wishing to make of Speyer a city, I thought to increase its honor a thousandfold by bringing in the Jews." Though the Church sought to degrade Jewish enterprise by forcing it into second-hand trade in clothes, by forbidding Jews to own land or till the soil, and [forcing them] to be usurers so it could profit by high taxes, still the Jews created new fields of endeavor: they introduced sugar, tea, coffee, tobacco; they traded with the Orient, wove silk, bound books; they were artists, artisans, goldsmiths, dyers, millers, olive-growers, vintners, tailors, chemists, metalworkers, doctors, scientists, scholars, soldiers, map-makers, navigators, gunsmiths, and explorers.

The Jews were kind masters who freed their slaves in their wills. They practiced the Jewish Law: "Mercy is the mark of piety. No man may oppress his servant. He must receive part of every dainty he eats; he must be degraded neither by word or act."

Denied the right of human society, the Jew turned to his books for comfort. Illiteracy was unknown to him. The Jewish system of education for child, youth, and adult was the finest in Europe. The Jew was a giant of learning among the ignorant pygmies of Europe. He had his own colleges centuries before the first German university was opened in Erfurt in 1379. Jews translated Greek and Arabic works, and their commentaries on the Bible paved the way for the King James version. Jewish inquiry and experiment laid the basis for the Renaissance, the Reformation, and modern science. It has truly been said that Hebraic mortar cements modern civilization.

Today we know that the new ghetto will fail to degrade the Jew even more than it failed in the Middle Ages, because today the entire world protests this effort to turn back the clock. Not only do the democracies oppose it, but even lands under nazi domination. How encouraging was that brave act of the Netherlanders in defying the Nazi tyrant by themselves donning the yellow badge which was ordered for the Jews. The world gained so much when the Jew was allowed to live in freedom that it cannot abide his enslavement. Philo, Maimonides, Spinoza, Heine, Mendelssohn, Ehrlich, Freud, Ricardo, Disraeli, Brandeis, Cardozo, and Einstein—all products of periods of Jewish freedom—belong to the world. Civilized people now realize that the world is a unit of which the Jews are a valuable part. Israel, the heart of the nations, cannot be destroyed without destroying the world as we know it. Religion and democracy are children of the Jewish genius. Destroy the parent and the children perish. No nation can long be enslaved, much less a religion. Those who seek to degrade us degrade themselves. We pity the persecutor who thinks he tolls the death-knell for Judaism; actually it is he for whom the bell tolls.

As long as democracy and civilization survive, the Jew must also live. As long as the Jew maintains his morale and self-respect by sound knowledge of heritage, he will live. As long as Jewish dignity warms the Jewish home, as long as Jewish integrity guides him in his enterprises, as long as his love of learning endures, so long will Jewry survive.

Rabbi Goode became increasingly active in the war effort, raising money for Bundles for Britain and the Red Cross, and participating in

War Bond drives. But still he was not content. His inner compulsion to help required that he be in the center of things. Accordingly, in January of 1941, he tried to join the chaplaincy in the Navy and was deeply disappointed when advised that no vacancy existed. However, when Pearl Harbor was attacked on that fateful December 7th, he applied to the Army and was accepted. He was commissioned First Lieutenant in July 21, 1942, took his training at the Chaplain's School at Harvard University and was sent to Goldsboro, North Carolina, on August 9, 1942, for his first assignment as Jewish chaplain of the Army Air Force base there. Still he was not entirely happy. He wanted to see action. He felt that he was needed where the men of America were fighting and he sought an overseas assignment. Finally, the orders came through and he was directed to Camp Miles Standish, Taunton, Massachusetts, a point of embarkation. When he learned that his assignment was to Greenland he pleaded for more active service. Destiny, however, had decreed otherwise.

Alex Goode, together with a thousand men and three other chaplains, was assigned to the S. S. *Dorchester,* an old, ungainly freighter bound for Greenland. The ship set out to sea in late January, 1943. A feeling of uneasiness permeated the ship, a vague feeling of being watched. The old freighter was part of a convoy, and after the second evening of February the fear intensified as the Coast Guard cutter blinked the announcement that they were being followed by a submarine. Planes also blinked to say that no help could be given at this time. There was a brief respite in the docks of St. John's, Newfoundland, after which the ships pressed on to their destination.

As the slow sea journey began again, the four chaplains went from man to man, offering a word of encouragement here, a reassuring pat on the shoulder there. The fear was real. All admitted to it, though they sought sleep as a means of handling it. Outside, the Arctic night was enchantingly beautiful, the sky clear and alive with stars. But response to the beauty of the night was not possible while this deep sense of danger persisted.

Just as dawn was breaking, the waiting was over. Straight and sure, the torpedo struck. In seconds many were dead, others badly burned, still others gasping for breath and searching for life belts. Whatever had been learned in the comparative serenity of training was forgotten as each man desperately tried to save himself. Life rafts were lowered into the icy waters and men jumped on, while the four chaplains went about doing their duty as best they could. In the rush to get to the lifeboats, many had forgotten to take life belts or gloves. One by one, the chaplains gave their own to those who cried out, "I've forgotten my belt." "Here," said one chaplain after another, "take this one. I have another. Here, take these gloves, I have another pair."

It all took a few minutes, the entire experience: 1000 men on board, 700 dead, 300 saved. The four chaplains—Catholic, Jewish, Protestant—remained on the ship. The last view was of the four standing on deck, arms linked, praying as the *Dorchester* foundered. A mighty wave washed over the ship and the praying martyrs were forever hushed.

A young sailor, when he returned from the war, told of the sight which had been indelibly impressed on his mind, the view of four men standing braced against the slippery deck, arms interlocked, praying together. Lieutenant John J. Mahoney, a young officer who was on deck, related his personal experience. He had heard the order to abandon ship. Responding quickly, he snatched his parka and life preserver and made his way to the promenade deck when he suddenly realized that he had forgotten his gloves. He chastised himself under his breath for his stupidity and began heading back to his cabin. Chaplain Alexander Goode overheard him swearing at himself and called to him. "Don't bother, Mahoney," he said, "you can have these. I have another pair." He pulled off his gloves and gave them to the lieutenant. The officer only later learned that the chaplain did not have another pair. He spent 80 hours in the freezing waters of the Atlantic and testified: "I owe my life to those gloves. I landed in a lifeboat that was awash, and for eight hours had to hold on in waters the official temperature of which was 30 degrees. My fingers would have been frozen stiff had it not been for the gloves. I would never have made it without them. As it was, only two of us survived out of the 40 that were in the boat."

Chaplain Abraham Ruderman, on February 21, 1944, wrote to the Jewish Welfare Board:

As we sat there, I recall seeing the ship going down. There must have been horror on their faces. They couldn't let go. As the boat keeled toward the starboard hundreds of red lights alone were visible—lights in the life preservers of the men. They looked like a long neon sign moving into the sea. For a short while the stream of light scattered over the water, and then they were no more. While in the boat the men prayed —they never prayed so hard in their lives. The cry of "Father in Heaven" pierced the very Gates of Heaven and their cries were heard. A few Jewish lads kept reciting the last verse of the "Shema Yisrael." Latin, English and Hebrew rose in one chorus to Him who hears and answers prayers.

Almost immediately, a movement arose to perpetuate the memories of these four men of God. The campaign drew quick response. America was ready to testify to this mighty act of faith and establish it as a symbol of American courage and unity. Eight years later, on the 3rd of February, the Chapel of the Four Chaplains came into being. At that time Dr. Poling said:

> The Chapel of the Four Chaplains is a Sanctuary of Brotherhood. Its three altars—Catholic, Jewish and Protestant—proclaim the unity of all Americans under one God. Its memorials and furnishings bear forever the names of men of different faiths who died as brothers-in-arms for the freedom of their fellows and for generations yet unborn. The message of the Chapel of the Four Chaplains is the message of these hero-dead— "The irreducible minimum for an adequate defense of America is American unity! Not uniformity! All race and faiths, all colors and economic degrees, living together as Americans all.

Two years later, on the tenth anniversary of the sinking, the Jewish Altar was dedicated under the auspices of B'nai B'rith. The writer, then Director of the Hillel Foundation at Temple University, conducted the service and delivered the sermon of dedication entitled "Embraced in the Arms of Eternity."

> *Ayle ez'krah, v'na'shy alai nishp'cha,* "These things do I remember and my heart is grieved. So begins the section on martyrology in the traditional Yom Kippur [Day of Atonement] service as congregants share, with reverence, awe and pathos that pierce to the very depths of their souls, the heroic experiences of the *Asara harvgay malchut,* Martyrdom of Ten Rabbis, who gave their lives *al k'dushat hashem* for the sanctification of the name of God.

> This hath befallen our people. With humble and mournful hearts we pray to Thee, O merciful God, view from heaven the blood of all Thy righteous. O make an end of bloodshed by men and wash the stain

away, O Thou King, Who sittest on the throne of mercy. So *ends* the section on martyrology in the traditional Yom Kippur service as congregants, with soft weeping warming the synagogue, resurrect out of the past and infuse with living presence the dauntless courage, the pious saintliness, and the blessed stubbornness of the Ten Martyrs who gave their lives "for the sanctification of the name of God."

So has it ever been since man first appeared on the horizon of history and initiated his quest for world environment, a society of peace and freedom. And so have consecrated souls stepped beyond the finitude of time into the embracing arms of eternity—the parchment of the Holy Scroll wrapped about them, enveloping their whole physical beings, burning, but the letters of the Sefer Torah [Holy Scroll], imprinted by hand, the souls, the sparks of divinity, easing from off the parchment, and soaring upwards towards the skies, defying destructibility, remaining forever inviolate, uniting heaven and earth.

Cabined within the confines of this beginning and end, there unfolds, before our very eyes, in all its tragedy and in all its glory, the panoramic epic of the Jew, his unbroken pilgrimage to every corner of the globe in search for the hand of friendship, and those of his people who in the process paid the supreme price for life and liberty—but not in vain. Within the boundaries of these annals of martyrdom, too, there spreads before our sight the dramatic story of America, its determination to offer refuge to those in need, its struggles to entrench this land as a home of the free, its perseverance toward the concretization of the ideals to which it is dedicated into living actualities, its blessed efforts to make freedom from fear, freedom from want, freedom to speak, and freedom to worship, everyday living experiences—drawing them from the state of idealism above and intertwining them into the very fabric of daily living —principles of democratic force propounded by the spiritual giant whose birthday occurs this day [Franklin Delano Roosevelt] and those Americans who in the process paid the supreme price for life and for liberty— but not in vain.

Here in this Sanctuary of Sacred Memories, in this Edifice of Humanity where *Nashki arah u'rakiah ahadade*—"where heaven and earth meet and kiss"—we gather to dedicate this Holy Altar to the sainted memory of Alexander Goode, Chaplain, High Priest in this Temple of Humanity. We meet tonight to recapture the spirit and establish rapport with the martyrs of the Twentieth Century, who lived, loved, and live still.

We convene to stand again on the deck of the *Dorchester,* see with our very eyes through strength of mind and purpose, and direct into our lives for determined action, the holy experiences of consecrated colleagues of the cloth. Fox, Poling, Goode, Washington. Even as we read in tomorrow morning's scriptural portion of the crossing of the Red Sea en route to the foot of Sinai to the Great Ideal, even so do our minds' eyes perceive brave men crossing the tumultuous waves of the ocean en route to the Great Ideal. The hour, the moment of spiritual power and might arrives: No questions asked, Are you Jewish, are you Catholic, are you Protestant, are you White, are you Negro. No questions asked! You need the belt of life—here, our belts for your lives. And then they prayed, engaged, integrated, arm in arm, they prayed to God:

"O make an end of bloodshed by men and wash the stain away, O Thou King, Who sittest on the throne of mercy." And what were the prayers that came from the mouth of him whom we draw into our hearts and souls and with whom we fuse this evening?—the prayers of all martyrs, Israel's watchword, incomparable in magnitude and depth, the Sh'ma Yisroel, Hear O Israel, the Lord our God, the Lord is One. Indeed, the Rabbis of the Midrash tell us, "He who recites the Shema brings to mind Israel's crossing of the Red Sea." And there they stood. *M'or gadol raiti bayam*—"A great light do I see in the sea"; the light of glory, the light of hope, the light of service kindled by the sacrifice supreme, to the end that the world might become a better place in which to live.

He who comes from B'nai B'rith, he who derives from the children of the Covenant, engraved with his life a *B'rit Yam*, a covenant with the sea; a contract, eternal and interminable, that the life which he and his colleagues gave be not found to have been for naught.

Yes, heaven and earth unite this evening. We consecrate this Holy Altar to the blessed memory of Alexander Goode, lovingly embraced in the arms of Infinity, tied to us with bonds of love and affection, and we vow with all the solemnity we can muster to our beings, we pledge fealty with all our might, that our lives henceforth, from this day on and forever more, be directed toward making good our share of the ideal for which this Ark of the Lord is being blessed this evening. Knowingly, consciously, without mental reservation, with presence of mind, our souls ascribe and affix themselves as signatories to this bond of life which cements us to the sanctification of Alexander Goode. And the witness that will testify to our meeting of minds and souls hangs suspended above us, the Ner Tamid, the Eternal Light which shines and shall illumine forevermore the Ark of the Lord; that Ner Tamid, even as the protecting clouds of glory that hovered over the paths of our ancestors in ancient days, that Ner Tamid, will serve as our guiding light, as we on earth kiss the heavens above and pledge our undeviating service to all humanity. We give our word, we give our hearts and our souls this evening, to build, to construct, to create, to erect a humanity that shall be free from the haunting ghosts of fear, a universe that shall be free from hate and torture and cruelty and war, a world that shall be founded upon love and kindness, understanding and equality. This Eternal Light, we pray, will be for us the prime mover in our unswerving determination to reach God, on rays emanating from these portals, to build for Him and for all His children on earth a world of freedom, sweetness and good. So said God to the poet [Thomas Curtis Clark]:

> Build me a House,
>   Said God;
> Not of cedar-wood or stone,
> Where at some altar-place
> Men for their sins atone.
> To me, your only sin
> Is to build my House too small:
> Let there be no dome
> To shut out the sky,
> Let there be no cumbering wall,
> Build me a House, a Home,
> In the hearts of hungering men—
> Hungering for the bread of hope,
> Thirsting for faith, yearning for love,
> In a world of grief and pain.
> Build me a House.
>
> Build me a World,
>   Said God;
> Not with a navy's strife,
> Nor with a host in arms,
> Compassing death, not life,
> Build me a World, said God,
> Out of man's fairest dreams;
> Heaven must be its dome,
> Lighted by prophet-gleams;
> Justice shall be the stones
> On which my World shall rise;
> Truth and Love its arches,

Gripping my ageless skies.
Out of dreams, on the earthy
   sod,
Build me a World,
   Said God.

We, the B'nai B'rith, together with all Children of God, respond to the call tonight. We shall build Thee a House; we shall build Thee such a World, O God.

Alexander Goode, giant of faith, was presented posthumously with the Purple Heart and Distinguished Service Cross. So long as men strive for freedom and defend democracy his name will live on in the hearts of his countrymen.

BIBLIOGRAPHIES

HENRY COHEN

"Henry Cohen," *Universal Jewish Encyclopedia*; III, 1941.

Cohen, Henry. *A Brave Frontiersman.* Baltimore: American Jewish Historical Society, No. 8 (1900), 59-74.

———. *One Hundred Years of Jewry in Texas, The Original Researches of Henry Cohen.* Dallas: Advisory Committee for the Texas Centennial Religious Program, 1936.

———. *Settlement of the Jews in Texas.* Baltimore: American Jewish Historical Society, No. 2 (1894), 139-56.

———. "What Constitutes a Successful Ministry," *Yearbook*, Central Conference of American Rabbis, XXXII (1922).

Dreyfus, A. Stanley. *Henry Cohen, Messenger of the Lord.* New York: Bloch Publishing Company, 1963.

Nathan, Anne, and Cohen, Harry I. *The Man Who Stayed in Texas.* New York: Whittlesey House, 1941.

Vorspan, Albert. *Giants of Justice.* New York: Union of American Hebrew Congregations, 1960.

DAVID EINHORN

"David Einhorn," *Universal Jewish Encyclopedia*; IV, 1943.

Kohler, Kaufmann. "David Einhorn," *Yearbook*, Central Conference of American Rabbis, XIX (1909), 215-70.

———. *Studies, Addresses, and Personal Papers.* New York: The Alumni Association of the Hebrew Union College, 1931.

Korn, Bertram W. *American Jewry and the Civil War.* Philadelphia: Jewish Publication Society, 1951.

Levinger, Elma Ehrlich. *Jewish Adventures in America.* New York: Bloch Publishing Company, 1954.

Marcus, Jacob Rader (ed.). "The Jews of the Union," *Civil War Centennial,* Northern Issue. Cincinnati: American Jewish Archives, XIII (November, 1961), 131-230.

Pessin, Deborah. *History of the Jews in America.* New York: Abelard-Schuman, 1958 (copyright United Synagogue of America, 1957).

Schappes, Morris U. *A Documentary History of the Jews in the United States, 1654-1875.* New York: The Citadel Press, 1950.

Simonhoff, Harry. *Jewish Notables in America, 1776-1865.* New York: Greenberg, 1956.

BERNARD FELSENTHAL

"Bernard Felsenthal," *Universal Jewish Encyclopedia*; IV, 1943.

Felsenthal, Bernard. *The Beginnings of the Chicago Sinai Congregation.* Chicago: Published under the auspices of the Executive Board of Chicago Sinai Congregation, 1898.

———. *The Jewish Congregation in Surinam.* New York: American Jewish Historical Society, No. 2 (1894), 29.

———. *Kol Kore Bamidbar.* Chicago: Sinai Congregation, 1898.

———. *On the History of the Jews of Chicago.* New York: American Jewish Historical Society, No. 2 (1894), 21.

———. *The Wandering Jew,* A Statement to a Christian Audience of the Jewish View of Judaism. Chicago: Chicago Pulpit Extra, 1, 1872.

Felsenthal, Emma. *Bernhard Felsenthal, Teacher in Israel.* New York: Oxford University Press, 1924.

Marcus, Jacob Rader (ed.). "The Jews of the Union," *Civil War Centennial,* Northern Issue. Cincinnati: American Jewish Archives, XIII (November, 1961), 131-230.

Philipson, David. *The Reform Movement in Judaism.* New York: The Macmillan Company, 1931.

Reform Advocate (Chicago), Felsenthal Centenary Number; December 21, 1921.

Stolz, Joseph. "Bernard Felsenthal," *Yearbook,* Central Conference of American Rabbis, XVIII (1908), 161-67.

———. "Bernhard Felsenthal," Publications of the American Jewish Historical Society, No. 17. Baltimore: 1909.

SOLOMON GOLDMAN

"Solomon Goldman," *Universal Jewish Encyclopedia*; V, 1941.

Churgin, Pinkhos, and Wolfson, Harry A. (eds.). "From Time to Time, Solomon Goldman—An Appraisal," *Bitzaron*, XXVII (May, 1953), 114-15.

Finkelstein, Eliezer Arye. "Solomon Goldman," *Hadoar*, XXXIII (June 29, 1953), 605-6.

Goldman, Solomon. *Crisis and Decision.* New York and London: Harper & Bros., 1938.

——. *From Slavery to Freedom.* New York: Abelard-Schuman, 1958.

——. *In the Beginning.* Philadelphia: Jewish Publication Society, 1949.

——. *The Jew and the Universe.* New York and London: Harper & Bros., 1936.

——. *A Rabbi Takes Stock.* New York: Harper & Bros., 1931.

——. (Maurice Samuel, ed.) *The Ten Commandments.* Chicago: University of Chicago Press, 1956.

——. *Undefeated.* Washington, D. C.: Zionist Organization of America, 1940.

——. *The Words of Justice Brandeis.* New York: Henry Schuman, 1950.

Weinstein, Jacob J. "Solomon Goldman," *The Reconstructionist*, XIX (June 26, 1953), 19-21.

ALEXANDER D. GOODE

"Chapel of the Four Chaplains, A Sanctuary for Brotherhood," prepared by Dr. Daniel A. Poling, Chaplain of the Chapel, and Rev. Walter H. White, Chaplain-in-Charge.

Fredman, J. George. *Brothers in Arms.* New York: Jewish War Veterans of the United States, 1945.

Goode, Alexander. "The Exilarchate in the Eastern Caliphate," *Jewish Quarterly Review*, XXXI (1940-41), 149-69.

——. *Toward Eternal Peace.* Unpublished manuscript in possession of Mrs. Theresa Goode Kaplan, Columbus, Ohio.

Postal, Bernard (ed.). "Jewish Chaplaincy Centennial Issue," *The Jewish Digest* (Houston), April, 1962.

Ruderman, Abraham. "Report of the Sinking." Report to the Jewish Welfare Board, February 21, 1944.

Thornton, Francis Beauchesne. *Sea of Glory.* Kingswood, England: The World's Work, Ltd., 1956.

ABRAHAM E. HALPERN

Bulletin, B'nai Amoona Congregation, St. Louis; various issues.
Jewish Voice, The, St. Louis; various issues.
Raskas, Bernard S. (ed.). *A Son of Faith; From the Sermons of Abraham E. Halpern*. New York: Bloch Publishing Company, 1962. (Rabbi Raskas generously made available a number of early St. Louis newspapers and Yiddish dailies consulted in the preparation of this volume.)
"Tribute to Greatness." Synagogue program, St. Louis, 1957.

KAUFMANN KOHLER

"Kaufmann Kohler," *Universal Jewish Encyclopedia*; VI, 1942.
Anniversary Service in Commemoration of the Hundredth Birthday of Kaufmann Kohler. New York: Congregation Emanu-El, May 15, 1943.
Enelow, H. G. "Kaufmann Kohler," *American Jewish Yearbook* (Jewish Publication Society), XXVIII (1926), 235-60.
Kohler, Kaufmann. "Hebrew Union College, and Other Addresses," Hebrew Union College *Jubilee Volume (1875-1925)*. Cincinnati: 1925.
———. *Jewish Theology, Systematically and Historically Considered*. New York: The Macmillan Company, 1918.
———. *Studies, Addresses, and Personal Papers*. New York: The Alumni Association of the Hebrew Union College, 1931.
Philipson, David. "Kaufmann Kohler," *Yearbook*, Central Conference of American Rabbis, XXXVI (1926), 170-77.

AARON KOTLER

Jewish Observer, The (Agudath Israel of America), I (November, 1963).
Jewish Press, The (New York), December 7 and 21, 1962.
Kotler, Aaron. "The People of Israel Need the Agudath Israel," *Dos Yiddishe Vort* (Agudath Israel of America), November, 1962, p. 4.
Seidman, Hillel. "Reb Aaron Kotler," *Young Israel Viewpoint*, December 14, 1962, p. 2.
———. "A Year Without Reb Aaron," *Young Israel Viewpoint*, November 22, 1963, p. 9.
"Special Issue in Memory of Reb Aaron Kotler," *Dos Yiddishe Vort* (Agudath Israel of America), January, 1963.

ISAAC LEESER

Davis, Moshe. *The Emergence of Conservative Judaism*. Philadelphia: Jewish Publication Society, 1963.

Englander, Henry. "Isaac Leeser," *Yearbook,* Central Conference of American Rabbis, XXVIII (1918).

Korn, Bertram W. *American Jewry and the Civil War.* Philadelphia: Jewish Publication Society, 1951.

————. *Eventful Years and Experiences.* Cincinnati: American Jewish Archives, 1954.

Johlson, Joseph (translated from the German by Isaac Leeser). *Instruction in the Mosaic Religion.* Philadelphia: n.p., 1830.

Leeser, Isaac. *Catechism for Jewish Children.* Philadelphia: Published by the author, 1839.

————. *Discourses.* Philadelphia: Published by the author; Vol. I, 1836, Vol. III, 1841.

Levinger, Lee J. *A History of the Jews in the United States.* Cincinnati: Union of American Hebrew Congregations, 1930.

Marcus, Jacob Rader. *Memoirs of American Jews, 1775-1865.* Philadelphia: Jewish Publication Society, 1955.

Morais, Henry Samuel. *Eminent Israelites of the 19th Century.* Philadelphia: Edward Stern & Company, 1880.

Pessin, Deborah. *History of the Jews in America.* New York: Abelard-Schuman, 1958 (copyright United Synagogue of America, 1957).

Simonhoff, Harry. *Jewish Notables in America, 1776-1865.* New York: Greenberg, 1956.

Wolf, Edwin, II, and Whiteman, Maxwell. *The History of the Jews of Philadelphia.* Philadelphia: Jewish Publication Society, 1957.

Wolf, Simon. *Address on the Life and Services of the Rev. Isaac Leeser.* Washington, D. C.: Independent Order B'nai B'rith, 1868, p. 13.

BERNARD L. LEVINTHAL

"Bernard Levinthal," *Universal Jewish Encyclopedia;* VI, 1942.

Goldman, Alex J. "100th Anniversary of Rabbi Bernard Levinthal," *Jewish Exponent* (Philadelphia), April 29, 1964, p. 25.

Levinthal Jubilee Volume (K'vod Hahamim). Philadelphia, 1934.

Matt, C. David. "A Great Rabbi Attains Four Score," *Brooklyn Jewish Center Review,* May, 1945, pp. 9-11.

————. "Rabbi Bernard Louis Levinthal," *Jewish Exponent* (Philadelphia), May 17, 1935, p. 20.

Mordell, Albert. "Rabbi Bernard L. Levinthal," *Brooklyn Jewish Center Review,* October, 1952, pp. 5-9.

————. "The Refugee Settlers of Philadelphia in the '90's," *Brooklyn Jewish Center Review,* April, 1952, pp. 13-17.

Nevins, Milton. *The Collected Poems of Rabbi C. David Matt.* Philadelphia: West Philadelphia Jewish Community Center, 1953.

MAX LILIENTHAL

"Max Lilienthal," *Universal Jewish Encyclopedia*; VII, 1942.

Elbogen, Ismar (translated by Moses Hadas). *A Century of Jewish Life.* Philadelphia: Jewish Publication Society, 1944.

Learsi, Rufus. *Israel: A History of the Jewish People.* Cleveland: World Publishing Company, 1949.

Philipson, David. *Centenary Papers and Others.* Cincinnati: Ark Publishing Company, 1919.

———. *Max Lilienthal, American Rabbi; Life and Writings.* New York: Bloch Publishing Company, 1915.

———. "Max Lilienthal in Russia," *Hebrew Union College Annual*, XII-XIII (1937-38), 825-39.

——— (ed.). *Reminiscences by Isaac M. Wise.* Cincinnati: Leo Wise & Company, 1901.

Simonhoff, Harry. *Jewish Notables in America, 1776-1865.* New York: Greenberg, 1956.

SABATO MORAIS

"Sabato Morais," *Jewish Encyclopedia*; VIII, 1907.

"Sabato Morais," *Universal Jewish Encyclopedia*; VII, 1942.

Davis, Moshe. *The Emergence of Conservative Judaism.* Philadelphia: Jewish Publication Society, 1963.

Finkelstein, Louis. *The Jews.* Philadelphia: Jewish Publication Society, Vol. I, 1949.

Korn, Bertram W. *American Jewry and the Civil War.* Philadelphia: Jewish Publication Society, 1951.

———. *Eventful Years and Experiences.* Cincinnati: American Jewish Archives, 1954.

Morais, Henry Samuel. *The Jews of Philadelphia.* Philadelphia: The Levytype Company, 1894.

Morais, Sabato (Julius H. Greenstone, ed.). *Italian Hebrew Literature.* New York: Jewish Theological Seminary of America, 1926.

Our Age (United Synagogue Commission on Jewish Education), IV (May 19, 1963).

Pessin, Deborah. *History of the Jews in America.* New York: Abelard-Schuman, 1958 (copyright United Synagogue of America, 1957).

Rosenman, William. "Sabato Morais—An Appreciation," *Yearbook*, Central Conference of American Rabbis, XXXIII, 1923.

Simonhoff, Harry. *Saga of American Jewry, 1865-1914; Links of an Endless Chain*. New York: Arco Publishing Company, 1959.

Waxman, Mordecai (ed.). *Tradition and Change; The Development of Conservative Judaism*. New York: The Burning Bush Press, 1958.

BERNARD REVEL

Eidenu (Memorial Volume). Published by Students of the Rabbi Elchanan Theological Seminary, New York, 1942.

Elbogen, Ismar (translated by Moses Hadas). *A Century of Jewish Life*. Philadelphia: Jewish Publication Society, 1944.

Hedenu (Volume in Honor of the 50th Anniversary of the Rabbi Elchanan Theological Seminary and Dr. Revel's 50th Birthday). New York, 1936.

Jung, Leo. "Bernard Revel," *American Jewish Yearbook* (New York), XLIII (1941), 415-24.

Revel, Bernard. *The Karaite Halakah and Its Relation to Sadducean, Samaritan and Philonean Halakah*. Philadelphia: Dropsie College (dissertation), 1913.

SOLOMON SCHECHTER

"Solomon Schechter," *Universal Jewish Encyclopedia*; IX, 1943.

Adler, Cyrus. "Solomon Schechter—A Biographical Sketch," *American Jewish Yearbook* (Philadelphia), 1916, pp. 25-67.

Bentwich, Norman. *Solomon Schechter, A Biography*. Philadelphia: Jewish Publication Society, 1938.

Davis, Moshe. *The Emergence of Conservative Judaism*. Philadelphia: Jewish Publication Society, 1963.

Gordis, Robert. *Conservative Judaism; An American Philosophy*. New York: Published by Behrman House for the National Academy of Adult Jewish Studies of the Jewish Theological Seminary of America, 1945.

Karp, Abraham J. *Conservative Judaism, the Legacy of Solomon Schechter*. New York: Adult Education Course, The Jewish Theological Seminary of America. 1963-64 Year of Dedication Series.

Levinger, Elma Ehrlich. *Jewish Adventures in America*. New York: Bloch Publishing Company, 1954.

Marx, Alexander. *Essays in Jewish Biography*. Philadelphia: Jewish Publication Society of America, 1947.

Schechter, Solomon. *Seminary Addresses and Other Papers*. Cincinnati: Ark Publishing Company, 1915.

———. *Some Aspects of Rabbinic Theology*. New York: The Macmillan Company, 1909.

———. *Studies in Judaism*. Philadelphia: Jewish Publication Society, Third Series, 1945.

"Schechter Memorial," Jewish Theological Seminary of America *Students' Annual*, III (1916).

Simonhoff, Harry. *Saga of American Jewry, 1865-1914; Links of an Endless Chain*. New York: Arco Publishing Company, 1959.

Waxman, Mordecai (ed.). *Tradition and Change; The Development of Conservative Judaism*. New York: The Burning Bush Press, 1958.

SAUL SILBER

Chicago Jewish Courier, The, September 3, 1946.

Fasman, Oscar Z. "Rabbi Saul Silber," *The Chicago Sentinel*, September 12, 1946.

"History of Chicago Jewry, 1911-1961," *The Chicago Sentinel*, December 7, 1961.

Jewish Record, The (St. Louis, Missouri), September 6, 1946.

Regensberg, Chaim David (ed.). *Gibeath Saul*, Essays Contributed in Honor of Rabbi Saul Silber. Chicago: n.p., 1935.

Segal, Y. "Rabbi Saul Silber," *The Forward* (Chicago), September 6, 1946.

Selected Essays of Rabbi Saul Silber. Chicago: n.p., 1950.

MILTON STEINBERG

Badt-Strauss, Bertha. "Thank You, Milton Steinberg," *The Reconstructionist*, XVI (April 21, 1950).

Kaplan, M. M. "Milton Steinberg's Contribution to Reconstructionism," *The Reconstructionist*, XVI (May 19, 1950).

Mandelbaum, Bernard (ed.). *From the Sermons of Rabbi Milton Steinberg*. New York: Bloch Publishing Company, 1954.

———. *Only Human—The Eternal Alibi*. New York: Bloch Publishing Company, 1963.

Noveck, Simon. "Our Spiritual Legacy from Milton Steinberg," *The Reconstructionist*, XVII (October 19, 1951).

Steinberg, Milton (Arthur A. Cohen, ed.). *Anatomy of Faith*. New York: Harcourt, Brace & Company, 1960.

———. *As a Driven Leaf*. Indianapolis-New York: The Bobbs-Merrill Company, 1939.

———. *Basic Judaism*. New York: Harcourt, Brace & Company, 1947.

———. (Maurice Samuel, ed.). *A Believing Jew; The Selected Writings of Milton Steinberg*, selected by Edith A. Steinberg. New York: Harcourt, Brace & Company, 1951.

———. "The Creed of an American Zionist," *Atlantic Monthly*, CLXXV (February, 1945).

———. "Gems from Steinberg's Writings," *The Reconstructionist*, XVI (April 7, 1950).

———. "Judaism and Hellenism," from *Hanukkah, the Feast of Lights*, by Emily Solis-Cohen, Jr. Philadelphia: Jewish Publication Society, 1937.

———. *The Making of the Modern Jew.* New York: Harcourt, Brace & Company, 1951.

———. *A Partisan Guide to the Jewish Problem.* New York: B'nai B'rith, Hillel Foundation (copyright 1945 by The Bobbs-Merrill Company).

———. "Theological Problems of the Hour," The Rabbinical Assembly of America, *Proceedings*, XIII (1949). Philadelphia: Jewish Publication Society, 1950.

———. "Toward the Rehabilitation of the Word Faith," *The Reconstructionist*, VIII (April 1, 1942).

ISAAC M. WISE

Berkowitz, Henry. *Intimate Glimpses of the Rabbi's Career.* Cincinnati: The Hebrew Union College Press, 1921.

Davis, Mac. *Jews at a Glance.* New York: Hebrew Publishing Company, 1956.

Franklin, Leo M. *The Rabbi—The Man and His Message.* New York: Behrman's Jewish Book House, 1938.

Korn, Bertram W. *American Jewry and the Civil War.* Philadelphia: Jewish Publication Society, 1951.

———. *Eventful Years and Experiences.* Cincinnati: American Jewish Archives, 1954.

Learsi, Rufus. *The Jews in America; A History.* Cleveland: World Publishing Company, 1954.

Levinger, Elma Ehrlich. *Jewish Adventures in America.* New York: Bloch Publishing Company, 1954.

Marcus, Jacob Rader. *Memoirs of American Jews, 1775-1865.* Philadelphia: Jewish Publication Society, 1955.

May, Max B. *Isaac Mayer Wise, the Founder of American Judaism; A Biography.* New York: G. P. Putnam's Sons, 1916.

"Message of Israel." Radio program, American Broadcasting Company, March 29, 1959.

Philipson, David. *Centenary Papers and Others.* Cincinnati: Ark Publishing Company, 1919.

———. "History of the Union College," Hebrew Union College *Jubilee Volume (1875-1925).* Cincinnati: 1925, pp. 1-70.

——— (ed.). *Reminiscences by Isaac M. Wise.* Cincinnati: Leo Wise & Company, 1901.

Simonhoff, Harry. *Saga of American Jewry, 1865-1914; Links of an Endless Chain.* New York: Arco Publishing Company, 1959.

Waxman, Meyer. *A History of Jewish Literature.* New York: Bloch Publishing Company, Vol. IV, 1941.

Wilansky, Dena. *Sinai to Cincinnati, Lay Views on the Writings of Isaac M. Wise, Founder of Reform Judaism in America.* New York: Renaissance Book Company, 1937.

Wise, Isaac M. "An Introduction to the Theology of Judaism," delivered at the World's Congress of Religions.

———. *Judaism—Its Doctrines and Duties.* Cincinnati and Chicago: Bloch Publishing Company, 1888.

STEPHEN S. WISE

Elbogen, Ismar (translated by Moses Hadas). *A Century of Jewish Life.* Philadelphia: Jewish Publication Society, 1944.

Goldstein, Sidney E. *The Synagogue and Social Welfare, a Unique Experiment (1907-1953).* New York: Published by Bloch Publishing Company for the Stephen Wise Free Synagogue and Hebrew Union College–Jewish Institute of Religion, 1955.

Kohut, George Alexander. "A Tribute to Stephen S. Wise," *Opinion,* IV (February, 1934).

Polier, Justine Wise, and Wise, James Waterman. *Personal Letters of Stephen Wise.* Boston: Beacon Press, 1956.

Sachar, Abram L. *Sufferance Is the Badge.* New York: Knopf, 1939.

Vorspan, Albert. *Giants of Justice.* New York: Union of American Hebrew Congregations, 1960.

Voss, Carl Hermann. *Rabbi and Minister.* New York: World Publishing Company, 1964.

Wise, Stephen S. *Challenging Years; Autobiography.* New York: G. P. Putnam's Sons, 1949.

Wise, Stephen S., and DeHaas, Jacob. *The Great Betrayal.* New York: Brentano's, 1930.

"Stephen S. Wise Memorial Issue," *Congress Bi-weekly* (New York), XXXI (April 13, 1964).

INDEX